Joyce Jillson's Lifesigns

WALLABY A Wallaby Book
Published by Simon & Schuster, Inc.
New York

Published by Wallaby Books
A Division of Simon & Schuster, Inc.
Simon & Schuster Building
1230 Avenue of the Americas
New York, New York 10020
Designed by Irving Perkins Associates
WALLABY and colophon are registered trademarks of
Simon & Schuster, Inc.
First Wallaby Books printing, September 1983
10 9 8 7 6 5 4 3 2 1
Manufactured in the United States of America
Printed and bound by Fairfield Graphics

Library of Congress Cataloging in Publication Data
Jillson, Joyce.
    Joyce Jillson's Lifesigns.
    "A Wallaby book."
1. Astrology. 2. Zodiac. I. Title. II. Title: Lifesigns.
BF1708.1.J55 1983   133.5   83-12064
ISBN: 0-671-43049-1

*This book is dedicated
to my mother, Beatrice*

Contents

8   *Contents*

Introduction

YOUR SIGN OF THE ZODIAC is determined by the position that the sun held at your time of birth. And just as the sun brings light and life to the entire solar system, so this body is the prime force and energizer in one's individual chart as well. It is no accident that we refer to ourselves, and to one another, solely by the name of the astrological sign of our sun. We are Leos, Aquarians, Geminis, Scorpios, Pisces, Capricorns, Aries, Cancers, Virgos, Sagittarians, Taureans, or Libras. Why? This is not simply astrological shorthand, but a nod to the incredible dominance that the sun sign plays in one's overall destiny. The location of the sun in a natal horoscope discloses and reveals an amazing amount of information about you. When this influence is thoroughly understood, you will notice that the sun's celestial presence illuminates every area of life, producing life agendas, directions, and situations which crop up over and over again. In fact, the solar influence is such a pivotal one that the sign of your sun is in might more aptly be called your "Lifesign."

Your Lifesign becomes the beacon of energy that colors all the astrological considerations to some degree. Actually, it is sometimes forgotten that within each person's sun sign, is another mini-zodiac. This inner zodiac is actually the framework of your existence, describing how you will do everything from expressing your individuality to how you will deal with other people and society.

The beauty of astrology is that it takes a holistic approach to a person. No one life event stands alone; they are all connected: Which is why the significance of your Lifesign is woven through the entire fabric of your life. Just as the zodiac is a wheel, so there is a circular motion to a person's activities and relationships. As soon as one life cycle is completed, new ones built upon earlier experiences are begun.

Sun sign astrology, which is what newspapers, magazines, and most books—including this one—practice, has often been unfairly criticized because it does not relate to a specific individual. To set the record straight, this is absolutely true. We are dealing with one twelfth of the population, and, yes, this does lump people together. But don't allow tired old propaganda to becloud the value of sun sign, or lifesign, astrology. People are segmented into groupings their whole lives. You are put into grade school with others of your same age; you retire at a certain

9

time; and if you work for a company, then you may attend company outings together, en masse. This categorization in no way invalidates these personal experiences, nor diminishes the lessons learned or the pleasures enjoyed at these common activities.

Astrology is the study of individuals; yet, the more I practice and work with clients, the more I notice that from politicians to policemen, and from movie stars to secretaries, we are all primarily concerned with the same basic needs. What are they? Money, love, relationships, security, career success, personal growth, and family matters seem to be uppermost in everyone's mind. Again, an individual may emphasize one aspect of life over another (however, if this is too imbalanced, for too long, a general uneasiness or unhappiness results), but, nevertheless, there is a consensus of what is generally important.

Throughout the ages, astrology has responded to the essentials in man's nature and to the undeniable lifesign directions in two ways: by its twelve-fold approach to personality analysis and forecasting, and by recognizing that much psychological comfort can be derived from being part of a group.

This latter point is more useful than immediately meets the eye. People gain much knowledge, assurance, and confidence by sharing common experiences. The ancient sages sensed that people wanted to belong to groups; and now science acknowledges the fact that as social animals, this is a powerful human need. Astrology provides group support for everyone. For while it does discriminate between who belongs to which sign, there is a place for everyone. All throughout civilization, and especially during early times, there were "royal" families and people who by birth were granted special privileges. Astrology was adapted and refined during these periods, and the twelve signs of the zodiac, provided a way for princes and peasants alike to circumvent the social restrictions imposed elsewhere.

Additionally, astrology deals with similarities in personality. We look for repeated patterns and experiences. Sometimes we find dissimilarities (often explained in one's personal natal chart) that seem to conflict with the lifesign descriptions found in this book. But then, would we be better off *not* recognizing the resemblances among people with the same sign strictly because there are times when the lives of these people do not conform? Should we ignore repeated coincidences? I believe not. Take the example of a delicate glass crashing to the concrete pavement. We *know* that the thin glass will shatter; we *do not know* the exact pattern that the slivers of glass will form on the concrete. To know that a glass breaks when thrown onto concrete gives us foreknowledge about life. But should we disregard this fact just because we don't know the precise position the shattered remnants will take? No, of course not. The same holds true for astrology and lifesigns.

The twelve-fold approach to forecasting and analysis is what this book will decipher. For within everyone's sun sign, there is a mini-zodiac; almost as if you had the benefits of all twelve signs interacting and working on your behalf. Astrology is so perfectly organized that the old occult dictum "As above, so below" is as applicable as an explanation for why astrology works as it is for why one's sun sign can actually be referred to as one's lifesign. The sweeping, totally enveloping effect of the solar rays is no more evident in the heavens than it is in an astrology chart. This "bringer of life," the sun, becomes, in astrological terms, the prism that colors, shapes, and deciphers all of life's possibilities, potentialities, and latent powers.

This mini-zodiac can be divided into twelve separate portions, called houses, in precisely the same way as the wheel of the zodiac is segmented into twelve symbols. These solar houses, that is, houses of your sun sign, divide everyone's life into twelve varied compartments, relating to individuality, finances, communication, home life, creativity, enhancement of daily life, relationships, transitions, personal growth, career, friendships, and the inner self. These are the chapters in your life.

Lifesigns takes into account this mini-zodiac within everyone's sun sign. Picture a clock with the hour divisions all converging at the clock's center. Now, the electrical current running the clock is your sun sign. (It doesn't matter where on the clock's face the electricity is applied, so long as it electrifies the entire clock.) This current will, in tiny ways, separate the accuracy of your timepiece from that of others, and the clock itself can come in all sorts of shapes and sizes. But no matter, the current must equally energize the hands to cover all twelve numerical positions on the clock, and in similar fashion, the sun functions in this way in your chart. This is exactly what takes place in sun sign astrology.

For centuries, astrologers and astronomers debated whether the sun's output of electromagnetic radiation was constant. Before modern times, scientiests really just questioned whether, at all times of the year, the same amount of energy fell upon the earth. Now we know that solar luminosity fluctuates. Astrologers believe that the variations of the sun's energy, solar tides, and seasonal changes, as well as the positions of the moon and planets, all contribute to what type of personality a baby born in any zodiacal month will have; and this personality or temperament must dramatically affect the course of this individual's whole life. These are just the beginning of the findings which, I believe, will once and for all validate astrology in the upcoming years.

Lifesigns recognizes that our lives are full of interconnecting cycles and phases, and that one's temperament contributes to how every element of daily living is perceived. By admitting these natural proclivities, you become the commander of your own destiny, rather than simply flowing with events.

There are no talents, abilities, or goals that are out of reach of any sun sign, and by focusing on how your Lifesign most easily achieves, attains and triumphs, you can short-circuit some of the rough spots. Misguided astrological interpretations about what you can and cannot accomplish are far too restrictive for this modern age. What *Lifesigns* hopes to do is to suggest areas and activities that resonate with your basic nature. However, the feeling and spirit of analysis are most important. The ancients comprehended that words were totally inadequate to explain spiritual experiences or even to fully express the wonder of our material universe. The patterns so important in astrology reflect basic archetypal ideas that *Lifesigns* will try to synthesize with modern civilization and technology.

The free-flowing feelings and impressions that weave the different aspects of your life together are as complex as you are. *Lifesigns* points out the thread of continuity that connects even the most disjointed portions of your existence, so that not only are you the master weaver, but you are also the artisan who can change the design at any time.

Chapter One
Individuality

THE FIRST SIGN OF THE ZODIAC, Aries, symbolizes the individuality inherent in each of the twelve signs. Like this leadership-oriented, innovative sign, we imprint our unique natures upon the world in an energetic, dynamic way. Aries has always been pictured as the ram, constantly battling to get the things it wants. In the same way, our style, personality, character and demeanor, signal to others what we are, and how we want to interact and blend with our environment. And, like the ram, those sparks inside a person full of life, energy, and uniqueness sometimes are so overwhelming and in need of expression, that instead of being in control of our lives, the drive to make our mark intrudes, creating roadblocks to success.

In astrology the first solar house has many of the characteristics of the Aries sign. We tend to associate impulsiveness, adventure, courage, and physical actions—all Aries characteristics—with the expression of individuality in *all* signs.

Besides individuality, the first house in astrology describes the way we present ourselves to the world. It is the outward manifestation of our character, yet it is an incomplete one because we choose how we want to be seen by others early on in life. The most sensitive people in the world may protect their vulnerability by appearing somewhat blunt or bold in the company of others. Therefore, individuality, as presented in this book, will *not* present all the intricacies of specific temperament; that is really a function of a complete astrological chart. The most obvious facets of personality will be outlined to give an objective perspective about actions, emotions, and personal goals.

Astrology helps us to perceive ourselves more clearly, and prods us, gently, to change those things that are not true reflections of our inner selves.

ARIES

PERSONALITY

Aries embodies the bursting energy that begins the cycle of the seasons with spring. As an Aries you are restless by nature, your energy spilling over into intellectual, emotional, and physical pursuits. And what is the core of the Arian personality, that which generates the energy you make use of? It is hard to define, and most Arians have given up trying—but it seems to be a desire to discover new frontiers, testing yourself in the process, while experiencing for yourself the lessons they have to offer. Don Quixote was surely an Aries. You aren't one to avoid a challenge; regardless of what anyone else might have to say, your motto is: "I think I'll just take a quick look for myself."

SELF-IMAGE

You understand that your occasional confrontations with others stem from the desire to keep problems from accumulating and bogging you down. You want them solved—now! You acknowledge yourself as being impatient, but for good reason; you seek less to rid yourself of impatience, than to inspire others to a faster pace and more open communication. The self-image of Aries centers around this idea of being an energizing ingredient in all situations and relationships. Your attention shifts quickly, so that you feel held back by friends or family when they continue to rely heavily on you for momentum after you have already moved on. When you see this happen, describe your perception to them calmly—exploding only causes them to cling more tightly.

PRACTICALITY

To an Aries work successfully completed creates a positive moral force, which the Aries sees as his or her contribution to a harmonious and productive business, marriage, or other relationship. There is an impractical streak in Aries, because this native will pass over important, though nagging, details in the rush toward a goal. Since this is an idealistic sign, Aries sets his or her sights high and enjoys straining for the impossible —or at least the unlikely. Aries works well alone or under direction, but communal efforts demand qualities this sign needs to develop. It is hard for the Arian mentality to grasp the advantage of group effort that succeeds, when they feel they could have done it alone!

EMOTIONS

Try to realize, Aries, that a shared sense of accomplishment will build connections, emotional stamina, and moral support that increase your rate of success and overall happiness. Can it be that behind the bluster and touchiness of Aries, there is a sensitive, compassionate heart? Aries knows this well and is at great pains to protect from hurt. To risk or not to risk! Aries may attack, but others ignore, quibble, deceive, look down their noses—all greater crimes in your eyes, Aries, than a passionate confrontation. Aries natives are not insensitive; actually, they regard others' reactions and emotions with great curiosity, wanting to incorporate the experiences of others into their own lives.

ATTITUDE TOWARD LIFE

Within your lifetime, Aries, you taste all the "isms," moods, and philosophies there are. Your attitude cannot be defined by limiting labels, and no sign rejects being pigeonholed more strongly than Aries. You do suffer from an insecurity that other signs often manage to avoid; but to counter this, you can summon up courage, faith, and optimism that can, but need not, possess a recognizable label. The most desirable change of attitude for an Aries is to let go of the idea that reversals and tests are personal affronts. Avoid resenting the good fortune of others when it is not yours as well. From the Aries point of view, others' strengths are your strengths—and others' weaknesses are their problem.

EXTROVERTS

Count on an extroverted Aries to lead the way! In professional life, you outdistance all competitors. Express no opinion as to why this is so, Aries. Verbal tact is not your forte. You wear your state of mind on your sleeve, which leaves you vulnerable to schemers who would undermine you. Your best response is to retain openness and not to seek revenge; that way you can have your cake and eat it, too. Look for a mate who matches your energy or has compensating strength to complement your irrepressible nature—you'll overwhelm someone meek, leaving you both unhappy.

INTROVERTS

Is there such a thing as an introverted Aries? Yes, indeed. This type of Arian stores his or her energy inside, utilizing it to burn away old stale habits and attitudes, preparing for anxiously awaited chances at love, money, and fame. An extroverted Aries never lets an opportunity pass —good or bad makes little difference. The quiet, introverted Aries wants only the best and waits excitedly in the wings, ready to pounce. Be careful that you don't pounce too suddenly or too hard—you'll defeat your purpose by obliterating your target.

TAURUS

PERSONALITY

Taurus plays builder to Aries' role of pioneer. You don't want to move hurriedly from discovery to discovery, but would rather flesh out a whole dream starting here and now. You know what you want and are ready to get to work and make it materialize. This is a role you enjoy. Why? Most Taureans would be hard pressed to find an answer beyond, "Because it's my work," "Because it's satisfying," or "Because it will look done when I'm done." The reason for doing something, for Taurus, lies not in any esoteric philosophy but simply in the job of doing a project well.

SELF-IMAGE

As a Taurus you have a strongly defined sense of purpose. You don't like to be questioned too closely; first, because you have an inbred sense of privacy and propriety, and second, because picking things apart for analysis is not your style. Live and let live is your motto; it tends to fail you, however, when you are put in a position of dealing with someone of whom you disapprove. Do Taureans seem just a bit complacent about their shortcomings? (It's true, you do have a few, Taurus.) Don't excuse yourself by saying, "That's just the way I am." Stubbornness should not be worn as a badge of honor. You learn best by examples, not by lectures —unless you've just had a good meal.

PRACTICALITY

Is Taurus ever anything but practical? Yes! But they'll practically never admit it. This sign deals brilliantly with what it perceives to be the most high-priority matter at hand. The impracticality of the Taurus native is the manner in which he or she seeks to make things happen—all engines fired, looking neither to the left nor right, bringing in all possible arguments and some impossible ones. When dealing with a Taurean employee, employer, friend, or family member, you must appreciate the need for compromise and to proceed with caution, using carefully and fully reasoned points such as, "Well, that looks great on paper, but. . . ." Normally peaceful Taureans see red if people or situations refuse to budge for them. This native is strong willed and can succeed in attractive and positive situations, keeping friends while still remaining in command. If he or she will channel the Taurean willpower into the best course possible under less pleasant conditions, there is almost no situation in which success cannot be achieved.

EMOTIONS

In the Taurean makeup, anger intrudes on a personality mainly concerned with a harmonious, supportive attitude. Taureans are so committed to the success of their romances that they can cling too closely—or demand to be clung to. Taurus could use a shot of Aries bravado in order to realize that emotional security doesn't stem from their partners'—or their—predictability; although if you ever pair up with an Aries, Taurus, you have permission to cling to whatever predictability you can find for dear life.

ATTITUDE TOWARD LIFE

You feel that stability is so important for you, that you will involve yourself in questionable or disastrous situations to preserve it. Don't ignore your needs in the area of new challenges, new environments; they may lie dormant, waiting patiently to be fulfilled, but they'll keep poking you periodically to make sure you haven't forgotten them. More casual, laid-back types—beware. This earth native elevates unimportant details to the status of major issues just to see things look "just so."

EXTROVERTS

Taurus is sociable and vocal when extroverted, though neither impetuous nor showy. You like to know that your presence is felt and appreciated properly. The Taurus extrovert can lean a bit heavily on the idea that he or she needs, deserves, or should expect popular approval of his or her physical and social appearance. But otherwise, Taurus, your organized, together vibe pulls people to you who respect your qualities while not hesitating to—as friends—point out errors.

INTROVERTS

To know what an introverted Taurus is like, picture a round, ruddy, diminutive gentleman, padding contentedly along to his bookshop, stopping at a cafe next door for his daily tea and biscuits with jam. He always goes at the same time, always the same flavor of jam. This person is jolly but is never one to offer one word more than is necessary. He is a bit wistful at the thought of the sparkle in the eyes of the girls who stop in, but basically he is too satisfied with his bachelor's life to do anything that might change it. One may envision, too, his female counterpart—every dish in its own place in the cabinet, she enjoys opening the doors to look at them. She might run an office, though from a behind-the-scenes position, keeping everything perfectly in order, inconspicuously the mainstay without which the outer structure would surely collapse.

GEMINI

PERSONALITY

Gemini is the sign that, like Alice in Wonderland, never stops discovering that things are getting "curiouser and curiouser." And like Alice who ventures through Wonderland, this air native is frightened only by the most bizarre events—and then only momentarily. No one recovers faster than a Gemini. This social gadfly livens up any conversation, dinner party, bus ride—any place or event where human beings can be found. Delight is the word that describes Gemini's reaction when he or she is invited (or allowed) to give free play to his or her verbal and intellectual abilities. Develop calming practices, Gemini—they will build your much neglected concentration span.

SELF-IMAGE

Geminis make sure they always have a supply of fresh self-images on hand. An immature Gemini can truly lack sincerity in his or her dealings with people and in self-presentation to new acquaintances. However, this is not usually the case; Gemini often perceives several core aspects of the Gemini personality and does express consistent motivations. Gemini explores what others might accept from themselves at face value, wanting to satisfy and fully experience all areas of self.

PRACTICALITY

Gemini's power of organization, along with an ability to catalogue details, gives this sign a head start on most people. Capable of sizing up all facets of the matter at hand, this air sign has its act together when meeting a client, planning the day's activities, or drawing up a work schedule. If the load is (or seems to be) too great, Gemini, your impatience can cause you to throw up your hands in despair, forget the whole thing, and go enjoy yourself at the beach. Everyone needs to do that from time to time—the only problem is that you sometimes take this break when the overload at hand is a serious relationship that might not be there when you get back. If you were born under this sign, ascertain whether you take on too many mundane details when you find that the urge to disappear presents itself frequently.

Your approach to people is a very practical one; you present a bright, interested face and help a discussion along with concise and logical suggestions. You are an asset to any business that needs someone who can be convincing. Beware, however, of a two-faced talent—that of being able to convince yourself of what may not be the right course of action!

EMOTIONS

Gemini dislikes feeling trapped, cornered, or overly committed. Your impulse to avoid such involvement is equally strong as your desire to bond with others in an open and affectionate manner. Business associates, family, and friends all know they can rely on you to welcome them at all hours of the night should they need to talk or just be near someone. Sometimes, though, they will underestimate the depth of your feeling in terms of how central a position they occupy in your emotions. It's not always comforting to be told that you would have done the same for anyone. But there is no need to feel guilty—just keep your emotional commitments clearly delineated in your own consciousness.

ATTITUDE TOWARD LIFE

Heaven to a Gemini consists of an eternity spent as a talk-show guest. You love carrying what to other signs is the burden of entertaining people in a spontaneous manner—to you it is effortless, comfortable, and utterly pleasing. "Will I be interesting enough? Will I appear nervous?" These questions may trouble you, but you know what the answer is— yes! An optimist at heart, you are definitely aware of the realities of life. You receive your share of hard knocks (sometimes a self-induced extra portion) but are too irrepressible to allow this to dampen your spirits.

EXTROVERTS

All Geminis can be considered extroverts to one degree or another. Your already prodigious verbal skills shine even more brightly if you are that dazzling social star, the Gemini extrovert. Your mate or lover needs an energetic, sophisticated bearing, both to properly appreciate you and to deal effectively (or keep up) with your high spirits. Less perceptive souls are left behind in a cloud of dust. You discover treasures where others see nothing unusual.

INTROVERTS

There is such a thing as an introverted Gemini and their rarity only makes them more of an enigma. Except for their darting eyes and hurried way of speaking, they won't appear to be Geminis! Instead of talking off the ears of others, their inner voices will be going at a lightening pace. These

Geminis usually have a scholarly bent, as there must be an outlet for the probing Geminian intellect. Their wealth of observation is saved for the right person and the right time; most often it is another air sign or a fire sign that discovers the hidden inner life of such a Gemini.

CANCER

PERSONALITY

Myriad and wondrous are the moods of those born under the water sign of Cancer. Cancerians love to revel in them, soaking up every last drop of essence they have to offer. Depending on the individual Cancer native, these emotional thunderstorms come and go fairly quickly, definitely leaving the air cleaner and brighter. Generous to a fault with friends, Cancerians nevertheless must fight off nagging little selfishness that whisper miserly and cautionary warnings in their inner ears. Cancer natives are deeply affected by the arts, particularly music and literature. You can and do use this passion, Cancer, to pull you into more productive and positive states of mind.

SELF-IMAGE

You visualize yourself as occupying positions of aide, confidante, advisor, and mother to your loved ones, friends, and family. Your real concern for your own and others' emotional balance is translated into this nurturing type of care. You are Florence Nightingale, Dear Abby, and Dr. Jonas Salk all wrapped up into one. Cancers may fib to themselves about their true motives in cases where something important is at stake; masquerading as a distinterested observer, you stalk, prove, and drop tiny but weighted bombs of acid criticism. Wit can be a lethal weapon or a coup de grace. For the most part, Cancer cannot help being frank about his or her true position and opinion (revealed by vibration if not by verbosity), a quality that makes enemies as well as (always more and loyal) friends.

PRACTICALITY

Motivation is the key word for Cancer when it comes to accomplishing goals. Cancer is perfectly capable of taking a hard view of what needs to be done—but also perfectly capable of then putting it off until doing it feels just right. As often as not this proves to be a true intuitive feeling, an accurate guide to correct timing. To strengthen the reliability of this faculty, try keeping a journal in which you record the sequence and interaction of moods and accomplishments as they occur. You can see whether you are repeating productive or unproductive cycles, learn to increase the sharpness of your intuitive perceptions and thereby your ability to trust them.

EMOTIONS

Sensitive to others' emotional states and receptive to the general feeling of any environment, the Cancer native is often dislodged from his or her own inner balance by the input received from others. Cancer often cannot bear to go ten minutes without a pout, depression, ecstasy, or tantrum. You absorb, as do all water signs, the emotional climate of whatever place you find yourself in, which makes it difficult for you to separate your own feelings from those of people around you. You might try some very precise questioning tactics when the atmosphere gets emotionally cloudy. Find out just who is protecting what and why.

ATTITUDE TOWARD LIFE

Cancer persons need to feel that there is a haven surrounding them, a secure base from which to move out into the world. While your sign neighbor Gemini travels only with what he or she can carry, you use the family station wagon and a trailer, or at least a large purse or briefcase. This is fine because you get to watch Gemini turn green with envy at your preparedness and patience (unless, of course, you are only going to the grocery store). Besides, Cancer wants to have a bag of plenty along at all times to shower gifts on friends. Cancer seeks material security to share with loved ones as much as for self-comfort.

EXTROVERTS

An extroverted Cancerian is often robust, but not necessarily in a muscular way. Although frowning upon rotundity is a modern American pastime, muses Cancer, the person who loved life's pleasures in the past felt duty-bound to indulge this love of the fruits of the earth. The Cancer extrovert is a buoyant type, willing to exchange much verbal support, quick to anger (or often just to pique), and quick to forgive although just a bit tough about forgetting.

INTROVERTS

The Cancer introvert is a sentimental soul, somewhat passive about getting out into the world to realize ambitions and dreams. This type can easily prefer the quiet of modest, single life, always maintaining a sweet, amiable face toward fellow workers and family. When married, this Cancerian often lives for home and family alone, seeming to require no other activities as outlets. To a large extent this is the true picture, but the mate of such a Cancer should gently nudge him or her into something that takes place outside the home once in a while—possibly volunteer work, home-based or part-time employment, or creative expression that can be shared with and appreciated by others. On the positive side, a Cancer turns his home into his hobby, constantly remodeling, improving, and planting so it becomes the neighborhood showplace. But alas, people rarely see it—when Cancers entertain, they stick to the same tried-and-true loyal friends.

LEO

PERSONALITY

Leo often views the antics of Aries, a fellow fire sign, with a frown. Aries is just too willing, observes Leo, to jump into a situation with eyes closed, hoping for the best. Leo, on the other hand, prefers (and is proud of it) a more stable approach. When Leo has scanned the situation at hand— and only then—will he or she make a move. Yet the Leo was born to gamble—but only after what they say was careful preparation. Leo is a passionate sign, dedicating the self to friends, loved ones, and personal goals with an energy that clearly comes from a powerful source. Sensitive to others' opinions of them, Leonians want all communication to be honest, although they may appreciate a bit of theatrics if it helps to make a point.

SELF-IMAGE

Leos envision themselves as sources of energy for others; people can come to them for advice, money, inspiration, or all three. If there is no money available, the advice and inspiration more than make up for it. Generous and forthright by nature, Leo enjoys being sought after as a person to be respected—or reckoned with. If your sign is Leo, you are willing to go to others for this kind of guidance as well, and to serve a short apprenticeship; however, you are anxious to move on toward your own independent stand or position. Focus on being thorough when dealing in practical matters—otherwise you may rush through a training period in a slipshod manner in order to appear knowledgeable as soon as possible, hurting yourself with this haste.

PRACTICALITY

Leo approaches objectives from a central focus and a primary goal. Then all related subjects are catalogued, including everything you feel you will need to learn or to deal with. In practical matters the Leonian ideal is nothing short of mastery—and often you attain it (and not hesitate to let others know you have done so). For all your independent nature, Leo, you are strongly affected by what others think about you, always seeking to demonstrate your abilities. Should the response not be positive, this casts a cloud of self-doubt over your proud and sensitive temperament.

EMOTIONS

Nothing matches the fury of a Leo scorned, to paraphrase the old saying. This reflects both positive and negative traits. Leo does not hide his or her feelings in relationships—people always know where they stand with this native. No elaborate or petty games are played. The strong reactions of the Leo nature stem from strong passions—no lukewarm romances here! However, it is difficult for Leo to separate the success or failure of external matters—from daily chores to romantic encounters—

from a sense of personal identification with the results. "Love me; love everything I do," says Leo.

ATTITUDE TOWARD LIFE

Like all fire signs, Leo has a restless, curious streak. You generate new interests and horizons on your own throughout life, not relying on fad or fashion for cues. Although you do keep posted on current trends, it is more from curiosity and the desire for up-to-date thinking than any need to follow them. You are essentially an optimist; difficulties are not ignored, but you won't be fazed or cowed into inaction by them. Once you have set a course you stick to it. It is likely that you should give more attention to the needs of others. You are very much aware of the importance of your friends, so don't let willfulness cause you to neglect them —or you may be left high and dry.

EXTROVERTS

The Leo extrovert can't help being in the role of teacher or mentor in some manner at some time. You possess the physical and emotional vitality demanded by such work, and you gain energy by interacting with people, especially students or apprentices. This sort of activity also assists you in focusing your own goals and attention, and provides you with a productive outlet for your abundant creative drives. Should you be preoccupied with any lofty position, you mentally undercut your charismatic nature so you are most impressive when you acknowledge the efforts of subordinates. Giving others the podium occasionally will add to your own knowledge and popularity.

INTROVERTS

There is no loss of gusto when Leo directs his or her attention to interior processes rather than outward pursuits. And certainly there is no reduction of the Leonian stubbornness quotient. If you are the more introverted type of Leo, you tend to work by yourself on projects or in a career where you are allowed a great deal of freedom of action. Correspondingly, you are less inclined to try to impose your patterns on others than an outwardly directed Leonian would be. Family and loved ones will learn to give this quieter lion the solitary time and habits he or she requires—and in return will receive constancy and helpfulness. Recognize that you do have to express your dynamic personality in some way —perhaps through a child or a dramatic approach to work.

VIRGO

PERSONALITY

Everyone has known a timid, reserved librarian. They read all the time, frown at giggling girls; their biggest emotional display is when they hiss, "Sshh, be quiet!" Perhaps it is a bit of an exaggeration to identify this sort of person as the archetypal Virgo. However, such a characterization points up some classical Virgonian traits. This earth sign prefers social interaction to take place in a highly structured environment. Virgo can take a more objective view of human behavior and interests in a "civilized" atmosphere. Virgo respects all honest efforts at making sense of this world. You enjoy the role of maintaining order, Virgo, where lazy browsers would reduce it to chaos.

SELF-IMAGE

Order is the key word of the Virgonian self-image. Virgos are the organizers of this world, and it would be a sorry place without them. Virgo may seem petty at times, but we all react that way when our toes are stepped on, our pet projects and ideals made light of. Their innate confidence comes from knowing they can handle just about any problem all by themselves. Virgo's grouchiness comes from concern—a serious concern over providing a fair and effective environment (world, family, or business) within which all people can best realize their potential. Watch out, Virgo, not to appoint yourself official martyr for all causes both within and beyond your personal control.

PRACTICALITY

When it comes to being 100 percent practical, Virgo does as poorly as anyone else, although he or she may hide this better than anyone. People usually picture a practical person as being a logical one, which as often as not isn't really the case. Therefore, Virgo is the victim of expectations manufactured by others. Virgo's goals when it comes to practicality center on two concepts: completion and utility. It annoys this earth native when interruptions result in sloppy or unfinished projects. In addition, emotions, talents, tools, and ideas all must be proven, and their practical value tested in the physical world; either they produce results or Virgo discards them. Because of this Virgos are pictured as being unfeeling— they are not. It is simply hard to argue with the efficiency that can be created with a bucket of soapy water, a dishcloth, and the easy accessibility of objects kept in their proper places. Yet upsets affect Virgos so strongly that they ignore difficulties of the heart, choosing to maintain outward control at the expense of deadening a part of themselves.

EMOTIONS

Virgos share the desire of all earth signs for stability. This extends, naturally, into their personal lives and is exemplified in the Virgo who is less of a hermit than Capricorn and more objective than Taurus (who simply dismisses relationships that might prove troublesome). Virgos seem shy and uninterested because they are hesitant to commit themselves emotionally—not because they are incapable of doing so. No one holds on like a Virgo who has decided that you are his or her chosen one. Possessing an inborn introspection, these natives are well aware of what will rock the emotional boat. They hold prospective partners at arm's length a while before saying yes because of this, analyzing them and waiting to make sure the attraction is mutual.

ATTITUDE TOWARD LIFE

Virgo enjoys many quiet laughs while picturing the wizened cynic he or she would rather like to be. But you don't live in a world of make believe, Virgo. You are all too aware of people's foibles and their potential for causing trouble. You'll even be so helpful as to make others aware of it as well. For this reason you cultivate a matter-of-fact attitude with which to deal with life's ups and downs. At the same time you maintain an allegiance to ideals that are lofty enough to help you to endure setbacks. Your inner vision usually manifests itself to others as humor rather than any sort of fiery bravado.

EXTROVERTS

The Virgo extrovert is quite willing to take on a leadership or managerial role, although pretending to hate it since he or she wants to be "just one of the crowd." To be truly decisive it is helpful for you to have fire or air signs as partners—they help to cut down the amount of time spent in planning. At home or work you want to be in touch with all details. Learn to delegate! Although willing to compromise, you can be touchy, needing to be approached cautiously. Perhaps the most annoying aspect of criticism from the Virgo in charge is that it is well founded. Virgos themselves don't mind being challenged—in fact, they may even enjoy it a little—as long as the approach is reasonable. Virgos hate arguments, but they just love to debate.

INTROVERTS

It's not easy being an introverted Virgo! You're pretty hard on yourself; a mild exterior is the mask behind which thunderous wars are carried on. Your watchful eye spots every flaw and failing—your own and everyone else's. An idealist at heart, you believe that your lofty ideals can be realized in the everyday world; when it doesn't happen, you take it hard. Virgo introverts may end up blaming themselves. Out of such difficulties, though, the Virgo introvert develops a very humane, humble view of life, one which allows him or her to derive great satisfaction from the simple truths of life. This Virgo is in touch with what is worthwhile in every friend and acquaintance, every event, all the tiny miracles and daily joys that contain the true significance of living.

LIBRA

PERSONALITY

Libra, an air sign, is one of the most naturally graceful and gracious in the zodiac. It is not that the anger of Librans never flares or they never insist on their own way of doing things; Libra will always seek a considerate, gentle way to attain whatever it is that he or she is pursuing. If you have a complaint about yourself, Libra, it is probably that you repeatedly find yourself putting too much emphasis on accommodating the needs of others while your own take the back seat. Equally at home as a sports enthusiast, a studious artist, or an analyst of human behavior (Libra is this in any capacity), you maintain a careful watch on your own performance, always striving to work at the highest possible level.

SELF-IMAGE

Librans see themselves as inhabiting a social and intellectual position that enables all that goes on around them to function smoothly. To a large extent this is correct. Strong social instinct and psychological insight make the Libran a valuable addition to a business, corporate board, even the United Nations! Where others bluster or give in meekly, Libra takes a middle course of compromise and patient, consistent effort. If you are a Libra, guard against becoming too wound up in mediating for others— it can tend to make you lose sight of your own best interests, which in turn will undermine your social effectiveness. Learn to strike a balance between selfish and selfless motives.

PRACTICALITY

Being an air sign, you tackle problems logically. You are best able to sort out your thoughts when there are other people around with whom to toss ideas back and forth and exchange mutual feedback. This can, however, cause unnecessary delays. Usually Libra is very capable of making sound judgments quickly; and since you search out all aspects of a given problem, your decisions are well founded in a practical sense. Your perceptions are not clouded by vague perceptions or volatile moods. But this detachment can lead you to engage in too much abstraction, and when this occurs, your practical sense suffers. Your rational approach, although a positive trait, can upset emotionally tense lovers or business associates who view the ability of air signs to make sense under pressure as heartlessness, or at least lack of sympathy.

EMOTIONS

Despite much bad press to the contrary, Libra has a very deep emotional life. You don't like advertising it for all to see and, above all, you don't like to lose control of its expression. The person who becomes Libra's mate needs to be persistent but never heavy-handed in drawing out Libra's emotional responses. Libras hate to display volatile emotions or their inner processes, and often become irritable at having them stored inside. Business associates rarely see the occasional outburst of this harmonious sign's temper. When asked to describe their gut reactions Librans can do so with a quiet articulateness that makes them seem more like something being read than an immediate and present set of real feelings.

ATTITUDE TOWARD LIFE

A great deal of exasperation accompanies Libra's constant propensity for mentally turning the possible motives of others over and over in order to fathom them. Doing so leads to two basic foibles in the Libran attitude: first, you want to step in and help, mediate, or offer consolation when trouble brews; second, you incline toward a feeling of superiority, wishing others would take your more careful and rational approach. As a result your actual response can vary from retreating into an ivory tower to being something of a busybody to exuding a winning, earthy, comforting aura to which others happily respond. Since your own views vary from moment to moment, you lack patience with those who never seem to change. Could this be, Libra, a bit of defensiveness?

EXTROVERTS

An extroverted Libra is always visible—or rather, audible. Your laugh and verbal enthusiasm pleases everyone. Not given to small talk, this type is a measured, serious, but charming person. You can share your abundant humor with people, although there is a certain amount of restraint that you must (and usually do) overcome. You do well in business; rather than being possessed by ambition you are endowed with curiosity and a strong drive to set things right. Spotting inefficiency a mile away, you correctly analyze people's abilities and weaknesses, and you do so without alienating anyone. You are able to gently reorganize a work force so that individual talents are put to maximize use and expressed with satisfaction. Then what happens? Librans have forgotten that all the fun is in making the changes, and following through is not pleasant for them at all.

INTROVERTS

The Libra introvert is apt to keep observations unspoken, to be content with being aware of his or her perceptions inwardly rather then feeling it necessary to suggest changes in the behavior or attitudes of others. What is perceived does need a channel, however, and writing is a natural outlet for the airy introvert. Music is another, but will often take second place to a written product, because performing the music may create such tension. Once or twice a year this Libra will speak to other human beings; the hesitation to do so occurs only because so few people take the time to communicate in the thorough, courteous, and rational manner of this sign. This problem also surfaces in the romance department, as the partner of a quiet Libran needs to have a similar conversation pace in order that real and satisfying communication can take place.

SCORPIO

PERSONALITY

Scorpio watches the world going by at the window, daydreaming of the way he or she would run the human zoo if suddenly put in charge. This thought preoccupies Scorpio to the extent that he or she might think that all this water sign's actions are power struggles. This is not so. Scorpio's messages encounter resistance because they are too true, striking home in sensitive spots, and nobody enjoys having their basic motivations questioned. In other words it is often the other party that initiates the struggle, assuming that Scorpio is on the warpath. Scorpio wants to be taken seriously but is much more interested in cooperation than obedience! You might try, Scorpio, taking breaks for sheer play to offset the impression you tend to give of being perpetually solemn.

Self-Image

If you are a Scorpio, you are fond of picturing yourself as the misunderstood hermit who needs to find shelter from the world's follies. Simultaneously, you imagine yourself as a puppeteer, running every show yourself. You aren't as grumpy as you would like to think; you are adept at camouflaging your wild, silly escapades—but you do have them! In fact, under pressure, your humor and spontaneous decisions prove so successful that you may seek out these stressful situations. Another aspect of the melancholy Scorpionic self-image is that often your touch of gloom serves to provide you with a quiet space in which to sort out priorities and difficulties and to generate and replenish creative drives. Don't wallow in your shadowy times—but don't think you must feel guilty about them either.

Practicality

"Waste not, want not" is Scorpio's philosophy in a nutshell. Scorpios often pare their wordly possessions down to a bare minimum, when things begin to strike them as being superfluous. Scorpios can become carried away throwing out everything in sight (people as well) in order to get rid of seemingly petty distractions. Your work attitude is similar. You will apportion your time with scrupulous care, because once you begin a project all resources are committed for the duration. If you have an impractical side, it is that you tend to focus on one thing at a time exclusively, letting other matters slide regardless of their importance.

Emotions

Scorpio always seems to be labeled as belligerent and obsessed with sex. You probably have known a Scorpio who fits this description. Scorpio's reputation stems from a strong focus on the inner, emotional life, which always seeks to explore every nook and cranny of his or her personality. Sometimes frightening or intimidating others with their aspirations, Scorpios work actively at what others dream about or hide from. Scorpio will also work with a mate or lover who is similarly willing to investigate the workings of emotional strengths and weaknesses. Someone who accompanies Scorpio on such a journey will discover this native's humorous and joyful side, rarely glimpsed by anyone who reacts with a fright-or-flight response.

Attitude Toward Life

The ideal state of being to the Scorpionic way of thinking is to be a still spot in the midst of chaos, a vision shared by Pisces. Unlike a Piscean, however, Scorpio is able to screen out distractions that interfere with the desired line of concentration. Scorpio might be described as fatalistic—

but this is not synonymous with being a defeatist. You are capable of lapsing from your usual rough-and-ready attitude into saying, "It wasn't meant to be, so why try?" when your mood is dark. More often, though, your fatalism translates into a sixth sense that allows you to pause, push ahead, or negotiate as needed. Others often see you as gloomy when all you're doing is sitting and watching the world unravel its mysteries.

Extroverts

The Scorpio extrovert is the culprit that gives all Scorpios a bad name. It's not that this type is more difficult to handle—actually, being outgoing relaxes some of the inner pressure that is characteristic of the sign. It's simply that this Scorpion runs into more lightweight folks who interpret any potent personality as a domineering one. Curiosity is strong in the extroverted Scorpio natives; they are full of questions, but they ration their answers carefully. Here is an extrovert who is not necessarily a talker. Strongly achievement oriented, you combine patience with drive, sticking with a project until it is completed, angering some with your need to get things done quickly. A weak-willed mate is not the one for this Scorpion; it's too easy to make all the decisions for such a partner and then tire of him or her because there are no challenges. Remember the Scorpio demands excitement from others, as boredom may erode his or her always shaky confidence.

Introverts

On the surface, the introverted Scorpio seems quite ordinary, aside from a few idiosyncratic habits that vary according to the individual. If it weren't for the black-silk top hat and polka-dot socks, you'd never notice this native. This Scorpion returns the stares with a blasé look that is simply marvelous. They have class and they know it. The show is actually for his or her own benefit, not for an audience. Generally quiet and helpful, the Scorpio introvert is strong-willed, although less confrontational than the extroverted type. They rarely get upset, but when they do, it is frightening.

SAGITTARIUS

Personality

"Count me in!" That is the war cry of irrepressible Sagittarians. Once you do let this fire native in, you'd better prepare yourself for the advice and commentary that Sagittarius is equipped and very willing to dispense. Rules and traditions fascinate this adventure-seeking person who cannot resist questioning and critiquing absolutely everything. While this amazes most others, to Sagittarius it's just part of the game of life. It is not that this native is an anarchist by nature—far from it. They will gleefully tear down and root out all the handed-down ground rules; but they will inevitably construct a new set based on personal preferences and ideals.

SELF-IMAGE

Sagittarians see themselves as adventurers, travelers on the highway of life. If this is your sign, you feel a responsibility to generate your own learning processes; thus you are an avid reader, a fact attested to by your many library cards and magazine subscriptions, not to mention some overdue books. Your opinions can be dogmatic, but you simply cannot resist popping the philosophical balloons of others. Having done so, you don't hang around to rub it in (or have your nose punched); your wish is for no hard feelings, as you desire only to be on your way when a new horizon beckons. You picture yourself as being tireless, but your level of irritability does rise when you overextend yourself.

PRACTICALITY

In practical matters, Sagittarians tend to slip away from a down-to-earth attitude easily. Being a great delegator, you'd ask someone to eat breakfast for you if you could. You possess endurance, not patience. You need to create, especially in your business life, a variety of short-term responsibilities that can be worked at on a rotating basis—the optimal situation for you. Otherwise you become quickly bored with a repetitive routine and you work inefficiently. Make sure your boss, partner, or coworkers see that your interests remain focused when you are in a position that allows you to make the best use of your talents and style. Many a Sagittarian who has not taken the time to talk such matters through calmly at work has lost valuable opportunities.

EMOTIONS

No one gets sillier, more starry-eyed, or filled with more wild energy when a relationship begins than Sagittarius. You adjust quickly to a new emotional atmosphere and are eager to share yourself and possessions. You are a true romantic. Your original intuition about a person tells you all you need to know. But as reality gradually intrudes upon the scene, it's often hard to keep that same shining image before your eyes. The secret to stabilizing your emotional life is to look for your biggest satisfactions in small things, not trying to see into the future. This helps in other areas of your life, too; once your emotions latch onto a project, it is as hard for you to maintain a constructive and objective outlook. Infatuation is a sign that perhaps you are being deluded, but that's half the fun for you Sagittarians.

ATTITUDE TOWARD LIFE

Ever-hopeful Sagittarians can't extinguish their characteristic optimism no matter how hard they try. You may be quick to announce that you have met defeat, but without any conscious effort your energy regenerates its momentum and you're back on your feet again. For all your attachment to ideals you are a survivalist at heart. You will modify your thinking to enable yourself to handle new situations. Be willing as well to admit that you have been wrong, if for no other reason than for others to see that you are human after all. You tend to feel, once you have acquired some new bit of knowledge, that you have had it all along; although this lacks accuracy it is a sign that you are dedicated to acting on your beliefs.

EXTROVERTS

Sagittarian extroverts wear their hearts on their sleeves and must talk about love and life to experience it. All the important ideas and opinions, all the little weird ones, too come rolling out unannounced. Outrage, bewilderment, amazement, applause, and tearing out of hair follow in your wake. The biggest pitfall for extroverted Sagittarians is that they are quite capable of zealously propounding views they do not hold! Yes, Sagittarius, you are just playing devil's advocate, but more somber folks won't appreciate the brilliance of this and will often react negatively. This is a danger to you in your work environment—don't let your hard-working image be undermined by coming off as a know-it-all.

INTROVERTS

The same flow of ideas that the extroverted Sagittarian verbalizes to all and sundry is turned over and over in the mind of the Sagittarius introvert; often it is later put into written form. Despite a more introspective approach to life, however, this Sagittarian also acts like a gadfly, striving toward, and usually succeeding in, influencing (and knocking for a loop) an even larger audience than that of his or her more outgoing counterpart. By engaging in an inner view of ideas, this Sagittarian develops both an impressive vocabulary and a perceptive intellect, which others will latch onto and promote.

CAPRICORN

PERSONALITY

Did you ever walk down the street and be discovered either tossing a candy wrapper away, or listening to a blaring transistor radio, and see someone frowning at you? There's no way to absolutely guarantee, but I think you just saw a Capricorn staring at you. This earth native is a watcher, an observer—at best, helpful with suggestions, at worst, judgmental. Capricorn's attention is always fixed on some aspect of the mechanics of everyday life, on the lookout for people's inefficiencies and errors. Capricorn, of course, is utterly free from unnecessary habits and idiosyncracies and must endure life in a world where everyone else engages in nonsense. That is one side of Capricorn. The other side is a childlike naivete which allows them to get away with just about anything, and a memory that is very selective, forgetting what a Capricorn doesn't want to know.

SELF-IMAGE

Capricorn's self-image is that of a Greek god on a mountain, surveying the folly of human nature from a perch of isolation and aloofness. If you are a Capricorn, you are aware of having a strong social conscience; however, you are often unaware of the effect you have on others—what they tend to see is a withdrawn person who just doesn't seem concerned. To some extent this impression is accurate—many Capricorns do prefer their privacy to the compromises of social life. But just as often the Capricorn serves to insulate a more tender nature from disappointment than one might think. Capricorn also tends to gloss over or underrate his or her ideas and opinions, producing a disarmingly shy or stubbornly authoritarian type, or one who alternates between the two. Capricorn, strike a balance!

PRACTICALITY

A born cataloguer, organizer, overseer, you are more aggressive than your earth cousin Virgo in practical affairs. As a Capricorn you have a strong "supervisor instinct"; often your innate reserve is all that keeps you from being overbearing. Your difficulty is that you misinterpret what others think of you, particularly in your work environment. In your rush to get things done, you forget how important social niceties are. By warming up your style, with a smile or a chatty telephone call, you get better results and more emotional satisfaction. Capricorn verbalizes, but not always efficiently. It is in underestimating the importance of personal relationships where the Capricorn is most impractical.

EMOTIONS

Capricorn's emotional life may seem muted to outsiders; this is because you feel that those who don't know you well need only to see your dutiful side when it comes to your behavior with a mate or lover. Your feelings of loyalty are strong, and even if you should be spending time elsewhere than with your partner, you are secretive for the sake of appearances. Unfortunately, Capricorn, you can also extend this secretiveness to your primary partner. You do prefer to end one relationship before beginning another, so your life is not without its share of emotional turmoil—and this, too, you approach in an orderly fashion.

ATTITUDE TOWARD LIFE

Happy or sad, feeling industrious or lazy, enthusiastic or depressed, Capricorn's primal response is to organize; this means you set up limits and time schedules for everything you deal with, be it an emotion, a hobby, or what to do on your day off. You don't like to feel that time or effort will be wasted because of lack of proper planning—no matter how unromantic it may seem to deal with emotions in this manner. Those of you who have Capricorns in your lives can rest assured—they experience all the feelings related to job, love, and sadness that the rest of us do, but they just don't want to handle anything in a frivolous way.

EXTROVERTS

The Capricorn extrovert channels his or her energy along two lines: accomplishment and instruction of others. You take each with equal seriousness, always trying to combine these two needs into one activity. In business, for example, you head instinctively for a managerial position— you enjoy the challenge of setting your sights high. When you have secured the position, you are then able to teach others the ropes, giving them the benefit of your experience. You may feel just a tiny urge to get preachy in this capacity; don't let it undermine your credibility. Politics is a natural area for you, as you enjoy playing to a crowd and are a skillful negotiator.

INTROVERTS

Like your rare neighbor the introverted Sagittarius, you find it much easier to put your ideas on paper than to express them verbally if you are a Capricorn introvert. Expression is a basic need, but being able to revise and refine written work affords the Capricorn mentality immense satisfaction. Those who love you will need to be outgoing but not brash in their approach to you. You make few obvious (or visible) signs that you are interested in a person or project, even when this is very much the case. Capricorns show their pleasure through actions. A word to the lover of an introverted Capricorn: he or she is worth the effort. The dry humor, loyalty, unique personality, and perseverance of this earth native are a delight to anyone who has the intelligence to share and appreciate them.

AQUARIUS

PERSONALITY

Aquarius, you may possess the most unconventional views on your block; you may delight in playing the agent provocateur, political activist or just plain pest. But beneath that wild exterior there is usually an equally wild interior! Aquarius is a naturally curious sort who questions any and all opinions and attitudes to determine whether they are relevant or outmoded. The problem is, of course, making a critical observation and having it result in a positive reaction that leads to change; Aquarius is more capable of accomplishing this than other signs. Although Aquarians dwell in the realm of ideas, they are far more determined than they appear and have great powers of persuasion. Socializing plays an important role in every aspect of their lives, as friendship is the one constant thing they depend on.

SELF-IMAGE

Aquarians see themselves as being a necessary polarizing or catalyzing influence on friends and society. To these natives, action and growth occur only when people have been challenged to define what they believe in. Things need to be seen clearly, and the Aquarian does this as much for themselves as for others. It's true that when Aquarius is around, things seem to happen in big ways—of course, not everyone enjoys an avalanche. It's also true that Aquarius occasionally lacks delicacy when interacting. Their motto is: "The truth, the whole truth, and nothing but the truth"—most of the time. Listening intently to that little guiding voice inside, Aquarians can alienate others unwittingly by coming across as overly critical when they are simply extremely interested.

PRACTICALITY

Although management techniques, the soothing of hurt feelings, and the handing out of praise and criticism in a balanced manner are not great Aquarian strengths, you are unbeatable, Aquarius, when it comes to inspiring others to employ you. You are able to utilize the talents of others effectively for their personal benefit and/or that of a group or business. As for yourself, your reserve of practicality lies in your drive to attain your goals, coupled with the ability to make decisions based on a quick assessment of what is in front of you. Often you will aim too high —you inspire yourself too easily! Most of us still wish we could grab the running start that Aquarius always seems to be able to conjure up.

EMOTIONS

It takes time for airy Aquarius to be able to feel the impact of events on his or her emotions. This may cause you to seem inconsistent to those close to you. You always discuss emotional difficulties very rationally on Tuesday. On Wednesday, when the topic is mentioned by someone else, you explode. This is less evident at work than at home or in a romance. Practice being more consistent at expressing strong emotions reasonably. And deal only with the person involved, Aquarius, as you sometimes let too many people in on private matters.

ATTITUDE TOWARD LIFE

Aquarius is the original idealist. This need not lead to an impractical approach to life; channeled correctly, an Aquarian's off-beat methods for dealing with situations that arise can achieve concrete results. Aquarians believe in communal action, recognizing that none of us ever really makes it alone. Those who compulsively reject aid only limit their opportunities. If ideals are the tools of Aquarius, enthusiasm is the fuel. But learn to laugh at your foibles, Aquarians, or enthusiasm turns to fanaticism. You want to march to the best of your own drummer, but not to the extent that you go off on a tangent.

EXTROVERTS

Visibility is the key word for an extrovert born under the sign of Aquarius. This native is not content to sit back and observe, nor to simply amass and catalogue details as the other air signs, Gemini and Libra, tend to do. Aquarians like to get not only their feet wet but their knees, chest, and elbows, too—this is not one to remain uninvolved! In their personal lives, Aquarian extroverts often supply the element that keeps relationships vital, sometimes refusing to restrict themselves to just one person. If you are contemplating becoming a mate of this Aquarius, you'll need to be able to respond constructively to close psychological scrutiny, for Aquarians have a different code for lovers than they have for themselves.

INTROVERTS

Turning a philosophical and analytical eye toward social issues involves the introverted Aquarian so totally that he or she will often rely on a whole circle of friends rather than a mate for companionship. Of course, this type of Aquarian is interested in an intimate relationship, but academic or political activity may consume so much of his or her time and energy that a lover will feel neglected, especially if not involved in a strong career interest as well. Someone with such interests, of course, is the ideal partner for the Aquarian introvert. These Aquarians are certainly not antisocial; making new friends and acquaintances is their profession. Often a traveler by nature, the introspective Aquarian can easily achieve what in politics is known as "name recognition"—having an impact on society at large even if it is by name only.

PISCES

PERSONALITY

If ever you should chance to see a group of people, children and/or adults, gathered around someone who has their undivided attention while relating a story, you'll probably see a Pisces at the center of that circle. This water native has an instinctive flair for adding a fanciful and spellbinding dimension to any tale, an imaginative quality which adds a satisfying depth as well to Pisces' personal relationships. Children are intrigued by Pisceans, although the reverse is not always true! If you are a Pisces, you may hesitate to commit yourself to a relationship or career, but once you have done so, you never stop searching for ways to aid its growth.

SELF-IMAGE

Your pleasant social face, Pisces, reflects an inner self-image that pictures you as both a teacher and a student in all situations. You seek the deeper meanings of events and ideas, imparting what you find to others when they are at loose ends. You are rarely overbearing or preachy, always meeting people and situations with an open, receptive attitude that assumes there is something new to be discovered. You can, however, be too well convinced that your attitude is perennially humble, losing track of any straying into a know-it-all frame of mind. It's hard for you to get stuck in such a position, though—your watery nature is too changeable.

PRACTICALITY

One can never read a description of Pisces without having to wade through numerous and detailed accounts of this native's impracticality.

It is true that Pisces is a dreamer, but often this quality enables him or her to visualize a goal and the steps needed to reach it successfully. In addition, Pisces has a knack for bringing in outside help, making an effort a cooperative one. Lazy? Maybe. Smart? Yes. In this capacity, Pisces, you are an asset to a business that needs an intermediary, someone who can spot talent and arrange for its most productive placement. You do tend to become impractical when your vision races ahead of your patience—then it becomes a matter of "I want it now or not at all!" Needless to say, Rome, the Transcontinental Railroad, the Pyramids, and Yankee Stadium were not built by a Pisces, but they probably conceived the original ideas!

EMOTIONS

Pisces' emotional storms, although slow in peaking, make as big a set of waves as anyone else's. You tend to let others take the lead in matters of the heart; you'd rather be approached than do the approaching. Prospective loves may take this passive quality as a sign that Pisces is not interested,—a mistake, but how are they to know it? People are waiting for cues from you, Pisces, and they have as much of a right as you do to assume that the other party should make the first move! Once in a relationship, you are an intuitive, supportive partner. It is important for your mate or lover to share some if not all philosophical views with you, as you will tend to drift away if empathetic communication is not immediately forthcoming.

ATTITUDE TOWARD LIFE

You appear to be more of a daydreamer than you really are. Often what is taken for a lack of attentiveness is really a process of gathering information and impressions through a soaking-up of the atmosphere of a place or the "feel" of a person. You must receive a strong emotional impression before you feel you know a person or understand a situation. For this reason you can be said to have a psychic attitude toward life. You use your invisible antennae and mind's eye to form accurate pictures of the world, contrasting with Gemini, who uses the rational mind, Taurus—common sense, or Sagittarius—philosophical ideas.

EXTROVERTS

Yes, there is such a creature as an extroverted Pisces. This type is more mild-mannered than most of the signs, but don't let that unassuming exterior fool you. Extroverted Pisceans have their goals very clearly in mind, and although they may not be pushy, they are steady workers and expert tacticians with a knack for gently turning a situation to their advantage without raising a speck of dust. If a lover thinks that Pisces follow his or her lead, a rude awakening is in store! For the Pisces extrovert's own good, though, they should use less covert methods of handling people and problems or loved ones could call them manipulators. Otherwise, Pisces, you'll start scaring off potential loves who are drawn to your artistic temperament.

INTROVERTS

The Pisces introvert is one of the top wishers, hopers, and dreamers of the zodiac. The hurdle for this native is to gain a stronger sense of definition. It may be pleasant to just tend your own garden, ignoring or going along with other people's schemes, but you are too receptive to their input, though, to remain uninvolved. Approaching relationships slowly helps you to focus on your own needs and to see how well they mesh with those of a potential lover. Although not assertive in business, you can hold your own in a number of fields—teaching, writing, financial consultation, and counseling. Once your attentiveness is engaged so that it does not wander too far afield as your mood changes, your work is as polished as it is inspired. Introverted Pisceans have an ability to project trust, and thus many people open up and confide in them.

CHAPTER TWO

Finances

THE SECOND HOUSE OF THE ZODIAC governs money matters, activities related to finances, latent abilities, and the accumulation of emotional and physical wealth. In ancient times these things were symbolized by the sign of Taurus; and the symbol for Taurus, the bull, became synonymous with wealth. This analogy continues even in this day, as a farmer's wealth is determined by how many farm animals he owns. With the bull's ability to procreate, and thus expand a farmer's possessions, this further outlines how wealth is viewed astrologically: this portion of the chart represents the ability to create wealth from present resources.

Everyone has a natural aptitude to earn and accumulate luxuries in life. However, because of childhood environments, societal pressures, and the apparent lack of opportunity, avenues of financial good fortune may not have been presented to you. Those who make early career and money-making choices can use astrology to blend their current financial situation with areas of good fortune that might have been overlooked.

All twelve signs have the potential for financial success. However, each sign interprets the terms 'wealth' or 'security' in a different fashion. For Taureans, Cancers, and Capricorns, wealth means large sums of money —preferably cash—that they can put their hands on at any time. For Virgos and Scorpios wealth means access to power and corporations. Their skills are in their ability to deal with other people's money, and part of the thrill of success has to do with the intellectual achievement attached to these maneuvers. Aries, Geminis, and Aquarians find that wealth is often equated with freedom—freedom to say 'no' especially. For Pisceans, Leos, and Libras, wealth means luxury. And for Sagittarians wealth allows them to take gambles, to risk, to forge into uncharted businesses and to back up their vision with action.

ARIES

EARNING POWER

Aries exhibits a dynamic ability to forge ahead into untried areas and wrest from them his or her livelihood. Anything that stimulates your pioneering and militant instincts, especially if it provides a solid challenge, will bring forth your finest capabilities. A military career could fulfill your need to lead and command and to surround yourself with equipment such as weaponry or high technology, for which you have an understanding. Architecture, telecommunications or anything related to design, repair and maintenance would make excellent use of your mechanical aptitude, while racing cars or motorcycles would bring in the element of speed and sound, which seems to nourish you like food. Your need to banish what you consider evil could make you an effective consumer advocate, motivational speaker or child, marriage and family counselor. Participating in weekend races or rallies enhances your social life and can yield prize money for the undaunted Aries. Avoid unchallenging occupations as they will merely frustrate you and waste the real gifts you could contribute to the world

POSSESSIONS

You see the material world as something to be utilized for building and creating. The objects with which you surround yourself will have utility in the present, or will have served a useful function at some time in the past. Antiques hold an appeal providing they are well-crafted and have proven themselves in durability and functional excellence. If you can continue to extend their usefulness in your life, so much the better. If not, a few pieces will nevertheless be appreciated in your home as monuments to creative craftsmen of other times. Gathering possessions for their own sake, or for the sake of personal security, is not your inclination. Neither will you collect them to make your environment a showplace for others. Fine, quality tools will inspire your deep satisfaction, especially if they are constructed of metal or fine hardwood.

FEELINGS ABOUT MONEY

Money to Aries becomes a tool for fashioning the scenarios of life. Although you appreciate it as a key to freedom from bondage to an inspired lifestyle, you would not be inclined to spend much time projecting the future growth of your savings account. With adequate cash flow the door remains open to new experiences, dynamic accomplishments, and personal freedom. You use funds to enhance life, to leap into the center of exhilarating activity. If supply of ready cash falls short, you tend to panic, fearing the worst. This fear permeates your thinking, making rational consideration of the situation extremely difficult. However, you will realize from past experience that you have weathered many extremes where money is concerned, and will likely make a brilliant move which will maneuver you back to the center of the playing field.

ATTITUDE TOWARD SPENDING

Although Aries is known to be impulsive where spending money on pet projects is concerned, you are likely to be true to your character as a fine strategist. You may have more than one project in progress at any given time, but the needs of each have been considered and the required expenditures planned in advance. Your impulsiveness is more apt to surface in considering investments for potential gain. If a get-rich-quick scheme is in the cards, your adventurous, optimistic spirit will dash to the fore, eager for a roll of the dice. This could be a major pitfall so use your dynamic intellect to analyze the situation carefully, perhaps seeking professional counsel from an investor or broker. Guard against too much optimism and foolhardiness where your financial foundation is concerned.

GIFTS

Giving and receiving are also ruled by the second house. Money dealings are in truth a matter of exchange of energy. In personal exchanges material gifts are often appropriate, requiring very little thought. Little thought, however, is usually what you put into your selection of gifts for others. Then you turn supersensitive when they seem a bit unappreciative. Try to slow down enough to penetrate their character and desires and select a gift that would please *them*. Allow time in advance of the last possible moment in which to shop. If this seems too overwhelming a task, perhaps a mutual friend would help with insight and shopping. Sometime at the beginning of the year, why don't you mark on the calendar all the coming year's birthdays, anniversaries, and other special occasions of family and friends, thus relieving yourself of the usual last-minute crises? Your own taste in gifts will probably be associated with movement and mechanical functions. A gift associated with one of your favorite sports would be well received.

LATENT ABILITIES AS FINANCIAL ASSETS

One of your most dynamic qualities is a bold, pioneering spirit. There is scarcely an area of life where this asset could not be used to stimulate and infuse new vitality, although you would find the greatest fulfillment in fields uniquely suited to your special aptitudes. Use this boldness to your financial advantage by directing your energies into fields relating to weapons. gauges, sharp implements, and speed. Repair and maintenance of machinery could also be a prime area for developing your innate abilities. As an engineer or designer you would have the opportunity to create new forms and eventually see them materialize through cooperative effort with others. The explosion of the information industry, through computers and other technological advances, would serve your natural talents well. Any device that speeds up business processes could be sold, marketed, or designed by you innovative Aries. Homemakers are able to turn cooking, decorating, or teaching skills into lucrative sidelines.

FINANCIAL SECURITY

If you desire to establish a secure financial base through a slow-growth stock yielding dividends, locate a good broker who is familiar with such investments. A Taurean or Capricorn would have good insight in this area. With a solid foundation you could justify a bit of gambling with short-term investments. By all means, however, resist the temptation to borrow against future earnings. Speculative types of investments have a compulsive attraction for bold Aries, and they could produce a good return if handled with insight and close monitoring. Examine trends in both the immediate market in which you are interested and in society at large. In unstable economic phases, and even during depressions, fortunes can be made by quick and insightful transactions. Take advantage of Mars' dynamic power to make contact with your target at the right moment.

TAURUS

EARNING POWER

Earning power for Taureans is substantial, provided they stay within the bounds of their own inclination to be slow and steady in all things. Impulsiveness where money is concerned is not your style. Unlike the daring and foolhardy Aries, you will investigate each financial opportunity with great care, scrutinizing every tedious detail in order to ascertain its true potential. Once your approval has been gained, the investment will become a solid focal point of your business dealings. Your desire to dabble in the marketplace could be satisfied by supporting local bond issues. They pertain to the local area of your home and will yield the slow, steady income that sets your emotions at ease. Your stability enhances your value in most fields of employment, although you will be most gratified in work connected with products of the earth.

POSSESSIONS

Taurus is very at home in the second house of money and possessions. As an earth sign you have a natural ability with substances of the material world. Solidity is a feature of everything connected with your life, from home furnishing to your substantial bank account, which is usually moderately stable. Your extreme prudence in handling money can deteriorate into overcautiousness if not carefully monitored. Never one to take a gamble, you would rather miss an opportunity than risk losing funds due to a hasty decision. People seem to intuit your good sense in business matters and will often turn the conversation in that direction in order to benefit from your counsel.

FEELINGS ABOUT MONEY

The sign of Taurus is the one that most enjoys having money for its own sake. Few things are more deeply satisfying to you than watching large amounts of money accumulate in a savings account marked with your name. A goodly amount of spare cash should be available at all times to satisfy your recurrent desires for indulgence. Cash in hand will permit you to partake of sumptuous meals at fine restaurants on a frequent basis. Money will allow you to furnish your home lavishly, assuring the beauty and comfort of which you are so fond. An expensive automobile and a wardrobe of exquisitely made clothes will naturally be in order to complete the picture of success and opulence. The final touch will be a well-stocked kitchen complete with natural wood, warm colors, and the best quality pans and cutlery.

ATTITUDE TOWARD SPENDING

Although not inclined to simply throw money away, you are happy to spend it freely when the right situation calls for it. Money, of course, is to be collected, but also to be spent in providing the accoutrements of fine living. You have little patience with those who incessantly purchase cheap trinkets and dust collectors. If one must have a dust collector, let it be of fine craftsmanship and preferably made from material other than plastic. You will spend freely on others as well as on yourself when the occasion is right. If you are a parent, you may be prone to buy the children a few more material goods than they really need. Who but a Taurean father would bring home ice cream sundaes for the family just before dinner is served? The ultimate purpose of money is to bring pleasure, as you see it, whether in the gathering or the spending of it.

GIFTS

In the selection and giving of gifts, it is the Taurean who really shines. If you are financially secure, you will allow your heart free reign and purchase rather expensive gifts for those whom you truly love. You enjoy treating yourself to quality merchandise as well as giving the finest and most tasteful of gifts to loved ones. This is not done for theatrical purposes as much as from a deep appreciation of the genuinely beautiful products of the earth. Your sense of aesthetics is exquisite, due to the harmonious vibrations of your ruling planet, Venus. If anything is unappreciated by you, it is the trivial of the material world. One quality item far surpasses in importance many gifts of less enduring value. The Taurean has the unique capacity to select just the right gift for others, being the best one in the family to do the Christmas shopping.

LATENT ABILITIES AS FINANCIAL ASSETS

The unique abilities given to those of your sign are well suited for achieving success in the material world. You are steady and dependable— certainly an asset in any type of work. Your affinity for harmony and beauty will enhance your position even farther as most occupations will benefit by these influences. You are destined to gracefully earn a living without having to make major compromises with your personality. Most likely, you have been graced with a rich and powerful voice, which could make a singing career a possibility. With your innate understanding of and attraction to money, you could do extremely well in the field of banking or working with financial institutions. Dealing in real estate would be in line with your earth element as would sculpting, which also draws on your sense of aesthetics.

FINANCIAL SECURITY

You should be a master when it comes to arranging for financial security. You will find it easy to steadily accumulate sound investments, to regularly make deposits in your savings account, and to set aside trust funds for your children. Neither you nor your family will suffer from lack in the future; insurance coverage and pensions will neatly take care of most of life's pressing needs. Your natural tendency is to live within your income, expanding it by degrees in a geometric progression. If an investment in stocks or bonds becomes desirable, you will be inclined to give the situation much careful thought before borrowing money for that purpose. Taurus will, in the long run, benefit more by carefully considered, long-range investments than by quick investments on the stock exchange.

GEMINI

EARNING POWER

Gemini's dualistic nature makes unique and stimulating methods of earning income attractive and very lucrative. You are quite ambitious, but in a mental way, often difficult for others to understand. Productivity— usually related to intellectual pursuits—will be greatest if flexibility is maintained in your time schedule, allowing you to jump from one relevant (or irrelevant) interest to another as inspiration leads you. In a cooperative effort with another who is able to see projects through to their culmination, you will be able to fulfill your intent of bringing form to your expansive ideas. Occupations that allow you to contact the public mind will be most satisfying both mentally and financially, and your youthful contemporary appearance will further enhance your earning power in these arenas. One caution, however, is to take care not to overtax your nervous system—the most likely part of your physical makeup to be affected detrimentally by stress.

POSSESSIONS

The flow of people and possessions (money included) through your life is accepted, but only on the basis of its usefulness in furthering your expanding circle of interests. If you find yourself responsible for a large sum of money, try to give serious consideration to how it should be handled. You tend to have a gambling urge and also are easily swayed by the ideas of others. Use your own instincts in deciding upon a course of action or seek professional appraisal of your intentions. Your money probably means more to them than to you. If you have a mate or partner who is rooted in the material side of life, you could benefit from a cooperative approach—your partner managing and you contributing brilliant ideas. Much could be accomplished in this way.

FEELINGS ABOUT MONEY

You may touch a dizzying multitude of places and things in your carousel ride through life, but rarely will you become attached to any of them. Possessiveness in any form is simply not a part of your character. Money is a useful tool for acquiring the luxuries you enjoy, and your involvement with it ends there. Counting your accumulation of wealth leaves you cold. Anything which is likely to tie you down to one place or limit your activity is viewed with disdain—even the traditional home in suburbia. An apartment in the city would be more in keeping with your lifestyle. Become aware of your high degree of sensitivity, accepting it as a part of your makeup that requires special consideration. Use your resources to create an insulation from excess agitation, which is extremely damaging to your nervous system.

ATTITUDE TOWARD SPENDING

Although you often move quickly where spending money is concerned, you seldom part with cash foolishly. Indecision is your worst enemy. If faced with the necessity to make a purchase, you may well end up with two items rather than one due solely to the fact that you could not decide which you preferred. You may frequently make small purchases that will always be tasteful and certainly contemporary. Some may consider your small investments frivolous, but you view them as appreciation of exquisite design wherever found. The element of surprise is a factor as well, exerting an intriguing, magnetic influence difficult for a Gemini to resist. As you are not known as a deeply emotional person, your attitude toward spending will be more an intellectual appreciation than a gut-level satisfaction.

GIFTS

Gemini is the original year-round shopper. Delighting in surprising friends with unexpected gifts, you will flit through stores waiting for that certain gift to catch your eye. Not only is this an enjoyable pursuit, but it serves to keep you in touch with the latest styles and trends. Whatever is popular at the moment will attract you strongly, whether as a gift for yourself or another. Your flair for delightful and unusual wrapping paper is unsurpassed—the wrapping being almost as important as the contents. A surprise gift from another will leave a lasting impression, especially if it is carefully selected and wrapped. Books, jewelry, and theater tickets would be appreciated by Gemini.

LATENT ABILITIES AS FINANCIAL ASSETS

Gemini's basic ability to process vast amounts of information with near-computer speed makes you a prized asset in buzzing offices or businesses where incisive, quick decisions are required on a momentary basis. Although your energy level may prove unsettling to those of earthier nature, your skill, competence, and quicksilver intellect will surely draw admiration from all quarters. To avoid frustration in dealing with plodding coworkers, try to delegate a carefully selected liaison person between you and the more sedentary members in your office. Your social fluidity and keen grasp of languages could open the door to work in foreign service of some sort. Your conversational skills could find a wonderful outlet, as diplomatic functions are greatly enhanced by the scintillating brilliance of the Mercurial mind. Your sense of style and contemporary fashion could be an asset there as well.

FINANCIAL SECURITY

The question of financial security is not one that weighs heavily upon you. An adequate checking account gives you freedom to move quickly through life's changing picture, but a well-padded savings account is not prominent in your plans. Faith in your own vast resources of intellect and communication leads you to believe that you are not likely to be vulnerable to stagnant, limiting situations. Focusing on the moment will seem more desirable than dealing with weighty projections of possible future needs. If you desire to invest for long-term earnings, consider a field related to communications or paper products—especially where paper may be used as a vehicle for public contact in a political, literary, or journalistic manner.

CANCER

EARNING POWER

As a Cancerian you will find your earning power enhanced by unique abilities that give a strength perhaps unexpected by others. In business you can be formidable, holding your position with great tenacity and skill. Although you may appear somewhat passive in other areas where your life's work is concerned, you are extremely shrewd and often surprise the world with your ability to bring projects to fruition regardless of obstacles or delays. Defeat in business matters is unknown to you as your inherent nature to hold fast will insure the completion and success of all ventures to which you apply yourself. A deep sympathy with the masses can lead to your prospering in fields where mass consciousness or historical perspective of nations is significant. Being a child of the moon, all occupations connected with bodies of water would evoke the best from your deep emotional bond with that element.

POSSESSIONS

Possessions are important to you—especially when they relate to the home. This, indeed, can become a major stumbling block as you find it virtually impossible to release anything you have accumulated over the years. Collecting is a favorite pastime for Cancer natives, but taken to its extreme you could become fenced in by voluminous possessions, which then become a source of helpless frustration. Allow yourself to satisfy the collector's instinct by creating a fine collection of antiques. The most appealing collectibles would be related to the sea or to ships, or perhaps cultural artifacts of historical value. Knowing your propensity for holding on to things, try to carefully discern an object's true and lasting value before incorporating it into your life; once it is accepted, fully enjoy its richness and beauty.

FEELINGS ABOUT MONEY

Cancer's relationship to money is always founded on an emotional need for security. Although you do not worship money as such, you recognize its ability to prevent anxiety and give much attention to being sure there is an adequate amount in the bank. You are a thrifty individual, not inclined toward capricious expenditures, yet at times the moon's influence may obscure your usually sound judgment. You would benefit greatly by observing monthly lunar cycles, noting particularly good or bad days to see if over a period of time they fall into an observable cycle. Be alert to new and full moon days to determine whether you are emotionally stable or unstable at those times. Feelings will be a strong motivating factor in your financial dealings, often lending excessive weight to your monetary decisions. Balance this by reviewing the hard facts as unemotionally as possible.

ATTITUDE TOWARD SPENDING

Cancer types have a marvelous sense of economy when it comes to spending money. You fluctuate widely from positive to negative moods, but your underlying good sense will usually save you from wasting money foolishly on unneeded items. Objects you spend money on will be in the traditional vein and will probably be of good quality. A house full of cheap trinkets would never satisfy you, but an extensive collection of good books would fulfill both your sense of aesthetics and of tradition. Keeping a secure insulation of money will be vastly more appealing than frequent shopping sprees, although you will enjoy the occasional foray into department stores to select a fine item for the home. A few personal luxuries will be worthy of your purchase and will enhance your sense of self.

GIFTS

Giving gifts will be one of life's true pleasures for you as you look forward with youthful enthusiasm to the recipient's delight in receiving a well-chosen gift. The receiver's potential appreciation will stir you to give much attention to buying the gift, although your tendency will be to look for something you like rather than one that would please him or her. Your deep need to satisfy others will come to your aid here as you remind yourself that you really do want him or her to totally enjoy your offering. An elegant gift means much to you, and this sense will cause you to select tasteful things for friends. If purchasing for one in the sign of Cancer, remember that women will enjoy very feminine things—perhaps a special scent of perfume or body oil, lingerie, or a garment made of fine fabric. Men will appreciate personalized gifts such as monogrammed handkerchiefs. An expensive-looking tie or set of cuff links would warm his heart, but it's best to avoid clothing as his tastes are particular and he simply won't wear what he doesn't like.

LATENT ABILITIES AS FINANCIAL ASSETS

One of your unique gifts as a Cancer native is a superb memory. None in the zodiac can excel you in power of retention of the details of past events. Even your own childhood is often recalled in vivid detail. This priceless treasure can open doors to deeply satisfying work in institutions that preserve historical records of civilizations and cultures. You could find fulfillment as a museum curator or in work with a local historical society. Your sensitivity and focus on things related to home and family could lead you to work in an occupation connected with children. In that capacity your ability to form rich emotional bonds would be a definite asset. The same sensitive nature could be directed to the healing arts, where your compassion and tenderness would comfort many.

FINANCIAL SECURITY

The financial security of your future will be of primary importance to you, especially in considering the possibility of illness or accident in later years. If health is threatened, you become obsessed and are capable of magnifying the condition entirely out of proportion to its actual seriousness, resulting in anxiety which further complicates the original condition. Knowing this, be sure to warm yourself with adequate health insurance to allay the possible worry, which will surely be detrimental to your sensitive nature. A good-sized savings account will have as much psychological as practical value. Your family's welfare will occupy much of your attention, and you will want to make arrangements for their future security as well. Be sure to plan well ahead for the cost of college education for the children.

LEO

EARNING POWER

Earning his or her daily bread can be more pleasure than work to the exuberant Leo. This individual will readily dive into the most demanding career, reveling in the thought of great accomplishments to be made, vast projects to be constructed, and large numbers of people to impress. If you are a native of this sign, you will do everything on a grand scale, including earning income. Hard work only seems to increase your energy, particularly if your work allows the expansion of your creative imagination. You are known for thoroughness and are not likely to make snap decisions. The final outcome of your deliberations will be carefully considered and sound. You are at your best in positions of management where your magnanimous personality and firm direction will magnetically attract support and cooperation from those with whom you work.

POSSESSIONS

Leo's possessions will be extravagant and tasteful, always of the highest quality and most dramatic visual appeal. Not one for trivia, you will surround yourself with warmth and richness, and then attract a bevy of appreciative admirers with whom to share your opulent environment. Review any part of Leo's life and you will find the same theme of quality, warmth, and drama. You take pride in showing off your possessions to others and will feel rebuffed if they are not properly appreciative. Leo will want to have an attractive car, fine clothing, a substantial desk in his or her well-decorated office, and a congenial home awaiting at the end of the day. Your ceaseless energy is also one of your possessions and should be kept vital by a few minutes alone at rest each day. Create a psychologically satisfying place in which you may commune with the inner person in a quiet environment.

FEELINGS ABOUT MONEY

Money is a wonderful thing to a Leo, enjoyed as much in itself as for the material objects and experiences it can purchase. You would be the one who, while dining with many jovial friends at the most elegant restaurant in town, would flourish a hundred-dollar bill with which to ignite your cigar. There will ensue a wave of awe and admiration—just what you had in mind, of course. An adequate, or more than adequate, amount of money in hand at all times will assure you the freedom to display your personality in the grandest manner. Your personality will be just as expansive without funds, but you will feel frustrated at the limitation placed on your generous nature. With your capabilities, the avenues to bountiful income should be wide open, giving freedom to your magnanimity.

ATTITUDE TOWARD SPENDING

You could be identified by the following old cliché: "The last of the big spenders." Leo natives manifest largeness in every way including their willingness to part with enormous sums of cash when the mood or situation dictates. If a good time is had by all, then virtually any expenditure will have been well worth it. Spending a goodly amount on yourself is done with equal abandon, not heedlessly of course, but with total satisfaction and no regrets. Despite outward appearances, you are not a spendthrift and certainly would not waste money on trivia or on individuals who did not appreciate your generosity. Life is to be lived to the fullest in your script, and part of that fullness includes enjoying the finest material goods life has to offer, and many good friends with whom to share it all.

GIFTS

As might be imagined, when it comes to giving gifts you outshine all the rest. Skimping on a gift to anyone, yourself included, would be unthinkable and—worse—could lead others to view you as stingy. If there is anything you are not, it is stingy! Generous, sometimes to a fault, you would rather do with less yourself than see others receive less than you feel they deserve. You are a somewhat impulsive buyer, and in your desire to impress others may spend quite lavishly on a gift. If the item to be purchased is large in size, so much the better. Having an artistic flair, you could design a flamboyant wrapping and execute it yourself with great relish. Your personal taste in gifts will run toward richness—garments of the most expensive fabrics, sizable costume jewelry, rings with large stones, a plush set of monogrammed towels, and decorative items in yellows, oranges, and golds.

Latent Abilities as Financial Assets

As a Leo native you are ruled by the sun, the life-giver and benefactor to all in its realm. Likewise, your innate understanding of authority can place you in positions where many can benefit by your true warmheartedness and desire to give freely to others. You are loyal and optimistic and naturally view situations with a broad perspective. These qualities coupled with a practical idealism and deep faith in what is right will especially suit you to an occupation requiring the responsibility for others. Teaching older children could be an excellent field for you, as would any craft or profession in the dramatic arts. Leo is the natural performer, desiring to be on stage at all times. Your philanthropic sense could incline you to a public life where your noble character would be a wonderful example for all.

Financial Security

Your bountiful enthusiasm, though welcome in most areas of life, can become a problem when trying to make financial arrangements for the future. You are all too likely to become enamored with what appears to be glamorous opportunities, failing to perceive their true nature. With existing financial pressures, you become worrisome, often moving hastily into ill-considered ventures. To avoid this mishap, discipline yourself to analyze every detail with utmost care. A reliable investment counselor could be just the right ally and would have time-earned knowledge to help you reach a wise decision. Real estate should prove a good investment for Leos as well as businesses dealing with automation. View others with care so as not to be taken too strongly by first impressions.

VIRGO

Earning Power

Virgo's earning power is greatest in occupations requiring precision and attention to detail. You are of unsurpassed value in a supporting role dealing with minutiae and giving help to all involved to assure the successful outcome of any endeavor. In a secretarial position your skills could find their true usefulness, as this type of work will fill your appetite for detail, as well as providing the daily routine in which you flourish. Your keen, analytical insight could indicate work in the scientific community, especially in a research capacity. With your desire for cleanliness and purity, the fields of health and hygiene could open to you, especially in areas that focus on nutrition. Your natural charitableness toward others would make you suitable for certain types of hospital work or nutritional counseling.

Possessions

Your natural sensitivity to detail will cause you to be highly conscious of all material objects in your life. Generally your possessions will be uniform in style and quality, attractively arranged, and well cared for. Collections of knickknacks will be unappealing as they require far too much attention in dusting and organizing. Your taste is refined and you appreciate quality, usually in a conservative vein. Your primary concern regarding possessions is that they be functional. Objects in your life are to be used, and in their usefulness you find their true beauty. Regardless of the number of possessions in your environment, you will know the exact location of each one at any given time. Although this trait may seem extreme to others, it assures the orderly, predictable lifestyle on which you thrive.

FEELINGS ABOUT MONEY

Money will be useful to you for what it can purchase to keep your life organized and in providing the materials needed to satisfy your creative urge. As part of a practical life plan, you will feel best directing a portion of your income into various types of insurance to establish a secure structure within which you may operate without excessive concern for the future. You will feel most emotionally stable with a reliable, steady income, without which you tend to worry excessively, overtaxing your highly sensitive nervous system. Your inventive genius will want to express itself through hobbies which provide a creative outlet for your boundless energy. Frequently these interests may require rather refined and expensive equipment such as a home computer or a quality electronic device. Here again, money will be your ally in furthering personal interests.

ATTITUDE TOWARD SPENDING

Natives of Virgo are quite frugal individuals. Although generally not miserly, your natural reserve will cause you to be cautious and thoughtful before parting with sums of money. Shopping is not particularly appealing to you in itself, but if you wish to purchase a particular item, you will give considerable attention to reviewing the offerings on the marketplace and comparing values with meticulous care. You will perceive expenditures for useful items as wise, but will have no inclination to clutter your life with unneeded paraphernalia. Public appearance is a point of consciousness to you, and the purchase of a neat and functional wardrobe will warrant your attention. Perhaps a tedious endeavor, you will prefer to select your own garments to ensure the harmony and utility of your wardrobe.

GIFTS

Exchanging gifts is an area Virgos would just as soon avoid. Not only are there too many questionable details to be considered, but the outlay of cash for a possibly nonpractical item causes resistance in your realistic nature. You may not be overly generous, but any gift purchased will be in excellent taste carefully considered. In order to avoid lengthy shopping trips and keep the gift sensible, you may decide to give a gift certificate —a gift you would enjoy receiving yourself. You will exercise the usual care in recalling the dates of birthdays and special events in the lives of others, yet won't be offended if a friend overlooks yours. When giving to a Virgo, avoid gifts of a personal nature as individuals of this sign have their own very particular taste and are not inclined to use anything that is not exactly perfect for them.

LATENT ABILITIES AS FINANCIAL ASSETS

Your particular focus in life centers around abilities that have high-market value—namely industriousness and highly developed powers of discrimination. You will excel at tasks requiring persistence beyond the average and will thoroughly enjoy delving into mountains of laborious detail that would be unapproachable by other signs. As a secretary to a dynamic business person, you would be a wonderful asset, or as a researcher in the scientific department of a university. You are an intrepid analyst and will thrive in any position drawing upon your precise insight and capacity to sustain a highly intellectual activity over long periods of time. Use your sometimes overfastidious tendency to your advantage in a field where utmost cleanliness is essential, but guard against this same tendency when manifesting itself as a hypercritical temperament in regard to your coworkers.

FINANCIAL SECURITY

You will be most content with a well-planned future that avoids nagging insecurities. You tend to worry excessively, which can adversely affect your high-strung nature, so plan for adequate security with insurance—life, health, and medical—and review the investment markets as a possible source of long-term income. Your overcautiousness could be a detriment here as the best opportunities may pass by while you are contemplating the pros and cons of the investment. However, once your timing is right, you can be one of the most fortunate of investors. If your inclination is toward personal business ventures, consider an area connected with paper in some way. Whatever you do, capitalize on your skill in analyzing details—this especially is where you can rise above the majority of individuals. Develop your timing and it will open the door to success.

LIBRA

EARNING POWER

Libra's peace-loving temperament is certainly an asset where earning power is concerned. In any work environment you will be one who adds beauty and refinement while everything is made more harmonious. Of all the signs you are most likely to flourish in a partnership. Born in the sign of balance, you will seek an equal sharing of work and rewards for you and your partner whether it be in business or a personal relationship. Your ruling planet, Venus, bestows upon you a deep desire for the beautiful, which would naturally incline you toward occupations focused on the aesthetic. You would do well as a hairstylist, a milliner, or a designer of women's fashions. Your taste runs toward the elegant, making you a superb candidate for work in fields dealing with personal luxuries.

POSSESSIONS

The delights of the material world hold an obvious attraction for you. Your reputation as a romantic is reflected in your surroundings, which generally contain as many traditionally elegant objects as you can reasonably afford. It is easy for you to exceed the limits of your projected budget —if an especially appealing item tempts you, your credit card will be used without delay. The richness added to your life will be well worth the expenditure. A pretty home is important to you, and as you love to share it with guests, you will have every reason to spend a little extra money to furnish it well. Whatever you own of a personal nature will be in good taste and will often include a few fine antique pieces, especially when it comes to jewelry. Although your wardrobe choices have a certain substantial appearance, there is an unmistakable airiness about every piece.

FEELINGS ABOUT MONEY

You find it extremely difficult to take money very seriously, however hard you try. Of course, you like to have an adequate supply in order to keep up with your elegant taste, but really you would be just as happy with a number of credit cards and a checkbook. Your finances tend to experience frequent fluctuations, due to a lack of sound planning for the future. It's not that you are irresponsible—you are merely busy living in the moment and aren't inclined to spend much time projecting into future financial possibilities. Although you hope your financial life will always run smoothly, you have great difficulty in deciding how to sustain this condition and usually end up not dealing with it at all until absolutely necessary.

ATTITUDE TOWARD SPENDING

Spending money is something you thoroughly enjoy. Your sense of romance and enjoyment of pleasant living conditions combined with an easygoing attitude toward life can often lead you into spending more freely than would be considered prudent by most. Being quite an impulse buyer, you are capable of running up rather large bills at the best stores, and often make purchases that would be considered frivolous by most standards. Although you may experience moments of despair when confronted with the bill, you quickly bounce back to your inherent optimism and choose instead to spend the time enjoying your purchases. The worst disasters are likely to occur when you shop with other impulse buyers, as this will surely motivate you to be even more liberal in spending than would normally be your wont.

GIFTS

Libra will delight in both the giving and receiving of gifts. Shopping is an art form to you, and when considering a gift for a friend you will call upon your resources to select a special piece that both reflects yourself and appeals to the recipient. You have a well-developed eye for beauty and quality and often select gifts of traditional elegance. A lovely piece of crystal or a fine antique ring or necklace would be typical of your choices. Any type of soap, oil, lotion, or other product designed to enhance one's beauty would be appealing as would a gift certificate for a beauty treatment. Practicality is not one of your major concerns in this area. You will no doubt select a sentimental card to accompany the gift, and choose the wrapping paper with utmost care so that everything will reflect your fine taste and sense of romance.

LATENT ABILITIES AS FINANCIAL ASSETS

Your innate sense of justice could lead you into unexpected fields ranging from diplomat to welfare worker. You are able to maintain an effortless equilibrium when dealing with the public, and although your personal life may be prone to wild fluctuations, the work environment seems magically immune from such inconsistencies. You do have sound business sense and manage to keep your wits about you even though tending to be a bit extravagant at times. Always amiable and courteous, you will impress people favorably wherever you are placed. You could do well as a manager, perhaps connected with stage productions, or as a musical director. Music feeds your soul, and work in that field could be healing to you personally as well as providing a marvelous creative outlet to enrich the lives of others. Whatever your work, try to avoid nonharmonious conditions as they will not allow you to expand as you would like.

FINANCIAL SECURITY

Hopefully, Libra, you will find yourself in a partnership with someone who naturally plans ahead for years down the road. This would relieve you of an aspect of life which you consider troublesome. Although you try to keep your life in good order and make wise investments when necessary, you tend to rely far too much on the advice of others. Being easily influenced by others, you could leave important decisions in the hands of those not skilled enough to handle them wisely. Your lifestyle could connect you with financiers, in which case you will have the advantage of learning from them. If not, be sure to obtain sound professional advice before risking any investment. Since you have been bountifully gifted with personal creativity, you may do just as well developing markets for your own creations rather than taking chances with more abstract investments.

SCORPIO

EARNING POWER

Scorpio's earning power is directly related to a main characteristic of this sign—intense energy and power. With this vast resource focused on income, you will be able to generate a livelihood in any field of your choice. Your preference in occupations leans toward work in which there is a mystery to be solved or some aspect of the unknown to be discovered. In this area you could be well suited to computer programming, as it is a discipline requiring both logic and a certain detectivelike skill. With Mars as your ruler, your income could be connected with a military career either on land or at sea. There is a deep, intuitive quality to the Scorpio native, which could incline you toward work as a psychiatrist or psychologist. Whatever your field, power will somehow be in evidence, and it is your task to use it wisely and ethically.

POSSESSIONS

An environment littered with possessions will mean little to you, as money will be seen more as a tool for buying power than as an avenue to vast possessions. You will enjoy owning objects of quality and will often acquire rather unusual items relating to the occult or in some way to the unknown. Your belongings will have a certain boldness about them, a certain intensity. You are not overly concerned with the public's view of your physical surroundings and you prefer to remain an enigma to others. Much of your ability to be effective lies in the air of mystery that permeates your character, so your less conventional possessions will merely serve to enhance your image. Although you have a streak of flamboyance, your basic foundation will be rather conservative, reflected in the practical and utilitarian quality of things in your environment.

FEELINGS ABOUT MONEY

You have deep feelings about money for the power it can bring, but at the same time find it less important than a project or cause in which you choose to immerse yourself. Foremost to you is giving your total energy to the focus of the moment, and if that is gathering money you will accomplish it with the greatest of zeal. Money is more likely to be viewed as something to use than something to have. You tend to become so intensely focused on the current, main event of your life that the amount of money available is relegated to second place in your concerns. However, you actively dislike failure of any kind; to the degree that money represents success or accomplishment, it will then become important as an asset. Money also provides you with the freedom to enjoy the occasional overindulgences in which you revel.

ATTITUDE TOWARD SPENDING

As a spender your overall tone runs toward the conservative, yet you are not beyond spending quite a bit on yourself or a friend should feelings indicate such a need. You have the power to methodically accumulate a large sum of cash rather quickly when your gaze has come to rest on a desired possession. Seemingly, you have the ability to generate money out of nowhere, creating your own source of income where a job didn't even exist before. You perceive this merely as a transfer from one form of energy to another, and you are a master manipulator of energy. In a sense, the concept of spending money is not real to you. Your fine tuning allows you to perceive in a deeper way that nothing is ever spent, but one energy is simply exchanged for another. Where others may see the outflow of money as a loss you perceive it as a process, a flow that draws new energies and events into your life.

GIFTS

Scorpios are notoriously difficult to buy gifts for unless you are extremely aware of their hidden depths. They love anything of dramatic character, but at the same time have an acute sensitivity to their particular brand of aesthetics. They will greatly appreciate a well-chosen gift, especially if it becomes a lasting reminder of friendship. There is a leaning toward the scientific in this sign, and the combination of that inclination with a love of mystery could indicate a liking for some type of science fiction literature or art. Scorpio may experience some apprehension connected with buying gifts for others, as he is most intent on finding the absolutely perfect gift for a specific individual. Generally your intuition will come to the rescue if you place yourself in a receptive state. Usually the inspiration comes unexpectedly, often as you are wandering through a store wondering what to get. Trust your inspiration.

LATENT ABILITIES AS FINANCIAL ASSETS

You will discover many unexpected areas in which your less obvious abilities can be turned into financial assets. Probably your intuitive insight into human nature will be your best guide in life, and though not a salable commodity in itself, you will often see a little deeper than most into the root of things with this capacity. This could lead you to work in unusual areas of healing, especially as they relate to matters of the spirit. You may be attracted to a career as a detective or a law enforcement officer, or even into the field of chemistry where mysteries await discovery. You like discipline and respond well to it, which could incline you to a military career or a profession as a doctor, dentist, pathologist, or surgeon—all of which require a high degree of discipline and skill. You must feel that your work is important in the world in order to bring the great strength of your character to life.

FINANCIAL SECURITY

Your plans for financial security are likely to be based on faith in your own ability and energy to create what is needed at the time, rather than investments in the future, which often seem a bit nebulous to you. The future is unpredictable, but the present is vital and alive. You thoroughly enjoy business success and feel confident in your ability to be successful both now and later. The ephemeral quality of the stock market will leave you cold, but you may be inclined to have one or two modest, steady, maybe blue-chip investments with an occasional dramatic business venture every few years. Investment in adequate insurance to cover possible emergencies will seem wise to you and will assure you the freedom to remain unconcerned with this facet of life. Although you do not expect unfortunate accidents, neither do you wish to be devastated by them should they occur.

SAGITTARIUS

EARNING POWER

Earning power for Sagittarius will pivot around physical, mental, and emotional freedom. Restriction is the surest way to place a halter on your unique, expansive type of genius. The key to maximizing your earning capabilities and the theme through which you render the greatest service in the world is: "Don't fence me in." The animal kingdom is dear to you, especially when it comes to work with horses or dogs. You could become a fine veterinarian or trainer of horses with this predisposition. Your income will most likely be earned in a field for which you have a heartfelt affinity, as the tedium of an uninspired occupation will never bring forth your finest offering. Generally your type is extremely well suited to work involving travel at a distance from the home, which capitalizes not only on your love of physical freedom, but also on your desire for excitement and innate urge to explore the unknown.

POSSESSIONS

Possession do not hold a great deal of meaning for you and more often become annoying inconveniences. The responsibility of stewardship of physical possessions is not one which you care to make foremost in your life. Your preoccupation with movement and travel further minimize the need of fixed objects around you, as your environment is the world itself rather than a house, family, or office. With the world as your home you still refuse to become possessive in any way, knowing that the deeper spiritual nature of all existence transcends man's desire to attach ownership to all he surveys. Even the small possessions that accompany you in your travels, such as keys, sunglasses, etc., are likely to be mislaid repeatedly as your mind is usually operating in other realms.

FEELINGS ABOUT MONEY

Your feelings about money are fairly neutral. It is just another object to be dealt with—one with which you'd rather not spend too much time. You can't seem to hold on to money, probably due to its lack of significance to you, and it quickly slips out of your hand to take care of mundane necessities or to purchase another serving of freedom in your active life. You feel some vague appreciation of its value as a key to freedom from the dull monotony of a routine job, and certainly you recognize its necessity as a lubricant for life's perpetual activity, but here your relationship with it ends. You don't care to manage it, collect it, or glory in it, and are perfectly happy to leave the money managing and accumulating to those more inclined to such pursuits.

ATTITUDE TOWARD SPENDING

The outflow of money is a rather slippery affair to you. Never one to be grasping, you tend to go to the opposite extreme where finances are concerned, seldom allowing money to stay in your grasp long before it flows back into circulation. If you find yourself heir to a generous sum of cash or worldly goods, you would be wise to locate a trusted estate manager to oversee the disposition of your wealth. You are simply not temperamentally suited to such pursuits, yet your highly developed sense of physical and spiritual integrity will make you realize that you must take responsibility in these concerns. You will be perfectly content with a regular income from your estate, knowing that the cumbersome aspect of worldly wealth is in good hands, and that you have fulfilled your responsibility of stewardship.

GIFTS

As a Sagittarian you will find the prospect of selecting gifts for others a rather awkward matter. This is not due to a lack of generosity, but to your more expansive relationship to mankind as a whole, making it slightly difficult to narrow your focus down to a single individual. Yet you wish to give to your friends and are quite pleased when they are appreciative of your selection. In this regard you are willing to make the effort to take extra time and shop carefully. Buying gifts for those of your sign is an uncomplicated matter. Since you are always mislaying small belongings, there is a constant need to have them replaced. You tend to be sports-oriented and are easily pleased by gifts that consider this. Anything of an outdoorsy character will surely gain your approval. A hand-knitted sweater would be a sure hit.

LATENT ABILITIES AS FINANCIAL ASSETS

You are interested in a broad spectrum of pursuits and can quite easily hold down two jobs at once, provided they both appeal to your interests in some way. You will view them more as adventures than as mundane employment. Your ability to effectively work at several tasks at once will likely lead you into the center of activity somewhere. Beneath the surface you have a deep philosophical bent and under the right conditions would make an excellent teacher. Your intellectual potential is formidable, enhanced by your capacity to store enormous amounts of knowledge for use at a later date. The world of academia could prove appealing provided there remains plenty of latitude for exploration of personal interests. You will feel a strong need to be physically active, which could provide a basis for employment in the sports field or could lead to a profession as an athlete or a jockey.

FINANCIAL SECURITY

You will not be enthralled by the prospect of making fixed plans for future financial security. You have a strong gambling instinct, which is certainly not the foundation from which to deal with matters of personal security. Even if a certain investment catches your interest, you may not want to stay around long enough to see the eventual outcome of your choice. The safest approach for you is to keep half of your money in a savings account at all times, then invest the other half if you feel so inclined and see how it goes. In investments of any sort you will do best in businesses or investments related to movement or faraway places. Imported products could be good for you, but avoid investments connected with airlines. Investments in racehorse facilities could be an area you might enjoy.

CAPRICORN

EARNING POWER

Of all the signs, Capricorn may well have the greatest earning power, not necessarily because of great talent or energy, but as a result of a driving ambition, which propels him or her forward over every obstacle. If this is your sign, nothing can keep you from reaching your desired goal, and you are most definitely goal-oriented. Your occupations will be taken with great seriousness, though you have a refreshing wit that offsets your otherwise unbearable heaviness. You thoroughly relish being in the public eye and could easily be attracted to the political arena where your abilities as a statesman would be used to advantage. A career will be a main focal point for you, often to the exclusion of other facets of life. Your rise in accomplishment will be through your own effort, but you won't have any qualms about using other people as stepping stones if they can assist your relentless climb up the social and professional mountain.

POSSESSIONS

Possessions will be a fixed part of your life, necessary to establish your social position. As with most things in your life, they will be used as supports for your further advancement. Generally you have a strong taste for the traditional, which reflects in every aspect of your life from clothing, to home, to automobile. Your bookshelves will be lined with the weightiest-looking volumes, preferably in matched sets bound in leather and embossed with gold print. Although you are an earth sign, many would consider dust to be your true element. Capricorn would be in heaven poring over the classics in ancient archives. It is not uncommon for musical instruments to grace your environment, as you are often musically gifted and find deep satisfaction in this expression.

FEELINGS ABOUT MONEY

Money to Capricorn is without a doubt the key to success and social acclaim. You will make financial plans and budgets in great detail, often projecting years into the future, and then stick by them with awesome rigidity. Unexpected change is not a welcome factor in your life. You are not likely to experience a frivolous moment where money or anything else is concerned. Financial security is essential to your emotional condition, and will be the foundation for your earning a steady paycheck throughout life. Money equates with status in your view, so the degree of your wealth will be a direct reflection to your self-image. You find it necessary to plan each financial maneuver in advance with utmost care, as only by careful planning will your intentions be realized.

ATTITUDE TOWARD SPENDING

Spending will be permitted only after the utmost rational consideration has been given, and only if there is an absolutely sound reason for doing so. Since money is the direct link to your social position, it follows that any unnecessary expenditure could possibly retard your steady pursuit of public recognition. Of course, it will be wise to spend money on certain quality items that will further your lifestyle. Often you feel more comfortable with things than with people and can find your material environment a refuge when emotional relationships become difficult. Investments yielding steady income will be especially attractive to you and are well justified by predictable returns from the marketplace. Spending in order to make money will be viewed as a sound practice, providing good results are assured.

GIFTS

You, as a Capricorn, have the unique ability to select exactly the right gifts for others. With considerable thought and unmistakable clarity of vision, you will be able to identify a gift suitable to a friend's taste and of lasting traditional value. Gifts from a Capricorn will be used and appreciated for many years. Although you are not inclined to spend exorbitantly, you can nevertheless be quite generous under the right circumstances. Your choices will tend to be of a practical nature—something that can be worn or used in your accustomed lifestyle. You, too, will appreciate a gift of utilitarian value. Trinkets and trivia will not inspire you in any degree. You would be pleased by a gift that would be useful in your professional life, perhaps a substantial briefcase or a subscription to a magazine connected with your business. You are not inclined to wear jewelry, but a fine, quality garment of conservative styling could be just right for you.

LATENT ABILITIES AS FINANCIAL ASSETS

Your natural desire for permanence and durability give you an innate understanding of things related to the earth. You are a dependable, hard worker and could do quite well in the field of agriculture. Earth-connected work of a general and practical nature such as large land and building enterprises could prove highly profitable. The capacity to make the most of all opportunities will work to your advantage in all large-scale undertakings. Your inborn dignity will be a powerful asset, as people will magnetically be attracted into your sphere of influence and will show a natural confidence in your ideas and abilities. Your serious approach to life could suit you to some areas of writing, while your sense of structure and form could give you talents as a designer, decorator, or upholsterer.

FINANCIAL SECURITY

Financial security is an area in which your greatest attributes come to the fore. Ever the plodder and the planner, you will find it extremely easy to articulate the most tiresome details into a well-rounded financial plan, which will secure you, your family, and your business far into the future. Every facet of life will be examined and inserted into its proper place in the scheme of ever-increasing stability and security. You tend to have many inward fears, which can cause you to be overcautious, but you learn well from the past and can rely on lessons learned by the mistakes of others. You are a splendid business person and will probably generate sufficient income through your work to provide adequate security, but you will be more at ease if you take things a step farther and invest in a few blue-chip stocks or reliable bonds, which yield a steady income.

AQUARIUS

EARNING POWER

As an Aquarian your earnings will come from areas not accessible to other signs. Your ruling planet, Uranus, bestows unique insight into the new, the dynamic, and the electrical. Your ideas extend even beyond the pioneering work of Aries into the totally avant-garde, particularly when expressed through the arts. Scientifically inclined, your work could be in new forms of communication, or in the design of equipment to be used in space exploration. The heavens hold a mysterious intrigue for you and it would not be uncommon for your scientific skills to be used in astrology or astronomy. A true individualist, you will not be limited by society's expectations, and, in fact, will be unlikely to give the opinions of others even the slightest consideration, not due to your own idealism as much as to plain indifference.

POSSESSIONS

Possessions play a minor role in your life and are more likely to be associated with limitations than with accomplishment. You will want to have access to any facilities needed to further explore your futuristic interests. The newest and best equipment becomes an absolute necessity and in that regard you may enjoy having your own laboratory or workshop and a wide variety of reference books. Your basic creature comforts will be minimal. You are always involved with humanity as a whole and thus may find it beneficial to create a refined atmosphere in which to entertain when necessary. More often your approach to personal and social exchanges will be casual, perhaps even leaning toward the eccentric. Although not personally attached to your environment, you do relish being viewed as different, and may take extra pains to cultivate that impression through your possessions and environment.

FEELINGS ABOUT MONEY

Money is expedience to the busy Aquarian. You thrive on the new and ever-changing and are not beyond manipulating society in certain ways to increase the cash flow that supports your appetite for the unusual. Although not an accumulator of money, you will often lend your personal support to causes that favor reform or advance the human condition in some way. Although you do not blatantly take advantage of others, you will use social or work situations to your advantage, viewing this as life's opportunity to further your great contribution. Personal independence is enormously important to you, and you will be sure to have enough money yourself—or have access to enough money—that you will never need to fear entrapment into dull routine.

ATTITUDE TOWARD SPENDING

Money will be spent whenever necessary to further your independent work or research. Life without expression of personal ideas is no better than death to you, so in this way money becomes a key to life. You are prone to occasional erratic behavior, which sometimes appears in your attitude toward spending. Usually a thoughtful spender, you can undergo periods of wild expenditure, investing in spur-of-the-moment schemes that are quite likely to fall flat. Your tendency to want to help others could make you available for loans to a friend in need. As long as your own supply remains adequate, you could allow him or her plenty of time to repay the debt. You enjoy art, music, and literature, and will not mind at all the expense of a social evening including dinner followed by the theater or a concert, especially if the theme is contemporary.

GIFTS

When buying for Aquarians, be sure to consider their likes and dislikes. They will appreciate your gift with warm thanks if it pleases them, but if not they can be most ungracious. Those of your sign are avid readers and will be responsive to a gift of reading material, either books or magazines, and may possibly enjoy tickets to hear a lecture by a future-oriented individual. Antiques usually please you but the item must be authentic. Likewise any artwork must be an original or at least one of a limited edition. You could well be an electronics buff and will appreciate an unusual piece of gear to add to your setup. When shopping for a gift for another person, take care to consider his or her taste rather than your own. So much time is wrapped up in your own thoughts, you can easily lose track of the interests of others.

LATENT ABILITIES AS FINANCIAL ASSETS

A less often noted aspect of the Aquarian's interest is his or her affinity for the ancient past, which could reap profits through work as a historian, or more likely, a researcher into the remote past. Probably most characteristic of Aquarian types is work in the field of inventions, especially in the field of electricity and new sources of energy. Your thinking is clear-cut, clinical; your intellect is capable of quite astounding feats, which suits you well to areas where new ideas emerge. Coworkers can often be at odds with you, for though kind and sympathetic to others, you seem rather distant, even aloof in an enticingly glamorous way. Whatever your work, try to make a place for yourself in an area where the full scope of your inventiveness can be used—for only in this way will you be completely happy.

FINANCIAL SECURITY

Future security is not a big concern for the Aquarian, as his or her future is intimately entwined with the present. Indeed, you are so much in the future in your thought processes that the present almost ceases to exist. Your real security is in the advancement and uplifting of mankind so that all may share in a creative, harmonious world. You don't seem to be one of the most fortunate investors, but with sound professional counsel you could make modest profits. Your greatest security will come through the use of your keen intellect, possibly through inventions which if handled well can yield future profits. Intelligent advice from an experienced professional would be helpful here, too, as far too many inventors lose the rewards of their ingenious inventions to shrewd businessmen and speculators who have a sixth sense for highly marketable products.

PISCES

EARNING POWER

Gentle Pisces was not cut out for the labor market and may not feel at his or her best doing strenuous physical labor or in jobs that are noisy. You are the dreamy, artistic, imaginative sort inclined more toward work that places value on your sensitive nature. You have an intuitive empathy with the suffering of others, which would indicate work in nursing or in one of the healing arts. You have the almost magical ability to relieve the suffering of others through your gentle touch and could even use this gift in work with animals. The arts will be your forte as they will allow expression of your highly active imagination. Harsh reality is difficult for you to cope with. However, with an artistic outlet you could find psychological satisfaction and earn a living simultaneously.

POSSESSIONS

Possessions drift in and out of your life like foam upon the sea. You appreciate the loveliness of each thing as it comes to you, savoring its uniqueness and often developing a sentimental attachment to it. If a friend admires something of yours, and you feel that they truly appreciate it, you could easily give it away, happy for it to be going to a good home. Life continues to bring gifts to your door and you continue to collect them until eventually your abode may take on a rather cluttered appearance. You do prefer to be orderly, but it's so difficult to cope with the practical routine of running your life. A housekeeper could be a tremendous help in keeping a general neatness about the home. Your taste is quite charming and anything you purchase for your environment will have a lovely poetic quality.

FEELINGS ABOUT MONEY

The handling of money is one of those gritty areas of life that calls for realistic thinking. You love to have plenty of money available to buffer you from the harsher aspects of life, and you are capable of earning a fine living. You will usually pay all the bills in the proper month but not always on the same date each month. Although it is difficult for you to see yourself clearly, you are aware of a strong tendency toward diffuseness in your life. Knowing this will help you to develop a financial zone of insulation to protect you from the larger waves of monetary chaos, which can become emotionally burdensome. A healthy savings account will do much to create a feeling of well being and stability in your ephemeral life. Your primary feeling about money is that it is a necessary evil that must somehow be incorporated into your flow of events.

Attitude Toward Spending

Spending money occurs for you with relative ease, although you may do so with a slight discomfort if finances are low. As you easily absorb the focus of those around you, it would be best to avoid the company of impulse buyers when shopping. You need a source of inspiration—often a friend or lover. Look for qualities of stability, good planning ability, and sound common sense in a close companion, then allow this one to be your inspiration in the rational stewarding of funds. Identify pursuits that allow you to escape from reality in creative ways such as through art, music, or participation in a dance group, then spend money on things that will enhance your development in these areas. Reading is another fine way to experience alternate realities, so invest occasionally in exciting novels, which can be emotionally therapeutic.

Gifts

Pisces enjoys both the giving and receiving of gifts, especially when connected with a romantic occasion. You have a love of luxury, but not always the means by which to indulge, so a plush gift from a friend could be quite fulfilling. You are magnetically attracted to things with an exotic flavor, especially if they carry the tones of faraway places with colorful histories. A gift in this vein will keep on giving as the fantasies and flights of imagination generated in the Pisces mind will be a gift of their own. You will be more appreciative of the "right" gift than one on which much money was spent without adequate thought. You will enjoy giving to others using your rich imagination to select a unique gift that could only come from a Piscean. Wrapping will be done with great artfulness and a flair that is exclusively your own.

Latent Abilities as Financial Assets

You have extreme flexibility and can mold yourself to many different work environments. Pisces rules the feet—an influence that could dispose you to work in the sale of footwear. Your vivid imagination could allow this to be carried even farther as a designer of footwear for theatrical productions. Costuming would be a fine area of work for you both in its connection with the dramatic arts and in the color, texture, and drape of fabrics, which mold beautifully to the fluid Piscean touch. Although discipline is foreign to you, you can easily immerse yourself in the rigorous discipline needed to be a dancer, as the emotional fulfillment received will be well worth the effort expended. Your strong need to identify with a source outside yourself could lead you into religious studies, which could become a deeply satisfying career.

FINANCIAL SECURITY

The possible security or insecurity of the future is something you would rather not have to consider, but alas, it simply must be dealt with sooner or later. It is most important for you to establish a good bank account or have a valuable collection hidden away somewhere. This will provide something to lean on and dissolve much of the agony connected with the cold reality of life. You don't want to be bothered with things of a financial nature, so work out the details of your economic life and stick to the plan without fail. You could make wise investments due to the accuracy of your keen intuition, but don't rely on this. You are equally prone to financial setbacks, so the only alternative is a well-planned investment in something that will yield predictable benefits. A practical-minded mate or friend could be helpful here, but use your intuition to guide you as well.

CHAPTER THREE
Communication

MANY FACTORS GO INTO THE STYLE of communication that works best for each of the twelve signs. Most important is how you accept others into your inner circle, and also how much of a need you have to communicate. This varies between the signs; although we all have some desire to relate our experiences and activities to others, these needs seem to go in spurts for some. Scorpios and Capricorns desperately want to discuss their plans and feelings with others, but can go for long periods of time without this rather than talk of someone who might disclose their secrets.

Aquarians, Geminis, and Libras all have the gift of communication; yet they, too, are sometimes careful about discussing intimate subjects. These three signs may go overboard talking about inconsequential matters and pull back when something close to the heart is mentioned.

No one sign is more successful than another, astrologically speaking, in communications. However, the temperaments of the signs predispose the more outgoing people to try more and different communication techniques, making them more likely to hit upon their optimum verbal style.

Communication usually refers to words, but this chapter will also consider nonverbal clues as part of one's style. The art of persuasion is inseparable from successful communication, and so areas of daily life involving compromises, negotiations, and finding solutions to problems cannot be avoided. Additionally, communication is an act of educating others as to your feelings or to information in general. The presentation of information and the way you accept teaching is related to your ability to communicate rather than intellectual considerations.

The third sign of the zodiac, Gemini, strongly influences this area of life. Symbolized by the glyph of the twins, many Gemini characteristics will be highlighted—for all signs—in this chapter.

ARIES

STYLE OF COMMUNICATION

Aries opens a conversation with one or more assertions and is certain to come up with a few more as the talk progresses. This fire sign native loves to bait an adversary in an argument—and often will unintentionally create an argument where none was present. You are stimulated by sustained discussions in which every point is thoroughly chewed at least once, provided that it remains lively. You can become emotional in such an exchange, and occasionally abrasive if the other party is impatient or the subject becomes dull.

COMPATIBLE COMMUNICATORS

Your greatest pleasure in verbal interchange is with persons who possess knowledge you would like to acquire on a particular subject; this often will be an older or more experienced person than yourself, or one who has accumulated more in the way of formal education. You learn much from these people and enjoy provoking them with your own points, which are thrust in with all the momentum of your involvement in the discussion. Sparks can fly when you debate with earth signs; you are calmer and more cooperative when talking to water signs, especially Scorpio. You get a kick out of sparring with the opposite sex.

ABILITY TO PERSUADE

Aries brings much enthusiastic energy to a conversation, along with an earnestness that is convincing in style and presentation. Watch out that you don't become too adamant or argumentative, as this will tend to cause people to resist valid points to which they might otherwise acquiesce. It is easy to get you into a lively exchange as your enthusiasm and mental processes—not to mention your hackles—are easily roused.

EDUCATION

Often self-taught and always responsive to experience, Arians assimilate and retain best that which reaches them directly on an emotional or instinctive level. You are convinced less by logic than by the strength of the appeal. A strong, natural curiosity keeps you learning constantly from your environment and from the way you see the environment affecting others.

DEALINGS WITH BROTHERS AND SISTERS

If you are an only child you develop a charismatic social ability, which brings you into close interrelation with your peers. You enjoy the give-and-take atmosphere that comes with having brothers and sisters; a large, noisy family is comfortable and happy for you, and you retain your amicable relationships with siblings throughout adulthood. This includes those sibling relationships which are friendly rivalries; they grow in depth and subtlety as you mature. The excitement of fast-paced communication is so pleasing to you that you may instigate quarrels with brothers or sisters to experience it; this can make for stormy times, but it is rare that resentment is held between you. In your family group it is usually you who stands out as the wild one, especially next to earth or air sign siblings.

Dealings With Neighbors

Aries likes to be on friendly terms with neighbors. As a child you probably visited adults on your block, and you still enjoy chatting over the back fence. The availability of someone closeby gives you an escape from family pressure or contact with humanity if you live alone, but remember that your neighbor's patience can wear thin if you drop in too frequently or complain too much about people or things in your life. You relish the crowded chatter of block parties and will approach others to get one started; yard and garage sales also appeal to your liking for interchange with those around you.

Decision-making

When you have a choice to make you will almost always be guided by what appeals to your sentimentality. This may frequently come as a surprise to others who only see the energetic, tough-skinned outer you. Once you have made up your mind to do something, your enactment of your decision is total—it's out with the old, in with the new, right now, no looking back. The same holds true for Aries in making commitments —whether or not you will agree to something depends on your emotional or intuitive response, and once committed you will remain loyal. This doesn't mean that you will be uncritical, however; you are not afraid to say exactly what you don't like about a situation. You expect the same loyalty and forthrightness from others and are indignant when they are not given.

Contracts

To an Aries a contract is almost an insult. Aries wants others to trust him or her and the terms "good faith," "honesty," and "simplicity" abound. Why? Aries feels that lawyers needlessly complicate and sometimes infringe on their natural deal-making talents. A memo from an Aries is as emotionally binding as is the most in-depth contract. However, once others refuse to live up to a deal you Aries will cancel it immediately. You are not the easygoing person who will let things ride for a while. An Aries should protect himself from others who take advantage of your penchant for making a deal quicker and with less forethought than any of the other twelve signs. By the same token you expect to be taken at your word, and it displeases you when others are unsure that you will follow through.

TAURUS

Style of Communication

The argument presented by a Taurus native rests on reference to tradition, valuing what he or she perceives as an unquestionable source. Personal interest also plays a dominant role in the way a Taurean makes a point, as if the person he or she is talking to must agree that what Taurus so deeply believes must be right. This sign is most comfortable when feeling totally confident of his or her stand, being able to say, "I just know." You can be shy in a group of strangers but will always attempt to put others at ease.

COMPATIBLE COMMUNICATORS

You communicate best with those who are fairly fast-paced but not harsh or negative. You appreciate Cancer and Pisces for their emphatic natures, although if they are withdrawn you are reluctant to approach them. You are a great storyteller, and as such are both entertaining and educational; mutual appreciation grows between you and someone who responds to this.

ABILITY TO PERSUADE

If you are convinced of the rightness of your position, Taurus, you put your whole being into the effort of persuading another to take the same view. You will certainly convince them of your sincerity but may lose the point—and their patience—as your persistence verges on the overbearing (sometimes it does more than verge). Despite the fact that you are an earth sign, you are not always practical in your thinking and will risk losing ground for emotional reasons.

EDUCATION

Abstract concepts can be difficult to grasp for Taurus; information is best received by you when it is illustrated by examples or demonstrated in real-life settings. Your effort to learn is undermined if you are offered a reward for it—habit sets in and you are disinclined to work on a nonreward basis. It is better to set up a system of self-discipline whereby you put off routine pleasures until you have applied yourself to the satisfaction of your better judgment. This holds true as well for helping a Taurus child to learn.

DEALINGS WITH BROTHERS AND SISTERS

Despite tussles and territorial conflicts between you and your brothers or sisters in childhood, solid friendship grows and lasts between you. Taureans find an increasing need for the companionship of siblings beginning from their twenties. When you raise a family you want those you grew up with to be on hand as aunts and uncles, and it is with great pleasure that you are an aunt or uncle to their children. If your brother or sister is a fixed sign, particularly an Aquarius, arguments tend to be intense—you may even come to blows—yet nothing breaks the essential bonds. Siblings of other signs seek your advice; you play the role of elder even when they are chronologically older than you.

DEALINGS WITH NEIGHBORS

Beneath your usually amicable exterior there is shyness; you jealously guard your habits and routines against interference and your sense of vulnerability against possible hurts. You therefore proceed with caution in bringing acquaintances into your confidence, although there are usually many in your neighborhood or work environment with whom you would like to be on friendly terms. Once you have begun to share yourself with another, you are a staunch and loyal friend who trusts that your giving will be returned. Taureans retain a fondness for those they have known as neighbors, which lasts over the years and survives long periods without contact.

DECISION-MAKING

Taurus arrives at decisions inwardly after careful, introspective deliberation. This can be frustrating to others when it comes to discussing what you have made up your mind to do—it always seems that you have decided in advance and that your position is immovable (true on both counts). Your sign has a reputation for slowness, which you don't always demonstrate. You follow many of your own values and refuse to consider altering your stand. This is fine as long as those values include flexibility so that you don't make errors through a rigid or limited point of view.

CONTRACTS

Good manners and presentation are paramount to you in evaluating new contracts—socially and in business. First impressions are lasting to a Taurean and can be replaced only by very strong contrary evidence over a period of time. You are conservative with your time and energy and therefore hesitate to commit yourself, which may cause others to think you are unwilling to give your word. The truth is that you simply want to be sure before entering into an agreement, so as to avoid backing out or letting someone down at the last minute.

GEMINI

STYLE OF COMMUNICATION

Gemini is a great communicator—whether or not this proves fruitful in relating with others depends on you. You are always ready for an exchange, but your weak point is discretion. What you cheerfully point out in fun (or just because you have observed it) may be taken as a deliberate barb by someone whose mind doesn't run along the same channels as yours. There is an old saying that three people can keep a secret if two of them are dead; but if the third is a Gemini, word will manage to get out.

COMPATIBLE COMMUNICATORS

Your sign is a democratic one—everyone you meet is accorded the same degree of respect (or disrespect). Gemini can always spot someone of outstanding achievement or one who has something to say that is worth hearing. You are animated by other air signs; you find water signs illogical but attractive. You enjoy provoking earth signs, but fire signs are capable of leaving you breathless—quite a feat! Sagittarius has actually been known on occasion to out talk Gemini.

ABILITY TO PERSUADE

Getting others to accept a particular point of view is less important to you than getting them to simply loosen up and express themselves. Your methods for this can run from gentle persuasion to inciting a riot. If you pace your verbal flow at a somewhat low-key rate so as not to overwhelm your listener, you can easily sway almost anyone to see things your way.

EDUCATION

The eyes and ears of Gemini are always open. You extract information from any environment you chance to be in—from a stuffy classroom to a political rally. You are happy as long as you are given a chance to voice your opinion and join the fun. Gemini is unsurpassed at amassing a wealth of detail, which would boggle the mind of another sign, but you need to balance this with a structured setting and a sense of direction to form parts into a cohesive whole.

DEALINGS WITH BROTHERS AND SISTERS

If you have brothers or sisters your household is a lively place, filled with lots of banter as well as lots of criticism. A sibling of the opposite sex is a harmonious companion for you; you share your innermost thought processes and learn much from each other. Through relating to siblings you acquire the ability to recognize the boundaries of others and respect them, especially as you mature and enter into family and social life on your own. Geminis who are the only children in their families frequently find a close friend who becomes a substitute sister or brother—a relationship that can last throughout life.

DEALINGS WITH NEIGHBORS

You are the neighborhood socialite—the more the merrier for Gemini. You will invent excuses to introduce yourself to even the most reticent neighbor, and with your gift of intelligent gab you may well succeed in making him or her your friend. It doesn't bother you if those in your environment don't share your views, attitudes, race, or even language— you will manage to establish a decent rapport with them at the very least. And if you can't coexist in total harmony there is always a good argument.

DECISION-MAKING

Decisions are the bane of Gemini's existence. You see every angle from every possible point of view, and it pains you to think of having to miss anything. So you postpone making up your mind and spend hours— even sleepless nights—fretting and weighing alternatives. You might find it helpful to write your options down on paper to get a satisfying sense of clarity before trying to make a choice. Set time limits for yourself so that you don't delay so long that you frustrate others as well as yourself. Discussion with friends may help, but too much advice only clutters your mind and adds weight to all possible choices. When you feel yourself burdened to the point of overload with thinking, a rare (for Gemini) silent period may occur; this is the time to isolate yourself and meditate for the answer you seek.

CONTRACTS

Geminis value freedom of thought and action so highly that they can balk at the idea of making commitments, fearing that doing so will inhibit them or tie them down. You can free yourself from this fear by realizing that each contract into which you enter constitutes nothing more than a new base from which to expand. You are a frank person; rarely is a Gemini guilty of deliberate misrepresentation of self. However, others may not see it your way if you give your word in all sincerity on Monday and expect them to understand on Tuesday that your philosophy of life has undergone a change.

CANCER

STYLE OF COMMUNICATION

Cancerians will let you know what's honestly on their minds. It may take months (they may all the while be attempting to tell you in various vague and indirect ways), but they do want you to know. As a water sign Cancer is not so much irrational as inconsistent; water signs have emotional natures, and emotions do have a logic to them. It is not in the makeup of a Cancer to be detached from the subject of a discussion, so the mood of the day colors the talk—sometimes including the opinion being expressed. Outgoing Cancers are very verbal and enjoy debating; the shy type prefers to listen.

COMPATIBLE COMMUNICATORS

The Cancer native likes a great variety of people, tending for contrast toward nonwatery types, Capricorn and Taurus in particular, who appeal to the Cancerian's instinctual and reflective nature. Libra might not be too easy for Cancer to live with, but Cancer responds to this sign's balanced judgment and refined, aesthetic sense. What Cancers wish to communicate flows like water into the receptive vessels of those with whom they share.

ABILITY TO PERSUADE

Your main drive, Cancer, is not to persuade others but rather to secure their understanding of what you seek to express. Whether they feel the same way is secondary to you. You sustain discussion easily and are easy to converse with, being able to concentrate for long periods and to follow the verbal ramblings of others. Your animated, articulate style wins support for you when you need it. You reach people through conveying a quiet depth in what you say, as well as by genuinely hearing and accepting their views, though they may not be your own.

EDUCATION

From childhood on, the Cancer native loves to read. Information on a wide variety of subjects is assimilated from books, the historical novel being a great favorite in particular. You are a reflective sign, so that one book, movie, trip, or comment experienced by you provides food for thought and deep dreams for a long time. Cancer is an excellent listener who can learn much from conversations others are having; it is also good for you to enter into the discussion yourself, as you receive new ideas from hearing your own thoughts externalized. Often a word casually spoken will take you on a long, intricately developed train of thought, unknown by the person who spoke it. Many Cancerians have a gift for writing, spellbinding others with these flights of the imagination and searchings of the soul.

DEALINGS WITH BROTHERS AND SISTERS

An older brother or sister frequently becomes the childhood idol of a Cancer person; this may be either an overt or a secret adulation. You watch this sibling with a sharp eye for traits to emulate or to store for future use. If the one you place on a pedestal should fall, he or she is not likely to regain this position in your eyes. Generally you will channel complaints through your parents rather than fighting it out with a sibling; this creates the danger of lasting animosities or differences that grow rather than diminish as you enter childhood.

DEALINGS WITH NEIGHBORS

Cancer leans toward living a secluded lifestyle and therefore may never really know those in the neighborhood or have a wide circle of casual acquaintances. You prefer to have one or two close friends nearby and don't crave more than these for company. A protective feeling insulates you and your home, making it difficult for you to share space with out-siders or be made constantly aware of their goings-on. You are disturbed if neighbors are noisy and usually are careful not to intrude on the privacy of others.

DECISION-MAKING

When you are convinced about something you don't hesitate to act; often it turns out that you should have waited, as split-second decisions or those based on whims abound with you and are not always correct. Talk things over with someone else before making up your mind—you talk yourself into things too easily. Cancer is one of the few signs that will actually listen to advice, and this sign will even follow it sometimes.

CONTRACTS

Fidelity is high on your list of values, making you someone who consis-tently keeps your promises and honors your commitments. Usually Can-cer does not agree to do things he or she is against doing—when this does occur occasionally, you will most certainly voice your objections and make your disapproval obvious. Cancer is quiet, but not silent; the details of agreements must be known to you before you enter into them.

LEO

STYLE OF COMMUNICATION

Leo loves to reach out and share with others; this sign will even draw a passing stranger into a conversation. You are articulate in your verbal expression and very much to the point—even blunt. A Leonian is confident and calm at best; at worst, arrogant and bossy. As a fire sign you have a streak of impatience that can inhibit your listening ability. Your own view of what is at hand is so firmly fixed in your mind that you are squirming for the chance to expound on it. You possess the ability to project your voice and attract the attention of all around you; people respond either positively, enjoying your presentation and wanting to hear more, or negatively, wanting to contradict or silence you.

COMPATIBLE COMMUNICATORS

Enjoyment comes to you, Leo, through a hot debate with Aquarius— also with Taurus or Scorpio if these two are so inclined. You drop any hard feelings more quickly than the latter two. If a Leo native lacks self-confidence, serious competition will generally be avoided in any encounter. You are a sociable creature, enjoying crowds and gaining much pleasure from a wide circle of eclectic friendships.

ABILITY TO PERSUADE

If you pace yourself and refrain from assuming a dictatorial pose, you are a most convincing talker. Your power of concentration, coupled with the air of assurance you wear so well, makes you persuasive despite a leaning toward the verbose. Leo is seen as an authority or expert even in areas where more expertise is possessed by others. You create the impression that you have everything under control and can impart whatever is needed to others.

EDUCATION

Leos learn from people, gleaning information more from discussion and active participation than books or introspective reflection. Despite this you are usually a good student, as you focus on grades and achievement. Whatever you apply yourself to will prove educational and informative —the key for you is having the motivation to give something its requisite attention.

DEALINGS WITH BROTHERS AND SISTERS

A strong, protective feeling marks your attitude toward siblings. Difficulties arise when you assume that you can force a brother or sister into doing something your way or seeing eye to eye with you. If you are an only child you tend to expect too much attention in a group; this may cause misunderstandings between you and your peers. Leo tends to team up with a sibling of the same sex in childhood and the teens. Since you are not afraid to travel your own path, you often willingly live some distance apart from your family. You may find that a congenial relationship develops between you and a sibling through the mail.

DEALINGS WITH NEIGHBORS

If you are friendly with your neighbors on more than a casual basis, you fraternize with them mainly by going to visit them rather than inviting them to your home. Visitors are screened carefully by you, and it is rare that you will invite a group of people over unless you are feeling particularly expansive. Even in this case the crowd is more likely to be made up of your friends or business associates and their friends rather than your neighbors. Despite this, however, you are generous and helpful in emergencies and don't try to avoid becoming involved when someone is in need.

DECISION-MAKING

When it comes to decision-making Leo is hardheaded and jolly at the same time—a trick Scorpios wish they had and Taurus can't see any use for. Leos will consider advice before deciding, but will insist that each point be thoroughly proved. You listen carefully and will follow advice if it seems valid, but you are somewhat reluctant to admit that you really need it. It is difficult for you to delegate authority when there is a choice to be made, as you feel that ultimately the final move must be made by you. However, this doesn't assist you in knowing what the right move will be.

CONTRACTS

A Leo will follow through on a contract or commitment, sometimes doing so foolishly after circumstances have clearly removed the need or the advisability of doing it. Personal loyalty counts with you in a big way, as does the confidence of others in your fidelity. Be sure that you give your word only when what is being asked is truly worthy of it—not to prove something or to impress someone (particularly the opposite sex). Leo's mind is not always pragmatic but functions superbly in legal matters. You can be misled by charisma in personal dealings, but when given a contract to analyze you are truly Leo the Lion!

VIRGO

STYLE OF COMMUNICATION

Virgo is soft-spoken and clear of definition, a descriptive talker, not so rigidly analytical (as is your reputation) as concerned with simple accuracy. Your explanations are precise, making sure the exact details of your point are communicated to your listener. This sign doesn't like to stand out in a crowd—turning into a phobia in some cases. As a result you may hold in angry or resentful feelings for a while to avoid making waves. This behavior won't last long, as your gripes are then likely to come out in acid remarks or sudden bursts of temper. You are sympathetic to the minds and educational levels of others and can easily adjust your conversation to talk with them.

COMPATIBLE COMMUNICATORS

Virgo prefers to communicate with people who don't come off as being too brash. Aries, Aquarius, and Leo natives may be kept at arm's length over touchy issues for this reason. A talkative Pisces, Libra, or Capricorn makes a good companion with whom you can while away the hours in conversation. You love to give advice, never giving it lightly, and you appreciate the response of those who receive it openly. You are apt to withdraw—or at least wish to—if someone makes a strong effort to convince you of something. Pay attention to what is being said rather than to the intensity of the tone, and you will have an easier time finishing your exchanges. What needs to be said will probably have to be repeated later if not completed now. It is better to clear the air for more harmonious communication by resolving differences as soon as possible.

ABILITY TO PERSUADE

A patient, painstaking talker, you are able to pepper a lecture with terse, caustic observations that are so carefully timed as to cause your audience to agree with things they never would have considered before. Virgos can display inconsistencies in not caring what another may think one minute and then becoming irate because they feel ignored or not taken seriously.

EDUCATION

The Virgo native is bookish, able to extract learning from the printed word even if reading is done with pleasure. You are observant of the interaction of people and derive much of your ability to judge character from watching others. You experience great satisfaction from a job well done and therefore excel in school and with your own projects. These can range from writing to carpentry to handyman plumbing, although particularly frustrating jobs may not be undertaken a second time. You appreciate a straightforward approach from those who instruct you; those who try to create exaggerated effects will make you mentally close down and not return for more.

DEALINGS WITH BROTHERS AND SISTERS

Often it is not until adulthood that Virgo will really get to know a brother or sister. There is less tumbling and rousting about with other children for Virgos; you are helpful to younger siblings and somewhat shy of older ones. In adolescence you tend to let relatively petty problems and differences keep a close relationship from flourishing. As you mature the real person seems to emerge from behind the face of the sister or brother you have lived with at a distance.

DEALINGS WITH NEIGHBORS

You are jealous of your privacy and anxious to avoid giving neighbors the wrong impression, so you keep the goings-on at your place sedate (at least in keeping with your self-image), which may not be as sedate as some would associate with your sign! Visitors undergo a careful scrutiny, and those who live near you may never see more than the well-kept exterior of your home. (The inside isn't necessarily so well-kept, either, another Virgo myth).

DECISION-MAKING

When it comes to making decisions, Virgo thinks carefully—often too carefully—taking so much time over small details that the overall view is missed. You will drag your feet if you feel you are being pushed to take the lead in a joint or group decision, or if you are hurried by someone in a heavy-handed manner. Or you may abruptly give up your own position to avoid a scene.

CONTRACTS

Virgo possesses the eye of an accountant, the mind of an efficiency expert. Given time to study a contract or prepare in advance, you are not easily deceived. Being literal-minded, you adhere exactly to the terms of any agreement, personal or otherwise. You are willing, however, to terminate a commitment over a minute issue or fine-print detail. In personal matters you tend to expect others to live up to unspoken agreements, which may never have crossed their minds. It is best to discuss your expectations, but you need to guard against a tendency to dissect personal interaction until it disappears. There is a happy medium—find it!

LIBRA

STYLE OF COMMUNICATION

Libra communicates in a series of carefully considered evaluations, delivered in an articulate and amiable manner. This sign favors group discussion as a problem-solving tool, perceiving that the varied opinions of those in a group will reveal all the aspects to be considered. You aim at a balanced presentation, often keeping your personal views in the background if you feel they are not essential to the overall picture. This modest trait is admired by others—it is a relief not to be presented with the ego first and foremost—yet your slant on things is generally most interesting and is enjoyed by others when you share it.

COMPATIBLE COMMUNICATORS

You avoid the company of loud and brash persons, as you regard vulgarity and abruptness as hindrances to communication. Harmony is your forte, and you will adjust yourself in almost any way possible to maintain it. You are fascinated by the ability of earth signs to go about their business simply and instinctively (or at least to convey this impression) while you fret and analyze. You establish your easiest rapport with Virgo, Pisces, and other air signs like yourself. Libra may not seek to be in a position of authority or leadership, but enjoys helping both children and adults to learn.

ABILITY TO PERSUADE

Your pleasantly outgoing demeanor with people allows them to seriously consider your point of view. Even when someone disagrees with you outwardly, he or she is moved by what you say and may come to concur with you. Your main asset is that you will almost never use a heavy-handed approach in trying to convince someone, regardless of the importance you attach to your position. This makes you a natural diplomat and an excellent mediator.

EDUCATION

Libra combines the Aries trait of self-teaching with Virgo's eye to social interaction as a source of learning. You benefit from gentle and consistent reminders of the pragmatic considerations of daily existence, as your inner world is often far from these things. If your idealism is crushed this can cause you to withdraw from group experiences, disillusioned with the ways of people and the world.

DEALINGS WITH BROTHERS AND SISTERS

Through childhood and adolescence—and in some cases in adulthood, too—Libra needs to build a persona and a reputation that are distinct from a healer of wounds and solver of arguments. Your needs can easily be overlooked by siblings because of your tendency to selflessly take care of the problems of others. You are slow to anger but explosive when the fuse blows at last. There is always the danger, too, that you will receive only resentment and black eyes from intruding on the disputes of sisters or brothers.

DEALINGS WITH NEIGHBORS

Libra takes pride in home and family and welcomes observers; this makes you sociable with neighbors and a gracious host or hostess. Block parties, card games, and dinner parties are all pleasant for Libra—the lover of cordial relationships. You need to refrain from observing too closely the troubles that may be going on in other families; you only want to help, but this may embarrass and alienate people. Like Aquarius, you attract all sorts of people to you and appreciate their uniqueness; this makes you someone with whom others are comfortable. Those around you who would ordinarily remain strangers may become acquainted with one another through your presence among them.

DECISION-MAKING

Libra is the balancer of the zodiac, and as a result frequently is quite unable to make a decision. One side and then the other is held up for examination, each side often dividing into two and then two more. If you are a more self-confident Libra type, your values are weighed against those of an illogical and frequently unpleasant world, causing you to defend rather than analyze them, which you can do in an illogical and not very pleasant manner. When you reach a decision which is satisfying to you, great relief and an elation permeates your whole day—or month. If the needs of someone else are at stake, you tend to make your choice with this in mind; this is commendable and can certainly be the right course of action, but make sure that you don't sell yourself short.

CONTRACTS

To avoid an unwanted confrontation, a Libra native may imply consent by saying nothing. This can cause others to consider that you have committed yourself, and then be seriously displeased upon learning you actually have not. Or—which is sometimes worse—you may find yourself going through with the terms of a contract into which you never really entered, also to avoid confronting someone with an unwelcome response or refusal. You have a good grasp of issues and problems, but often the resolution you will propose is too idealistically constructed for the situation at hand. You are happiest when dealing with those who share your high regard for ethical integrity and can blend it with a realistic attitude toward applying it to the matter at hand.

SCORPIO

STYLE OF COMMUNICATION

Scorpio presents a pleasant surface manner but has little interest in small talk. Nonverbal communication in the form of stony silence can be the sole indicator of Scorpionic displeasure. Words delivered like boulders, with or without anger, come forth when this native feels compelled or pressured into speaking. You save your verbal efforts for major encounters or showdowns, preferring to let your vibrations tell those around you what you think of a particular subject or person. You are articulate in a slow-paced manner, which is the external manifestation of an inner struggle to find exactly the right word. Emotional issues touch off a free flow of talk, which many Scorpios rarely exhibit under ordinary circumstances.

COMPATIBLE COMMUNICATORS

Scorpio communicates best with people whose sense of humor is highly developed and who have weathered much in the way of experience. You respect the painful yet rewarding processes people go through to gain depth and wisdom. You seek out controversial talk, welcoming tests of your own view; a quarrelsome Aquarius or an opinionated Leo or Sagittarius makes a great sparring partner. For closer, more intimate sharing you gravitate toward Pisces or Capricorn, with whom you can share silence, although you may have difficulty relaxing in silence with the opposite sex.

ABILITY TO PERSUADE

Impatience causes your temper to flare, quite often in some Scorpios. It is a most unusual Scorpio who makes a good public relations person—you won't hide your true feelings and cannot pretend interest when there is none. You stick to an issue until it is resolved, revealing a reserve of energy for debate or argument that can make you the victor through sheer endurance. In serious debate you are philosophical, somewhat scholarly, and can be extremely biting and sarcastic.

EDUCATION

Your opinion of the worth of a subject determines your willingness—and therefore your ability—to absorb information on that topic. You glean information from a variety of sources—books, people, observation. What you learn from a good teacher who expects much and doesn't pamper you will stay with you for a lifetime. Elephants and Scorpios never forget—unless they want to annoy you.

DEALINGS WITH BROTHERS AND SISTERS

Scorpios are jealous of brothers and sisters on their own turf on the home front, not wanting them to trespass or invade their privacy. This does not stop them, however, from being loyal to the core where siblings are concerned—a Scorpio will defend them regardless of whether they are right or wrong and settle up with them privately later. At first these natives have difficulty accepting stepbrothers and stepsisters or adop-tees, but if their personalities prove compatible they will form a bond as close as that of a blood tie. Childhood and adolescence see Scorpio in many skirmishes with siblings, often brought on by this sign's impatient response to them.

DEALINGS WITH NEIGHBORS

You want privacy where neighbors are concerned—if not the whole house or apartment to yourself, then at least a private room. Scorpio revels in a mental image of an unknown, secret hideaway, and if money permits you may even have one constructed. Actually you are very socia-ble if those nearby meet your standards, if not, they're out on their proverbial ear. This doesn't tend to attract droves of neighbors into friendships with you. The friendships you do make tend to be deep and lasting.

DECISION-MAKING

Close scrutiny is given by you to all details of a decision you are faced with making. Although you may do it at lightning speed, you do not make choices lightly. Scorpio condenses the deciding process, sifting through the alternatives and tossing out extraneous factors to get at the root of the matter. Problems can arise if you ignore those who are close to you while you are deliberating, making them feel they are not being taken into consideration. Your decision is influenced most heavily by a gut-level response, involving your impressions of the people with whom you are dealing and how you will live with the outcome.

CONTRACTS

Scorpio keeps up a perpetual evaluating process, regarding contracts and commitments between self and the world. You want to know what's in it for you; depending on your personality and the situation at hand this consideration may be selfish or simple and honestly realistic. When the time comes for personal commitments you enter them willingly or not at all. You like to have arrangements made on your own terms, which can cause you to become uncooperative and quarrelsome. You are capable of understanding the positions of others; it is helpful if you slow down and remind yourself at crucial moments to consider them. Agreements you contemplate making should be thoroughly checked out and clarified by all concerned.

SAGITTARIUS

STYLE OF COMMUNICATION

Sagittarius natives communicate in leaps, bounds, and generalities, yet always cut right through to the heart of the discussion. You cause rumpled feelings when you trample the toes of someone to whom you tell an unwelcome truth—"My, you look terrible today." You are then puzzled when your straightforwardness is not well taken. Sagittarius likes to relate everyday matters to large-scale philosophical and political issues. Precedent is important to you in all considerations. You have the desire to inspire and educate others.

COMPATIBLE COMMUNICATORS

Sagittarians communicate with everyone, though a prudish Virgo or a hidebound Capricorn can be a bit irritating and cause you to lose your Jovian goodwill. You can have great talks with quick-thinking Gemini and Aquarius. Your fellow fire signs, Aries and Leo, create a love-hate ambivalence with you—you love the energy but hate the results, which rarely bring agreement.

ABILITY TO PERSUADE

Sagittarius can talk a bear out of its skin. You convince yourself so easily that it is only one step to convincing someone else. Goals are lifeblood—you have boundless energy for debating or selling to obtain whatever you desire. Your remarks can be ill-considered but are never hateful.

EDUCATION

You are imaginative and inventive, but painstaking research bores you. You prefer information that condenses and synthesizes ideas into a few terse comments or descriptions. You are full of both questions and answers. You abound with hunches that are equally likely to be ridiculous or right on target.

DEALINGS WITH BROTHERS AND SISTERS

Sagittarius is likely to fraternize with the neighborhood kids as much as with his or her own siblings; you may even prefer relating to your brother or sister in a group situation rather than individually. You are affectionate and playful with them at home, unmercifully critical of their faults but quick to forget all offenses. Your love of travel causes many of your sign to move far away from siblings as adults.

DEALINGS WITH NEIGHBORS

Sagittarius is famous (or infamous) for dragging in stray dogs, abandoned cats, and strangers off the street. If you are comfortable in your surroundings, your sociable nature makes your place the center of activity in your neighborhood. You can reach out too quickly or too much, only to find that you later want to extricate yourself. Also your sign has been known to invite a pack of folks over and then leave—returning after an annoyed mate has cooked for them and cleaned up. You are anxious to make everyone feel welcome, and you love to hear the stories each one has to tell.

DECISION-MAKING

You love, in your expansive way, to give advice and counsel; you can even go so far as to advise patience—something you have great trouble maintaining when there is a decision to be made. Your criteria for resolving dilemmas of choice are often dogmatic; you do not reflect or construct a critique so much as search for a precedent in your personal experience and values. When this is found you follow it to the letter; if there is none to be found you will seek it in the experience of others. It is not easy for Sagittarius to admit mistakes; a tendency toward arrogance makes you reluctant to modify your stand. A Sagittarian will make a statement of opinion that carries with it a ring of absolute authority and confidence, and then will brazenly state just the opposite a short time afterward as if there had never been any doubt that this position was the only one with any validity. When called on this, you will respond with a charming smile and acknowledgment, as if the turnabout was most natural and logical. The amazing thing is that you almost always seem to get away with it! However, when the rug finally goes out from under Sagittarius, it can do so with a vengeance.

CONTRACTS

Exuberance over a new business or personal alliance or agreement can cause Sagittarius to overlook important details. You will be unpleasantly surprised to see what you've gotten yourself into later. When you're at your best, you shrug and make the best of it, and will come clean about your mistaken conception or hasty move. At your worst you accuse the other party of misrepresentation. When you are solidly behind a decision you are tireless in your efforts and cooperation, although you are definitely not uncritical of the methods of those with whom you are involved.

You may fuss a great deal and threaten to break contracts, but generally you will stick to something, though you may be complaining all the while. You dislike being the one who quits, and may try to annoy a partner into becoming exasperated with you and dissolving the partnership. But for the most part, if the indivdiual or group with whom you are associated continues to tolerate you, you will do the same for them—and even manage to make everyone feel that there are more good times than bad.

CAPRICORN

STYLE OF COMMUNICATION

Capricorn, you are most at ease with what is within your own mind when it comes to expressing your thoughts. Before you speak you know these thoughts with clarity, but you tend to slow down in externalizing them or feel that you are not being fully articulate. In truth you are a most precise observer of the traits, quirks, and tricks of others—and your own—making you a very humorous, wry, and witty talker when you choose to be. When the need arises it is Capricorn who communicates a verbal form that is free from emotional bias. A caustic streak can intimidate others.

COMPATIBLE COMMUNICATORS

The Capricorn native enjoys communicating with reflective and boisterous types by turns. Libra and Cancer provide you with nourishment for your soft, inner nature, while Leo or Scorpio types are satisfying with their incisive and assertive stances. This interesting dualism goes farther, as you can be coldly non-indulgent with what you consider to be petty individuals, yet are fascinated by the instructive worth of what everyone you meet has to say—even those whom you reject.

ABILITY TO PERSUADE

Persuasion is not your forte, at least not in an obvious form. Capricorns lecture, extrapolate, improvise, but rarely present an out-and-out attempt to sway another. This excludes, of course, Capricorn lawyers, who make convincing cases with their pragmatic, unfanciful delineation of facts.

EDUCATION

You are reticent and shy with strangers as a rule; friends and family see your charm, which is uniquely your own, often a bit eccentric. You are a social observer and a great respecter of books and study. Capricorn delves deeply into history, synthetic works, and interdisciplinary forms of learning. You listen well to lectures and retain what you hear, also taking copious notes. A warm, very human teacher helps you as a student to seek out the company of others and to be more accepting of their shortcomings. Although an earth sign, you are not always strongly mechanically inclined but live in the realm of the intellect. Your deepest respect goes to the established and proven authority on a given subject or in a particular field, though you may take a dislike to one in a high place due to a personal mannerism or characteristic that is repellent to you.

DEALINGS WITH BROTHERS AND SISTERS

In relating to brothers and sisters, Capricorns take cues from their parents and treat them similarly, evaluating their worth as it seems to be reflected by parental authority. You tend to favor siblings of the same sex as yourself and are shy of the opposite sex—especially a siblings's friends —in childhood and the early teens. There is argumentativeness on your part and a tendency to be withdrawn; these are not signs of dislike but rather an indication of the Capricorn child's need to take time to mull over problems, to decide whether a fault lies with you or the other person. You value the loyalty of a sister or brother and bestow it likewise for life, regardless of differences.

DEALINGS WITH NEIGHBORS

You are polite and proper with neighbors but don't like to have them too close. You enjoy a cordial exchange of views, but this develops into a real personal relationship only in rare cases. Business associations on the other hand can well be formed by Capricorn through discussions with a neighbor, the legalistic and formal terms of business maintaining things at a respectful distance with which you are comfortable. You like to chat over gardening or bringing in the mail, but only a true liking for your neighbor will elicit from you an invitation to come in for coffee or prevent you from graciously turning down such an offer yourself.

DECISION-MAKING

Family ties, business loyalties, personal friendships—all these count far less when it comes to decisions than Capricorn's eye to the reactions of the questioning public. You strongly resist coming to any resolution that is unorthodox or even unusual, wanting all arrangements to be well within acceptable limits to the most conservative of observers. You are not heartless, as detractors may accuse you of being; it is simply that proprieties must be observed. You take your time in reaching a decision; this is not procrastination or indecisiveness but a careful and studious way of avoiding error and taking the long view.

CONTRACTS

In making new commitments, Capricorns feel that they must not break old molds or precedents. You don't want to propel yourself into a situation which is too new or to involve yourself too quickly. Seeing terms in print is helpful and reassuring to you, as this minimizes the danger of misunderstandings and mistakes. A danger that does sometimes trap you is that of missing opportunities through perfectionism—your mind wants to see all eventualities covered down to the minutest detail. You do not commit yourself lightly, and when your word is given it is scrupulously kept. Capricorn honors the terms of an agreement to the letter and is deeply hurt or offended when this courtesy is not reciprocated.

AQUARIUS

STYLE OF COMMUNICATION

Aquarius relies on the observations of others to throw his or her own views into perspective. This sign watches the way in which people arrive at a position or decision and forms a picture of the whole process along with an impression of the persons involved. You are an avid talker, one who gets great enjoyment out of being a bearer of news. Aquarians follow discussions closely, concentrating on all implications of what is being said; you may even do so to the point of absentmindedness as to other appointments, chores, or projects that have been scheduled.

COMPATIBLE COMMUNICATORS

Aquarius can casually communicate to nearly everyone. However, you are a fixed sign and as such need people of similar outlook to sustain a close rapport. You like individuals with a flair about them—Leo, Gemini, and Aries in particular satisfy your taste for spicy conversation and unencumbered ideas. Earth signs can rub you the wrong way, seeming too deliberate, even ponderous.

ABILITY TO PERSUADE

It is central to the Aquarian personality to get people to reach a consensus where any group of several minds is working or talking together. Often you will make such an effort to bring this about that you are unable to relax sufficiently to be convincing. Aquarius makes a better lecturer than a salesperson, as the enjoyment of expounding on a particular subject can be satisfying for its own sake, but the pressure of having to succeed at a sale can remove all enjoyment from describing the value of what is being sold. People are impressed by the bright, outgoing Aquarian demeanor; you may be opinionated but are a willing listener and are actually more easily swayed than able to sway others. Even more than trying to convince another person, an Aquarian tries to make his or her own position understood—to himself as well by putting forth these arguments.

EDUCATION

When you are interested in a subject you are an attentive and eager learner. As a student you can be given extra work in a favorite field and will produce your best results. What does not interest you requires much effort—not to comprehend but to pay attention. Aquarius is attracted to unusual subject matters and tends to pick obscure topics for study. You can work on your own but need to air your efforts before an audience afterward.

Dealings With Brothers and Sisters

Aquarius has good relationships with siblings, leaning toward those of the opposite sex for deeper communication. Age and interest have to vary tremendously to prevent you from sharing adventures and outings with your sister or brother. Often Aquarius will seek out friends in the neighborhood or at school for younger siblings to play with, or create a circle of kids of varied ages in which you and siblings participate. Your restlessness or unique lifestyle can separate you geographically from brothers and sisters in adulthood. Looking back on childhood you are likely to perceive similarities between yourself and other children in your family, which you had not noticed before, or which you even may have regarded as differences.

Dealings With Neighbors

Friendly interchange with neighbors enlarges your group of friends and provides you with a variety of news and views. Too many people around you can frazzle your nerves, and you can begin spreading yourself too thin. Your sign has the propensity at times to wander in different directions, gossiping, debating, and generally gadding about. You don't slow down until you are asleep on your feet, at which time you are apt to become grumpy and unreasonable.

Decision-making

Aquarians approach decisions impulsively. Unlike Virgo, who sees the trees but no forest, you see the whole forest but neglect to consider the trees. You tend to become abrasive when others balk at the prospect of taking risks or acting quickly. As a fixed sign Aquarius finds it hard to modify an attitude; often you feel that you see a situation clearly while someone else clouds or clutters it unnecessarily. This may be true, but remember that the other person needs to go through whatever process is necessary to arrive at a satisfactory answer. You are able to move fast when this is required; you stick to your decisions through obstacles and challenges.

Contracts

The Aquarian native is not easily snowed into a commitment that he or she does not want to make. This doesn't stop you, however, from trying to pressure others into making them when it seems important to you. You don't want to seem unafraid to tackle any new venture and will present full explanations and detailed reasons for any hesitation you may feel. Actually your intuition may be warning you to hold off, until the reasons become clear later. It is helpful for Aquarius to seek counsel in sifting through fine print, as this bores you and is therefore difficult for you to concentrate on. Ask Capricorn or Virgo—they will be delighted to assist you with details you prefer to skim over.

PISCES

STYLE OF COMMUNICATION

The way Pisces communicates is not necessarily the vague, absent-minded, muted style that is associated with this water sign. Pisces can be voluble and long-winded, maintaining an intellectual discussion perhaps longer than most. There is indeed the silent type of Piscean, the quietest of all quiet ones, but this quality does not characterize everyone of this sign. Pisces gets on the wavelength of others, picking up their emotional stance; this deepens and stimulates discussion, bringing to the surface more levels of what is actually being dealt with. These natives have a mobile and fluid style of speaking that captures the imagination.

COMPATIBLE COMMUNICATORS

Like Virgo, your zodiacal opposite, you avoid confrontations with the aggressive representatives of Aries, Leo, or the intense Aquarius. Other water sign folk are compatible with you in talk, although this is because of style rather than similarity of opinion. You share with Aquarius a uniqueness in your way of looking at the universe. Pisces seeks out imaginative, inspirational thinkers and talkers, as these enable you to converse at your own level.

ABILITIES TO PERSUADE

Since you pick up on the vibes of others, Pisces, you can intuit how to proceed in communicating with them. What you lack in aggression you more than make up for in subtlety. Your ability to persuade others really depends on how much of an introvert or extrovert you are. It is not unusual for you to enter a discussion with one point of view in mind only to come away convinced of the rightness of the other person's position. If you are a bold Piscean this is because you have viewed the matter fairly and have been truly swayed; if you are the reticent type, this can also be the case, but you may simply not have gotten up the gumption to state your own opinion.

EDUCATION

Pisces is a good self-starter in unusual and unorthodox fields of study, as your fascination carries you along with seeming effortlessness. Like Capricorn, you are attracted to synthetic works and enjoy searching out threads that connect and unite different subjects. Young Piscean natives need much positive reinforcement of their accomplishments in order to feel the outside world is interested in them.

DEALINGS WITH BROTHERS AND SISTERS

If Pisces chances to be a spoiled child, he or she will learn to covertly manipulate situations with siblings in order to come out on top. A self-reliant Piscean is soft-spoken and gentle, so that brotherly and sisterly relations are affectionate and sympathetic without concealing an effort to dominate. Pisces will welcome a stepparent's child or an adoptee more readily than most other signs, especially if that person is in any way in need of empathy and support. A Piscean only child may gravitate toward those among their friends who have family problems or are melancholy in order to comfort and cheer them.

Dealings With Neighbors

You have either a strong attraction or repulsion toward your neighbors, being either a recluse among them or an outgoing, chatty participant in neighborhood affairs. You welcome novel personalities, new foods and wines, music, but you need space for silence and would rather remain separate from neighbors than have this violated. You need to spend time on your own and not just soak up the habits and styles of others. Watch your impulse to reveal secrets too soon as well as a tendency to get in over your head with a clique.

Decision-making

Pisces puts off making decisions, telling people to wait so as to be alone to mull things over. Given the necessary calm in which to ponder, you are able to see through details to the end result your choice will be. Overdependency on the opinions of others may cause a Piscean to give up too much in the way of personal power. When you are strong in a decision, it may seem eccentric or fanciful to others, but it is seen and felt as solid by you. Once your mind is made up you can find all sorts of reasons to present to others in defense of what you have chosen, although with Pisces there is always a chance that you will change your mind as long as it remains possible to do so.

Contracts

You easily grasp the whole significance of an agreement you are being asked to make, but as we all do on occasion you can miss the mark regarding the end result, missing opportunities and offending friends by rejecting reasonable demands. You do not shrink from obligations; you only need to see them in perspective and evaluate them as being fair and then will carry them out faithfully. An uninvolved ear can be the answer when you are unsure as to whether or not to commit yourself; the advice of such a listener can help you find the middle way between refusing an equitable offer and being talked into accepting one that would not be good for you. Talk out both sides to hear how each sounds—often simply verbalizing your own thoughts to someone who has no stake in the result will give you the clarity you need.

CHAPTER FOUR

Home Life

IN ASTROLOGY, the fourth section of the chart refers to home life, sense of security, and the way people deal with others and material holdings that add to their well-being. There is also an underlying theme related to home life and the effect the environment has on a person. Throughout one's life, the home is not only a place, but a psychological atmosphere.

The sign of Cancer, symbol of the home, the mother, and the family, governs this fourth section. The astrological glyph of the crab is quite fitting, for as a crab grabs onto and clings to that which it captures, so do people fuse with those elements which signify home.

Because the mother in a family has traditionally supplied all this nurturing, this part of everyone's life is colored by the mothering instincts of those around them now—even youthful expectations of what a mother figure should provide. Today, with mothers and fathers both participating in the child-rearing, the home environment reflects a new dimension of contributions to family stability traditionally associated with women: caring, emotional support, understanding, and the protection of the family's home life and reputation.

This chapter illustrates how emotional needs color the way people deal with their closest family members, and how they can successfully create a home atmosphere which brings out their best, most content selves.

A theme of stability is present throughout this section of a person's life. The historical significance of owning a family homestead or land holdings, along with the ability to pass this stable gift to descendants, connects generations to one another.

ARIES

IDEAL HOME ENVIRONMENT

The Aries native, though dynamically outgoing and active in group and other social interaction, highly values a sense of home. The individualistic nature of this sign expresses itself in your desire for privacy, which makes your home your castle. You have an inner self, which may be missed by those who do not know you well, and this private self needs a home space in which to relax and reenergize. This is not to say that the fiery side of your personality won't come through in the way you put your home together—it most definitely will. The flashiest and most unconventional furnishings are often to be found in Aries' homes, complete with the flamboyant red tones of Mars, your ruling planet. Yet often you will have a quiet room done in soothing blues or other soft colors, reflecting that inner self few people seem to see. Many Arians, influenced by Moon-ruled Cancer in your solar fourth house (the home), decorate their homes exclusively in these soft hues.

SENSE OF HOME

A periodic urge for new beginnings keeps some of you moving from place to place, choosing new and varied locations in which to live. Your generous nature prompts you to give away objects of art, rugs, kitchen items, and just about anything a friend might chance to admire in your home. However, you are most attached to a few things having sentimental value for you and are inclined to brood if one of these is lost or broken. Remember that what goes is always replaced, frequently in novel and surprising ways. Learn to let go—as you so often advise others! Aries folk love the company of others, and your home becomes a center of social activity to your delight. Your couch or floor (or both) may frequently be occupied by guests passing through town, in personal transition, broke, or in the process of finding places of their own. This is especially the case with your Aquarian and Sagittarian friends. If you are tiring of the company of one or more visitors, find a way to tactfully advise them that it is time to move on. Don't wait until you're going crazy wishing they would leave—this could bring forth an angry outburst and alienate a good friend whom you would miss later.

FAMILY LIFE

You may have made up your mind early in life that you want to be married or single, as the case may be. And as often as not you will wind up doing what you thought you would not do—and being very happy with your choice. Actually Aries does well in either the wedded or the bachelor state. Everything depends on your intuitive feeling of what is right for you. Ask yourself what your true feelings really are, and refrain from doing what seems to be the right idea simply because it is your first. It may well be that your original plan will suit you just fine, but reflection often will show that second thoughts yield the best results.

PARENTS

Young Arians are fortunate if they have parents who can help them channel their exuberant and often headstrong energies. Aries adults, when becoming parents themselves, may grow closer than ever to their own parents—or reconcile estranged relationships with them—as they realize how much of themselves is put into the raising of a child. Your link with your father has probably been quite a strong one, and you can trace some of your own strong points or problems to his attitude in your childhood. Those of you who grew up without the influence of a male parent are likely to have felt this as a definite sense of something missing in your lives. Aries men do well to keep this in mind when bringing up their own offspring; you have more influence on them than may be apparent. Don't force your children to follow your inclinations. Gentleness is a much more powerful stimulus to a child; and each child is his or her own person, to be guided yet not designed by you. Aries mothers call on their inner reserves of patience in dealing with their children. Offspring observe you—be a good role model in the channeling of anger, in communication rather than blame or withdrawal.

EMOTIONAL SUPPORT

The Aries person needs to feel loved, yet not in a clinging or restrictive way. You appreciate feeling that your family really listens to you and that your needs are respected. Aries men tend to be somewhat fixed in their level of chauvinism; you may find that your daughter as well as your wife spots this in you and doesn't take too kindly to it. Aries women are likely to have business or social interests outside the home; if these are encouraged and the household duties are shared, you will deeply enjoy coming home to this supportive atmosphere. Arians of both sexes respond to strong emotional support but should not be coddled or babied. They will pull away from a pampering relative even after having whined a bit, seeming to invite this treatment.

OLD AGE

Resist a tendency to boss children and other family members. Build relationships with them that are based on mutual respect; this may necessitate living apart from family for your independent temperament. Your self-sufficiency combined with a sense that you truly value them as people will keep your children as staunch friends in your later years. Senior citizens of your sign often prefer to live in the company of others their own age rather than depending on children or other relatives. Your sense of having fulfilled your personal goals in life will be the source of your happiness in old age. This has little to do with success in the eyes of others, but is based on artistic accomplishments, good friendships, a sense of having brought order to your life, or having made peace with the universe within yourself. Your sense of purpose should be channeled into these aims, known only to yourself.

PROPERTY AND REAL ESTATE

Aries may or may not be inclined to pursue the acquisition of property. If you have interests in this area, work at developing a sense of decorum in your dealings. Your drive may gain wealth for you but your temper could cause you to lose everything else. You have a good intuitive sense about people and the fairness of deals you may be offered; use them well and you will reach your goals.

TAURUS

IDEAL HOME ENVIRONMENT

As a Taurean you like your home to be spacious and airy, giving off the comfortable feel of stability. You tend toward suburban or country living; those of you who are city dwellers will build and maintain an oasis in your home space, causing visitors to forget they are in the city. You enjoy traditional styles in furniture, as they give off an aura of solidity and permanence along with a grace that is always fashionable. Both men and women of your sign have a flair for interior decorating; the bull-in-the-china-shop cliché about Taurus is disproved by your delicate touch and subtle combinations. You will find that greens and soft metallic hues lend your home the atmosphere you desire. Many Taureans love antiques, making the home a treasure trove of beautiful objects both functional and decorative. Be sure to share your lovely space with others. Your home can be warm and inviting; overcome a tendency to keep newcomers away or to feel that you cannot accommodate the needs of visitors.

SENSE OF HOME

Earthy Taurus possesses a sense of home that is among the strongest in all the zodiacal signs. Whatever your outside activities may be, your home is truly the center of your world. You may even find yourself stopping for a few minutes at your house or apartment between appointments when a trip home is not really necessary just to get the feeling of being centered and of starting off again from your own space. Venturing too far from home, or staying away too long, can be disorienting to you. You feel the need to maintain a sense of the familiar, to be surrounded by your own things and in control of your surroundings. Enjoy them by all means, but try not to let your horizons be limited. You can reestablish your center wherever you go—indeed, you carry it within yourself.

FAMILY LIFE

Household duties are very satisfying for you, and you derive relaxation from maintaining the nest you have created. You desire an orderly routine of day-to-day living, and this can cause you to lead a solitary life unless you are flexible. Of course, having a partner who is comfortable and compatible with your needs is a great help. Any situation causing emotional strain in the home can be particularly difficult to deal with, as you always wish to maintain an atmosphere of peace where you live. Remember that you as well as others can be contributing to disharmony, and be aware that although it may be hard to give in or to compromise this is often the way back to the calm that you crave. Don't pout when things don't go your way. Some time by yourself is useful in regaining your equanimity, but avoid giving family members the silent treatment or playing the martyr. Those whom you are close to will respond to your warmth and good humor.

PARENTS

If your parents engage you in contests of the will, you need to watch yourself in adulthood; this tendency could unfavorably influence your own children or cause problems with adult relatives. Develop the reasoning side of your nature, and this will be an example for your offspring. Taurean children do best when able to develop a full relationship with both parents; if you are a single parent of a Taurus child, find someone of the opposite sex who can provide your child with the experience of knowing a loving adult who sets a good example in addition to your own. Start early to accept the fact that your children will need to grow away from you as they mature. They will remain closer to you if you encourage their independence.

EMOTIONAL SUPPORT

Taurus, you may not seem particularly aggressive or domineering, but you may very well expect total agreement from your mate and obedience from your children! Discuss your wants and expectations with your mate —preferably before marriage—and leave your children room for their own preferences. Taurus men can give an outward appearance of an easygoing casualness they don't really possess; inwardly they tend to view life through a set of assumptions as to how things should be, and tempers flare when others don't fit in with these views. If you are dealing with this phenomenon in Taurean relatives, use soft persuasion in which your point of view touches their hearts. They do want the happiness of others, but they need to feel it as being as immediately important as their own. Women of this sign are cautious, may be overprotective both of mate and children. Both male and female Taureans, no matter how they may be feuding with siblings or other family members, will loyally defend them in any confrontation with the outside world.

OLD AGE

The continuity of family traditions and values is extremely important to Taureans in later life. They greatly enjoy being grandparents and may display a carefree manner with grandchildren that did not appear with their own children. Grown children of older Taurus people will keep a harmonious relationship with them if they are able to help them see that the family spirit is being carried on, although outward forms and customs have become outmoded. Older Taureans like to be consulted by their children, to feel respected and needed by them. Their advice is practical and freely given—but don't ask for it if your mind is more or less made up already, as they will assume that you are asking because you intend to do what they say!

PROPERTY AND REAL ESTATE

Taurus loves to have property or real estate with a history, and will work to restore an old home to its original beauty. But make sure what you plan to buy is really worth the money you spend—this is one area in which your famed practicality can desert you. Use your calm and assured demeanor to your advantage when working with real-estate people or private owners looking to sell their homes. You are able to back it up nicely with your sound pragmatic judgments and observations. In fact, you can be an excellent real-estate person yourself.

GEMINI

IDEAL HOME ENVIRONMENT

The delights of the big city are just your cup of tea, providing you with the heady atmosphere of crowds and a sense of perpetual busyness. You like big windows that look out over the bustle of traffic, and the noise generally doesn't bother you. If you are a family-oriented Gemini you gravitate toward a suburban setting, with grass, trees, and privacy, but not too far from civilization. You prefer small quarters to a place that is too big; a mansion would boggle your mind as you struggle to fill each room in a way that would satisfy your aesthetic senses. Display your eclectic tastes in your home furnishings. You have a skill for successfully combining styles that have little in common from a more consertive perspective. It is your touch that unifies them. Bright, open rooms with lots of sun please you, as do clear yellows, whites, and reds. Balance with blues and pastels to ease the nerves when the need arises.

SENSE OF HOME

Home to you is a central location from which to move out. The urge to wander may move your home base from place to place to satisfy your love of continual variety, but you need your own space to ground you as too much input can burn you out. The Gemini enjoys making his or her home a place where all are welcome, friends and strangers alike. Don't let this make you a doormat—know your priorities and stand up for them.

FAMILY LIFE

The day-to-day routines of home life can get on your nerves, Gemini, as you need to be intellectually stimulated almost as much as you need to breathe. You have all the energy you need, however, to maintain your home—just make sure you also have outside projects or some sort of interchange with family members that keeps your mind busy. Actually, if you can create the latter situation you love to be part of a large or extended family. Group discussion, games, and the like make your home a place where you truly love to be. Geminis are to be found in profusion in communal homes and sharing apartments or houses with groups of friends. Your natural talent for mediating between people when problems arise in the household makes you a beloved aunt or uncle and a parent who shows no favoritism. If single, you are in demand by your married relatives to help with the kids or an occasionally recalcitrant spouse.

PARENTS

The Gemini child, being a naturally social person, has an easier time than most if raised by stepparents, grandparents, aunts and uncles, or other parent substitutes. They readily accept being raised by a single parent but need contrasting examples to choose from. Having close friends participate in family life is a boon to the parent of a Gemini, as these youngsters possess such an abundance of energy that one adult can be overwhelmed. A Gemini parent has the best chance of keeping up with Gemini offspring. With mental Mercury as your ruling planet, you question parents and other authority figures, not out of disrespect (unless you deeply feel you have been unfairly restricted) but because of your restless and often insatiable curiosity. When you become a parent yourself it is frequently your spouse who handles mundane disciplinary matters rather than you. Let your children get close to you during your quieter moods; without realizing it you may often keep them at a distance through the high and constant level of energy you exude. This is particularly the case if you have a Cancer or Capricorn child, as these will withdraw if they feel you are putting them off.

EMOTIONAL SUPPORT

Your automatic process of analysis enables you to shed light on the nature of family problems and upsets, but be sure to empathize with family members during difficult times. Often they may feel that you are simply dismissing their feelings with your concise and emotional statements of what you perceive to be happening. Since you are truly gifted at explaining, sit down with your loved ones and tell them how you experience what is going on. If they understand that you need the objective perspective you display in order to fully assimilate your experience, they will be more understanding of you. And if you keep your words and tone of voice as gentle with them as you like theirs to be with you, they will feel that you are seeing their position without condemning or belittling them.

OLD AGE

The older Gemini is alert and intellectually active and can give advice without wanting to exert control over others. Watch your level of activity to avoid overstressing yourself, and you will long remain younger than your years. You want lots of company and may choose to live in a rest home for this reason when elderly—but rest is the last thing you will be looking for! The company of children is more enjoyable to you now than it may have been at any earlier time, and you enchant the young ones with long and tall tales spun out of your wry humor and seasoned experience.

PROPERTY AND REAL ESTATE

As a rule Geminians are not particularly interested in accumulating property and may be renters all their lives. However, you do have an uncanny knack for advising others whose interests lie in that area. You love to compare and to search out all possibilities, and your chatty sociability brings opportunities to you. Ironically, your disinterest in accumulating material goods seems to attract possessions to you, and you may wind up with one or more homes, which you can rent, sell, or live in. The condo craze may be the exception to this disinterest of yours, and you can fill your building with friends with whom you happily pass the time.

CANCER

IDEAL HOME ENVIRONMENT

Cancerians enjoy the country, the suburbs, and urban settings—all that matters is what is to be found inside the home. These natives will be extremely picky about the details of the interior of the nest, and will often completely remodel a home to suit their tastes. The list of requirements is a mile long, and Cancer will not be satisfied until each one has been met. Silver, white, black, and watery shades harmonize with the Cancer temperament. You are likely to be quite fastidious in your housekeeping, but actual cleanliness takes second place to having everything in a precise, highly organized order. Someone else might not be able to perceive the order, but Cancer knows where each thing is and is satisfied.

SENSE OF HOME

To one born under the sign of Cancer, the home represents a safe haven in the midst of the hubbub of the world—an indispensable retreat where time moves more slowly and the feeling is one of safety and security. As a result the more introverted Cancerian can become something of a recluse, seldom venturing forth to deal in the daily matters of business or the marketplace. Even the more outgoing types may at times be a bit compulsive about maintaining the privacy and sanctity of the home environment.

FAMILY LIFE

A need for closeness in family life characterizes Cancer, both male and female. You love to feel that you are nurturing those you love, and that you are receiving this same nurturing from them. Through this you gain the strength for outside endeavors, for it is rare for even one of your sign to desire or be able to maintain an existence totally separate from the world at large. Small chores are satisfying to you, even more so when the duties of the home are equally and harmoniously shared among family members. Petty annoyances can be escalated into cataclysms when you fall into a complaining mood and pursue them beyond their true size and significance—perhaps this has something to do with the crab symbolism of your sign! Try to let go of minor grievances before they are taken out of proportion.

PARENTS

Your mother is likely to be the parent to whom you are closer; a gentle, empathic father is a big plus for a Cancer type, and Cancer men are among those who are capable of expressing their masculinity in a gentle, paternal fashion. Harshness on the part of parents causes the Cancer personality to retreat and to feel helpless; if this was the case in your childhood, endeavor to use your experience when you become a parent to draw your children out and put them at ease rather than inadvertently repeating the pattern. Parenting is natural to both men and women of your sign. You are a great candidate for becoming a substitute parent to your children's friends and other young people who cannot relate spontaneously with their own parents.

EMOTIONAL SUPPORT

It is important to you that you have emotional support in the home, and you readily reciprocate. See that this positive trait does not degenerate into possessiveness, especially of your children, or overdependence. You verbalize complaints, and this is good. Concentrate on accuracy and objectivity here, and your family will work with you on desired improvements in your interaction. When you feel you are not receiving enough emotional support, you tend to attack those you love in covert ways or to use unfair methods of getting your way. It is better to deal with problems out in the open to avoid multiplication of misunderstandings and undue prolonging of discomfort. Remember that your spouse, siblings, in-laws, and children are just as anxious as you are for harmony to be restored. Don't let that harmony be sacrificed just to get a few more jabs in.

OLD AGE

You will give much attention to building a nest egg, and this stands you in good stead for your old age. Now is the time for you to have the pleasure of grandchildren coming to visit. You will want to have your family around you as much as possible, and if you have maintained an open rapport with them in which thoughts and feelings are freely aired this will be a warm and happy time. The treasures of a lifetime—both material and spiritual—will be shared by you and your loved ones. You will radiate that sense of loving security that has been so dear to you, and that you have earned.

PROPERTY AND REAL ESTATE

Your changeable moods may cause you to suddenly decide that you simply must have a particular house, piece of land, or part of town to live in. For the most part those of your sign are able to align your wants and needs with the money or circumstances needed to secure them. But you need to avoid feeling that you have somehow been cheated if not every detail of your dream manifests readily.

LEO

Ideal Home Environment

You love to see your dreams become reality, and this is highly evident in your home. Leos are always building, choosing, or renovating their "dream house." Every detail will have been envisioned by you and then done to a T. You like your home to be on display, so that even if you live in a rural setting it will be visible—not hidden away. If you are an urban dweller, the interior of your home will be as large and gracious as you can afford. Your tastes in decorating run to the modern, even to the avant-garde, and feature deep shades of all colors. When sharing a house or apartment with friends your space can readily be identified by your individualistic touch.

Sense of Home

Leo natives tend to base their choice of a home setting on that which will fit in with business or career orientation. If your work does not demand a great deal of mobility, you will build and appreciate a sense of putting down roots and really settling into a home. If you must move frequently you may take along a portable mini-home in the form of a collection of items which you set up wherever you go, creating your own atmosphere of familiarity. The most temporary dwelling will bear your unique signature. You are proud of your creativity in putting together an attractive living space and delight in sharing it with others. Your social life is most pleasing to you when it is centered around your own castle.

Family Life

You enjoy having a fixed, regular routine in your home, but in order to be satisfied it must be one that you have set up yourself or at least had a major share in the process. You can be restless and withdrawn when there is disharmony in the home, and those of you who share living space with friends may often be tempted to go and live alone to have things more to your liking. Chances are this won't really suit you—you like the company of others too much—and you will sooner or later (probably sooner) find yourself establishing another shared situation. Air your views in advance to avoid conflict later.

Parents

As a family person you begin by expecting your parents to be sterling examples of all that is honest, successful, and socially gracious. You believe that the outward expression is indicative of what a person has on the inside, so that what meets the eye is extremely important. Your parents, siblings, and even your mate if you marry may mistake this attitude for simple materialism on your part unless you explain your way of thinking to them. A Leo child will return in kind the emotional input he or she receives; kindness is rewarded with kindness, anger with more anger and a stubborn resolve. Children of this sign lean toward the parent of the same sex. As a parent you do your best when providing a consistent, rational steadiness for them to rely on, rather than demanding their respect and obedience.

EMOTIONAL SUPPORT

Despite your self-assured demeanor, you need to feel that you are uncritically supported by loved ones. Be open to honest grievances on their part as this will speed restoration of the mutual appreciation you thrive on. You are willing to be an equal sharer of burdens and responsibilities once love and loyalty have been tried and found strong and enduring. Remember that this can be done without making unrealistic demands or overworking yourself to demonstrate your own good will. Your biggest contribution to happy family life is your readiness to take the initiative in solving problems; in this you may be emotional but never deceitful or petty. You are happiest in a close family situation, often one that includes in-laws and sometimes siblings who come to live with you after you marry. If you are a single you enjoy spending time with friends' families and partake of family living with and through them.

OLD AGE

Old age brings you a fullness of experience that you wear well, often blossoming into an impressive dignity, which attracts the respect and liking of others. You can become the patriarch or matriarch of your brood, but take it easy here if you live with your children—you have raised them to be self-sufficient and to think for themselves, and they won't take kindly to an overly authoritative attitude. Your sense of humor is jovial and well-seasoned, giving you an expansive outlook on life that brings joy to yourself and others.

PROPERTY AND REAL ESTATE

If you are planning to purchase a home or property, you are unafraid to take risks and will have a creative approach to obtaining exactly what you want. Your business ties should enable you to contact intelligent and sociable salespeople and others who can advise you. You do well when listening to several points of view and molding a coherent plan from them. Leos who have been apartment dwellers for years often develop the desire for their own home in later life. You want to relax at the end of your life with solid holdings of your own, and in a place where you can continue to entertain and display your talents.

VIRGO

IDEAL HOME ENVIRONMENT

Your dwelling is in the best of taste, never garish. You prefer warm, understated earth tones accented with yellows and greens, the friendly colors of nature. The Virgo home reveals signs of culture and excellence, having an almost librarylike quietness and refinement whether or not you have pursued an academic life. Contrary to the stereotyped notions about your earthy sign, you may very well prefer to live in the city, having a widely eclectic, high-paced, artistic, and intellectual lifestyle. You may change locations a number of times before finding the right home to meet your exacting needs.

SENSE OF HOME

Virgos go to one extreme or the other in the housekeeping department, tending to be either fastidious—even compulsively neat—or downright sloppy. You enjoy entertaining and parties in your home; when not inviting a crowd you prefer the company of only one or two friends in addition to your own family. You are a thoughtful host or hostess and usually manage not to be overly concerned (if you're the neat type) with possible damage to your domain by guests. This is not to say that you won't have the carpet cleaned as soon as they leave—even if you had it done just before they arrived!

FAMILY LIFE

You have a domestic urge, often felt from childhood on, and derive great satisfaction from establishing a nest. This can be detoured somewhat if your early life was difficult, particularly if your parents quarreled frequently. The family atmosphere on which you thrive is one in which your own special needs are met without struggle; you take care that the needs of others are given this consideration by you. A somewhat delicate nervous system can make you irritable or fretful if the home routine is disturbed too much or interfered with by in-laws or busybody friends. You may store resentment without being straightforward about airing your grievances, tending to be silently hostile around the house. It is better both for you and your loved ones if you describe what is bothering you, as this will relieve your inner pressure and help them to rectify the situation—or at least let you know what their response is to your complaint. They can't do this if they don't know what's on your mind. Don't feel that it is unfair of you to say that something rubs you the wrong way; it certainly isn't fair to let people know something is wrong but refuse to tell them what it is.

PARENTS

The influence and example of a gentle, firm father or father figure is a boon to the Virgo in childhood and adolescence, enabling him or her to meet life without building a wall of reserve or becoming a complainer. You are more accepting of your mother's moods than your father's, internalizing her feelings as your own approach to parenting. Should you and your spouse be staying together only for the sake of a child, especially if the child is a Virgo, divorce would be preferable to continual exposure to argument and ill feelings between you. As a parent the Virgo native should make sure to display the deep love that is felt for the child or children; this love is certainly present, but your child may not always perceive it through your collected exterior. Temper your inclination to criticize with affection and you will find there is less that you feel like criticizing.

EMOTIONAL SUPPORT

To give you the emotional sustenance you need, your family needs to know that your seemingly aloof attitude is not one of distance from them. Remind them of this yourself. You need time and space to clarify your thoughts and reactions, to find solutions to problems, and it is easier for you to accomplish this if no one is trying to force you into a confrontation before you are ready. This is absolutely valid, but don't let it become an excuse to postpone confrontation indefinitely. Virgos need the help of those around them to draw their attention above the level of details, which can become stumbling blocks if concentrated on too much or too long. If you have a Leo around the house, this one will be a help to you, rounding things out with a sunny disposition and little regard for minutiae.

OLD AGE

All grandparents are Virgos. You are concerned, helpful, indulgent as you never were with your own kids, doting, crotchety, and a wee bit prone to saying, "I told you so." The typical Virgo grandma is not overbearing but may seem extremely watchful. If asked what is wrong she will invariably reply, "Oh, nothing." You have a robustly active inner life, which enables you to flow gracefully into the reduced physical activity of old age. Keep a wide perspective on life and its changes and you will find yourself always in demand by your loved ones.

PROPERTY AND REAL ESTATE

Natives of the earth sign Virgo have a conservative philosophy of home and hearth. They like to remain settled or rooted and prefer to hold on to property—or even simply to remain in the same setting—rather than changing locale for prestige or monetary purposes. You don't care for wheeling and dealing but your sharp eye for practical value will enable you to put those roots down in real stability. You will move if you see that it is solidly worthwhile to do so.

LIBRA

IDEAL HOME ENVIRONMENT

Libra's ideal home has clean, straightforward, architecturally attractive lines. You prefer a plain, elegantly simple design to anything ornate or ostentatious. If you have a choice you will generally tend toward urban life—a townhouse or condominium—where you can feel yourself to be a part of a busy flow of humanity. You enjoy having a yard or garden, not necessarily to putter in but to balance and complement the home. Librans love their homes but will move without regret if it is desired by their mate.

SENSE OF HOME

As an air sign you devote much thought to home conditions and inter-relationships. Many of the problems you experience may be due to your reticence in taking an active role. Continue to consider things carefully as you do, but try to be more decisive. You feel the need for your surroundings to be orderly and want all family members to participate in maintaining this state. You regard your home as a sanctuary and may find it difficult to be comfortable with visitors you have not chosen yourself. This can be particularly bothersome when your teenagers bring home their friends. One solution can be to set aside a time of the day or week when no one enters your space—preferably a private room or corner belonging excusively to you—balanced by another time when you devote your attention solely to a social visit with your youngsters and their guests. You may find that your receptivity to them shows them more to your liking than you thought—and this goes for some unfavorite friend of your spouse, too!

FAMILY LIFE

You have a strong sense of family ties, and your closeness with siblings increases in adulthood. Many Librans live with a brother or sister even after one or the other marries. If you are setting up your own household after sharing a home with a sibling, you may have to put extra effort into helping this one feel that no real separation is happening. Chances are your mate shares your approach to most things and will welcome the presence of your family, enjoying as you do the warm atmosphere of a crowded table with much babble and laughter. This is provided, of course, that there are no unspoken animosities between relatives, and that you know exactly who will be present! Many Librans are gourmet cooks, a great contribution to a happy family.

PARENTS

The Libra child depends on the solidity of the home environment and finds it difficult to handle when parents separate. Correspondingly, Libran adults do not have an easy time carrying the single parent role. Sharing a house or apartment with another single mom or dad often proves to be a wonderful solution. Plain speaking about your inner feelings sets a positive and lasting example for your children. You are among the fairest of parents and will never play favorites or make decisions carelessly.

EMOTIONAL SUPPORT

Harmony-loving Libras tend to maintain a surface image of contentment in order to avoid argument and discord at home. You will sacrifice your preferences to do this and are slow to anger. However, this invites the danger of loss of temper when the last straw finally comes. In-laws can be helpful here in drawing out your real feelings and assisting in making them known to your immediate family. You should make the effort also to express yourself directly. Often a short spat can clear the air for a lasting and unpretended calm, which is well worth the temporary struggle. You feel loved and appreciated when your needs are met with understanding and affection, so it certainly pays to share them with those who care for you.

OLD AGE

For most Librans the perspective turns to one of serenity with advancing age. In looking back over your life you will derive deep satisfaction from being able to see that you shared your inner self with others at crucial times. It is very possible that you will live with your children, as ties with them will have remained close. You take a verbal but diplomatic role as an older family member, and this is appreciated—especially in mediation between your kids and their kids. If you have no family with whom to live, you accept a rest home environment fairly easily. Seek an outlet for your talents—without doubt they are needed—and you can use them to enhance life for everyone around you as well as for yourself.

PROPERTY AND REAL ESTATE

In buying a home you can put off decisions indefinitely in order to make enough comparisons to satisfy yourself. Don't miss out on something you really like just to take more possibilities into consideration. And remember that weighing and pondering may come more easily to you than to your family—they may be tearing out their hair waiting for you to make up your mind.

SCORPIO

IDEAL HOME ENVIRONMENT

Whether a Scorpio's home is large or small, modest or opulent, it has a visual, atmospheric impact that can't be missed. It is usually characterized by some unique element in architecture, placement, interior design —or all of these. Color schemes vary widely with the individual Scorpio, but lean primarily to deep hues, dark reds, and blues. Your dwelling displays strong textural contrasts, often utilizing metals, wood, and leather.

SENSE OF HOME

Your home is your personal creation. Although you happily make use of hand-me-downs and bric-a-brac, you never take what you can't use and you discard what has no place among your possessions, not liking to be a hoarder. An innate restlessness may cause you to make many moves, and your enjoyment in putting together your castle never fades. It is satisfying to you to have your own business, which can move with you when you desire a change. Often your office space will be in a specially designated part of your home rather than at a separate location.

FAMILY LIFE

Scorpio enjoys both a close give-and-take family life and the pleasures of solitude. If you remain single or have a partner but no children, your time is pretty much your own. If you become involved in raising a family, arrange your home so that you don't seem so much of an isolationist when taking time for yourself. An alcove or niche with your desk or armchair in it, where you are by yourself yet still visible, is helpful. You can establish a do-not-disturb schedule and still have your family feel that you are with them. You have strong feelings about what is and isn't out of bounds—this can pertain to territory, possessions, time, routine, or all of these. Don't allow yourself to be too finicky as this can border on the idiosyncratic or even obsessive.

PARENTS

The Scorpio child thrives on a close, vital relationship with both parents. However, if the parents are too watchful or critical of them they can develop an obstinate, almost warlike attitude, which continues into adult life. The in-laws of a Scorpio do well to really get to know this native if they wish to avoid conflict. You are not petty, Scorpio, but you know what you are about and can't be manipulated or bought off—and woe to the one who is caught trying! As a parent, you should take care not to let confrontations with children or disciplinary methods blow up into earth-quakes. Let your kids know that you need your privacy and will respect theirs. Your offspring are likely to have a Scorpio streak themselves and will give you positive response if you are honest with them and not hostile.

EMOTIONAL SUPPORT

Scorpio often feels misunderstood or underestimated by his or her family in general, or may simply have such a different lifestyle and set of values that little in common remains. Your refusal to live by any standards other than your own may well keep you on rocky terms with all but one or two close relatives. Use these friendly contacts as a liaison with the rest, as both you and those from whom you have become estranged will be happier if the distance between you is eliminated. Some Scorpios may feel, but never admit to, the need for this reconciliation. This would be too bad, as unhealthy emotions cannot be beneficial especially when carried a long time. A family counselor could prove of great help if you and others decide that it is worthwhile to bring private feelings into the open in the interest of peace.

OLD AGE

As Scorpios grow older they tend to become set in their ways, preferring repetitive routines to major change and familiar methods to new ones. If you have children you may find now that your attachment centers on one child or grandchild. Don't feel guilty or try to force yourself to change this—simply be fair and courteous in all relationships. A deep level of generosity may manifest in you now as never before, as you enjoy seeing wealth or property passing from one generation to the next.

PROPERTY AND REAL ESTATE

Don't be overly demanding when surveying houses or condos with an eye to buying one of your own. You may never find one that already suits you perfectly before you buy it, and will most certainly revel in turning one that comes close into what is just right for you. The same goes when selling your home—be reasonable in your expectations.

SAGITTARIUS

IDEAL HOME ENVIRONMENT

The larger your home the more you want to stay there, Sagittarius. Or perhaps it is that the more of a homebody you are the bigger you want your place to be. Your sign tends to prefer houses to apartments when in a town or suburban setting, and palaces when living in the country. A Sagittarian apartment-dweller will usually be someone who travels quite a bit and who has friends in all sorts of city and country settings with whom to visit. This includes extended visits, and the footloose Sagittarian may well be a world traveler. Soft gray tones serve as the background for red tints and purple shades, which the Sagittarian home displays in bold patterns or solids.

SENSE OF HOME

You either move regularly to new locations or create a busy life wherever you have your roots. Your home can be a busy organization of many people; visitors and phone calls abound. Your domestic life is conducive to a multiple family or extended family setting, and if you can't afford a new mansion you'll find and renovate an old one. Any family lifestyle suits you as long as it never becomes intrusive or suffocating—if it does you become claustrophobic and rebel. Menial duties may seem too trivial to you; however, share in doing them anyway, as this is the only way in which others will feel you are pulling your weight. And ultimately you, too, are only satisfied with yourself if you have done your fair share. Sagittarians hate to be pinned down to one place, and may make a boat, motor home, or wooded cabin a second home. Sometimes they have their own retreat, which even family and friends are not allowed to visit. They hate clutter of any kind and prefer a simple, modern-looking home.

FAMILY LIFE

If you have teenage children you become the understanding parent who converses with their friends as they wish their own families would. It is occasionally possible for you to mediate between these adolescents and their parents, but for the most part your views are more liberal than most. Your home is the safe haven where the kids can be themselves without necessarily bringing other adults into the picture. Your energetic nature loves the outdoors, and you can have a great time taking your kids and their friends hiking or camping. Sagittarian parents make great scout leaders and PTA members, provided they can avoid shocking the more conservative of their colleagues with their liberated ideas. Even if you are not home as much as you would like, you set a fine example for youngsters; they will never forget the sense of fair play that you display.

PARENTS

Sagittarian children pay close attention to parents and use them as role models, sometimes following their examples all too well! This is the prototype of the child whose parents exclaim, "Where did you pick *that* up?" Divorce or separation of parents rarely unsettles them as long as the absent parent remains available and is not maligned verbally by the other. As an adult, Sagittarius retains the need to be held to commitments and to be reminded that others consider it important to be able to rely on them. If your parents stressed this to you in a positive manner you have a better chance of remembering it now, but there probably will always be times when you are tempted to let a promise or an appointment slide by unattended. Work toward overcoming this inconsiderate behavior; the Sagittarian who succeeds in doing so builds a strong and exemplary character, which is charismatic and inspiring, especially to your children.

EMOTIONAL SUPPORT

The best emotional atmosphere is one based on trust and mutual respect. You find your real anchor within yourself and expect the same in others. If intimates do not treat you with the respect you deserve, you become unpredictable and are apt to go off on binges or flights of fancy. Because your adventuresome nature may be a bit more than in-laws can put up with, you tend to keep them at a distance. If they are kindred spirits, you may become closer to them than even to your spouse. It is not unusual for you to form long-lasting relationships with members of this new, extended family. Friends of the family participate in your home life, adding verve and excitement to even ordinary occasions. Sagittarians adore the unknown and may invite foreign exchange students to spend time with their family, finding that these guests add to holiday experiences. Your house may become a meeting place for "regulars" who think of it as a second home.

OLD AGE

By the time Sagittarians become senior citizens, they realize how their wandering urges have been expressions of inner curiosity about themselves. Now you no longer search for some nebulous answer in new homes, new jobs, new cities or countries, and new partners. Your sense of humor has ripened; you love life in a deeper way; you radiate warmth and the wisdom that characterizes the highest potential of your sign. The older Sagittarian who has family ties generates a robust optimism and a positive vision for the future of the young. Pace your physical activity and keep it up—it will make your body hardy and your disposition sweet.

PROPERTY AND REAL ESTATE

You are not concerned with ownership since Sagittarians care most about ease, comfort, and especially convenience. You prefer to rent or lease a dwelling. If you own your home it must be one which can be expanded to meet new needs. The apartment or rented house you occupy can be tiny, as it generally serves only as a home base for your adventures. You have much energy with which to search out the spot that will make you happiest. Balance it with pragmatic evaluation of what you see—if you can't manage this by yourself take a Taurus along.

CAPRICORN

IDEAL HOME ENVIRONMENT

Persons born under the sign of Capricorn prefer a quiet, subdued atmosphere, which prevails throughout the decor of the home even if it is a grandly elegant dwelling. Capricorn abhors anything gaudy and loves the efficient and the understated. Luxury doesn't interest you, Capricorn, but you find a real delight in outfitting your surroundings with all the amenities that are functional. You have the knack for turning a necessity into an object of loveliness. You lean toward traditional designs of simplicity; if your interests lie primarily outside of the home, your dwelling may be completely devoid of ornamentation—and only the most basic of furniture. Capricorn's home colors run to tans, dark blues (even verging on black), golds and silvers—all muted. You can be an industrious gardener or landscaper, making the outside of your home well-groomed and attractive.

SENSE OF HOME

The home life of a Capricorn may center around a study or workroom, as these natives are always deeply involved with their vocations or avocations. You like to feel the presence of familiar things around you, and to you this means your work. Your career is represented in the decor of the home, though never ostentatiously. You prefer to receive friends and associates in this work space, as the rest of your home is regarded as an inner sanctum, which you like to reserve only for those to whom you feel close. Yours is not an "open house" living space because too much hubbub in your personal surroundings makes you want to retreat. This attitude may cause a bit of difficulty at times if your mate or child is more of a socializer than you are; this is when your private room comes in handy. Find a balance with family members so that you neither hide out in your corner nor endure too much gabbing with a frozen smile and gritted teeth.

Family Life

Capricorns are usually neat housekeepers, but they sometimes go through cycles of carelessness that surprise and dismay family members. They are prone to losing things around the house; undoubtedly the first person to hunt for his glasses, which were perched on his nose, was a Capricorn. This sign has a deep reverence for family tradition, which prevails even when relations are not particularly cordial.

Parents

The Capricorn native is ruled by rules, dictated to by dictums. You have too much respect for authority, deferring to those in positions of power even when your own opinion or decision would be better. For this reason, lectures and disapproval from your parents may have darkened your self-image with guilt or self-doubt. Use this experience to avoid doing the same with your own children, expecting them to follow you unquestioningly because you are the parent. The father often has the most lasting influence on the Capricorn child, and what he imparts in the way of the value of cooperation is decisive. If Capricorn is shown consideration and courtesy in life his or her best nature comes to the fore.

Emotional Support

Capricorn is more emotional than usually is apparent, requiring displays and verbal assurances of love and affection. You are a patient listener, but you can be sure that your practical mind is putting together its own version of what is being said. Nod in agreement to Capricorn's preferred approach to solving a problem and he or she will follow you anywhere. This sign possesses an innocence that presumes acquiescence, and can growl or recoil in shock upon learning that it is not present. If the emotional needs of family members are not expressed a Capricorn may be blissfully unaware of them. However, once they are presented they will be met with consideration—provided they are deemed reasonable.

Old Age

Capricorns thrive in their later years of life because they are able to let go of responsibilities they have carried since their very earliest years. They want desperately to be financially self-sufficient, but become more and more emotionally needy, sometimes reverting to a childlike dependence. This emotional attachment includes the mate's relatives, and deepens as Capricorn grows older. Despite this, a bit of eccentricity makes the Capricorn prefer living alone in old age rather than moving in with children. Sharing a home with a brother or sister may be more acceptable. A rest home or retirement community is a reasonable alternative for some Capricorns, as long as they don't have to participate in too many of the activities. As grandparents, Capricorns are well loved, even though little ones may be a bit intimidated by their fixed routines and a tendency to alternate jokes and nonsense with grumpy silences.

PROPERTY AND REAL ESTATE

The Capricorn native may often generate a concealed worry that is visible only as a certain fussiness or irritability around the house. This can be caused by a fatalistic attitude toward the success of ventures outside the home or over the maintenance of the home or grounds. Capricorn has a strong sense of the responsibilities of owning a home and may feel inadequate to the task of keeping it up. Once this fades, a wealth of practical ideas flows forth to more than meet the situation. You would do very well with real estate as an avocation, often making money from improvements you have made to your home. This interest in real estate could turn out to be very lucrative in later years.

AQUARIUS

IDEAL HOME ENVIRONMENT

It is likely that Aquarius will try a number of different home and lifestyle situations through the years. This is a matter of exploring your ideals regarding home life, in all its different aspects, by experimentation. Often an Aquarian settles down in an older home, which can be redecorated in a novel and unique manner. You also enjoy purchasing a brand-new place that features some striking new architectural design. Aquarian colors for interior decorating include deep shades of blue, green, or purple.

SENSE OF HOME

Your home is a blank canvas for you to paint. Aquarius loves to work from scratch, putting together his or her own blend of traditional and modern decors. You enjoy being at home and receiving visitors; friends are to be found there on a regular basis. You are a neat housekeeper for the most part, as physical disorder around you makes you feel mentally jumbled, and this is something you realize sooner or later. An Aquarian will periodically go through all stored possessions in order to discard what is not needed. Be careful, as it is easy for you to throw away something in a burst of enthusiasm that you will miss later on. Above all you need to have a home where you are comfortable inwardly. There may be periods of time when you are someone's houseguest or sharing space for the sake of convenience, but this can't last indefinitely for an Aquarian. You will inevitably leave these arrangements to create a situation where you are truly at home.

FAMILY LIFE

Aquarius is willing to try various living arrangements: single parenting (Aquarian women are in the vanguard of single women deciding to have children), extended family (still a novelty to most Americans), shared parenting with other families, and open marriage in some cases. The key isn't necessarily what's new for this day and age, although much that reflects the time is Aquarian, but what is new and interesting to you personally. You adapt very well to changes in environment and conditions; keep in mind that this is not necessarily the case for those with whom you live. Include others in your preparations and plans—doing so tries your patience but helps keep things together. You may often find yourself in the role of bringing estranged family members back onto speaking terms.

PARENTS

A close, lively relationship is possible between Aquarian children and their parents, and also between Aquarian parents and their offspring. Children of this sign select the most unique traits of their parents to make their own. This child will readily accept parental divorce or being raised by someone other than the parents, but always retains a sensitive spot that yearns for a more traditional situation. Children of Aquarian parents may also wish that their dress, lifestyle, or views were more like those of their friends' parents. If this is handled with love, respect, and humor your child will grow out of it into an appreciation of your individuality.

EMOTIONAL SUPPORT

Aquarius can live alone but prefers company. Being solitary too long can create habits which then seem odd when the Aquarian does pair off or begin sharing space. You need a partner or friends who understand and respect your need for rationality and order along with your urge to continually redefine or alter your work, home, or living patterns. You will happily remain with a mate who does not stifle your sense of freedom. However, if this is threatened you are capable of simply vanishing without warning from that person's life. You believe in the value of verbal communication and require a free flow in this department in order to coexist harmoniously with anyone. In-laws are welcome in the Aquarian household but cannot pry or interfere without bringing on a confrontation. Relationships with siblings are close and remain so throughout life.

OLD AGE

Aquarians retain their flexibility long past the age where others have settled into fixed roles. Just bear in mind that it is unnecessary to make changes for their own sake or to maintain an avant-garde image. You experience some difficulty in assuming the housekeeper-grandma or gardener-grandpa role—you have too much to say! You lose nothing and indeed can benefit from listening to cautionary advice. It may seem restrictive but can help you to avoid going out on a limb. Your undying spontaneity is enjoyed by children, but older folks may lack patience with it. You insist on living where you can be your own boss, often preferring a dog or cat for companionship over children or other relatives who would cramp your style.

PROPERTY AND REAL ESTATE

Once your Aquarian mind is fully on the subject of acquiring your own home you have boundless energy with which to go about it. Make sure to do it when in this enthusiastic frame of mind; otherwise your attitude will sour and remain an unpleasant association for you when doing similar things in the future. Don't feel that you have to rush into buying a home right away—sudden opportunities or inheritances are likely to present themselves. Your ability to generate enthusiasm in yourself and others will help you find what you are looking for.

PISCES

IDEAL HOME ENVIRONMENT

If you are a Pisces you probably have an inner picture of your dream house, evolved in your thoughts from childhood and adolescence. Your home life is dominated by this image throughout adulthood, and any home you have before the one that fits your ideal will constantly be compared with it and found wanting. This is not to say that you cannot be happy until you are living in the place of your dreams—each dwelling you inhabit will possess touches of it, and even if you should never actually materialize what your mind sees you will dwell there in your imagination. For Pisces this is not a depressing state, nor an escape into fantasy. It is an oddly practical way of having what you want despite all obstacles.

SENSE OF HOME

Whatever the size or location of your home, Pisces, it serves you as a shelter from the buffeting of the mundane world. Country meadows appeal to your sense of beauty and quiet. If you live in an urban setting you will nonetheless maintain a certain amount of seclusion—your place will be set far back from the street, or be in a loft or along an isolated alleyway, or require a mazelike route of approach. Your senses are pleased by soft-lined, fairly ornate architecture and decor. Rich earth colors, darkening to black, are satisfying to you, as are light shades of green, blue, and rose.

FAMILY LIFE

In your family life you are a softening influence on others, tending to be a better listener than you are a mediator as you are distressed by conflict. Remember that retreating to step out of the way of confrontation can put distance between you and your loved ones. You have a gift for accurately verbalizing your thoughts, and this flows smoothly when you are serene. Use it under stress, combined with your characteristic gentleness, and it can work wonders. You are more concerned with beauty than neatness in the home, and may even see beauty in a certain amount of disorder. A hectic, crowded household disorients you with its barrage of impressions, noise, and demands. It is important for you to let in-laws know that your home is your own—don't let your needs be swept into the background through politeness.

Parents

A Piscean father is a beneficial, empathic balance to children. This same soothing empathy in mothers of your sign builds in children a good sense of trust and security in life. Piscean children have strong psychic bonds with their parents, which make it somewhat difficult for them to accept stepparents. The new parent of such a child must be unusually sympathetic and caring to form a happy relationship; this should be taken into account by the natural parent of a Pisces who is planning to marry.

Emotional Support

Pisces needs encouragement to discuss any undercurrents of discontent in the home with other family members, as otherwise he or she can develop distorted pictures of what is happening. Pisceans are masters of subtle manipulations, so relatives of these natives need to carry a double-edged sword—on the one hand empathy with Piscean moods and hunches; on the other hand a hard-nosed insistence that holds them to promises and previous arrangements. Pisces can only live happily with those who respect the amount of time spent in exercising the imagination, who recognize that the realm of imagining is a real place, and who see and appreciate the gift for enhancing the everyday reality with what they have found there. Only then will Pisces feel truly sheltered and accepted in the home.

Old Age

As you grow older you grow more and more into the enjoyment of daydreaming and the pleasures of being by yourself. It is a good idea to set aside specific times to devote attention and energy to family matters. Hopefully you will have grandchildren, as you make a warm and giving grandparent and one who does not interfere with the way your children are bringing up theirs. Date books and written reminders come in handy for keeping you posted as to your schedule; without them the time can flit by and appointments be missed without your noticing. Before you retire, make any reconciliations that are necessary with your children, as this is a wonderful time for you to share hopes and dreams with them and your grandchildren. You will surprise yourself when you look back over your lifetime—you have put together so much to love and treasure now.

Property and Real Estate

Pisceans can move restlessly from place to place, but should—and usually do—exercise great care in planning and preparing for moves. You may not have a strictly pragmatic approach to finding and buying your own home, but rather a protective concern, which allows you to grasp practical details and long-range financial arrangements. If you are selling a home, try not to allow vague impressions cloud your thinking, as this can cause delays and errors. Check out your hunches on a factual basis.

CHAPTER FIVE

Creativity

THIS FIFTH ASPECT of a person's many facets, creativity, is most imbued with a feeling of fun and relaxation. Creativity in astrology means everything from the joy of procreation, to romantic conquests, the thrill of participating in sports events, and, of course, the emotional satisfaction from all artistic endeavors.

Leo, the flamboyant sign of the artist, teacher, lover, and sports enthusiast, fits into this area of life perfectly. Why? Leo is also the symbol of the child. And it is a return to childhood and to the pleasures of play or make-believe that makes someone exceptionally creative. The lion, especially the lion's tail, is depicted in the astrology glyph for Leo. Astrologically speaking, the lion represents the taming and directing of our unconscious so that the power of this majestic beast can be harnassed through the use of human willpower.

Creativity surfaces through a conscious effort to gain some objective while maintaining a playful attitude. Think about lovemaking, sports, children, art, and showmanship—all activities which take conscious planning so that the children inside us can be free to create and express themselves.

Astrological lore does not differentiate between the fruits of a person's body (a child) or the fruits of a person's mind (a creative attainment). Romance is also a function of creativity. When a marriage or relationship becomes boring or less fulfilling, it is often because the fun of romance is lost in all the adult functions that couples must perform to exist in the everyday world.

Great artists live in this portion of their personalities almost to the exclusion of the other parts of their lives.

ARIES

CREATIVE TALENTS

A sense of newness characterizes the creativity of Aries. Your personality is fueled by the wonder you feel for life. Your creative efforts strive to express and prove the validity of your self. The Aries native tests the boundaries of whatever field is being explored. This sign is stereotyped as using up all of its energy at once and never completing what has been begun—certainly this is not true of such Arians as Johann Sebastian Bach.

THE ARTISTIC ARIES

Zealous Aries, when artistically inclined, prefers a career that promises active, demanding involvement rather than a behind-the-scenes utilization of talents. You would rather perform than teach, but if you enjoy teaching each class is a performance. You bring abundant energy to what you are doing and are capable of creating new dimensions in your field that no one has thought of before, causing jobs and projects to appear where there may have been none. The sensual aspects of your creative activity please you the most; you would prefer, for example, to create sculpture with your own hands instead of the abstract planning that goes into architecture.

MARKETING YOUR ABILITIES

Aries is a tremendous self-promoter and will also work to promote others. You create enthusiasm around you with the force of your own. This native is able to cast a critical eye on his or her own output and to strip away excess baggage and unnecessary frills. Beware, however, of a tendency to exaggerate, convincing yourself but alienating people who might have helped if presented with a more believable picture. A public relations person might be helpful to you, or you might consider learning to meditate to calm and center your energies before taking them out into the world, in order to give a more tranquil self-presentation.

SHOWMANSHIP

Arians love the thrill of showmanship and display, but by pushing themselves too hard, they are in danger of getting choked up or overcome by stage fright at the last minute. Of course, a certain amount of this is good as it keeps you on your toes, but again this is where a self-quieting technique might serve you well. If you have a good focus on the needs of the artistic community of which you are a part, this will channel some of your drive and enable you to avoid stressing yourself (and others if that is your tendency) too much.

SPORTING LUCK

An Aries will pick the hardest slope the first day he or she is on skis—and about 50 percent of the time will get away with it! This is infinitely puzzling and annoying to more timid souls (and to Aquarius who inevitably breaks an ankle). You are a born gambler, and a deep well of concentration makes you quite at home in a casino or on a steep granite mountainside.

ROMANTIC CONQUESTS

Aries is the human prototype of what is romantically known as the wolf —males and females alike. This comparison goes beyond the obvious in ways which are usually overlooked—in the wild a wolf keeps one mate at a time for life. Aries does have the desire to dedicate the self to a loved one. Your fiery nature is impatient, though, and it is not likely that you will choose to remain celibate before settling down. You are not the type to hesitate when someone is attractive to you, and you tend to be overly enthusiastic in the face of the resulting involvements.

CHILDREN

You love children and probably plan to have them someday, but you can easily get carried away with the idea of them only to find that the reality is woefully different. You can benefit tremendously from pre-birth counseling to reveal your hidden thoughts, feelings, intentions, and expectations relating to family life. If you have friends with kids, spend time with them to get a realistic view, which will guide you in deciding such things as when to start a family, how many children, and how far apart in age they should be.

When you undertake parenthood this can be the situation that finally makes you an adult. You are a young parent regardless of your age, participating in the kids' fun and loving to take them on outings. Your famous Aries anger is probably not damaging to your offspring—it may be loud but evaporates and is quickly replaced by hugs and kisses. Do be careful of impatience, though, as children can be easily wounded by the feeling that you are brushing them off, considering their needs unimportant. A childless Aries may "adopt" a niece, nephew, or the child of a friend to spend time with. Or you may consider the fruits of your creative work as your children, putting into them the energy others give to actual offspring.

TAURUS

CREATIVE TALENTS

Taurus, like Aries, prefers direct contact with an artistic medium to the planning or designing side. If you are a writer your work is tied to some philosophy or cause as it must be purposeful to you. If you paint you are a bright, varied colorist who works within accepted boundaries—not avant-garde. Taureans make great storytellers (a practice now gaining much success as a field of its own) and are adept at acting when so inclined. Your sign boasts many well-known artists in all fields; some notable examples are the actors/actresses Jack Nicholson, Anthony Quinn, and Audrey Hepburn, and the musician/composers Peter Ilich Tchaikovsky and Duke Ellington.

THE ARTISTIC TAURUS

Taurus explores within given limits or standards, rarely having a radical outlook but expressing in an original and dedicated manner. You are a conscientious worker, although you can lean in the direction of self-indulgence, as you tend to fixate on needs that are comparatively trivial and attach prime importance to them. Don't cut yourself off from group support by refusing to compromise—that support is needed and you may even end up coming to the conclusion that a revised product is better after all. Your sign may experience some difficulty getting started on a project, but once this inertia is overcome you work energetically to completion.

MARKETING YOUR ABILITIES

A streak of shyness may inhibit you as far as the marketing of your creative work is concerned; or a tendency toward complacence can muffle your drive. Aside from these surmountable obstacles—when your determination sets them aside—you are a confident and tireless publicist and demonstrator. You have a down-to-earth, step-by-step approach that leaves no stone unturned in the pursuit of what you are after. You present yourself well; your calmly cordial and engagingly practical manner make it unnecessary for you to have any agency represent you.

SHOWMANSHIP

Taureans have a fully developed appreciation of their own talents, often including a glamorous self-image, which may border on conceit but is never harsh or brash. A droll sense of humor underscores your contacts with people, enlivening every performance—rehearsal or business meeting—and winning converts for you. You are willing to work hard and diligently to perfect a performance, from a walk-on to a lead role to saying just the right thing to clinch a deal; and if you are nervous you are the only one who knows it. As a child you probably entertained your family and their guests with songs and dances, loving their approval and the delightful feeling of making them laugh. You never lose this desire to perform; it matures with you.

SPORTING LUCK

Taurus is a bit cautious when it comes to new or bizarre adventures; if you chance to get involved in one and wind up on top your surprise equals your delight. However, it won't make you any more inclined to take risks the next time. You feel more comfortable with activities in which you can work toward a predictable goal for a specific reward, and in these you are unstinting in your effort. Those around you may view you as lucky; actually what they see is not luck but a purposeful and practical sequence of the setting and acquisition of your goals.

ROMANTIC CONQUESTS

A Taurean is a romantic at heart, having an idealism in love matters that belies the down-to-earth pragmatism you display regarding almost everything else. Watch out that you are not won over by glittery show or try to get results by attracting others by this method. Although your nature is sensual, you are not a rover; the romances into which you enter are always approached with the possibility that you have found the one around whom your love life will revolve. Both men and women of your sign have a sort of laid-back attitude, letting relationships come to them rather than seeking them out. Once you give your heart, you are faithful and easily hurt by any slights you receive from the person of your affections. You have a certain naivete when it comes to love; this serves you both negatively and positively, making you appealing yet also vulnerable.

CHILDREN

Taurus possesses a great natural affection for children; your sign would not be likely to have a child (on purpose) if single, but married Taureans who deliberately remain childless are rare. You give a lot of love to your offspring, but you need to restrain a tendency to regard them as your possessions. You will have more real influence on your children if you do not try to control them but encourage them to think their decisions through for themselves. They will certainly benefit from incorporating your pragmatism into their own personalities—don't cause them to reject it by overemphasis. You expect respect and obedience from your children. It will help you and them if you avoid being too authoritarian; earn their respect by reciprocating it and they will be much more inclined to follow your wishes.

GEMINI

CREATIVE TALENTS

Gemini's first approach to any project is to carefully analyze what is to be achieved and how to organize things best. This process enables you to discover what the material you are working with is all about. It translates into an abundance of work in the literary field, both in poetry like Geminis William Butler Yeats and Bob Dylan, and in prose like Thomas Mann and Arthur Conan Doyle. Gemini's brightness also projects itself well on the stage; you are capable of creating a rapport with an audience that keeps them hanging on your every word and gesture.

THE ARTISTIC GEMINI

Gemini is a talker, personable and witty, explaining everything he or she does and thinks. An exuberance that is captivating and fascinating comes through whatever is expressed by this sign, giving its natives an extra attraction, which can fix them in the memories of all who see them. Marilyn Monroe and Judy Garland were two such Geminis. You are a hard worker, often in danger of pushing yourself beyond your limit. You will keep going until you are frazzled inside and even then will sometimes refuse to quit, making things difficult for those around you. Whatever field your talents lie in, you are prolific, restless, and eager to explore. A logical coherence distinguishes your works, making them edifying as well as entertaining.

MARKETING YOUR ABILITIES

When bringing your creative work into the marketplace you readily generate a positive feel that inspires confidence in backers and audiences alike. Your free flow of conversation makes you an engaging person, and you carry with this an ability to know when to advance and to whom. You understand intuitively how to back away from producers or publishers who are unconvinced of your talents; more often than not you will devise a way to slip in the side door with a new approach. There is a danger of spreading yourself too thin, as you have difficulty limiting the quantity of your projects and so can fail to give any one the energy and concentration needed to carry it through.

SHOWMANSHIP

Whatever field you are in, Gemini, you are a charmer. Your presentation of yourself may not always be developed beyond a glib, even shallow, performance, but you are always entertaining. It could even be said that Gemini finds it too easy to amuse others, so that you are rarely forced to work at expressing your depth or your real potential. You can't stand the thought of getting into a rut and repetition bores you, so you continually surprise your public with unexpected gimmicks and ventures.

SPORTING LUCK

Geminis love to gamble—the social, cordially competitive card game and the exciting race appeal to them. You also have an uncanny (to others) ability to concentrate on two or more things at once—the activity being engaged in as well as the undercurrents and surrounding scenery, too (not to mention the thrill of being held in suspense and the satisfaction of winning). The first game player was without a doubt a Gemini. You may lean away from the more grueling sports such as swimming, hiking, or football, preferring the fast action and deftness of basketball, fencing, or the breathtaking thrill of skydiving. Gemini has nine lives, possessing a delicate but lithe physique that can't take hard knocks but will hold out as long as the mind remains interested.

ROMANTIC CONQUESTS

In romantic matters Geminis are too curious for their own good. Bob Dylan wrote: "I fought with my twin, that enemy within . . ."—a Gemini describing the sign of the twins. You know what you want; the problem is that all your logical approaches get sidetracked by the multifarious possibilities abounding in your head. You lavish attention on your current love and expect the same in return. Fire signs give you the most trouble, but just about all your romances are rapid-fire sequences of hot and cold. When you settle down at last no one is more surprised than you are. You have trouble admitting it, even to yourself, but you feel a need for security in your love life. You may be attracted to the silent type as a complement to your own garrulous nature, but to get serious you need someone who can converse with you at nearly your own speed.

CHILDREN

Perhaps Gemini exercises caution nowhere so much as when contemplating having children. You enjoy being around little ones and are at home in the company of teenagers, but you reach the end of your rope quickly in the patience department. However, when they're your own kids you can't send them home! When you do have kids you are the one who sets the pace—they have to run to keep up with you. You share your career interests with them and join with them in sports, clubs, and other activities. They renew your own youthful exuberance. Take care to be sure that a quiet child gets enough attention from you and feels your loving approval.

CANCER

CREATIVE TALENTS

Cancer brings to any creative field a soulfulness of expression that comes from the heart. In music you are an articulate and poetic lyricist; your listeners are moved often to laughter and tears. The need to dramatize life situations leads many Cancerians to the stage; Jimmy Cagney, Peter Lorre and Donald Sutherland are notable actors of this sign. Writers born under Cancer produce works that resonate with unique personal voices: Buckminster Fuller, Marcel Proust, and E. B. White are only a few famous writer names of this nativity. The field of painting, too, boasts many Cancerian artists, expressing in a human, warm style such as that of Rembrandt or Rubens.

THE ARTISTIC CANCER

The special beauty of a Cancerian creation comes from the fact that you see what you create as a part of yourself. You resent any interference with your work, detesting to do rewrites or having an editor or director alter what you have done. Some artists of your sign never bring themselves to put their works before the public eye or ear because it is too painful for them to let go of their creations. Your artistic work in any field expresses the real you and therefore reveals you clearly, but you carefully erase your footprints to delay your audience from tracing them too quickly to your secret heart. When working with others your empathetic nature makes for a true blend, producing a whole that seems greater than the sum of its parts.

MARKETING YOUR ABILITIES

An emotional need for safety and security clashes in the Cancerian makeup with the desire to advertise and make your work visible. You have a wealth of creative ideas for a very effective presentation, which should be utilized through a representative if you are too retiring to implement them yourself. Your sense of timing can be swayed off the mark by changing moods, including the well-known rage of the temperamental artist. Within the Cancer personality pragmatism alternates with unrealistic ideas and whims; between these you may sometimes find it difficult to reach a middle ground. If you surround yourself with people you can trust this creates a stability from which you can draw. Air signs are good companions in your artistic life, appreciating your work and able to interface well with the commercial world.

SHOWMANSHIP

You may not declare yourself before the world in a roaring manner like your Leo friends, but despite temporary eclipses of depression or self-doubt you emerge with new strength and vision to bring into whatever spotlight is upon you. You love publicity and you hate it, vacillating constantly about how much or little to reveal about yourself. At times you want to be available to the public, signing autographs or shaking hands; and at other times you prefer to shut yourself away, letting others do your talking for you even over the phone. No matter what your mood, however, when you are on stage all anyone sees is a self-assured person, radiating the warmth of human experience in your intensely personal style.

SPORTING LUCK

Cancer's timidity at the prospect of high risks makes this native a reluctant gambler. You avoid chancy gaming, as everything in your experience is taken so personally that a loss unhinges your emotions too easily. It is hard for you to keep an objective eye on anything you are involved in; you much prefer recreation to strenuous sports and easygoing, social gatherings to competitive events. Surprise luck may follow you. Cancer may be the one to pick the lucky number or find the lost bill, winning in unexpected ways.

ROMANTIC CONQUESTS

Love at first sight was invented for Cancer. If the feeling is obviously mutual you are ready to wear your heart on your sleeve, to change your looks or the place where you live, to do anything to please your loved one even if he or she isn't asking you to change a thing. But if you are unsure of the response you will receive, Cancer, you are capable of concealing your love—sometimes for years. What never occurs to you is that you may seem forbidding or unattainable, and you too may have a secret admirer who is afraid to reveal his or her love for you. Cancer natives tend to fantasize about those in whom they have a romantic interest; this can cause you to grossly misjudge them or misperceive the nature of your involvement. You possess a natural ability to put intimates at their ease. When you are comfortable you reveal your emotional self to loved ones and draw their feelings into expression as well.

CHILDREN

The Cancer nature is protective and nurturing of loved ones, making you someone who thrives on parenthood. You are happy with a large family, having the patience to see to the needs of each child in a loving and careful way. Your feelings for your children are always clear in your mind as is their importance to you; other commitments in your life, taking your time and energy to the point where you overextend yourself, can make you into a crabby Cancer for real. Be good to your kids and yourself, and avoid planning to do too much in too little time.

LEO

CREATIVE TALENTS

Leo is the sign associated with the fifth house of the zodiac—creativity. Natives of this sign thrive on their talents and on receiving positive feedback from them. Acting is a natural for Leos, particularly live theater and television, which affords audience rapport. Notable Leo actors include Dustin Hoffman, Lucille Ball, and Robert Redford. Leo writers present definite themes, usually with a strong social message or with a philosophical bent—James Baldwin is a good example. As a musician Leo prefers to run the show, as demonstrated by the perfectly Leonian Count Basie. Leos also make gifted directors and producers, being able to see the impact a work can have on an audience and to guide others toward achieving it.

THE ARTISTIC LEO

Leo wants to be visible, noticed, and rewarded for creative effort. It's up to you, Leo, whether your desire for public acknowledgement will result negatively in conceit, arrogance, and gross overestimation of your talents or positively, making you a consciously directed and highly motivated artist whose gift to the world is that of excellence. You are generous with your time and money, especially to fellow artists. This tendency can also include your passing judgments when you allow yourself to assume that you can or should dominate them.

MARKETING YOUR ABILITIES

You possess a calm, self-assured manner that makes you an influential talker, good at spirited parley when bringing your wares to market. Perseverance gains for you what others miss by giving up too soon; you win what you pursue by sheer dogged persistence and couldn't care less if you seem a bit pushy. You do need to watch this, though, as you can lose opportunities through an overdemanding attitude. It's good to let people know that you think you're great at what you do, but it's better to give more demonstrations and less self-congratulatory talk.

SHOWMANSHIP

Showmanship? Leo invented the word. You love the spotlight, and you probably got Virgo to invent that for you, too. An excellent sense of timing puts your audience in the palm of your hand, whether you are on a stage or in your living room. People may say, "There's Leo, showing off again," but they stay around to look and listen more often than not. A good judge of an audience's mood, you play the moment to the hilt. Whether you win them over or make them furious, they are not likely to forget you. You are a versatile performer, drawing on a variety of resources to achieve the effect you desire.

Sporting Luck

Leo is adventurous but will stop short of real risk—you are not timid so much as reluctant to fall down in view of anyone. No one dislikes feeling foolish as much as Leo; you will practice privately for weeks on end in order to make your first public performance seem effortless. And once you have mastered your sport, watch out—the risks take on a new meaning for you. A dramatic flourish is your perfect cup of tea, drawing you to the thrills of racing cars or parachute jumping—anything for a good show.

Romantic Conquests

Leos love being in love, so much so that they can forget to pay attention to what the loved one is saying or feeling. You discuss your intimacies with friends, partly for aid and partly out of pride, and this can cause problems. It is rare that anyone will appreciate being aired for the inspection of others, especially when (and this can too often be the case with Leo) you may not be engaging in any conversation of real depth about the relationship with the other person involved! A double standard lurks in the background of many Leo romances, affecting male and female alike; the Leo man wants to feel adored and superior, and the Leo lady —regardless of women's lib involvement—enjoys being on a pedestal and walking through a door someone has opened for her.

Children

A Leo parent provides a stable and loving authority for children. You relish this role, which makes your relationship with your offspring a strong and mutually affectionate one. As long as you are doing more than playing the part of the ideal parent—being a role model rather than a real person—you will maintain a happy connection with your children. Don't think you need to appear larger than life to them. They will need to see you as being sympathetic and human, so they can envision adulthood as something into which they can progress at their own rates without having to change their basic feelings about life. Leo parents tend to compete with teenage offspring of the same sex as themselves, feeling that these young ones are somehow taking over what once was the parent's province. Look ahead and let the kids have their part of the world; there is always new action for Leo to be the center of. Many Leos take in orphans or participate in community projects that benefit children, as you have an inborn desire to aid others; you also make a good stepparent, accepting the new child as your own.

VIRGO

Creative Talents

Despite a reputation for being conservative and cautious, Virgo writers have a strong liberal bent, a powerful longing to see wrongs righted and for everyone to live in mutual tolerance. These Virgonians possess a powerful imagination, which leans toward the mystical. The works of Leo Tolstoy, Upton Sinclair, and H. G. Wells all express the Virgo's deep reflections on life and humanity. Musicians of this sign gravitate toward composition and teaching rather than conducting or performance, preferring to dwell in the sphere from which the music is created and to impart to others their knowledge of this sphere.

THE ARTISTIC VIRGO

Virgo brings to art a fascination with form and structure, frequently displaying the skeleton of what is represented without fleshing it out with color. Your social conscience peeks out from behind the artistic curtain, as a drive to aid others is central to your self-image regardless of your field. Perhaps this desire is what makes so many Virgos inventors—you want to create that which people can use to better their lives. Your inventions are always very practical yet unique, the type of thing that moves folks to say, "Now why didn't I think of that?" Although no one else may see it, you are self-critical to the extent that you may hinder yourself where your talents are concerned, taking a long and tortuous route to obtain confidence that will enable you to present your work with an easy mind.

MARKETING YOUR ABILITIES

You clearly see the steps needed to bring your talent or product into marketability, but you are prone to seemingly endless excuses and phobias that hinder action. Your critical tendency is by no means reserved for yourself, and by the time you are through evaluating all that is lacking in agents, clients, or publishers there may be no one left for you to deal with. Often, too, you will place your trust in someone who has experience or expertise but lacks the integrity to deal fairly with you. The result is stolen material, letdowns, and disillusionment. Virgo may repeat this error, failing to examine the motivations of others and seeing only their apparent successes. You can see what's going on with prospective associates if you look, and you'll be surprised to find that when you begin interacting with them on a human level you'll find more to like than you thought possible.

SHOWMANSHIP

Virgo has a sense of humor that can be subtly tongue-in-cheek or bordering on the gross (a similar phenomenon to that of Virgo's meticulous or nonexistent housekeeping). You have great timing and will mentally rehearse a line for long periods which you wait to drop at precisely the right moment. You can remain silent for days with guests and then astonish them by bursting into a song-and-dance routine that leaves them in stitches. Many Virgos prefer to deal indirectly with the public rather than experience the emotional exposure of seeing their works come before the eyes of strangers.

SPORTING LUCK

In sports Virgo prefers mental gymnastics or those physical activities based on grace, finesse, and coordination such as tennis. The gambling instinct is a forbidden pleasure that you hide carefully. You avoid it like the plague or do it on the sly; you may keep yourself from even thinking about it for years and then binge (and lose) periodically. Losing can cause you to become discouraged with life in general, bringing to the forefront of your consciousness all that you feel is unfair in the world. You are much better off playing chess for the love of it.

ROMANTIC CONQUESTS

In the romance department, Virgo, you are apt to find yourself in entanglements that you feel are not of your own making; this is not so. You must develop a consciousness of your own needs and desires; they are there and you are acting on them, but often they don't fit some concept of yours and so you don't acknowledge them. You are choosy and demanding but will listen to the ideas or complaints of a loved one. More difficult than listening is making a change requested by a romantic partner—this can be what makes or breaks a relationship for you. You seek depth of communication and also stability in love; you don't give your heart easily but when you do it is for keeps.

CHILDREN

No matter how demanding a career is, Virgo loves to round life out with family and children. You do not attempt to push children into any preconceived mold but have a natural eye and ear for their needs. The noise and exuberance of young ones may cause some Virgo natives to shy away from the experience of parenthood, but not the thought of demands on your time or a fear of responsibility.

LIBRA

CREATIVE TALENTS

Libra enjoys the role of commentator and plays it well regardless of what field of talent or interest he or she may inhabit. Libran talents are far-ranging, and there are prominent Librans in every creative arena: Barbara Walters, Phillip Berrigan, and John Lennon all have in common the gift of presenting to people that which makes them think. Musicians born in this nativity create a blend of distinct styles, reflecting a deep desire for harmony, which goes beyond music into human interrelation. George Gershwin combined classical music and instrumentation with blues and jazz in a pioneering style that changed the evolution of contemporary music. Actors of this sign possess a particular charisma that makes them stand out in a unique fashion: three such personalities are Marcello Mastroianni, Brigitte Bardot, and Charlton Heston.

THE ARTISTIC LIBRA

As a Libra you see yourself as providing multiple views and an eclectic use of materials through your creative work. You share with Virgo a strong humanitarian instinct, but in a much more overt style. Visible results are important to you, and you are more often than not a perfectionist, feeling an almost physical discomfort when perceiving disharmony, distortion, or incompleteness. You tackle controversial subjects with humor and perceptiveness, revealing the silly, often tragi-comic way human beings forget their essential unity with one another over these issues.

MARKETING YOUR ABILITIES

Your approach to selling or publicizing your creative work is colored by idealism regarding the way it—and you—should be seen by people. You may prefer to leave this to others who can represent you, honoring your sensitivity but not being subject to it themselves. A native intelligence enables you to see what needs to be done, but you would rather not have to push the buttons yourself. Be very sure that you choose agents or managers you can trust, as your desire to have things taken care of can leave you vulnerable to deception. A very self-aware Libran avoids this danger with a composed, carefully worked out self-presentation.

SHOWMANSHIP

Libra is showy in an elegant, understated way. You evaluate yourself carefully, presenting a face and a talent that show only strengths. It is a rare Libra who employs the tactic of showing mistakes or nervousness to an audience to win them over. Rather than praising yourself, you let your presence do your talking, leaving an indelible impression. Gimmicks and verbal acrobatics are simply not your style; the identity with which you meet your public is your own—the same one by which your friends know you, intensified or magnified only as is tasteful and appropriate.

SPORTING LUCK

The Libra native thrives on teamwork games and the social aspect of sports and play. You are not personally aggressive so there is no satisfaction for you in activities which provide outlets for the hostilities of others. You like to focus on the stylizing of the body with dance, yoga, and swimming. You enjoy walking, energizing your body while appreciating the beauty of nature. The folks you see jogging on busy city streets are not Libras; you welcome new ideas but avoid all that is pretentious, anything that smacks of latest-craze ostentation or mania.

ROMANTIC CONQUESTS

Libras seek out romantic relationships, often feeling incomplete or only partially alive without some romantic interest in their lives. Libra is known as the balancer of the zodiac; this makes you a lover of harmony but also someone who has difficulty reaching final resolutions where affairs of the heart are concerned. You are apt to tolerate too much, building your own secret world to reign in rather than meeting a problem head-on. Such a relationship may finally end in a burst of temper on your part, leaving the other person stunned, learning of your discontent for the first time. Matched with someone considerate, you flower, no matter how different or unconventional (this both fascinates and perplexes you) this person may be.

CHILDREN

Libra is a naturally gracious parent, creating a home atmosphere that gives children the sense of harmonious peace, which you cherish yourself. Watch out for a tendency to preach to children—they must make their own mistakes and recover from their own falls in order to grow. You are a protective, sheltering parent, striving to bring the best influences into the home environment. Your strongest point is organizing family activities which develop the social conscience of your children. You are willing to put forth the effort required to make your children's home one of excellence and good feelings, although their messiness and the drain on your attention can sometimes frazzle your nerves and make you long for a tranquil vacation.

SCORPIO

CREATIVE TALENTS

Painters abound under the sign of Scorpio, serious and possessing a powerful vision that puts the depths of their inner life onto canvas; three such artists are Claude Monet, Georgia O'Keefe, and Pablo Picasso. In writing, political and religious ideas are the impetus that moves many Scorpios; this sign desires to affect its audience deeply to convert large numbers of people with the intensity of the Scorpionic presentation. Robert Kennedy brought this intensity to the political arena; Grace Kelly won renown both as an actress and as a sparkling figure of royalty; Art Carney's acting, both dramatic and comedic, cuts through to the core of human experience.

THE ARTISTIC SCORPIO

Scorpio's internal clockwork perpetually turns over impressions, drives, and influences to churn out a stirring and touching human testimony. You desire to move others by giving them an experience that transforms them. Your sense of humor runs as deep as your serious side; depending on your degree of introversion or outgoingness it can be tongue-in-cheek and self-effacing, pouring out in a steady stream of commentary and one-liners, or taking the form of biting satire or wild practical jokes. Dick Cavett is a good example of a Scorpio comedian, skillfully drawing out the feelings and thoughts of others while creating word pictures of the foibles of humanity and the ironies of living.

MARKETING YOUR ABILITIES

Your Scorpionic self-knowledge guides you to calculate deliberate moves and techniques that propel you toward success. Keep an eye on yourself in your relations with others so as not to—consciously or unconsciously—try to own or control them for your own ends. Results will always be better if those who are in a position to assist you do so through their own volition, because they believe in the worth of your work. You combine pragmatism with your deeply felt personal drive, making you a good promoter of your creative efforts as well as an accomplished artist in your field.

SHOWMANSHIP

Where the appeal of others may be based on a flashy presentation, yours is based on guts and a tough delivery, which doesn't mean coarseness (though it does occasionally apply) but rather an air of experience and indefatigable survival. A Scorpio can radiate self-assurance or pull at the hearts of an audience by exquisitely portraying the loner each one of us is inside. Don't get wrapped up in your interpretation of a role to the extent that you lose touch with your real purpose—to reach those who are watching, reading, or listening.

SPORTING LUCK

Scorpio enjoys sports that can be engaged in alone; rock climbing, hang gliding, and surfing appeal to your self-sufficiency as well as to a certain sense of matching yourself against the universe, which comes only from danger. Tough mental as well as physical demands appeal to you; if the chessplayer sitting like a rock for hours, deep in concentration, is not a Pisces, he or she is a Scorpio. Your sign drives the hardest—putting forth an almost superhuman effort—and then is totally disinterested in whatever reward or prize is given. What interests you is your own analysis of your performance; if you are satisfied is enough of a reward.

ROMANTIC CONQUESTS

The fabled Scorpio sex drive usually don't manifest in your being a collector of amorous trophies or leaving behind a string of broken hearts (not that you aren't capable of breaking a heart or two). You simply are not interested in anything superficial. The glamour of one-night stands rapidly fades if sampled; you prefer real communication. You may, however, be exacting in your requirements for even the most preliminary introductions, choosing to avoid those who do not meet your standards in appearance. An inner fantasy life is where many of your desires and projections regarding love and sex are worked out, often never being mentioned to another.

CHILDREN

If you are an extremely introverted or solitary Scorpio, you may do better to remain childless—unless a strong desire to have children draws you out of yourself, or if you have a mate who can handle your need for absorption in your work or creative projects without resentment and shoulder most of the child-rearing without your active help. Otherwise your children are your heart's delight, filling your days and your thoughts. They may tire you but you don't feel it nearly as much as natives of other signs. Any frustration caused by offspring is more than offset by the joy they afford you, and you have a constant empathy with them that renews your patience. Scorpios find it difficult to be separated from their children by divorce or other circumstances; the thought of not seeing them, or of having their main influences come primarily from others, is very painful to you. Your habit of self-evaluation makes you set a good example for young ones; a tendency to criticize or expect perfection is balanced by the fact that you require much of yourself as well.

SAGITTARIUS

CREATIVE TALENTS

The creative drive of Sagittarius is to present an articulate overview, which will provide inspiration and information to an audience; this holds true throughout all fields of creative endeavor. You make each artistic work a social critique, reflecting your specific hopes and desires for a better world. Morality is conveyed through the portrayal of human situations shown as if each one represented the whole reality. Often Sagittarius acts as the organizer for the efforts of others, synthesizing them into the realization of a vision; Walt Disney was such a Sagittarian. If your nature is not too restless for sculpture or painting, you can turn out striking works that illustrate your free spirit. Your abundant energy produces the visible and amiable type of popular musician; three Sagittarian examples are Dave Brubeck, Arthur Fiedler, and Frank Sinatra.

THE ARTISTIC SAGITTARIUS

The style of Sagittarius is that of sweeping identification with a particular philosophy. You are likely to have periods of intense creative turnout alternating with fallow periods in which you produce little or nothing. The in-between times may be longer than those of artistic activity; you spend them searching and dabbling in new mediums or sideline interests, which can dissipate your concentration and drive, causing you difficulty in returning to your focus. Although you are by no means conventional, you are rarely a radical or avant-garde type; you draw from many sources to put together a work that bears your distinctive stamp.

MARKETING YOUR ABILITIES

You believe in your work and its worth, and you communicate your enthusiasm well to prospective buyers or backers. You have trust in your ability to carry others along by the sheer exuberance of your approach. This can make you vulnerable, as you are often too ready to believe praise and may miss that the wool is being pulled over your eyes. Be sure to have copyrights and contracts strictly in order so as not to be deceived by unsavory people or situations which contain hidden traps.

Showmanship

On stage or in the marketplace you may have a shyness that belies the abundant energy within you. This does not manifest as awkwardness or visible stage fright, but rather as a diffidence that others find charming. Once into a role you can tend to upstage others, intentionally or otherwise. Watch your tongue with those you wish to impress—Sagittarius is famous for suddenly coming out with a comment that is ill-received to say the least, unwittingly insulting one person or everyone in the room. Good humor, often seasoned with bawdiness, shows your expansive nature; the exuberance of Sagittarian Bette Midler is certainly visible. You are enduring and resilient, a real trooper, loving to make people laugh.

Sporting Luck

Sagittarius possesses much physical energy; many of this sign are active in athletics, dance, running, and other aspects of physical practice. A characteristic grace makes your movements seem effortless, and you master techniques quickly and easily to the envy of earth sign folk. You are attracted to social sports, from the refinement of baseball to the roughhouse of soccer. You are willing to take risks, which makes you an exciting player to watch. You are a good competitor and a good loser as well, who never stints on effort and who loves the game for itself.

Romantic Conquests

In love matters Sagittarius follows a predetermined ethical formula. The ethic, however, is strictly your own—whether your ideal is the one love with whom you mate for life or a multiple relationship with all the unconventional ramifications one would only expect from you or Aquarius. Romance provides you with a constant field of investigation of the dynamics and growth of the self. You possess a curiosity that is rivaled only by that of Gemini, and yours probes deeper, being concerned with the inner workings of mind and emotions. Your lovers may feel neglected, as sometimes you seem enamored of your own reactions and responses, dilemmas, and paradoxes more than you are interested in the feelings they have or the ideas they express. You are capable of carrying on hours of intense discussion about your relationship with the person involved, bringing out each detail as if it had significance on a grand scale, and then picking up your keys, saying, "I'll be right back," and disappearing for two days.

Children

Sagittarians love the verve and spontaneity of children; you share their sense of play and are adored by them, as they feel comfortable with you as they often can with no other adult. You will have kids early in life, late, or in the middle—or all of these. Nothing is more pleasing to you than having a veritable nation of them around you, building your dynasty! Your life at home will run more smoothly if you first work at moderating and regulating your life pace and then starting your family. A few Sagittarians (or any other signs for that matter) are fortunate enough to have a mate who is willing to stay home and raise a brood while you gad about elsewhere, popping in now and then to give them treats and smiles and leaving your long-suffering partner to handle clean-up, discipline, and such without you.

CAPRICORN

CREATIVE TALENTS

Capricorn's nature expresses itself in spontaneous and exuberant talents, which are combined with a care and thoroughness that make for perfection. Capricorn will make revision after revision, searching for just the right phrase or gesture. You may need to work on leaving well enough alone as you can revise or rewrite until nothing is left. As a writer you are moralistic on a universal scale; Kahlil Gibran is one of many distinguished writers of Capricorn nativity. You also make a fine editor, both of your works and those of others. The idealistic-pragmatic dualism you bring to your creativity expresses itself comedically, as in the case of Danny Kaye, or with a pungent seriousness such as that of Faye Dunaway. Capricorn is a good organizer; a Capricorn architect is capable of envisioning and then overseeing a complete project almost single-handedly.

THE ARTISTIC CAPRICORN

You are a good improviser, rhapsodic at times, but your staple fare is understatement—skillfully executed—with an orderly eye for form. You can be absolutely obsessive when it comes to coherence; if all loose ends are not tied together you are ready to throw the entire project out and start over. You enjoy cross-referencing knowledge from one field to another and making extensive outlines from which to work. Although you are fair and respectful with others you prefer working on your own and having your own say.

MARKETING YOUR ABILITIES

In marketing creative work Capricorn is concerned not so much with the intake of money as with the correct presentation and the potential for prestigious placement. You plan publications and showings in the most ideal manner possible; your perfectionism can make you unreasonable here, as you find it difficult to settle for anything you feel is less than best. This may cause delays or disagreements for you but it also guarantees that your work will always bear your own unmistakable mark.

SHOWMANSHIP

Capricorn is a dry wit, a polished storyteller, able to clown around in an affable and endearing manner while never completely losing a certain air of shyness. Your basic nature is too quiet and idiosyncratic for you to be a one-person show for long; this may keep you behind the scenes most of the time, bringing out your showmanship only at rare (and delightfully surprising) moments. A desire to see a work performed or presented in its best possible way overshadows any prima donna tendencies you may harbor. A rare gift in an actor, which others admire, you feel that the show is first and foremost. As a director you are at your most garrulous, a hard driver who tolerates no nonsense but will endeavor to make clear the reasons behind the instructions given—not out of personal consideration so much as a desire to have the most understanding applied for the best results.

SPORTING LUCK

Capricorn exercises a natural caution and conservatism in sports and games, being enthusiastic yet not flamboyant. You work as hard at play as you do at nonrecreational activities, valuing effort for its own sake. You share with Scorpio a predilection for loner-type sports such as bicycling, swimming, and cross-country. You possess both endurance and grit, taking things step-by-step with care and consideration. Other signs may get restless and leave you behind on outings and adventures, but for you the joy is in doing it your way.

ROMANTIC CONQUESTS

When it comes to romance, Capricorn carries an innocent babe inside through old age. You are romantic to the point of worshipping your mate —not that this keeps you from being moody or noticing (and complaining about) the faults of your loved one, but the spark you felt in the beginning remains. Capricorn loves the warmth and sensuality of a sexual relationship, and this may be where a great part of your emotional life, so often held in due to shyness, is expressed. However, many Capricorns choose to remain celibate until the right person comes along. Likewise, you are faithful once your heart is committed to one partner. You are not afraid of the challenges within love relationships; for Capricorn a difficult situation affords its own satisfaction as a worthwhile problem to solve. You may appear at first (or second) glance to be aloof or demanding even when you are the pursuer, but one who learns of the Capricorn lover's inner warmth and affection will have found a truly giving and responsive mate.

CHILDREN

Capricorn is capable of understanding small children as few others do— indeed the newborn baby's face, combining a wizened and balding look with impish grins and wide-eyed innocence, is very Capricornian! With older children you tend to lead them along your own channels; your loyalty may be to what you consider proper form rather than to their needs. Take great care in this, as it will cause your child much pain if your love and understanding are replaced by coldness due to your having a concept of right behavior or ambition, which his or her nature cannot fulfill. Capricorn often waits until later in life to have children, after the initial demands of a career have been met.

AQUARIUS

CREATIVE TALENTS

The verbal inclinations of Aquarius produce many speakers and writers. These natives have strong political and historical interests, being actively concerned with the state of the world and its betterment. Writings by Aquarians emanate social criticism, often combined with or thinly veiled by fantasy; satire pours from the Aquarian pen like water. Lewis Carroll, Sinclair Lewis, and James Michener are three notable authors born under Aquarius. You possess the ability to describe what you see or feel with precise articulation; you are so descriptive, in fact, that you may find it difficult to simply paint or draw your subject—there is so much detail that you consider relevant, there ends up being no room to picture it all without the aid of words. For all their social interest and personal unconventionality, Aquarians contain a streak of shyness about the revelation of private feelings to others, which actors of this sign must work to overcome. James Dean and Mia Farrow are two contrasting examples of the Aquarian actor, having in common the presentation of the mood of a generation.

THE ARTISTIC AQUARIUS

Aquarius likes the commentator role and enjoys being a bit eccentric before the public eye. You search for ways to break out of socially imposed boundaries, seeing them as narrow and feeling them as restrictive to your inner freedom. Your work can have a strident tone or tend to rely on platitudes, which become tiring even when they are radical ones. Putting a balance of feeling in with your strong thoughts softens your message and makes it easier for others to comprehend. Indeed, your intention is to point out a common human identity.

MARKETING YOUR ABILITIES

You have no trouble grasping principles and concepts concerning mass audience marketing and techniques, but you may find your personality unsuited to carrying them out. The weight of details of etiquette, the game of withholding your real intentions, are oppressive to you and may cause you to either shy away or blast your way through. You can run hot and then cold, enraging others with your inconsistency. You are happier finding a trusted representative who has a real appreciation of your work; with such a helper you can either stay home and avoid the marketing scene altogether, or go along and watch your rep show you off. From this vantage point you see the whole process as amusing and fascinating, and can fascinate others with an occasional comment or humorous aside, free from the burden of selling yourself.

SHOWMANSHIP

Improvisation comes to you with some difficulty, especially when you perform alone. With a partner or group with whom you are comfortable you lose a certain shy stiffness and your spontaneity begins to flow. In the same way time and experience are your keys to finding the right timing for putting your humorous concepts into play. You bring intelligence and insight to a performance, captivating an audience without overwhelming them with volume or gimmicks. Your glamour lies in the enhancement of your own characteristics rather than the meeting of an established type of image; this is something the Aquarian performer intuitively knows and of which he or she takes advantage.

SPORTING LUCK

Aquarius brings concentration and quick thinking to games and play. Two Aquarian athletes with characteristically different personalities were Hank Aaron, quiet and shy, and the jaunty and flamboyant Babe Ruth. Both achieved excellence and revealed Aquarius' love for hard hitting, demanding sports. Those Aquarians who are less physically inclined enjoy the same demands on the mental level—games of skill being preferred over those of chance.

ROMANTIC CONQUESTS

Aquarians are often the moving force in romantic relationships. It is likely to be you who instigates contact, keeps the relationship moving, and ends it if it is to end. You will put forth much effort to make things work between yourself and a romantic partner, displaying a patience in the time you spend, which sharply contrasts with a tendency to let fly with a verbal barrage when exasperated. Aquarius will stick a difficult relationship out, seemingly beyond its chances to attain or regain harmony; yet there comes a moment, often abruptly, when you have had enough, and you are capable of simply vanishing from the other person's life without a trace. You need to feel free to pursue your own interests and to spend time with your friends, but you are concerned almost unreasonably that your partner be happy with your relationship. Aquarius is apt to have many romantic involvements before settling down. Once experimentation and searching end, you are in most cases monogamous and even something of a homebody.

CHILDREN

Aquarius is the parent who remembers his or her childhood vividly— probably your social conscience originated with a critique of your parents and their injustices—and swears to repeat only the right things as a father or mother. Parenthood brings you a sympathy with your own parents, which you may never have had, as you begin to see yourself in your child. You may wait to have kids until a bit later than most, as you need to finish savoring your freedom before taking on responsibilities.

You are a loving parent but need to guard against becoming impatient or irritable with offspring over minor issues.

PISCES

CREATIVE TALENTS

The creative talents of Pisces manifest in deep, soul-expressing works. Your concern is with plumbing the depths of feeling and experience, as evidenced in the writings of Pisceans Anais Nin and John Steinbeck. Pisces brings to acting an ethereal yet sensual appeal: examples are the Piscean actors/actresses Jean Harlow, Michael Caine, and Ursula Andress. Zero Mostel and Lou Costello exemplify the shy boy who is mischievous at heart. Musicians of this sign can be leaders who stand at the center, directing others, such as Lawrence Welk and Glenn Miller. You may wish to remove yourself from the spotlight and concentrate on the center within, as in the case of George Harrison.

THE ARTISTIC PISCES

Pisces delves into hidden emotions, exploring the dark, murky places but also soaring into the heights of glorious poetic affirmations. You bring much subtlety to your art; the famous mime Marcel Marceau is a Pisces. Spontaneous eruptions contrast in Piscean creativity with delicate movements and a carefully considered approach. Your work is infused with a sense of the mystical and always contains some element of the spiritual.

MARKETING YOUR ABILITIES

Despite the Piscean reputation for being perpetually spaced out, you have an intuitive grasp of the state of mind the public is in and are capable of acting accordingly. You are able to maintain more of an even keel emotionally than other water signs, and so can reap more practical benefits and maintain a course of action without alienating others.

SHOWMANSHIP

Unless you are extremely shy, Pisces, you love to show off, invent, improvise, and clown around before an appreciative audience. Even if your career is far from the world of show business, this propensity will show itself with family and friends. You take a role to its limits; actors of your sign can identify so totally with a character they are playing that it actually seems to replace their own personalities. You need to employ discretion in order to avoid going overboard and losing touch with audience response.

SPORTING LUCK

You are a good planner and schemer, which aids you in competitive sports in which strategy is involved. If you have not as yet learned to play chess you may have a real treat in store for you if you decide to do so—this game is a Piscean's delight, as Bobby Fischer could tell you.

Although you sometimes appear timid and retiring, many of your sign have a fearless streak and will boldly embark on bizarre adventures. Others will imagine them and write about them with the realism of actual experience. Attractive to the brazen Pisces are such thrillers as skydiving, mountain climbing, and deep-sea fishing. You are equally at home in low-key recreation, such as hiking or simply strolling in accompaniment to daydreams. You lack the killer instinct to bring in big money from sporting or gambling, although the risk involved does not particularly bother you.

ROMANTIC CONQUESTS

Pisces falls in love with love and is always ready for the right person to appear to fit a favorite fantasy of the ideal lover. When the moment calls for passion, your response is right there, unfettered by propriety as others may know it and not caring to see beyond the moment. If you are not careful you can become involved in multiple relationships, actually living several lives at once. Romantic as this may sound to your unconventional ears, you will find it draining of your energy and unfulfilling to each and all the relationships in question. However, you are capable of being quite philosophical when you go from a collection of lovers to none at all. There are always more to come, and you are happy being alone in your own world. If you tend to cling to a relationship once it has begun, you may require a bit of time and space in which to heal and regroup your energies before beginning a new one.

CHILDREN

Pisceans are fascinated by children but may not be inclined to spend the time they require in terms of the everyday details of watching that they don't get into mischief and putting things back together when they do. If you feel this might be a problem for you, you might give some thought as to whether you really want your own kids or would be happier spending time with nieces, nephews, the children of friends, or those you can give limited time to in a community situation. Your easygoing qualities will provide them with a nice complement to their own parents' worry and watchful eyes—and afterwards you can go home without the aggravation! If you are comfortable devoting the constant time and effort needed in parenthood, you make a serene and benevolent mother or father, fostering the creativity of offspring and nurturing their sensitivities with your own. You need to watch that you don't overindulge them or leave them totally without restraints, as this will fail to prepare them for the world in which they will live.

CHAPTER SIX
Enhancement of Daily Life

THE NECESSITIES OF LIFE and the daily activities are summed up in the sixth house. Long overlooked by astrologers, it is the portion of life that we are aware of the most, but because of this familiarity, its importance is down-graded.

Virgo is the sign associated with utility in astrology. Just as Virgos are workaholics, meticulous, careful, health-oriented, and quiet, they still achieve greatness because of the diligent and persistent ways in which they go about accomplishing their goals. The glyph for Virgo is the symbol of a virgin woman. Inherent in this pristine state is all the potential for future fecundity. The woman often is shown carrying wheat, because this is also the symbol of the harvest and of the bountiful benefits of waiting (as farmers must) for nature to follow its natural, successful course.

Health-related matters fall into this category, because one of the ways we can enhance our aliveness is through prolonging our youthfulness both in body and mind.

One important warning: *No information in this section is meant to replace the need for competent professional medical advice and attention. Before utilizing any suggestions in this chapter, you should consult your doctor or health professional.*

Chores—repetitive work of all kinds—and adjustments can all be made easier and more enjoyable by putting your personal stamp on these activities.

This is the last of the six chapters dealing with your individual view of life. Chapters seven through twelve all relate to the influences of other people and your public, joint enterprises, which in turn influence your personal decisions, activities, and perceptions of the world.

ARIES

HEALTH

A first glance at Aries immediately paints the picture of glowing health, youth, and vitality. Ruled by Mars, you are the beneficiary of remarkable power and drive, which support your energy flow throughout life and give strong support to your speedy recovery in the event of illness. Aries rules the head and brain, activating your fine mentality. This part of your body will be a focus in the cyclic flow of life force and will be the point at which any imbalance will first manifest. Your opposite sign Libra could indicate the kidneys as an area that should be kept in the best of health. The subrenal glands, whose function is to pump adrenaline into the bloodstream in the event of an emergency, are ruled by Aries and come into action in times of anger or quick expenditure of energy. The influence of Mars ebbs and flows, though your drive for ceaseless activity relentlessly impels you forward. Here is the point at which common sense must take control. Tune into the times that your body would benefit by rest and structure these spaces into your yearly cycle of activity. Viewed as creative rejuvenation, this will be palatable, even to your hard driving nature.

PERSONAL APPEARANCE AND FITNESS

The Aries individual displays a clear-cut strength in all physical features. A remarkable number of you carry the broad, high forehead and fully arched, strong-boned nose associated with the ram, symbol of your sign. The eyes have a direct, penetrating gaze and are often deep-set under heavy eyebrows, which tend to grow toward each other in the middle. The mouth is firm above a slightly pointed chin, and tends to be large but rather thin-lipped. Cheek bones are high set. Teeth are usually long and sometimes irregular or slightly protruding. The hair usually has reddish highlights accenting a fair or ruddy complexion. Your vitality is good but can be weakened by excessive use of alcohol, which overtaxes the liver. The Aries mind is master of the body and will go far toward maintaining health and a dynamic driving force, which influences all areas of your life.

ROUTINE WORK AND DAILY CHORES

Aries is the sign that equates with action, and is perfectly suited to physical, mental, and emotional expressions. One might safely say that you are a human dynamo. You will approach all areas of life with a bold enthusiasm, especially responding to the new or undiscovered. Your power to visualize is strong and often leads you to complete work in your mind long before it is physically accomplished—a tendency that can cause you to lose interest in the work before it is actually done. Development of patience and perseverance will allow you to continue nourishing your mental creation until it becomes a worldly reality. The awful truth is that civilization's greatest creations have been the result of tedious labor, which has followed the original inspiration. The total satisfaction of seeing the manifestation of your idea will be well worth the effort you put forth in its development.

JOB ALIENATION

The Aries native is heir to a vast, unceasing supply of energy and vitality —a situation that suits you well to active and demanding work. If there is anything that will cause an Aries to feel alienated from his work it is a stifling, non-demanding position, which requires tedious repetition or focuses on things already known and developed. Although you enjoy a certain amount of solitude in order to clarify ideas, your physical activity level is so high that it must be expressed through movement in order to avoid bursting forth as anger or impatience. Competition spurs you on to even greater heights, and the dynamic energy of a busy, noisy atmosphere will only serve to increase your productivity. You may have difficulty in relating to a job where you must always be a follower, or where your pioneering ideas are rejected in favor of stagnant traditions. You must be free to express your own direct, uncomplicated way.

HANDLING CRITICISM

When faced with a critic you will probably react in two ways simultaneously. On the one hand, you will secretly appreciate his or her directness; on the other, you will react sharply and decisively to the attack. You seem to feel that with a loud enough display you can somehow neutralize any hostility directed toward you. The intensity of the disturbance will most likely cause your critic to back down simply to bring the scene back into some semblance of sanity. Anyone who annoys you, regardless of their position of authority, will receive a strong, direct response stating exactly what you think. Caution is not part of your makeup, and this lack of discretion can at times please you in dangerous situations. Although not accepting of criticism yourself, you can dish it out more often than necessary due to your bold and impatient nature. You seldom become angry but will never fail to let people know exactly where they stand with you and in no uncertain terms.

ADJUSTMENTS IN LIFE

As an Aries you are highly adaptable to changes, but for different reasons than most people. Everything you do is motivated by the dynamic energy of your ruling planet Mars. Living in the past is not for you, and though you may be wholeheartedly sold on a certain thing at one time, you can change your mind and jump totally into a new view without any further consideration of your former state. The past is dead and life is to be lived in your opinion, so why go back to useless considerations of things that no longer pertain to your life? There is a new world waiting to be explored and conquered, so why should you cling to what has gone before? You insist on being first in everything and will not accept the slightest disloyalty from anyone. If even the vaguest hint of betrayal is present, you will immediately discard the offending person or situation with a clear and tactless outline of exactly what is wrong. You hardly need to adapt to the new as you are already in it before you have the chance to think about it.

TAURUS

HEALTH

The Taurus native gives the impression of strength and solidity, appearing to draw his or her nourishment from the very earth itself. Your sign rules the throat and neck, indicating that you should be aware of the well-being of this area as well as becoming conscious of the thyroid gland, which, if adversely affected, will incline you to being over or underweight. Venus, your ruling planet, is connected with the throat, kidneys, and lumbar region and also effects the parathyroids, which help control the calcium level in body fluids. Be cautious during the virus season, allowing yourself a little extra protection in the throat and neck area. If you are bothered by some minor bodily imbalance, put your mind at ease by consulting a trusted doctor as to care and healing. You are extremely resilient and recover quickly from any illness. Your well-developed sense of taste and appreciation for the fruits of the earth often incline you to excess of physical pleasures. Remain aware of the value of moderation in all things, as misdirected energy can lead to a serious imbalance in the body.

PERSONAL APPEARANCE AND FITNESS

The Taurean look is substantial and appears to be united with its earthy foundations. Fullness is the most apparent characteristic, graced by charm and a warm kindness of expression in your facial features. You will most likely enjoy a thick head of hair, which adorns a thick yet graceful body. There is a gentle intensity about the eyes, which are dark and round. A full, sometimes bulbous nose and full, curving lips round out the face, which is underscored by a firm chin. Teeth are close set and squared. The neck is bull-like and extends to a rather pear-shaped body, which is thicker at the hips than at the chest. Supported well by solid legs, there is not a hint of weakness anywhere in your appearance. You are strong yet gentle and with a curbing of overindulgence can remain hearty well into life. With a focus on regular exercise, you can avoid becoming excessively bulky in later years.

ROUTINE WORK AND DAILY CHORES

The overall character of the Taurus native is solid, stable, and fixed. These foundation traits will influence every type of work that is done by you. Once you have thought a situation through slowly and carefully, you will bring it into reality through deliberate, persistent work and the power of sheer determination. Any opposition to your desired goals will be gradually and completely worn down by the tenacity with which you hold to your course. You have a deep enjoyment of material goods and are quite willing to work hard in order to enjoy the fruits of your labor You will hold on resolutely to people and things that are dear to you, and will gladly work to ensure that your loved ones are secure and well cared for. If the fruits of your work can in some way further beauty and harmony, you will be doubly pleased—a trait that often leads Taureans to become patrons of the arts.

JOB ALIENATION

The Taurean is a rather pastoral type in many ways, preferring to avoid the chaos and confusion of the city. Security is the lens through which you view life, and any occupation that deals with the nebulous or unpredictable will make you quite uncomfortable. The stability of a conventional office, or a business or industry with predictable demands and rewards, will be most satisfying to this one who appreciates firm foundations and time-proven endeavors. Your aesthetic sense is strong, indicating that work in a harsh or unattractive environment could set up discordant vibrations in your nature. If you experience anger connected with your job, be aware of this as an indicator that your bountiful vitality is being withheld internally to the point where it is becoming destructive. It is essential for you to modify conditions to allow this overabundance of life force to be used in creative outlets; otherwise it can turn inward and cause great damage to your health.

HANDLING CRITICISM

The Taurean is not one who takes criticism lightly. Ruled by Venus, planet of beauty and harmony, you prefer to surround yourself with the more pleasant of life's manifestations, of which critical-minded people are not a part. You think well of yourself and would like others to do the same, and are put off by those who feel compelled to air their negative views of you. You can be quite patient with their outbursts—up to a point—but when that point is reached, anyone with the slightest sense had better run for cover. Your patience is legendary, but when the raging bull is finally prodded into action, it will trample everything and everyone in sight, venting a deep, inner torment that has destroyed his or her sense of peace. Your patient tolerance with the small-mindedness of others conceals the depth of your pain, for you are a sensitive individual and, despite outward appearances of being calm, you can often be deeply wounded in your inner being.

ADJUSTMENTS IN LIFE

As a Taurus you are noted for your great adaptability. A solid and steady earth sign, you prefer life to be constant and predictable, and find it extremely difficult to relate to radical change. Even if a change seems wise, something in your fixed nature resists the very process of letting go of an established situation and having to build a new foundation. The element of risk is not one with which you feel comfortable, and any necessary change will be more easily handled if the transition has been well thought out and planned to result in a secure or potentially secure resting place at the end. Once you have engaged in the considerable thought process required before actually making a change and have carefully considered every practical aspect of the situation, you can allow yourself to step forward, but only as far as you need to and only with a full commitment to rooting yourself firmly in the new situation.

GEMINI

HEALTH

The Gemini native is the very image of lightness and airyness. Focal areas of your body are the nerves, arms, hands, shoulders, lungs, and capillaries. The quick perceptions of your mind are supported by the energy flow through the nervous system, a function of the body which you must take care not to overtax. Your ruling planet, Mercury, influences respiration, the brain, and the complex and delicate interconnections of the body. In the glandular system, the thymus gland is emphasized. Your high-activity level necessitates a rejuvenating supply of quality food, even though your temperament may influence you away from time-consuming food preparation. Keeping a supply of nuts and dried fruits on hand will allow you to fulfill some nutritional needs while zipping from place to place. Your blood needs adequate oxygenation through healthful breathing practices, which could be incorporated into your daily travels to and from work. An air ionizer could offset the effects of air pollution and work in enclosed areas.

PERSONAL APPEARANCE AND FITNESS

The Gemini appearance is often rather birdlike with small bones and a striking intellectual look. The body gives the feeling of a straightness and is often taller than average. The face is a thin oval with a square forehead. Eyes are bright and inquiring under arched eyebrows. Usually, the eyes are hazel. The nose is thin with fine and sensitive nostrils. Cheekbones are high and the jawline and chin are prominent and pointed. The mouth is thin and lacks a decisive look. Teeth are fairly large and can be uneven between pale lips. Curiously, the right and left profiles of the Gemini are noticeably different in keeping with the dualistic aspect of this sign. The hair grows quickly and is generally fair in color. You are active in many areas, and with extra consideration of your sensitive nervous system, you will be able to maintain a brisk level of activity throughout life.

ROUTINE WORK AND DAILY CHORES

As a Gemini you are a naturally industrious person but have a tendency to scatter your energies. Widely diversified in interests, you are inclined to allow multiple interests to interfere with the stability of partnerships or fixed situations. Travel is a delight for you, providing both the activity and the mental stimulation you require for personal balance. Variety is essential to you so be sure to plan change into your life even if it is not part of your usual work. Such diverse activities as vacationing in a new place or a shopping trip to a new or unique store will fill the need to experience the new and changing. You are strongly oriented to work of a mental nature, but have a fine dexterity and can easily develop mental concepts through the work of your hands. Keep yourself in areas where the intellect will be stimulated and this will give you the sense of fulfillment necessary to see you through occasional tedious parts of life.

JOB ALIENATION

One of the fastest ways to develop job alienation in the Gemini is to give him or her monotonous work. Although long-term employment plans are not characteristic of your sign, analyze the job market with an eye to finding work that will include plenty of diversity. A position that stifles your intellectual abilities, or one that exerts pressure on your sensitive nervous system will cause intense stress in your life. If circumstances have corraled you for the moment, break the tension by running before or after work, or even taking a rope with you and jumping a bit on coffee breaks or at lunch hour. If stranded at home with young children, a jump rope or small indoor trampoline can do wonders to release built-up nervous tension. There could be job-related problems connected with your tendency to leave tasks unfinished in your rush to become involved in something new. This tendency can be modified by joint endeavors with a coworker who is good at completing work.

HANDLING CRITICISM

Gemini is not the easiest of personalities to understand. To many people, they are disturbingly unpredictable and inconsistent, hence the nature of their criticism. Too much criticism and misunderstanding frustrate the Gemini terribly and cause distortions in an otherwise creative temperament. Normally, you have a high sense of moral ethics, but this can all too easily be turned into the negative by others who are overcritical. If criticism limits your freedom of expression, you become nervous and inadequate, soon breaking the bonds of limitation as you move off to a new environment without a regret. One must realize that Gemini absolutely needs to give his or her fine mind and wit a workout, and be also aware that he or she will not hold still for a great deal of criticism. Once you have been severely offended you will depart the scene permanently, for though you seem lighthearted and good humored, you are nobody's fool and are not about to hang around where you are not appreciated.

ADJUSTMENTS IN LIFE

It is not likely that you will ever adjust to a life of limitation and stagnation. No matter how tight the vise, you simply cannot exist without movement and intellectual creativity, and under the most limiting of circumstances you will still find a way to free your energies. If there is too much oppressive confinement, your dynamic mental energies can turn to negative creations, thus it is wise to allow the Gemini his or her natural freedom or you could find yourself regretting trying to bridle this whirlwind. Basically, you adjust fairly easily and without deep emotional trauma. It is not that you are insensitive, but your outgoing tendencies will quickly provide other interests so that not much time will be wasted in mourning the past. A life of isolation is not in the cards for Gemini, and any change that deprives him or her of companionship will be adjusted to by quickly acquiring new and interesting acquaintances. In your path of life it will not be unusual to find many discarded former friends, as your acceptance of new companions is often at the expense of the old.

CANCER

HEALTH

As a Cancer prototype you will find health greatly influenced by your moods, which are in turn influenced by the Moon. Zodiacal anatomy points to emphasis on the stomach and alimentary canal, breasts, solar plexus, pancreas, and diaphragm. Although your stomach can survive a range of extremes in food, it is particularly sensitive to your emotional state and can, under stressful circumstances, become the nervous stomach. Lunar influence causes you to become upset and worry more than most—a fact of life that can be balanced by using the discipline available through your strong mind to help control emotional extremes. Cancer natives love to cook, and the bountiful fruits of your labors can often lead to being overweight. Design your diet to include a large variety of fresh fruits and vegetables, perhaps stir-fried or in creative salads. This will steer you away from starchy and fatty foods, which are so stressful on the liver. Surround yourself with healthy people, as this by absorption will strengthen your own health.

PERSONAL APPEARANCE AND FITNESS

Cancer natives are generally of medium height with a fullness about their bodies. The bone structure itself is small, but the fleshy parts are rounded, giving a sense of softness. The arms and legs are short, and the neck leans toward heaviness. The head is large and round, reminiscent of a full moon, with well-proportioned features and rather fine brown hair. The large, round eyes are quite expressive and are often in soft shades of blue or gray. The mouth is lovely, giving the impression of a rosebud and concealing small, evenly spaced teeth. Although the neck and jawline are full, the chin itself is small. Cancer natives have a beautifully soft pink skin, which tends to bruise rather easily. The facial features show an affectionate nature, but also a tendency to worry, which may show in a downturned mouth. Cheeks are usually flat and the nose not prominent. Make your life as secure as possible in order to minimize a worrisome nature, which can adversely affect health.

ROUTINE WORK AND DAILY CHORES

You are assisted in approaching the practical, work-oriented side of life by a strong sense of values and a sixth sense that tells you when certain endeavors should become priorities. You have the valuable ability to examine an undertaking in your mind, creating and recreating in different ways to see which will be the most workable. You are industrious and persevering and are quite as willing to use these fine traits in the employ of another as for your own personal matters. Work will be pleasurable and deeply satisfying for the Cancer native, though in the business world you can be notably tenacious and effective. As a child of the moon your moods can fluctuate widely and are likely to strongly affect your capacity for work at any given time. Emotional upsets are the factors most likely to detract from your ability to accomplish what you wish. Preserve a harmonious home and all other aspects of life will benefit.

JOB ALIENATION

A most important feature of Cancer's working environment is a calm atmosphere. Any irritation, unrest, or discord in your place of employment is likely to bring out the worrisome side of your nature and considerably overstress your fluctuating emotions. The moon is likely to have considerable influence on your mood of the moment, and that changeability must be factored into your business world in a way that will minimize any negative effects of moodiness. Coworkers may consider your words harsh at times and your behavior extreme, as you have been known to sometimes be insensitive to the feelings of others. Conversely, you can be easily devastated by the comments of others, even if they are not intended to be hurtful. Work that allows you time alone, focusing on your personal interests, can be very positive for you. Also consider your desire to nurture others and try to establish a job-oriented outlet for this fine quality.

HANDLING CRITICISM

Cancer is not one of the signs that deals well with criticism. Of deep emotional nature and high sensitivity, the sharp arrows of verbal assaults will go straight to your tender heart, causing terrible pain. You do have a tough, protective shell, which helps prevent you from crumbling right before the very eyes of your critic, but the barbs will nevertheless penetrate your defenses, sometimes causing your snappy temper to surface. If insulted, you are not apt to be forgiving but rather to plunge into the depths of self-pity, bemoaning your fate and blaming the one who treated you harshly. You have a strong instinct for self-preservation and will often, by solicitous behavior, avoid drawing forth criticism. If others do not approve of your actions, you tend to worry excessively and can become quite unstable at certain times.

ADJUSTMENTS IN LIFE

Adaptability is not a natural trait in the Cancer person. Noted for your tenacious grasp, you will struggle until the bitter end to hold onto people and situations just as they are. As security is everything to you, any departure from the stability of the existing situation represents a threat and is viewed with suspicion and fear. Conversely, in your own familiar home, you can be surprisingly adaptable, particularly where children are concerned. Your desire to nourish and protect the home and family is extremely powerful, and changes for the betterment of the domestic situation are more easily accepted. One of the most difficult areas for you to adapt to appears when the grown children decide to leave home. This is your life's most difficult adjustment and may never be completed fully as you will often recall the past family life with deep nostalgia.

LEO

HEALTH

The Leo native seems to possess great solar energy, which radiates outward almost visibly. With the heart, spine, and back as prominent areas you will be graced with unusual resources and physical vitality, but you must in turn reciprocate with extra consideration to these parts so they may continue to serve you well throughout life. You have the capacity to extract maximum nourishment from the food you eat, and consequently do not need to consume vast quantities in order to maintain proper nutrition. Solar influence gives you substantial longevity and amazing recuperative powers. Illness equates with weakness in your book, so any ailment will be attended to with speed and in complete compliance with the doctor's orders. Your love of activity keeps you in good health, but be sure to maintain a wise balance of renewing rest so that you can continue at an efficient level.

PERSONAL APPEARANCE AND FITNESS

The virile Leo shows strength throughout the body, but most especially in the flashing eyes, which are striking and direct. The flesh is usually firm over a tall, large-boned frame through which movement expresses a catlike grace. The head is large and aristocratic and set upon a strong neck. The broad, open forehead and full cheekbones are well curved and indicate leadership strength. Eyebrows are arched and the nose slightly hooked above shapely, sensuous lips. The teeth are large and the jawline and chin cleanly formed. Leo's skin has a golden glow and freckles easily when exposed to the sun. You have great vitality, which could incline you toward overexertion or overindulgence and could be detrimental to your heart. Although you do well in sports, there is no need for you to practice athletics throughout life. With wide dietary practices and moderation in all things, you can retain youthful exuberance.

ROUTINE WORK AND DAILY CHORES

Leo, a fire sign, is ruled by the sun, giver of life, energy, vitality, and authority. This indicates the native's approach to life in general and work in particular. Your capacity to work is especially accented in the emotional and physical realms and the rewards of work are increased by a dynamic personal magnetism. You are able and ambitious and can easily reach the heights to which you aspire. Physical strength is a great asset to you and gives an endurance beyond the ordinary, which is just what you need to keep up with your expansive, stimulating lifestyle. There is a tendency to overtax yourself due to the enormous amount of work you expend in striving to reach your goals. It would be wise to be sure that your desire for action and accomplishment does not direct you into impulsive speculation or gambling. Good judgment in any type of activity will produce more lasting results than careless behavior.

Job Alienation

A satisfying job for a Leo must allow for broad expression of his or her natural exuberance and enthusiasm. You will feel like you are shriveling and dying if placed in a position where the stupidity of inorganization of a superior limits your own creative flow. Although usually viewing the events of life with optimism, you can be severely cramped if depression does creep into your thoughts. Though not often noticed by others, you are quite sensitive and easily hurt, but conceal it well under your magnanimous nature. Your true inner need is to accomplish all things with quality and professionalness, and to the degree that your work inhibits this tendency, you will find it deeply annoying and unsatisfying. There is a tendency to be close-minded and fixed in your opinions, but with awareness of this you can make a conscious effort to be receptive and thoughtful when presented with the ideas of others. Although you are a natural leader, the negative side of leadership—a tendency to be pompous or intolerant—could cause discord in your work environment, so wisely cultivate the positive, benevolent aspects of authority.

Handling Criticism

Leo is certainly not a member of the zodiacal family that would be expected to respond passively to criticism. One usually does better by humoring a Leo than by criticizing him. As a native of this sign you will desire respect and will not be at all happy with any actions from others that offend your dignity. You basically believe in your right to rule the world or whatever constitutes your world at the time, and will roar loudly if anyone seeks to infringe on that right. Criticism of the Leo shows a definite lack of respect and can throw you into such a rage that you become incapable of rational judgement. By your expansive and capable outward appearance, you seem to be invulnerable, but such is not the case. When your wisdom and generosity are not appreciated, you are wounded to the core, but it probably won't last as your naturally forgiving nature will shine through allowing the drama of life to proceed.

Adjustments in Life

You are a broad-minded sort and don't find it too difficult to accept change in your life. The most important thing to you is that life should be lived fully, but not especially in any one particular way. You can become quite sad if the breakup of a relationship leaves you alone, as loneliness is one of the hardest things for you to bear. The drive of your warm, outgoing nature won't allow you to be alone for long, however. The passion for life returns and you quickly move yourself onto center stage again to continue in the great drama of life. One adjustment you will probably not have to make is to living or working with shabby, worn out equipment or furnishings. This will be too much for you and can only be surpassed by having to be around pessimistic people. You won't have to adjust because you will find it intolerable and soon take yourself elsewhere.

VIRGO

HEALTH

Virgo is the sign associated with cleanliness and purity, and of the body parts rules the nervous system and intestines. Outwardly, natives appear reserved and unemotional, perhaps even cold, but inwardly there is a tendency for nervous tension to collect and produce imbalances stemming from worry. It is important to bear in mind that energy must flow. This is especially significant to earth signs who tend toward emotional blockages. Mind and body are intimately connected and any imbalance in one is sure to affect the other. Worry generally disturbs the body's digestive system, so to insure proper digestion of foods, arrange to dine at unstressful times of the day and in relaxed conditions. Rest is extremely important to you and should be structured into your daily routine. By nature, you are self-sufficient, even to the point of rejecting help from those who would attend to your ailments. Fear can be a source of illness, but once removed, health quickly returns. You have a marvelous resiliency and can recover well when emotional stress is absent.

PERSONAL APPEARANCE AND FITNESS

The hard-working Virgo is slender and graceful but not without strength and endurance. The Virgo face is kindly in appearance with an air of clean intelligence and a somewhat fastidious demeanor. The facial features tend to thinness, although the nose is often slightly large in proportion to the face. The oval-shaped head is high of forehead and ends in a pointed chin. The jawline itself is broad and the lips well-formed and distinctive. Overweight problems will not plague Virgos as they effortlessly stay slim all through life. The neck is long and graceful. A lovely, ivory tint to the skin adds to the delicate beauty of the Virgo. You are by nature interested in health and should have no problem discerning the proper nutrition to keep your body in optimum working order. Your mental energy will be with you throughout life but do take care not to overload your sensitive nervous system.

ROUTINE WORK AND DAILY CHORES

Virgo has been known as the workaholic of the zodiac. Your ability to remain in an active state for extended periods is truly awesome and, surprisingly, you seem to gain more energy rather than less from this endeavor. You are highly oriented to helping others, and the inner satisfaction received from this may well be what keeps your motor going at such a pace. You approach work in a methodical way and can quite easily continue with uninspiring work for extended periods, receiving your satisfaction from the conscientiousness with which the work is accomplished. Your powers of concentration are excellent but lean more toward the intellectual rather than the physical. Mentally quick, you can easily become overcritical. You will work to keep your environment orderly and hygenically clean as these qualities are absolutely essential to your mental health. Although your drive is not great, you have the ability to persist until the goal is accomplished.

JOB ALIENATION

Those in the sign of Virgo are excellent workers, but can find difficulty in coping with their highly analytical natures. A talent for perceiving details can be used effectively in most jobs, but if it becomes a focus in personal relationships with coworkers, it can turn into a most exasperating, nit-picky approach to every facet of life. You often tend to feel restricted and inhibited and tend to worry excessively over the smallest details. This magnified concern is usually transferred to your nervous system, causing you to be overly high-strung and edgy with others. Employers may expect that with your talent for accumulating detail, you will be able to organize it as well. However, this is not necessarily the case. Rather than live under the pressure of false expectations, try to make your focus a gathering of detail, leaving the structuring data to a coworker. You will do well to focus on being a stabilizing factor in your work place.

HANDLING CRITICISM

The Virgo is a sensitive soul and does not have built-in defenses to fend off criticism from others. You are a worrier by nature and can become extremely nervous and upset if you feel inadequate or disliked. You strive for perfection in all things, and this tendency can at times be annoying to others who may be critical of what seems to them an over-fussiness. In this desire for perfection you also may be at odds with yourself, expecting more than humanly possible then worrying if you can't meet your expectations. If criticism does come your way, you will view the accusations in the most meticulous way, evaluating each point but sometimes failing to realize that others are viewing you through different eyes than those with which you see yourself. You are a most discriminating individual and, in fact, can become rather hypercritical yourself, as others do not usually come up to your extremely high standards in some areas.

ADJUSTMENT IN LIFE

Adjustments to new situations are not always easy for the Virgo. You thrive on routine and regularity, feeling marvelously secure and competent when things are running along smoothly in a predictable fashion. Change, however, upsets these patterns and causes you to have to cope with the formless, which is not one of your innate gifts. The nebulous realm of transition opens a Pandora's box of what you see as potentially hazardous conditions, which need to be dealt with and somehow organized into a new, predictable structure within which you can again safely function. Fortunately, you are by nature an extremely reasonable person, a characteristic that will come to your aid in having to cope with changes in your life. Your considerate nature and eagerness to help others can inspire in others a desire to help you in time of need, and the help of another could be just what you need to get through times of adjustment with as much facility as possible.

LIBRA

HEALTH

Libra, sign of the scales, generally reflects this symbol in the outward appearance of balanced health. Planetary focus in your body is on the kidneys, gall bladder and back, on the action of body liquids in general, and on the equilibrium of the parts. Exercise is essential for you in order to keep the kidneys functioning well, and this is particularly important as you tend to be one of the less active signs physically. A predominance of fruit, salad, and lean rather than fatty meats will protect your kidneys from the overstress of filtering out heavy substances from foods. Drink plenty of water and juices and use discretion in the intake of sugar. You outwardly retain your beauty and healthful appearance even when ill, so will probably not generate much sympathy from others regarding your ailment, but you will be most appreciative of get-well cards, flowers, and inquiries about your condition. Be attentive to your own welfare and attend to any symptoms that may occur immediately. In this way you will retain your glow and free yourself and loved ones from unnecessary concern.

PERSONAL APPEARANCE AND FITNESS

The elegant Libra tends toward tallness with a medium bone structure and sloping shoulders. There is a natural slimness to this sign, which shows in slender hands and legs and is in complete harmony with the Libran grace of movement. The head is long and refined with a small face, which is classical in appearance. There is not the slightest hint of coarseness in the Libra's face from the calm, yet expressive eyes to the long, finely sculpted lips. The cheekbones are high and the chin well-formed. The nose is long, straight, and pointed with delicate nostrils. The neck, too, is long and elegant. An alabaster complexion completes the look of elegance and refinement. It is important that you transcend the lack of enthusiasm you feel for activities requiring exertion. Guide yourself into an environment that will stimulate your physical activity and in this manner health will be preserved.

ROUTINE WORK AND DAILY CHORES

Those born under the sign of Libra are not the most energetic of souls, but manage to keep life in order due more to their desire for beauty and harmony of environment than desire to throw themselves into work. You tend to look down on menial work and would do better at distasteful tasks if the endeavor were shared with another who perhaps could inspire you to give a little more. You thrive on cooperative efforts and strive to divide work on an equitable basis. It is said that laziness is a Libran tendency, so to stem this tide, consciously involve yourself in some regenerative activity such as yoga or another moderate form of exercise. What you must realize is that energy begets energy and regular activity will establish positive patterns in your life. Yoga is designed to achieve balance in the body and would be a natural expression for those born in the sign of balance.

Job Alienation

As a Libra it is essential for you to work in pleasant, attractive surroundings. Environments that are cluttered, poorly designed, or dirty will grate against your basic inclination toward the beautiful. Harsh sounds and arguments at work can be extremely devitalizing and cause you to feel a helpless despondency with conditions. Your skills lie in a natural tact and diplomacy and the ability to make others feel happy and relaxed. Because of this you would do quite well and find deep satisfaction in a position specializing in public contact. Your fairness and sense of justice will endear you to coworkers, but people can become alienated if your resentful side becomes apparent. You may have difficulty with jobs requiring hard-driving decisions, as your tendency to be ever evaluating the balance of factors can make it difficult to arrive at firm decisions. Working alone often does not bring out your fine quality of cooperation in partnership, which could be a most valuable asset in the business world, and would in addition fulfill a deep, inner longing.

Handling Criticism

The Libra native is usually quite upset by any form of criticism, even when it is not directed at them. Unpleasantness is to be avoided at all costs, and when faced with the reality of criticism from others, Libra simply doesn't know how to handle it. In order to avoid any kind of negativity, you will go overboard to satisfy everyone in your environment so completely that there will never be a cause for criticism. The opinions of others influence you greatly and any criticism will not only offend your sense of harmony, but will be taken deeply to heart as an inconsiderate assault. You will recover, of course, striving to balance the scales and return to a harmonious relationship as quickly as possible. You are not likely to be critical of others as this, too, would upset the equilibrium so important to your peace of mind.

Adjustments in Life

In one sense adjustment is the keynote of a Libran's life. Your symbol—the scales—indicates the ceaseless balancing and rebalancing, or adjustment to a state of equilibrium. Although you are of changeable temperament, the necessity to adapt to new circumstances can be quite trying for you. First of all, any change is a departure from the comfortable state of balance, which you prize so highly, and there are so many influences to be considered that it is extremely hard to decide just how the new situation should be established. You are of an easygoing nature, which allows you to be accepting of others and of change itself, but also sometimes makes common sense secondary to pleasantness. Fortunately, you have a profound sense of justice, which helps you make adjustments with an eye to fairness for everyone involved.

SCORPIO

HEALTH

Ruled by the planet Mars, giver of all energy, Scorpio individuals will appear to be healthy and sound. The focal point of your body is the reproductive organs, lower digestive tract, eliminative processes, and pigmentation, such as the red color of the blood. The private nature of this area of the body, and the Scorpio tendency for secrecy, can be a hazardous combination in matters of health. Be alert to any signals of imbalance in this sector and make certain to relieve any emotional pressure that you might be internalizing, which could manifest as an unhealthy condition. Herbal eliminants will generally be more harmonious with the Scorpio makeup than will chemical cathartics if constipation should be a problem. Although you thrive on intense activity, you receive great nurturing through nature and will balance your active life well with frequent times to commune with nature in a totally undemanding way. Gardening can be quite therapeutic for natives of this sign. Hot foods are best avoided, and your food intake should be regulated according to the degree of energy you expend.

PERSONAL APPEARANCE AND FITNESS

Strength and intensity are prominent characteristics of the Scorpio's physical appearance. Usually large boned, the height will span from medium to tall, with the look of dark swarthiness being quite common. The eyes are penetrating to the point of being unnerving to others and have a look of the secretive. The forehead tends to be large and wide, though rather shallow in depth. The eyebrows are full as are the nostrils, the bridge of the nose being slightly raised. Cheekbones and chin display a roundness, and the jaw is very strong. The mouth is full, firm, and sensual, showing deep determination. The overall face has a sultry look. Scorpio is heir to a strong vitality, which keeps you fit and active throughout life. Any illness will be tolerated briefly, but not long before you leap back into the action again. When you rest to recover health, you rest completely, having an inner sense of what will heal you.

ROUTINE WORK AND DAILY CHORES

In order to work effectively and use the intense energy of this sign in its highest capacity, the Scorpio native should be aware that he or she absolutely needs times of quiet and communication with nature. You have a great capacity for inspired work, but to keep your powerful intuitive flow moving freely, you must take time to receive energy from the universe so that you can channel it into the affairs of men. You are courageous by nature and can extend this trait to supply the courage to give up certain personal satisfactions in order to take care of the mundane. You are capable of willing sacrifice for others but must be careful not to develop an attitude of martyrdom. The Scorpio has great powers of concentration, which enables you to delve deeply into mental or spiritual matters while fulfilling mundane obligations. Utilize the time spent in undemanding work to organize and ponder the many details you have observed and recorded about a situation that interests you.

JOB ALIENATION

The Scorpio worker needs very much to feel that this particular job has a real value in the world. Any kind of work perceived as trivial will only arouse your scorn and will not likely draw forth the vast stores of energy to which you have access. Jobs with hazy outlines or a strong, speculative nature will be difficult for you to take hold of and could become a source of deep frustration. Work requiring little effort will only numb you and tend to bring out the resentful, stubborn, sarcastic side of your temperament. In your sign particularly, energy unchanneled in creative ways quickly becomes destructive both to yourself and others, so it becomes quite important to align yourself with work that allows you to express your full intensity in constructive ways. An additional depth of satisfaction will be achieved if your work makes use of your powerful intuition to extract knowledge that is in some manner hidden. Take care not to overpower coworkers with the intensity of your personality, especially if your mood is momentarily negative.

HANDLING CRITICISM

As a Scorpio you are likely to meet criticism in one of two ways. You could react in a completely controlled, unflinching manner and more or less give the impression that your critic is completely beneath you and so unworthy—that his or her remarks don't ever bear recognition. The other response will be the famous retaliatory string administered with lightning speed and deadly accuracy. You know by instinct precisely where to strike in order to mortally wound the adversary, and if he or she does not visibly crumble immediately, you will know with your infallible, sixth sense that the string has hit its mark. You can see it in his or her eyes. The potential critic would be wise to consider very carefully before striking out at the Scorpio, as this native will never forget and probably never forgive. The Scorpio who has managed to control this deadly response and channel the energy into a positive vein will accept just criticism more easily, if not with total humility, but will silently retain the memory of false accusation or mistrust and never share a confidence with the assailant again.

ADJUSTMENTS IN LIFE

Adjustments in the Scorpio's life are handled in diverse ways, depending upon the areas that are affected. When changes in work or home environment present themselves, you exhibit an unusual flexibility, releasing the former situation and directing your energy into new areas of creations. The intensity with which you can begin anew is quite awesome and will keep you so busy that there will be little time to mourn the past. Adjustments affecting your emotional or personal life will be somewhat more difficult. You feel emotion quite deeply and with a consuming passion, which you tend to internalize when the situation is not open to outward expression. This inward accumulation of energy, which can all too easily burst out in a destructive manner, can at least make you quite difficult to live with.

SAGITTARIUS

HEALTH

As a Sagittarian you are likely to be an active person, a characteristic that helps keep your physical body running smoothly. Mental and physical activity are both essential to your well-being and emotional peace. If you find yourself in a sedentary or confining occupation, create time for frequent exercise, preferably in the open air. Sagittarius rules the liver, hips, thighs, and due to the influence of Jupiter, the pituitary gland. You have a strong constitution and are especially venturesome, which could lead to accidents or strained muscles. Your independent nature prevails in illness or in health, inclining you to a graceful acceptance of a few aches and pains as part of life and nothing to arouse alarm. Natives of your sign have a tendency to put on weight around the hips and thighs, so be attentive to the quality of foods in your diet to fend off this possibility. City dwellers may enjoy belonging to a health club, which will provide both physical exercise and relaxation.

PERSONAL APPEARANCE AND FITNESS

Sagittarius is often the tallest of the signs, well-boned with firm flesh and an often stocky build. The face is oval and has a distinctly aristocratic appearance. The long head has an appropriately high forehead and not particularly prominent cheeks. The jaw and chin are firm and strong. The frequently almond-shaped eyes are wide set with a candidness about the gaze. There is a long, straight Greek nose, with rounded nostrils and a broad tip. Curly hair is not uncommonly seen in the Sagittarian and is likely to be fair in color. The mouth is arched with strong teeth—rather broad and flat. The outdoorsy look is enhanced by a healthy, clean complexion. The ears, hands, and feet are often larger than usual. Your desire for movement, travel, and fresh air will lead you to enough activity to maintain your physical fitness. You have great stamina and can remain active and survive under extreme conditions, providing you retain what you consider to be your freedom.

ROUTINE WORK AND DAILY CHORES

As a fire sign you are gifted with great driving power, though often the mental drudgery necessary to make projects work causes you to become impatient or procrastinate. You are ambitious, but not always to the point of forfeiting your independence to embark upon a career. Mundane tasks do not warm the heart of the free-ranging Sagittarian, although you will not usually worry a great deal about dull jobs not accomplished. A challenge is what you seek—to the degree that you are able to see challenge in the commonplace—and will be able to direct your energy toward its accomplishment. Any kind of claustrophobic situation—be it mental or physical—will be deadly to your temperament, so when life demands a certain amount of tedious work, be sure to balance it with a goodly amount of physical movement through sports, walking, or travel. Motion seems to increase your ability to think, so if desk-bound try to walk around the office or outdoors to stimulate your creative processes.

Job Alienation

Although the Sagittarian possesses a fine capacity for work, he or she can be totally turned off by a restrictive or limiting environment. Your intellect is strong and it, too, will benefit greatly by a job that draws you out mentally. Sincerity and open-mindedness are yours, but when overly pressured you can become tactless and irresponsible. Jobs requiring intense focus on detail may prove stifling, as you are more inclined to see the large, overall picture and will be happier in the macrocosm than the microcosm. Your career must be challenging and expansive or you will surely feel a sense of alienation and frustration, which can eventually cause you to break away into something more fulfilling. If confined to dull conditions for the time, involve yourself in an active sport, or perhaps take up work with horses as a hobby. Also, be aware of intellectually inclined coworkers who might provide a stimulus to your mind.

Handling Criticism

Although the warm friendliness of the Sagittarian is appreciated everywhere, there are some aspects of your personality that tend to draw criticism. You are equally tactless with everyone and have a unique trait of knowing each person's most vulnerable point. Your optimistic nature saves you from falling into fits of depression when criticized, but there is one area that is absolutely sacred to you and will arouse your ire if attacked. This is the area of your personal honesty. You are the very soul of integrity—a quality upon which you place high values, and anyone who questions your dedication to truth or your personal sincerity had better be prepared for a fiery verbal response. You may tend to say more than you mean in these encounters, and can often be quite harsh on others, but only for a moment before your friendly nature returns.

Adjustments in Life

Change is an easy thing for the Sagittarian to accept. As a matter of fact, you thrive on it. The most difficult adjustment you will have to make is to lack of change. You are not possessive of either persons or situations, nor are you inclined to worry about things. If personal relationships become too restrictive, you simply leave them. You are not flighty, but you are by nature unable to adjust well to stifling or limiting situations. Your strong optimism leads you to feel that any compromises you may decide to make will have some worthwhile, redeeming factor that will make the situation acceptable. Your tendency to overlook details can be a saving grace in times of necessary adjustment. It will allow you to focus on any possible positive potentials without becoming overly involved with negative trivia.

CAPRICORN

HEALTH

Those born in the sign of Capricorn are noted for unusual longevity. Natives have planetary energy focused in the knees, bones, and teeth, and it is these areas that should be given extra consideration in order to preserve health and freedom of movement. Capricorns are noted for their tremendous willpower, which can be a distinct ally in rising above the tendency toward negative thinking, becoming detrimental to the physical body. Your ruling planet, Saturn, influences the gall bladder and the spleen and limits the circulation. It is often said that Capricorns are born old and grow younger with the passage of time; it does seem that the sun gives a strengthening aspect to your health as you increase in years. It is important to keep your circulation active, as this is vital to the efficiency of all body processes, so make sure to get adequate exercise and plenty of vegetables in the diet.

PERSONAL APPEARANCE AND FITNESS

The Capricorn's body is characteristically long from the torso and neck to the rather slender arms and legs. The face, too, is long and thinner at the bottom than at the top, and often displays a grim formality. The eyebrows are heavy over deep-set, round, small eyes, which have a look of shrewdness. The nose and mouth are long—the latter being rather thin-lipped. The jaw and chin are small and reflect the perseverance of the ambitious Capricorn. You have a tendency toward dry skin, which can be helped by good diet and extra skin care. The face overall conveys a feeling of serious weightiness. Due to your desire to climb both socially and economically, you will remain active in the pursuit of your goals, which helps with general fitness. However, if you spend much time behind a desk or are otherwise immobilized, be sure to schedule in a modicum of physical activity in order to keep your system flowing freely.

ROUTINE WORK AND DAILY CHORES

As a Capricorn you have a remarkable capacity for plain, hard work. Your impetus and persistence are phenomenal, particularly when it comes to a task that will elevate you in the eyes of others. The mundane requirements of life are done with the same plodding, carefully considered regularity that you apply to your business or career. You feel best with solid foundations and do not begrudge any time required to investigate and organize your affairs so that everything will remain secure, predictable, and growth-oriented. Your willpower is extraordinary and gives you the capacity to deal with any of the world's mundane events, providing they are of a practical nature. The systematic approach of the Capricorn native assures that everything undertaken will be done with an almost disconcerting thoroughness, regardless of the amount of tedium involved.

JOB ALIENATION

Capricorns tend to be very stable in their jobs, but can become alienated if there is not an adequate amount of security and regularity to provide a solid ground for advancement. You approach your job with cool calculation, but even with all your planning you still find things to worry about. Hardship connected with your career can be borne on your sturdy shoulders, but lack of fulfillment can lead you into persistent states of depression. If your job requires a lot of superficial social obsequiousness, it will soon drive you into another means of earning your income, as there is no solid place to plant your feet. You could easily become overexacting, demanding an excessive amount of conformity from those with whom you work. This could create an environment not totally in gear with your approach, and therefore, rather disturbing. If you are temporarily locked into an unsatisfactory work environment, balance your needs by extra time to read, paint, or enjoy music.

HANDLING CRITICISM

The Capricorn nature is not designed to handle criticism very gracefully. Although you are not prone to emotional displays, you are extremely easy for a perceptive person to read, and the pain felt in your emotions will register plainly on your face. You would rather it didn't show at all, but it does in a look of introverted seriousness accompanied by several moments of thoughtful silence. Teasing is not a form of humor to which you respond, either, and rather than getting into the lightness of the mood you feel that you have become the scapegoat. You seem on the surface to be even-tempered and emotionally steady, but underneath you can be deeply wounded by mistreatment of a verbal nature. You love to feel appreciated, and when confronted with unappreciative remarks, you take them deeply to heart as serious wounds. Your own approach often makes you seem critical of others, though you do not always intend to be so. Your nature inclines you to view the weighty side of all matters, which often comes across as pointing out what is wrong rather than what is right.

ADJUSTMENTS IN LIFE

Capricorn will view any changes to be made in life with the utmost serious and practical consideration. Having to deal with frequent adjustments will be quite difficult for this steady individual, as he or she feels best when all things in life are safe and predictable. The easiest kind of adjustments to handle are those relating to career or business, as they will generally be changes that will in some way further the climb to higher worldly plateaus. Adjustments in emotional situations are far more difficult, as matters involving the feelings do not always respond to logic and cold, common-sense analysis. Capricorn can become quite frustrated in these areas and may even turn away from the source of discomfort, returning to the security of the more rational business world. Being rather rigid and inflexible makes adjustments quite difficult, but any changes made will be based on some type of logical foundation.

AQUARIUS

HEALTH

As an Aquarian you are heir to reasonably good health, though perhaps not as robust as some of your other zodiacal companions. Your sign rules the circulation, the shins and ankles, and often a sensitivity to cold weather is present. Being an intelligent and quite imaginative individual, you can easily become so engrossed in what you are doing that eating and sleeping are nearly forgotten. As you are generally focused on matters other than physical, you can become negligent, resulting in physical or nervous disorders. Illness is a sign of weakness to you and if required to convalesce, you will do so unwillingly, refusing to acknowledge your limitation. Realize that rest and a nourishing diet are essential for maintenance and repair of the body, and take the time to eat and sleep well, as this is truly your life-support system. If illness requires the use of drastic healing efforts, you could easily become interested in healing techniques, which are either esoteric or in some way new to our culture, such as acupuncture.

PERSONAL APPEARANCE AND FITNESS

Aquarians are usually quite handsome individuals having a distinguished appearance. Height is moderate with a large head and high forehead and regular features. The lively eyes are well-shaped, as are all the facial features. Below the wide-set eyes is a beautifully formed aquiline nose with fine and sensitive nostrils. This particularly outstanding feature gives Aquarians their superb profile. The chin is neat, though often a bit fleshy. The strong nose and wide yet thin and sensitive mouth give an air of nobility to natives of this sign. The complexion is a fine, ivory color, completing the picture of refined strength. Your altruistic nature keeps you actively involved in the affairs of humanity, which stimulates your intellectual as well as physical well-being. You move quickly, though not always gracefully. Be sure to give extra care to keeping your legs and ankles in good condition, since you spend so much time using them.

ROUTINE WORK AND DAILY CHORES

Aquarians have a marvelous ability to accept whatever life hands them and deal with it in an intelligent and thorough manner. Your capacity for concentration is so highly developed that often the task at hand will consume you wholly—to the point where you forget to eat, sleep, or consider others in your environment. You are able to plow through the necessary requirements of life, even though they may be dull, and to fulfill your duties with skill and dedication. You will be happiest if there is an intellectual challenge in your life, so even if you must pursue less than inspiring work, allow time to exercise your mind either in private hobbies or research, or in an endeavor connected with the betterment of mankind. Civic organizations could be a constructive focus, or work with groups who volunteer to teach new skills to adults or children.

JOB ALIENATION

As an Aquarian you have a great capacity for originality and are likely to feel stifled in a job that relates only to the known and explored. Work in which there is no flexibility, no opportunity to carve your own path will never bring forth your finest abilities and will leave you with a nagging, unfulfilled feeling. Interrelationships with coworkers will probably not be troublesome for you, but it could be for them. Although you are friendly, there is a detachment in your nature that some can interpret as a personal affront. Those of conventional bent may become exasperated with your leaps into the forefront of humanitarian causes, and this could be troublesome in your work environment. Your unconventional tendencies can, in some cases, go overboard into meaningless extremism, which is not always an asset in the business world. Allow your independent spirit plenty of freedom during off-work hours in order to make better use of your energy at your place of employment.

HANDLING CRITICISM

Aquarius is basically an unemotional sign and is far less influenced by criticism than most. There is no question in your mind about the rightness of your own opinion, whether it concerns yourself or the world at large. Criticism from others merely demonstrates that they are out of touch with the real situation. Not that you are impervious to the penetration of sharp remarks, but you will not likely give them much weight. You may often come under fire for your extremism or interest in attachment to radical reform, but to you this can only indicate lack of vision and general stodginess on the part of the assailant. Since you thrive on being different and even eccentric, those arrows meant as criticism may actually be seen by you as compliments. Your dispassionate nature saves you from fiery retaliation, as you are not at all inclined to make scenes.

ADJUSTMENTS IN LIFE

Being essentially a realist, the Aquarian will no doubt face adjustments in life, but for the most part the rest of the world must adjust to them! Many adjustments that cause difficulty for others do not concern the Aquarian because this native lives a good part of his or her life in the future, not the present. This characteristic requires him or her to adjust to a rather lonely lifestyle, as the rest of us dwell in the present or past. Your mode of adjustment to this situation is to keep right on doing the same thing since living in the present would require travelling backwards in time. One of the Aquarian's favorite ways of dealing with any kind of force or discord is simply to leave. However, if the Aquarian feels he or she is right about the point of controversy, nothing will change his or her course. You will quietly and determinedly continue to follow your own plan of action regardless of public opinion.

PISCES

HEALTH

Pisces is the most sensitive sign of the zodiacal family and can easily reproduce emotional imbalances on the physical level. Your sign rules the feet and to some degree the lungs, while your ruling planet, Neptune, governs the general nervous system and the thalamus, which controls the transmission of stimuli between brain and sense organs. You are extremely susceptible to external influences and should take care to surround yourself with healthful persons who have a positive outlook on life. Though often appearing outwardly passive and at peace, you can be quite emotionally high-strung and thus exert undue stress on the body's maintenance systems. Some outdoor activity, even daily walks or gardening, would be rejuvenating for you, especially if you live near the water. City dwellers could experience sensitivity to air pollution and should do everything possible to protect the lungs from unnecessary stress. Drugs of any kind can adversely affect you, so strive to find forms of healing that utilize herbs and nutritious foods.

PERSONAL APPEARANCE AND FITNESS

Pisces comes in a variety of body styles depending upon your proximity to the following sign, Aries. Often Pisces is short and rounded, but just as often, taller and firmer. There is a lovely, ethereal look about people of this sign, especially apparent in the mistiness of the large, round eyes, which are quite expressive and beautiful. The nose comes in a variety of styles as does the body, but all are attractive and often lean toward the aquiline. Pisces carries a large round or oval head with the broad face also displaying a roundness. The sensitive lips are generous and can be sensual. The small teeth frequently have a gap in front. Feet are small and the hands are nicely formed and expressive. You can remain active and fit if you pay particular attention to your environment, keeping it harmonious and peaceful, allowing yourself plenty of time for quiet and solitude.

ROUTINE AND DAILY CHORES

Dealing with the more rigorous aspects of day-to-day reality can be rather trying for Pisces. You are not a conformist, and disciplined, regular routines don't do much to cause your creative juices to flow. You have a superb imagination and strong intuitive sense, which together allow you to see subtle aspects of life often unnoticed by those with stronger, more earthly orientation. You can be ultimately successful in dealing with some of life's drudgeries if you use that expansive imagination to fit mundane necessities into a creative or artistic context. For example, if you find it difficult to embark upon a regular exercise program, arrange to exchange health-oriented massages with a friend while listening to music. If cooking the daily meals seems dull, cultivate an herb garden outside the kitchen door and use it along with edible flowers to garnish and flavor foods. Bring your rich imagination into daily life.

JOB ALIENATION

As a Piscean you may find it easier on some levels to be content with your work, and more difficult on other levels. By nature you are inclined to be easygoing and nonintrusive, not feeling it worth the energy to battle your job placement. On the other hand your extreme sensitivity will make you aware of a whole world of innuendos that most people don't even know exists. If your job requires a lot of hard-core earthiness, you may find yourself feeling confused or oppressed by the demands. You are quite adaptable and compassionate and could easily experience emotional discomfort in a job that requires cold, analytical relationships with people or information. You will do best in a field where your sympathy and innate healing abilities will be appreciated, or where your artistic nature can express freely without intimidation from others. If you are in an uninspiring or difficult job, seek to find a role model among your coworkers. You are easily influenced and highly responsive to external influences, which in this case could be an advantage that could allow you to take on their characteristics.

HANDLING CRITICISM

Tenderhearted Pisces is without a doubt the most sensitive to criticism of all the signs. You are well aware of this sensitivity, and for protection have built what appears to be a shell of indifference around yourself. The shell is not terribly thick, however, and could more accurately be compared with surface tension on a body of water. Some of the most painful emotional wounds for you to bear are the rejection by a loved one and harsh criticism of your artistic or dramatic creations. If the works of your hands and imagination come early in life, the assault could leave such deep scars that you may never again express your creativity in a public way. Later in life you can feign indifference when darts fly in your direction. It takes a lot to arouse your temper, but when activated your responses can be extremely caustic. Generally, however, you prefer the path of least resistance, allowing sharp remarks to flow by you as leaves in a stream.

ADJUSTMENTS IN LIFE

The Piscean's approach to making adjustments is first to withdraw into seclusion in order to reflect, soothe the emotions with music or poetry, and try to prepare for a confrontation with reality. It is extremely difficult for you to put things in a coherent form and view all considerations with critical analysis. Being of more intuitive bent, your conclusions are likely to be arrived at in a manner that even you cannot identify. Whenever possible you would rather take the easy way out than try to sort out the confusing facts in a semblance of order. You have a tremendous asset in your great adaptability, which allows you to mold yourself to new situations without too much wrenching pain. You prefer to live in your watery, dreamy world of seeming success, but if blatantly confronted with personal failure you will probably just create another image within which to live.

Chapter Seven
Relationships

ALL PARTNERSHIPS BETWEEN PEOPLE who perceive themselves as equals fall into this relationship section. In astrology the seventh house is 180 degrees away from the first, and it is the balancing element that makes us less self-involved and more emotionally complete. Although one's individual nature is never compromised by a good relationship, there is a necessary blending much like beautiful counterpoint in music. Just as two or more independent melodies retain their own structure, nevertheless there is an overall harmonic theme. A similar counterpoint is also found in good relationships where contrasting personalities often bring out undeveloped talents in each other.

In astrology we assume that marriage and all comparable relationships are between equals. Each person must bring to the joint association an equal contribution, and when this doesn't happen one person is usually more involved—and more committed—than the other.

However, this is not a hopeless situation, for people change, and by making slight adjustments in what you bring to a relationship, the scale of control can tilt, making the relationship more balanced. Libra is the symbol of marriage in astrology, and its glyph is the scales of justice. The up-and-down motion in all relationships is reflected here, but also the idea of justice. And what is more just than finding and loving a partner who is truly an equal?

But romantic equals are just one part of life, and so you can use this section to understand all relationships. Remember, too, that unfavorable relationships, such as between competitors or foes, are also represented here. By focusing on the positive elements of these associations, you can alter your activities to minimize the harm these uncooperative people can do to you.

ARIES

THE OPTIMUM PARTNER

The most suitable and congenial partner for Aries is one who is not scared away by your periodic rages and fits of temper, or turned away by your hermit phases in which you prefer to deal as little as possible with anyone. Your partner should also be one who matches you in loy-

160

alty, guts, and spontaneity, or you will tend to feel unmatched, although you may remain steadfastly in the relationship. A complementary personality suits you through persistence, a no-tantrum temperament, and a broad prospective on life. The Aries man needs a woman who can face him in all his moods—quietly yet without being submissive or coddling. Aries women need men who don't have a nineteenth-century view of the woman's role; your mate must see you as more than a dutiful housewife and give scope to your independent spirit.

MARRIAGE

Aries willingly accepts the challenges of marriage; they appeal to your idealism and you take pride in making things work. However, you may prefer the change of pace afforded by short-term relationships, or the sense of not being committed in an absolutely final way when you live with a partner but are not married. If you are truly a reclusive type, you may limit yourself to dating, but it is not likely that you will avoid romantic/sexual relationships altogether. You seek a mate who is active, alert, and has common interests with you so that you will not become oppressed by spending years in his or her company.

MARRIAGE WITH THE DIFFERENT SIGNS

When it is Aries plus Aries in love and marriage, there's never a dull moment. What looks to others like warfare is to you and your Aries mate nothing but playful banter. This can be a fruitful union for you, as each Aries partner has shadings of character that complement the other.

You may be fascinated by Taurus simply because this one seems so very different, but in truth you are probably too close for comfort—both are stubborn and want to see things done their way.

Marriage with Gemini calls for some sort of anchor, otherwise most of the time you'll find yourself miles apart—and this can mean literally! You spark each other in an inspiring way, although Gemini can tax your patience.

When direct, irrational Aries is matched up with methodical, often obtuse Cancer, things are romantic but confusing. You underestimate Cancer while he or she overestimates you; both can feel grossly deceived when the truth is out. You have highly emotional natures in common, which must always be taken into consideration.

You and Leo respect each other's fiery qualities and learn in proximity how to avoid trespassing on each other's forbidden territories. You are mutually amused by your similarities, which are readily seen. This is one of the best combinations for you.

When you and Virgo get together, your vastly different natures may seem to complement each other, but remember that time will take its toll. Virgo tones you down but gives in too much, suppressing his or her feelings and building a false sense in you that it is all right to take advantage.

Aries admires Libra's combination of tact and expressiveness. Libra in turn admires your forthrightness and optimism. If you share common goals and lifestyles (Aries can sometimes forget that this is important) this can be a good one.

You and Scorpio match each other in the dogged pursuit of goals; if these can blend, it will be okay. Otherwise Scorpio can engage you in a drawn-out battle of wills—although you also respect each other's pugnacity!

With Sagittarius there are bound to be some sexual fireworks, but there is some doubt as to whether you both can stay in one place long enough to set up a home and family. A live-in situation is the usual arrangement for this combination and might be a good idea as a first step before the commitment of marriage.

Capricorn needs much that you have to offer—and this is mutual—but marriage may not be the way to acquire it. Capricorn's silences and dry wit can be maddening to a confronting personality such as Aries. You are reflective, but you do it on the move, fast-paced; Capricorn moves slowly, step by step.

Aquarius brings you a good combination of a forward-looking attitude and a wide range of interests that you appreciate. If the two of you can accept each other's types of occasional spaciness, tangents, and eccentricities, you have much humor and affection to share.

With Pisces you find mutual inspiration; you feed each other's imaginations, but your combination may be too volatile for you to deal with for long. There's just too much Pisces pull to your Aries push.

BUSINESS PARTNERSHIPS

In the business world earth signs make good partners and coworkers for Aries, providing a steadying and pragmatic perspective. Each needs, however, to see his or her own role clearly in relation to the other's; a second opinion is good for Aries in choosing a close associate, as you tend to jump at first impressions. Remember that these may be specifically calculated to impress you.

HANDLING COMPETITION

Aries never turns down a challenge—sheer bravado may lead you where angels fear to tread. Aries gets to the heart of the matter, going for what is really worthwhile, which is good. You can also pursue minor grievances as if they were major issues, which is bad. You may find strong friendships arising out of competition with others. Friendly yet heated conversations, which constantly border on (and sometimes cross the borders) arguments, can continue for years.

OPEN ENEMIES

You run short of patience quickly, which can cause friction with adversaries; if it occurs frequently it will not fade. You are likely to form an attachment to victory for its own sake. A different type of personality will find it difficult to understand your goal. Aries are not interested in making converts but rather in seeing things happen according to their convictions. If agreement cannot be reached, it is your opinion that someone needs to vacate the premises—and chances are you don't mean yourself, although you are certainly capable of stalking out with a slam of the door. At least conflicts don't lurk beneath the surface with Aries; they are always in view, never tucked away in a drawer. When someone is on your mind he or she will soon know it, and you expect to be confronted by anyone who has a bone to pick with you.

TAURUS

THE OPTIMUM PARTNER

Taurus relates best with a partner who has an emotionally based personality yet is not loud, pushy, or hypersensitive. You cannot be fought head-on. Subtlety is needed, along with the patience of someone who paces his or her own activities and has a need for times of silence as you do. The Taurus man will do best in the long run with a woman who has a will of her own and is not easily stared down. You fall for flattery easily, Taurus males, so let's hope your lady isn't that type! The Taurean female thrives on a relationship with an emotionally sensitive man—one who is not overindulgent of her delight in shiny baubles.

MARRIAGE

You share with your neighbor sign, Aries, a hidden idealism, which you may not be keeping a secret, but it is not usually associated with your sign. You are highly romantic and want a lasting relationship based on similar backgrounds and interests. While others may actively seek to isolate and work out points of friction, you are more likely to wait for your partner to do this. Your mate can be very surprised when, after years together, you suddenly reveal a pet peeve, which has remained unresolved because you didn't want to be the one to cause a scene. Once committed you are in it for the duration, but you won't tolerate abuse.

MARRIAGE WITH THE DIFFERENT SIGNS

In a marriage with Aries, Taurus will experience day-do-day confrontations over minor details. The Aries tendency to push you is annoying, although this fire sign does appeal to you with his or her impetuousness. You may assume that you can calm and direct Aries, but chances are this won't be the case. Neither of you can let a matter rest, which doesn't bode well for peace.

With another Taurean, similar outlooks provide a natural ease in the relationship; yet difficulties can arise to overshadow this if both partners are not objective enough—you may simply be too much alike to see one another clearly. If you can maintain a mutual self-evaluation you can sustain a harmonious balance.

You enjoy Gemini's brightness. Each of you finds in the other the fascination of talents and perspectives, which differ due to the contrasts between earth and air personalities. In marriage you need to be aware that mutual envy does not lead either partner to play the martyr when the other receives recognition in the world.

With Cancer you have a good basis for long-term growth. Taurus is in tune with the Cancerian's protectiveness and concern for stability. You are able to expose each other's fussiness in a pleasant manner, replacing touchy spots with humor and good will.

Taureans share the step-by-step approach of Leo, but neither side retreats and compromise is unthinkable for both of you! You can develop mutual trust and respect, which will allow each of you some needed room. This is likely to be a long road, but if it's worth it you can make it work.

Ah, Virgo—what a relief for earth signs to find each other! Virgo's habits may annoy you at times, but when you think of what other people are like this becomes very minor indeed. Your aesthetic sense and sensual enjoyment of life blend with and complement the Virgonian good manners and critical mind—a full scope for a happy marriage.

You and Libra effortlessly attain a placid surface. Libra will indulgently smooth over your oddities, and you love it. The possible drawback is that he or she will smooth over too much for too long—until unpleasant feelings emerge. If you can mutually arrange from the beginning to air complaints with tact, everything will be fine.

You may cast a wary eye on your zodiacal opposite—Scorpio, suspecting hidden motives. They are there, but you may find them not at all distant from your own. With Scorpio for a mate you can spend hours plumbing one another's depths. Struggles may ensue, but this is a relationship that can last.

The flair and joviality of Sagittarius impress you and put you at your ease at the same time, but a truly deep accord is hard to come by. The first question is how to keep the same pace—and you may never get to the second question.

A union between Taurus and Capricorn is built to last. You may be infuriated by this native's alternating scowl and twinkling eye, but mutual good humor prevails. This is the romance that lasts from the first kiss through many years.

You and Aquarius are both fixed signs, and this means fixed attitudes and determination, which can cause you to lock horns frequently. But this airy native may be more in accord with you than you realize; often the obstacle is that you won't let go of your conviction that you are right. If you let Aquarius explain—they love to—you might find you want to stick around.

Taurus, you may have trouble fighting the assumption that you should direct Pisces' life. The watery Piscean character goes right to your big heart and softens it. The tranquility of Pisces may seem like aimlessness to you; you will encounter plenty of resistance, though, if you try too hard to mold this one. In any case there is no shortage of affection here.

BUSINESS PARTNERSHIPS

Though earthy and practical, you tend to rely on personal ties and family considerations a bit too much for good business. Your stubbornness can be difficult for partners; you may be able to dominate, especially with water signs (scratch Scorpio), but what you really need is not someone who will back down but another strong voice to whom you will listen. You are protective of company interests, tending to see others as not being responsible enough or as taking too many risks. You put your heart into a partnership or group enterprise and work steadily and sincerely for its success.

HANDLING COMPETITION

Taureans may seem to have thick hides, but actually they are easily hurt, especially by social putdowns or loss of face. You compete fearlessly if you are truly confident of your position; otherwise your complaisance quickly fades before the unblinking social eye. You don't stint in the effort department, and are motivated by the desire for reward both in business and socially.

OPEN ENEMIES

Usually you can avoid sparking trouble or increasing existing problems, but you don't back down when confronted. You know instinctively that silence is your best tactic under pressure, as you don't possess a really diplomatic touch; you are too blunt, taking things very personally and easily egged on by insults or accusations once you have been engaged in verbal battle. Often you will win such arguments through sheer dogged persistence, leaving your adversary exhausted and making a mental note to leave you alone next time.

GEMINI

THE OPTIMUM PARTNER

Gemini's best partner is one who has an inquisitive outlook, is athletic mentally if not physically, and is filled with the spontaneity Geminis love to relate to and own. A good organizational mind is a plus for Gemini's mate, able to handle the wealth of detail pouring forth from this airy native without overloading. To balance Gemini, his or her partner needs a calm, pragmatic outlook in crises, to be able to think and act while Gemini raves at all the possible ramifications of the situation, which can be imagined. The Gemini man responds best to an independent thinker, a woman who can keep up with him—and maybe even challenge him occasionally. Gemini women are happiest when paired with men who accept but do not pander to their frequent shifts in mood and attitude.

MARRIAGE

Gemini's need for security—usually hidden or denied—surfaces when the issue is marriage. You may expect that being married will in itself solve problems for you automatically, but you will have to learn from experience that this is not necessarily the case. You bring your abundant energy wholeheartedly into married life but may view marriage as a state of being taken care of, presenting no pressure on you to come up with solutions by yourself. You envision a spontaneous flow of activity and affection and may be taken aback at the inevitable periods of struggle, which are essential to the growth of a relationship.

MARRIAGE WITH THE DIFFERENT SIGNS

You and Cancer are bickering neighbors who, when all is said and done, love each other after all. Cancer's pouts may seem to drag on endlessly. You thrive on change while your Cancerian mate likes to set up secure routines. Finding a middle ground will do you both good.

The bigness and brightness of Leos attract you, though you will most likely find yourself tripping over the Leonine stuffiness and self-satisfied air from time to time. This sign is a good stabilizer for you.

Virgo may be just too serious for you to live with, moralizing where you explore, dismissing what you would justify. You do share intellectual interest and can have great lengthy discussions, but often your moral and ethical views do not coincide. The physical relationship can be tricky as well, timing always seeming to be off. Virgos (males and females alike) are notorious for the famed bedroom headache.

With Libra you are quite harmonious, although the instant rapport you experience may be diminished by the day-to-day happenings of marriage. The airy Libran nature is compatible with yours and serves to slow a frenetic Gemini down to a reasonable pace.

If contrasting qualities make for attraction, you and Scorpio have a marriage made in heaven. Challenges abound and do take their toll, but they are not insurmountable—thirty years from now your friends will be shaking their heads and wondering how you did it.

If you marry Sagittarius, one of you had better be rich. Plan to spend your life together as world travelers, or your mutual energy will start an atomic reaction. If your careers can blend you can handle each other's pace and have a lot of fun.

You had better take your time and search out the depths of Capricorn before deciding on marriage with this sign. On first impulse you may clutch at the stable social face of this earth native, but Capricorn deals in secret codes and careful pacing, and this could drive you crazy, Gemini. Capricorn does have down-to-earth qualities you can emulate to your benefit, but you are likely to spend all your time trying to find out what's going on in his or her mind.

Aquarius makes an adventurous, interesting partner for Gemini. You admire the Aquarian's long view and hard-driving mental habits, and this one won't let you take too much for granted.

Pisces can be even more elusive than Capricorn; expecting matter-of-factness, you repeatedly misinterpret what Pisces is saying. This can be a nice physical relationship, and a pleasant one socially, but just try getting dinner made. . . .

The get-up-and-go of Aries fits your style; and even the confrontational attitude of this fire sign suits you most of the time, fitting with your verbal orientation. You do, however, squirm under too much pressure and may be too evasive to satisfy Aries' demands.

Neighbors make the best enemies, and Taurus sits right next to you on the zodiacal wheel. It's too easy for you to bait, mislead, and outrun Taurus, although you are attracted to this earth sign's stability and sensuality. Taurus wants you to behave, likes to be apologized to—and may not be your permanent cup of tea.

With another Gemini the energies are similar to what you would find with a Sagittarian—the atmosphere around you may leave others breathless, but to you it's home. You need to set up quiet times in which to feel calm and get your bearings, as most major problems facing Gemini stem from a too loose arrangement of managing the mass of detail created by the combination of your personalities.

BUSINESS PARTNERSHIPS

In business Gemini fares well when there is a definite structure to work within and coworkers who are congenial. You thrive on the mutual exchange of ideas; often a good plan comes to you out of a discussion with an associate or partner. Make sure your coworkers are not too cautious —this will keep you perpetually impatient—and also not too authoritarian in temperament—this will cause you to be rebellious and argumentative, always feeling cramped by the other's presence. Geminis do well as the visible representatives of a company, handling clients and the public in a friendly and competent manner.

HANDLING COMPETITION

You hate to lose, Gemini, but when you do you keep a cheerful face. You thrive on competition, which brings you to focus tremendous energy on whatever may be your chosen goal. Your even-tempered response to wins and losses gains you allies—a most useful practice in business.

OPEN ENEMIES

Gemini's energetic verbosity can alienate or anger others easily, but usually you can restore calm just as quickly if you choose. You have a tactful touch, which you employ or withhold depending on your opinion of the person you are dealing with. Your weak point is gossiping to uninvolved parties, revealing the secrets and confidences of others. You undoubtedly know by now that displeasure results from this, but still your tongue tends to be loose. Try not to be too glib when confronted; adversaries will cool off much more quickly if they feel that you are taking them seriously.

CANCER

THE OPTIMUM PARTNER

Cancer's best partner is one who responds to this native's expressions of mood and is sympathetic and consoling without pampering. Cancerians will take what they can get in that department. It's best to be matched with someone who will give what is needed but not pour it on. You need a clear view of your own needs and limitations, so that your inner world and that of your mate remain well defined. A good partner for you is one who takes reasonable stands and sticks by them.

MARRIAGE

Marriage, home, and family are closely tied together for Cancer. In other respects you may be radical, but as regards domestic life you are comfortable with traditional ideals and practices. To have a satisfying home environment is so important to you that you will separate from a husband or wife for the sake of entering or searching out a preferable situation. Within the marriage relationship you expect to work to build up a safe haven in which you feel at ease and insulated from the anxieties of the world.

MARRIAGE WITH THE DIFFERENT SIGNS

Marriage with one of your own signs has many advantages in the way of mutual understanding and a basically common approach to life. The drawback is that you may lose objectivity about your own behavior, a problem that is multiplied by the combination of two watery natures. Squabbles are frequent, though not necessarily of the serious variety, if you don't mind the noise.

Leo puts on display what Cancer hides away for later—so you may feel that your Leo partner is always in the spotlight. Leo inevitably takes the lead, and it is hard for Cancer not to resent this. But regardless, you share much in the way of emotional communication and both of you put a lot of energy and love into the relationship.

Cancer and Virgo make a nice match; both have a certain inclination toward quietness and introversion and are thoughtful partners—as well as having a crabby, somewhat nit-picking side. Usually you manage to trade off on bad spells, each one cheering or tolerating the other, and most of the time that relationship is a comfortable and harmonious one.

With Libra you are likely to have a calm surface with turmoil underneath. Libra doesn't engage Cancer in enough of a showdown to really express grievances. Cancer doesn't receive assurances as to boundaries on behavior and can become overly complaining. You may feel that you are in a patient-analyst relationship rather than a marriage.

If you wed a Scorpio, there may be times when you have knots in your stomach due to wondering what he or she is doing. But as you share watery natures, the Scorpio motives won't escape you for long. In the long run things will probably turn out fine; this marriage can rise above its ups and downs.

Sagittarius always seems to be shooting arrows into your sensitive hide. This doesn't exactly make for the quietest of homes, but both of you solve problems and ease tension through a great mutual sense of humor. All the possibilities for longevity are in this relationship, including ways to slow Sagittarius down for security-minded Cancer and to toughen up Cancer's sensitivity to those unintentional ego-deflaters this fire sign is always coming up with.

You draw out much that is good in Capricorn; this sign is your zodiacal opposite and is quite complementary to your personality. Capricorn may not be too thrilled over the mutual revelations of gut-level emotion that go along with marriage to Cancer, but if this hasn't prevented the marriage, it's not likely to end it, either. You appreciate the depth of this earth sign.

Aquarius doesn't trample your feelings as blithely as Sagittarius but is less likely to feel apologetic afterwards. This air native will insist on completing a discussion down to the last detail. Actually, this is good for you, Cancer, because you can get into the habit of not discussing enough. This is a strong relationship, though not necessarily an easy one.

Don't get lazy if you have just married a Pisces. There are immediate problems that should be tackled for future harmony. Together you weather much by holding tight and seeing where the wind takes you. Pisces is a bit scattered to your way of thinking; you have a stronger focus.

With Aries things are stormy. But, of course, making up is fun. This relationship is the hackneyed picture of the red-faced man and the strident wife. Learning to control your tempers is a lesson you both need— it could be said that you deserve one another.

Cancer and Taurus make for a homey atmosphere; both are softies at heart. You may need to convince your manipulative Taurus to use more above-board tactics or at least to be more communicative. But since you've been known to sulk till you get your way, this twosome may work out very nicely.

Cancer plus Gemini equals lots of lively fun, although for the Cancerian it may be nerve-wracking much of the time. Gemini teases you, particularly about your phobias. This speedy air sign cannot take things as seriously as you do. You will probably end up dropping some of your rituals in order to keep pace.

BUSINESS PARTNERSHIPS

You have a protective sense toward your business colleagues, although this is somewhat held in check by a suspicious streak regarding their motives. You can be rather petty in matters of protocol, causing rifts with associates. Unless you are quite shy, you will speak your mind and welcome discussion in which the views of partners can be heard along with your own. Don't take their criticism personally—realize that they, like you, are working to make the business prosper. It is reasonable to expect that each one's point of view, yours included, will be modified in a partnership or group effort.

HANDLING COMPETITION

You are not comfortable in on-the-spot, one-to-one competition where all can see and judge. This may make you avoid necessary testing and proving of yourself, which could further your own interests. You do have a vengeful side to your character, which needs to be contained as more often than not, it will cause only trouble. When threatened you hold firmly to your own stand. You will also defend friends and business partners against their adversaries.

OPEN ENEMIES

You go out of your way to avoid confrontations. Your distinct loyalties make you very aware of the "other side," and you never forget an insult. Once things have cooled down you would just as soon leave well enough alone, but you will always have in mind the tactics you wish to use in the event that trouble recurs.

LEO

THE OPTIMUM PARTNER

Leo's optimum partner is very responsive, one who freely expresses his or her feelings about what Leo says and does. Leonians judge their own importance by the reactions of others; a native of this sign needs someone with a sharp mentality who presents challenges of new ideas and astute evaluation. Leo enjoys being able to discern what is really going on with a partner, recognizing what is put-on behavior and what is for real.

MARRIAGE

Watch out, Leo, for a tendency on your part to be attracted to surface glamour in marriage—a situation that has all the socially approved appearances but no real substance. You love to be correct in the eyes of society and to be admired by all. You are loyal to the idea and vision you have of marriage and will push to make them manifest, sometimes to the detriment of the relationship itself.

MARRIAGE WITH THE DIFFERENT SIGNS

In marriage with another Leo things are fine if your ideals are similar; if not, neither of you is likely to change course. Compromise makes or breaks this relationship. Both will want to pursue a chosen career or lifestyle that may be more important than making a marriage work.

If you and Virgo are both traditionally minded, this match falls into a comfortable pattern, particularly if the man is Leo and the woman Virgo. Otherwise, or if the signs are reversed, Virgo's lack of self-advertisement annoys Leo; and a meek Virgo may cling too much—even for the adulation-loving Leo.

Libra shows you a greater scope for your actions, although this air native may not be decisive enough for you, which you interpret as lack of trust. You are able to assist each other with many things, having both similar and complementary abilities.

Tough-minded Scorpio will expose your follies and puncture your Leonian pride. You and this water sign appreciate each other's strong will, but perhaps this one is best admired from a distance, although a strong sexual attraction may make doing so difficult.

You and Sagittarius have a jolly old time. You enjoy each other's penchant for overstatement and usually don't take each other to task for it.

Sagittarius may be a bit restless for Leo but can serve to pick up your pace in a positive way.

A scholarly Leo may find Capricorn attractive, but more often than not you will see this sign as being a wet blanket. Your expansive self-revelations embarrass stolid Capricorn. This combination provides a wide spectrum of interests if it can be lively enough for you.

With Aquarius you have many dramatic moments and much pathos. This relationship can weather just about everything, both of you being dedicated to the ideals of marriage and living them out when the partner is the right one. This is a quick-moving fire and air mix, trading off on strengths and weaknesses, bringing surprises to both.

Leo will chafe at the slow transitions of Pisces, which seem to you to be vagueness. You prefer confrontation to Pisces' rather evasive wait-and-see approach. A mature Piscean has much to offer you in the way of a wider and more objective outlook—water and air are considered to be the rational signs.

You share with Aries a vital, fiery optimism, but both of you are also great sulkers. You can benefit from Aries' wide range of interests and experience.

Leo and Taurus trade withering insults and huffy complaints. If your backgrounds and careers are in alignment, this can be a strong and durable match despite obstacles. However, both your fixed natures need these external similarities in order to jell together.

Leo enjoys Gemini's agility in resolving seeming impasses; the attraction here is pronounced but may prove to be superficial. Gemini's objectivity and attention to detail aid you in putting domestic matters into perspective.

Both Leo and Cancer want all the attention. Some of your gestures, which are fine for you, don't satisfy Cancer. Emotional misjudging is the biggest problem here. You toughen Cancer up in a way that is beneficial; after a while, this water native should know and be secure in your admiration—if you always make sure to show it.

BUSINESS PARTNERSHIPS

You are generous with your time and effort in business partnerships, and the success of an enterprise is vital to your self-esteem. You may tend to draw too much influence to yourself, as when prestige is involved. However, it is hard for Leo to know when he or she is on overload. You are loyal to legal agreements and sensitive over issues of rights.

HANDLING COMPETITION

In competition Leo always rises to a challenge, appearances being of prime importance. It is possible for you to put too much of an emotional stake in areas that are not vital. Losing comes hard to Leo, but you keep a dignified face regardless. Exercise restraint in the social arena, as you can be in danger of losing an objective self-image and speaking or acting foolishly to your own chagrin.

OPEN ENEMIES

In an adversary situation Leo draws together his or her social circle for aid. This is natural and helpful, but be aware that a clique-type leaning does not get out of hand, causing you to see enemies where there are none or to magnify disagreeable situations into more importance than they deserve. Your stubborn nature does not let you give in easily to conflict. Once wounded, you do not forget, although you are often quite naive concerning the motives of others until they have grossly misled or wronged you.

VIRGO

THE OPTIMUM PARTNER

For you, Virgo, the best partner is someone with whom you share quiet and meditative times, and with whom you have intellectual interests, vocation, or hobbies in common. Someone a bit more verbose than you draws you out of yourself, as does a partner who likes to be active and moderately on the go. A Virgo man needs a mate who won't pamper him and who isn't always trying to fix what she perceives as being wrong with him. A Virgo woman is best off with a man who is not the domineering or exploitive type, but who none the less will stand up to her critical comments, though without undue anger or pettiness.

MARRIAGE

In marriage Virgo seeks a shelter where he or she can straighten out kinks of emotions or mentality and protect and mold a family. This view may be too cozy to stand up to reality. Your view of home life as a situation where everyone is in dire need of your help will only bring resistance from loved ones. A harmonious atmosphere for you and your mate to maintain a mutual understanding—renewed consistently by discussion and sustained by affection—will create the safe haven you desire.

MARRIAGE WITH THE DIFFERENT SIGNS

If you should marry another Virgo, you can have a relationship that is mutually delightful, matching one another in habits and outlook. There may, however, be a certain closed quality in communication, which makes it difficult to unlock problems that need solving.

At first Libra looks very glamourous and warm to Virgo, but later you may see this air sign as a detached intellectual who stifles real reactions and responses. This is caused in part by your earthiness and sometimes acidic comments.

You and Scorpio are very different but can put together a relationship where differences work to mutual advantage. Scorpio may overawe you in the beginning, but you will come to identify with his or her passions and moods, as you view yourself as carrying a hidden inferno inside that no one sees.

With Sagittarius you converse well—and that's about it. This native infuriates you with half-finished projects, outrageous statements, and an impetuousness you regard as silly, though you do admire the verve and vision of this fire sign.

Capricorn shares with you a dry, literary wit and a near-worship of decorum—according, of course, to personal standards. You are both monogamous at heart, which makes for faithfulness and longevity in your relationship.

Virgo and Aquarius are the odd couple. Both have idiosyncratic patterns and phobias that the other cannot fathom, and each delights in exposing the foibles of the other. You can, perhaps, establish a better dialectical form of communication than any other pair of signs.

Virgo chafes at the leniency and gullibility of Pisces, but from the combination of your mutable natures, a happy liaison can result. You and your zodiacal opposite are both socially concerned and rely on instinctive responses to comprehend the needs of others.

Aries can be difficult for you in somewhat the same manner as Aquarius. Your fundamental impulses are quite different in quality, yet you admire Aries' level of activity, though you may see it as fools rushing in. You definitely see yourself in the angel role as opposed to your view of Aries.

You and Taurus both proceed carefully to reach solutions. However, each may have a bit of smugness regarding the other's shortcomings—without looking too closely at his or her own. This combination makes for a comfortable and relaxed sex life.

You dislike Gemini's restlessness and seeming duplicity and are not interested in the social flashiness this native exhibits as an air sign. You can, however, enjoy stimulating and knowledgeable conversation with Gemini.

In a marriage with Cancer you have a partner who shares your love for a secure and homey setting. Both of you are thin-skinned and will crab and snap to hide wounded feelings. If kind attention is given to one another, there is a nice blend; otherwise, there can be a continuous exchange of verbal sniping.

Virgo may fall for Leo's bravado and general display and then be disappointed to discover a mere human being underneath. Remember, Virgo, that it was you who indulged the fantasy! As neighboring signs you have much to give one another, but effort must be made to do so.

BUSINESS PARTNERSHIPS

In business relations you are conscientous and knowledgeable, tending toward the conservative. Partners and associates know you can be trusted, although you may hold on to suspicions yourself out of sheer caution. Hesitations and shyness are apt to cause losses for you in the way of making impressions; it may be good for you to have an up-front person as your partner in ventures that require much contact with the public.

HANDLING COMPETITION

Open competition is an ordeal for Virgo; you enter into it ruefully and nervously. You come through looking good in business and social tests by preparing in advance—your weak point being direct or unexpected confrontation. Often you can later think of a graceful gesture or kind word that would have been helpful, and will berate yourself at length for not having thought of it when needed. Your strongest point is conveying your honorable motivation to one with whom it counts, which will excuse much for you in the way of social reluctance.

OPEN ENEMIES

Virgonians insist that they have no enemies—and so ignore the need to take action to either forestall or defuse an impending social calamity. You do not wish to prepare for battle, and preparation is your strongest defense. The result of this is the very confrontation you abhor. Once hurt or insulted, you want to get even, although you may not acknowledge this. Those in an adversary relationship to you are people you see frequently yet who undermine your position through incessant criticism. Other foes include colleagues whose work fails to live up to your high standards and whom you have publicly accused or denounced in a fit of perfectionism.

LIBRA

THE OPTIMUM PARTNER

For Libra the most fulfilling partner is one who can share your interest in people, investigating their motives and behavior. A must, too, is someone who will take Libra to task for too much inconsistency and evasiveness, and who possesses a stable orientation in order to give assistance with frustrations and indecisiveness. Both men and women of Libran nativity are accommodating to the needs and desires of their mates, making the optimum partner for this sign a strong yet gentle person who can flow with Libra while, at the same time, providing something of an anchor.

MARRIAGE

Marriage is ruled by Libra. The nature of this sign is to share, to balance views and desires with one another. You will put your own preferences aside or sacrifice your own interests in order to make a relationship run more smoothly—the equilibrium of your marriage is your main concern. A permanent, monagamous relationship is extremely important to you, but you will not settle for less than what you want in a partner in order to have one—a marriage prospect must have much more for you than a casual affair could offer.

MARRIAGE WITH THE DIFFERENT SIGNS

When you are married to another Libra, your life is an endless sequence of accommodating gestures. "Please, after you!" "No, no, I insist—you first!" "Oh no, I wouldn't dream of it!" This does produce a harmonious household and maintains those nice feelings, but sometimes more action is needed than you two are inclined to make.

Scorpio seems quite uncooperative to Libra; your offers of conciliation don't move this water native. Scorpio moves on his or her own time. These two signs will keep a commitment to one another, but Libra may need periodic space to figure out what's going on.

You give too much rope to Sagittarius, and this sign will invariably hang himself. However, you are patient, and Sagittarius is endearing, and the lines of communication remain open. Remember that you can be more decisive—Sagittarius will accept it.

Capricorn, like Scorpio, seems to have a perverse resistance to your efforts to negotiate. Capricorn will discuss a matter with you but dance away just short of a resolution. Capricorn's idea of a harmonious life is a rigorous one, conforming to set patterns—this doesn't mix too well with your liberal ways.

Aquarius seems so cavalier about protocol and feelings—this sign just crashes right on through. If you resist the temptation to scold, your shared airiness reveals solutions. There is good mind-to-mind communication here.

"Quit bugging me," whines Pisces when Libra tries to uncover the reason he or she has been insulted, ignored, or laughed at. Pisces evades, and you don't pursue hard enough. Both sides are easygoing and can connect, but watch out for unresolved conflicts that surface unexpectedly.

Surprisingly, mild Libra and intense Aries can make a go of it; both seek balance as they view one another from opposite sides of the zodiacal wheel. Each can be irritated by the other, but there is mutual understanding and you know how to reach one another.

Taurus's dependence on habit and tradition frustrates you; yet you are pleased by the orderly, if idiosyncratic, slow pace of this earth sign. The mellow Taurean earthiness—even the rages—add necessary dimension for an air mentality. Similar backgrounds are always a boon in living with a Taurus.

Gemini likes to shine for your appreciation, and glitter can cover up problem areas through mutual appeasement where a showdown would be better. This is still an excellent combination, sharing mutual interests and artistic inclinations.

Cancer's irrationality is likely to drive you berserk. This sign can give you emotional depth, a frankly stated need for security, and a verbalization of fears—all traits you can learn and benefit from. Although a big romantic blaze is kindled here, long-term peace is hard to achieve.

Leo encourages and supports, pushes and directs Libra. It is better to break the habit of asking for this one's opinion! This is a good match; you can tone Leo down and demonstrate your fine communication tools.

You and Virgo bicker constantly over trivia. You may agree on all major issues and have great mutual attraction, but you can't seem to stop picking—two perfectionists in a detail factory.

BUSINESS PARTNERSHIPS

When choosing business partners, you have quite a good eye for those who will be of real help to you in furthering your interests. Often you allow them too much say-so, motivated by the desire to always be polite and fair. Your natural tact dissolves difficulties; in a group venture or association you will be the one who keeps the others from fighting.

HANDLING COMPETITION

Competition tends to unnerve you, being happier with joint efforts for mutual gain, or with contractual agreements stating the rights and responsibilities of all parties. Be careful not to allow yourself to slip into underhanded methods to avoid or minimize competitive strain. You are very much concerned with maintaining decorum and will sometimes sacrifice the winning position—with relief—in order to sustain or restore calm and cordiality.

OPEN ENEMIES

Rather than engage in hostility with others, you let off steam in other ways, choosing avenues of artistic release or even just talking to yourself. It is hard for you to admit your own part in creating a problem, as you do not wish to be associated with disharmony—even in your own eyes. You are adept at rallying friends to your case, making the position of your adversary appear unfounded and unreasonable.

SCORPIO

THE OPTIMUM PARTNER

The best partner for Scorpio is one who has a delayed anger response, giving time to hear or make explanations and to resolve issues, making sure to calmly state what he or she has felt to be unreasonable. Scorpio's mate should not back down for fear of a flare-up, as matters will not improve without real communication and Scorpio doesn't respect timidity. This fixed water sign is not responsive to a quiet partner, one who is not restless or fidgety and knows how to be self-assertive.

MARRIAGE

Scorpio expects much from a mate, requiring a lot from yourself and others. Problems that arise in your marriage stem from fixations, attitudes kept hidden from your partner, which nonetheless govern your approach to life. These tend to take the form of intolerances, fixed views and goals, which you desire (without conscious thought) for your spouse to share. You have a deep commitment to the ideal of marriage and will work long and hard to preserve it.

Marriage with the Different Signs

Marriage with another Scorpio is powerfully good or bad, or can alternate between these extremes; generally there is no middle ground. Arguments between you are short and blunt, because you understand each other's motives all too well. Somebody has to start talking when there's a problem—proceed carefully and things will go well.

Scorpio plus Sagittarius is potentially the best match between neighboring signs. You become infused with the contagious energy of Sagittarius, and you have a pretty big store of it yourself. There is strong physical attraction here, and friendly companionship, although this sign's lack of precision bothers you.

You have the patience Capricorn requires, and this earth sign reciprocates as well as bringing wit and wisdom to help things move along. Personal manias and odd habits are mutually tolerated surprisingly well.

You admire Aquarius for the free-spirited and humanitarian qualities this sign is known for, but this is not often a basis for marriage. Light romance and humor can be scarce here. You meet—or collide—in sudden shifts and tangents; you can feel oppressed by Aquarius' penchant for analyzing ruthlessly where you would simply let things take their course.

Pisces works well with you in marriage; a Piscean lightens you up, loosens old habits. You have in this relationship the security that allows you to express yourself comfortably. Pisces may wander in the realm of ideas a bit much for your tastes, but don't push him or her to be molded into your own views—it won't work.

The influence of Mars shows up in your relationship with Aries. A lot of ground can be covered with many lessons learned—the heat is on high for all the changes you want to go through. You share a creative spark that can make for a very frank, knowing, sensual marriage, although each of you needs some time spent in solitude.

If you and Taurus can avoid the following type of discussion: "That's just like me, except . . ." this one will last because you and Taurus are just alike, except Scorpio carries security around in a little hidden box; Taurus identifies it with externals—and both are hidebound as only fixed signs can be! Both are willing to work problems through to a satisfactory resolution.

Gemini rattles your bones. If you respond to airy, inquisitive energy— good. But don't marry expecting Gemini to quiet down. This sign brings you an enjoyable parade of ideas and situations—it just all goes by too fast for you with too much nonstop activity.

Cancer will take you to task if you are garrulous, and you don't appreciate being taken to task. But through the empathy of water signs, this native has already predisposed you to compromise. A natural sexual responsiveness is here, but it needs communication in order to be kept free of knots, which arise through emotional misunderstanding.

There is a chemical attraction between Scorpio and Leo, and a simultaneous mutual respect for each other's needs in the way of private space and habits. But if there is not a good sense of pacing and issues are pressed too hard, collisions occur too frequently for comfort. Watch out for unexpressed lapses into unhappiness or depression that cause distance between you.

Virgo may seem petty and argumentative, but he or she will also show you how to ask for it. The perceptions Virgo has of inner processes and motives are similar to yours, and you appreciate this sign's earthy stability. You may be tempted to try to run Virgo's life, but don't do it—the reaction will be more than you bargained for.

You may have trouble feeling that you have really captured Libra's attention, but the style of this air native leaves you with the impression that you have been reduced to a type. These signs often share philosophical, spiritual, and artistic interests.

BUSINESS PARTNERSHIPS

You select business partners so carefully that you can let many acceptable people go by. Your instincts regarding the right choice, and whether current partners are treating you fairly or not, borders on obsessiveness. Your initial view is usually sound but you don't like to make the effort to modify or compromise. You value personal loyalties over paper legalities, and your own loyalty is unshakable, although you may quarrel or dispute methods with partners.

HANDLING COMPETITION

When challenged in competitive situations, you have an initial indignant attitude, which can cast a cloud over all involved, dissolving any atmosphere of friendly rivalry. You measure opponents microscopically, planning and scheming all angles and approaches. At your best you hold yourself to a high ethical standard and will not backbite or hold grudges; but if you are unfairly dealt with, you are relentless in your pursuit of retaliation. You are often quite disdainful of the social status resulting from victory; for you the personal satisfaction is the whole ball game.

OPEN ENEMIES

Scorpio will resort to threats and rudeness without a second thought when feeling insulted or wronged. You never forget such a blow and you are slow to forgive. Your reactions can be awkward, as you will sit and stew, distorting the real nature of the conflict and therefore your manner of dealing with it. Scorpio can be duplicitious with those he or she considers enemies—presenting a smiling face but wearing a grimace inwardly.

SAGITTARIUS

THE OPTIMUM PARTNER

You need a hardy, relaxed partner, Sagittarius, one who isn't frazzled by your enthusiasm, jocularity, bustle, and high optimism. The most suitable mate for you is someone who is capable of maintaining an overview of events and attitudes, who has much patience and knows how to apply the brakes to your Jupiterian excesses. This definitely is not to say that he or she should be a wet blanket. A good match for you must have some exuberant energy to expend, must be buoyant like you, and not hypercritical.

MARRIAGE

Sagittarians view marriage as an arena for growth. You may feel that it's all right to pursue outside needs—after all, you're still married, aren't you?—and still maintain a commitment to marriage ideals. However, it is an unusual partner who will agree, and you are likely to spread yourself too thin for any of the growth you have in mind. You like the idea of introducing your partner to new people, ideas, and places. Often you don't form a clear pre-nuptial picture of what you expect from marriage —but you love to be surprised!

MARRIAGE WITH THE DIFFERENT SIGNS

There's plenty of movement and excitement when you marry another Sagittarian, but don't let the momentum carry you apart without realizing that it's happening. Tempers and abuse fly in this relationship—as fast as humor and goodwill.

Sagittarius and Capricorn are one of the most difficult side-by-side matches. You leap and bound, but Capricorn gripes and grumbles and refuses to follow or come to your rescue. You both love to debate and engage in intellectual discussions together, testing out your favorite ideas, but Capricorn punctures too many of your Sagittarian balloons.

Aquarius helps you to pin yourself down and work on mistakes. This sign has the tenacity to stay with you through hours of discussion—you may even feel that he or she follows you too closely, as will surely be the case with your actions! You can find much enjoyment here, but don't take advantage or you may find yourself on your own when Aquarius has had enough.

You and Pisces are intrigued by one another, seeing each other as exotic. Pisces hedges and hesitates, though, and makes you feel that you are on display in a jar. This water person isn't the grouchy or critical type, but you sometimes think you would prefer it—then you could get him or her to talk more.

Aries challenges you by approximating your energy level as no one has ever done before. Your problem is synchronizing your surges into some semblance of mutual timing. There are spats in this combination, but little need for long, tiresome explanations. There is no boredom here.

Sagittarius and Taurus get along well, especially physically, with an easy attitude toward day-to-day worries. But you are likely to drop hints regarding Taurus' self-improvement, and Taurus has an authoritative air, which can be a perpetual mutual rankling, with you being disdainful and Taurus condescending.

In you Gemini finds the perfect audience to entertain and amuse. The similar commitment you and this native share in regard to marriage is hard to come by, though as often as not, this can make you both feel that a short-term arrangement is preferable! You and your zodiacal opposite see each other's inner workings clearly and identify with them.

Cancer always seems to be out of sorts about something you've done or said, and it's hard for you to understand why. Still, there is much you can learn from one another, which will cement your union. From you Cancer learns to be bold and take risks; from this water sign you learn consideration and nurturing.

With Leo a fiery competitive sense can get out of hand. Leo, constantly requiring attention, is one who can tame your restlessness. Avoid the rut of feeling that you are always the irresponsible one who makes mistakes.

Virgo wants to bring you down to earth but finds it hard to do so in a pleasant way. This sign acts too wisely—when obviously you are the one who has the view from the heights! Learning each other's language is the trick in this one.

Libra is an enjoyable match for you, having an appeal to your better sense that sways you. This sign can fall into a pattern of holding back, watching and waiting for your response; don't abuse this quality. Libra is more organized than you, and an attempt to rationalize your way out can be devastating.

You and Scorpio can manage to be together without seeing each other. Scorpio stays hidden until you show your true colors through all that bluster; this unnerves you, as you wonder why he or she doesn't offer more. Scorpio's seriousness can benefit you, building a solid marriage if exchanges are frequent, acknowledged, and responsive in tone.

BUSINESS PARTNERSHIPS

The Sagittarian charisma attracts many business colleagues from whom to choose a partner or partners. Discretion doesn't always come into play in forming an alliance—need this be said to Sagittarius? Partners admire your vision and enthusiasm, and resent having to handle details without much help from you and to mop up your messes. You may accept a less fixed, lower-paying placement in order to be with cordial associates and to retain your freedom of movement.

HANDLING COMPETITION

Your personal momentum is so engrossing that you can miss seeing that someone is in a competitive stance. You are good-natured, win or lose, although sometimes showing insecurity in snippy remarks that leave others more hurt than you intended. You recover easily even from a loss that stings, and are soon looking ahead to the next challenge.

OPEN ENEMIES

It is not unusual for Sagittarius to be taken aback by hostility on the part of another; you can see that this person is very serious about something you have done, but you can't see just what it was. More than likely, it was unintentional—your antagonist is undoubtedly smarting from one of your off-the-wall remarks or some inconsiderate treatment of his or her time. You may not be able to assess what the proper response should be, but you are not short on resilience or imagination. You can leave the problem behind in the dust, building up a whole new framework in which to deal with this bewildered person faster than he or she can pursue you to tear down the old one.

CAPRICORN

THE OPTIMUM PARTNER

Capricorn's most suitable partner has a perceptive sense of humor and is willing to give you time to put together responses—whether verbal or active. The best bet for Capricorn's mate is someone with energy to draw out this reserved earth native, but who also enjoys having an independent side and does not cling too much. You need a partner who will support your professional life and goals but is not obsessed with status and signs of privilege; you can rely too much on these and should have a balance in the attitude of your husband or wife. You are happiest with a quiet person, though one who appreciates your humor and also provides some.

MARRIAGE

You may allow social standing or wealth to be the main factors in choosing a marriage partner, but you have a powerful romantic bent. You can be idealistically naive in this, having in mind a perfect partner who combines the romantic and social elements you desire. Although you are traditionally minded, you prefer divorce to drawn-out marital difficulties —your respect for institutional authority makes this acceptable. Many Capricorns wait to marry until somewhat later in life than other signs, to allow themselves time for schooling, career, or just getting enough of being single.

MARRIAGE WITH THE DIFFERENT SIGNS

Marriage with another Capricorn isn't a bad idea; you are sympathetic to each other's needs for quiet and independent activity. The romantic interest is there, though perhaps not in a blazing way; if personal cycles coincide the home fires are kept lit. Another Capricorn may be the only one who appreciates your criticism.

With Aquarius both partners see the marriage as a challenge—and it is. Aquarius pokes you, leads you on, rebels against your sensible rules and habits. You can use the loosening up but perhaps not the constant warfare.

Capricorn finds an understanding and complementary partner in Pisces. Pisces never presses you on decisions but expects the concern and care you are glad to provide. Don't berate Pisces for being too easygoing —you can stand to let a bit of it rub off on you.

Aries startles you with snap moves and judgments. You envy the ground Aries can cover, but are too reflective yourself not to see immaturity and bad decisions on the part of this fire sign—and you let Aries know it. This becomes a running battle, if not held in check.

Capricorn respects form and tradition; once you have found Taurus you have these to your heart's content. You and Taurus are a beautiful match, dedicated mutually to the ideas of romance, marriage, humor— and the will to succeed.

If you get Gemini to stand still or coalesce it will be the feat of the century. Gemini changes from day to day and you find this unforgivable. Despite the glamour, charisma, and the promise of challenges to meet, Gemini may not give Capricorn enough to hold on to.

You and Cancer recognize one another's need for security and articulate expression. This water person may fret over what you consider trivialities, but he or she is a good listener and a great source of feedback for your ideas. Both of you alternate between quiet and talkative moods, creating a nice balance.

Capricorn admires Leo's self-confidence and no-nonsense attitude. You are willing to be very supportive emotionally and financially, but watch that you do not channel all your energies into furthering Leo's interests, as you are bound to become discontent, hold grudges inwardly, and develop erratic behavior. Leo brightens you up.

As fellow earth signs, you and Virgo are able to let one another's quirks go unnoticed and take the exceptional right in stride. Count your blessings, Capricorn—Virgo will need your attention but not in obvious, direct ways; you will be free to give it in your own manner.

You admire Libra's social ease but are surprised to discover insecurity underneath; you take this as a sign of weakness and tend to be unsympathetic to Libra's concern for the balancing and blending of points of view. Your shyness resists the outgoing qualities of this air native; you do love the Libran talk and perspective.

If you and Scorpio take time to understand each other, a marriage can work. There will be run-ins, but rarely in a hair-tearing, shouting match. Hours or even days can pass without a word being spoken—this is fine, as long as you check in with each other periodically and not let dark feelings linger. Don't maintain a Capricornian shield of apparent unconcern.

"Now, what've you done?" you ask Sagittarius, hand on your brow. You see your own motives as possibly irrational but justified by tradition and habit; you find no such justification for the motives of Sagittarius, and often he or she can't explain, either. All the same, this sign will pick you up and regenerate you.

BUSINESS PARTNERSHIPS

Capricorn is the original shrewd, competent executive. Others willingly allow you the helm; you can jeopardize this by feeling too infallible, shrugging off or ignoring what is offered by needed friends and compatriots. It is easy for you to fall into taking on too much responsibility, becoming overloaded, particularly by personnel problems. Learn to delegate some of the work to partners.

HANDLING COMPETITION

You are rather grim about competition, not given to vengeance but digging in with all your strength. You marshall your resources, casting aside any notions of leniency. Slow and steady wins the race—the tortoise must have been a Capricorn, too. Obsessive secrecy won't help you.

OPEN ENEMIES

In a showdown you don't back away; you go at it tooth and nail. Others are surprised at how, minutes after punching it out with an adversary (usually this means on a verbal level), you drop the matter totally and are prepared for business as usual. You can unwittingly cause rifts by having your whole focus on your own world, neglecting simple acts that would prevent trouble.

AQUARIUS

THE OPTIMUM PARTNER

The best marriage partner for Aquarius is someone who moves with this sign's radical shifts in direction pertaining to career, politics, or artistic ambitions. Aquarius' mate needs to be flexible, not too reactive, to give time for the far-out Aquarian sails to lose wind and then gently help steer toward a middle path. He or she should share with Aquarius a wide-ranging curiosity and the adaptability to new situations, which is a characteristic of this sign. Most of all this versatile person needs to be able to pierce the rational persona of Aquarius and see the emotional nature underneath—the one Aquarius is forever describing and can sometimes obscure with description.

MARRIAGE

Aquarians quite often have multiple marriages, seeing each one as working at a different stage. An erratic type of Aquarian will grumble about decisions, feeling convinced that no solution is possible, and then let the partner do the deciding. Otherwise Aquarius keeps issues in the spotlight, working on them until resolved. By flying in the face of what others assume are right choices, you put yourself on the line regarding marriage, often selecting a bizarre companion to prove a point socially—resulting in anything from an astonishing success to a catastrophe. Your intuition has probably provided you with a feeling of what marriage should be for you; if you hold to this, neither settling for less nor building it up into an impossible ideal, you can make a strong, lasting marriage.

MARRIAGE WITH THE DIFFERENT SIGNS

Aquarius plus Aquarius can be the perfect combination or a bore—you tend to lose objectivity regarding your own thoughts and actions, becoming a single Aquarian unit. If you can keep synchronized, you can stand each other's pace; otherwise you are mutually disruptive.

Pisces will question your goals and be maddeningly noncommital. Although you share the same interest in new trends and experimentation, your daily habits and moods generally work against each other. Your meeting ground is the realm of ideas, not the practical world.

Aries' surges of energy and creativity match your own, and this fire native will try to derail you if you are too obstinate. You have instant friendship with Aries; sometimes this combination works better remaining just friends or in a short-term romance, due to your both having restless natures. If you meet when both are ready to settle down, there is a good foundation on which to build.

Taurus is someone with whom you can match wills. This sign pulls you down to earth and tests your ideals face to face. Your conceptions about marriage can differ greatly, and it can be too difficult for you to reconcile.

There is a charismatic attraction between you and Gemini; you need to pause to see if your fellow air sign is what you thought you saw at first glance. You and Gemini can talk things over thoroughly and harmoniously in situations that would turn into disputes with most others.

A need for a safe inner circle, sometimes nearly invisible to Aquarius, is satisfied by Cancer. You draw Cancer out, which is beneficial to this water person—but can you live through it? Cancer evades, pouts, complains, or enthusiastically joins in with you, never knowing which till it happens.

With Leo there is an immediate challenge and an immediate physical spark. This fire sign will force you to be consistent with—and often to restructure—the priorities of your spoken goals and commitments. This is one sign that won't try to hide from your searchings and observations.

With Virgo you experience being brought to heel, standing still to undergo Virgo's explanations of how and why you have hurt and offended this earth sign—and it bugs you. Virgo's tendency to be self-disparaging is also annoying to you. He or she does have a good eye for social relations, and you can fill time together with interesting talk. The romantic tie is nebulous and needs much attention to remain accessible.

You and Libra are harmonious; you enjoy being able to take a stand representing both of you. Libra will assist in formulating policy but is content to let you be the shock troops. You will need to take time to make sure that your straight-ahead manner is not abrasive to Libra's sensitivities, particularly regarding sexuality.

Scorpio has a magnetic effect on you, which is just fine with Scorpio. Watch out that you don't put yourself in a slavish relationship to this

one; Scorpio will either ignore you or move right along with the dominant role. Make sure your stands on issues are the ones you really want
to make; Scorpio will let you thrash about until you surrender through
exhaustion, and for Aquarius this is no easy matter.

Aquarius and Sagittarius share an open viewpoint, although Sagittarius may hide controlling patterns that you can't accept once you see
them. The optimistic, adventurous nature of this sign appeals to your
own love of expansion. Sagittarius is less willing than you are to stick to
resolutions.

You are infuriated by Capricorn's irrational reliance on accepted form
and ingrained habits. If Capricorn shuns social glitter you admire, identify with and enjoy this individualistic stance. If he or she is an aggressive
climber, you criticize what to you is a crassly materialistic attitude. Peaceful interaction is hit and miss.

BUSINESS PARTNERSHIPS

Aquarius should join with business partners who understand and can
work with your bursts of energy, who appreciate your attraction to new
ideas and methods and see ways to benefit from them. Your choosing
ability can be hampered, basing choices on ideology rather than the real
potential for mutual cooperation. You thrive on the exchange of ideas
and interactive feedback afforded by working closely with others and are
usually happier with a partner or partners than on your own.

HANDLING COMPETITION

You tend to stiffen up in competitive situations, being too intent on and
critical of your own performance. You don't resort to insult, petty attitudes, or dishonesty and are deeply disappointed to encounter these in
others. You have no bone to pick with competitors but may feel that
those who are in a position to judge are incompetent or biased.

OPEN ENEMIES

When Aquarius makes enemies, it is through being outspoken and stubbornly refusing to move from a position or opinion. You work through
negativity much faster than most, leaving anger behind while the other
person is still hurling invectives in your direction. You are willing to
argue a point through to its resolution, believing in the power of words
to solve problems. You are not a planner or schemer of strategy; you rely
on improvisation and an element of surprise, which affects you as well
as your adversary.

PISCES

THE OPTIMUM PARTNER

The optimum partner for Pisces is imaginative, to match and blend with
the Piscean imagination, and is also someone who can step back and act

as a stabilizer, not pulled into phobias or fantasies generated by you. A talkative type is fine, though not critical or gossipy in a way that is directed at Pisces, who would respond by withdrawing for long periods of time. Pisces' mate needs to be self-motivated regarding improvements and changes, as Pisces generally won't push for these. A romantic, impulsive person suits the Piscean temperament, as does someone with artistic talents and learnings.

MARRIAGE

Without realizing it, Pisces, you may prize your independence so much, enjoying life at your own pace and in your own style, that you actually avoid marriage, thinking of it as an eventual bond rather than an immediate possibility. You have lofty, if somewhat vague, ideals and expectations regarding this commitment; it will be helpful to you if you articulate them to yourself—writing them down is a good way—as this will assist you both in choosing a partner and in living with one. When you do meet a strong marriage prospect, explain what you have concluded and stick to it. Otherwise you can easily find yourself looking for a new mate not long after settling in with the first one.

MARRIAGE WITH THE DIFFERENT SIGNS

Perhaps marriage with another Pisces is too much of a good thing. Both may avoid confrontations, not wanting to waste time in petty quarreling, but legitimate issues should be resolved. If neither of you brings your discontent into the open, you will drift apart, the source of the problem becoming increasingly hard to define.

Not all Aries people are warmongers, Pisces, and you do have an inpetuous side yourself. The problem here is that there's no one to put on the brakes. You can have delightful times, but Pisces can lose touch with Aries through the differing natures of these two signs.

The daydreaming side of Taurus and this sign's appreciation of beauty agree with your Piscean nature. Although Taurus is stubborn, you find it easy to move him or her through an intuitive sense of motives and patterns. However, don't get into manipulating Taurus, as you'll soon become bored. This is usually a good combination sexually.

Gemini's perpetual motion and constant mental engagement absorb you to the point that you can lose focus of your own needs. Although you love all that spontaneity and curiosity, you are always having to fend Gemini off. It is too easy for Gemini to talk you into things.

Cancer's grumpy moods reflect a perception of troubles that you might miss; don't discount them automatically without listening. This combination tends toward a quick courtship; you provide one another with mutual support against a big, troublesome, non-watery world.

You are simultaneously attracted and put off by the vibrancy and strutting of Leo. Your signs, though dissimilar, make strong connections. You need direction and plain speaking on your part, and calmness, caution, and an attempt at foresight on the part of Leo.

You divine Virgo's convoluted intentions, habits, and reasoning; this sign has the knack of drawing exact descriptions and explanations from you—no small accomplishment! Your physical relationship may be slow in reaching a mutually satisfying peak, but both you and Virgo have the patience and willingness needed to get it there.

Libra casts a discerning eye on your silences and is sympathetic to your idealism. This sign is outgoing toward all in a democratic manner that may ruffle your feathers—you want a feeling of specialness and uniqueness. You and Libra may not be direct enough with each other in solving problems.

Storms ensue from the combination of Scorpio's drive and intensity and Pisces' contrariness and tendency to be haughty when confronted. However, your watery nature enables you to weather and accept the contrary waves of this relationship. Don't hover over Scorpio; take him or her seriously enough not to offend.

Sagittarius is forever dropping those well-intentioned critiques that sting sensitive Pisces. The self-righteous, pompous air of Sagittarius can make you unwilling to engage in the necessary give and take that make a relationship work. Sagittarius does respond to your creativity and impulsiveness.

With Capricorn you get the chance to play the engaging, mood-lightening fool, and it is a pleasant role for you. Make sure that Capricorn returns the favor—you will probably fare better than this earth native as you are able to pass by grumpiness and eccentricities. You can share with Capricorn the quiet, devoted life you both love.

Aquarius may press you too closely. Both of you are prone to tangents and oblique reasoning, but Pisces is hard-pressed to maintain contact with the Aquarian's twists and turns. Often this is a romance that does not lead to marriage.

BUSINESS PARTNERSHIPS

You have a quickly synthesized overview that is valued by more detail-minded people and makes a good complement for them in business partnerships. These organized types are the ones you work with best, providing the routine necessities while you supply the imaginative input. Your hunches and intuitions are tempered by their caution or confident risks. Don't get wound up in a private universe, because partners will either just walk away or walk away with your business.

HANDLING COMPETITION

Slight of hand on the part of Pisces can defeat a challenger before he or she knows what has happened. Only an extremely timid Piscean runs and hides, but most natives of your sign conceal their moves and responses when feeling threatened. You never forget enmity shown toward you, although grudges and spiteful retaliations are rare. However, you always remain wary of one who has dealt with you in a hostile fashion, preventing the chance of a repetition. When faced down, you are articulate in stating what has hurt or offended you and why.

OPEN ENEMIES

Open enemies? The Piscean doesn't have any. Why? They prefer secretive, behind-the-scene backstabbing, while out in the open everything is sweetness and light. If they must fight, a Piscean will use every trick of the underdog. If fact, they are so successful with this role, they may find that after victories a loss is needed just to get back their equilibrium.

Chapter Eight
Transitions

ALL INTIMATE ENCOUNTERS, life passages, and joint enterprises unfold in this eighth house of mystery. How willing are you to merge your assets and share your confidences with others often sheds light on how rich you feel within, the depth of your self-confidence and, therefore, your generosity of spirit. For this reason, negotiatons and compromises are the outward manifestations of how secure one really feels.

Financial dealings are also reflected here; actually, all types of mergers should be assessed against this backdrop. Why? In all long-term financial relationships, you are best advised to look to the person behind the venture, rather than at the venture itself. How the signs respond to unconscious motives can be glimpsed in this section. You can also look at this portion of the chart to tell about a person's sexuality.

Although inheritances really have as much to do with others' actions as one's own, don't overlook the opportunities, which may not be strictly financial in nature, that you face. Recommendations, promises, and legacies, involving heirlooms rather than trust funds, can be uncovered. There are possibilities for inheritances aside from those gained through relatives: scholarships, grants, and just plain hand-outs come in the ways indicated by this chapter.

In astrology you determine the amount and the frequency of your luck, and this area of your life is no exception. It is just as impossible to tell if someone will inherit a million dollars or a thousand—a chart only reveals that it will appear to be a large sum of money to you.

This is the section of astrology devoted to endings of all kinds. But keep in mind that the symbol of this Scorpio house is the phoenix, rising from the ashes to soar above the clouds. For those who feel at the end of their ropes, depressed or disillusioned, guidelines presented here will be extremely useful.

ARIES

TURNING POINTS

Aries doesn't find it easy to let go of old patterns; especially if you feel that you have a score to settle with another party. You will tend to hang on until you are satisfied that things are finished according to your specifications. Advice won't budge you, nor will seeing the atmosphere change before your eyes into something quite different than what you have been accustomed to. Once you have gotten around to accepting the inevitable, you move to adjust and rebuild more quickly than any other sign, with the possible exception of Gemini. The mature Aries avoids a characteristic predisposition toward a persecution complex, setting off bravely for new adventures with the past firmly in the past.

INTIMACY

You may find that you are somewhat stiff and awkward in the initial stages of a romance or when you first become part of a social crowd. You are keeping the cap on a volatile emotional and sexual nature until you feel enough at home to express yourself without worry. You need someone who responds with equal fervor; otherwise you can develop a falsely bloated ego around the idea that you are simply too powerful and overwhelming for the other person to handle. In a secure setting your drive can be channeled into affection and tender, considerate actions, replacing the bluster of the courting stage.

RELATIONSHIP ENDINGS

When confronted with endings, Aries all too easily resorts to an attitude of self-pity, unreasonably lashing out as if the ex-partner or associate had done everything out of vindictiveness. Actually, it is this stance of the angry victim that is vituperative. On the good side, Aries is adventurous and willing enough to move along when it's over and begin a new venture—or a new life. You will face an ending realistically as long as you are able to put together a romantic view of your new freedom with which to console and inspire yourself.

NEGOTIATIONS

Negotiations are often sore spots for Aries—they are all points of honor and hurt feelings. You can benefit greatly from enlisting the aid of tried and true friends in such situations, or from obtaining legal help when it is appropriate, relying implicitly on them. Remember that a reputation of being willing to bargain will bring more opportunities to you.

JOINT FINANCES

Your initial eagerness for investments and deals must be tempered with reason; another opinion, preferably that of a totally disinterested person as far as the deal itself goes, comes in very handy. You have as good a head for the figures as anyone and can be decisive where another sign would allow problems to accumulate through inaction. If you put these talents to work for you in money matters, you can go far. Keep in mind, particularly with your mate, that hesitation in spending and borrowing is not automatically a demonstration of poor financial sense. Often something that must be done immediately or lost is better forgotten, and friends and reputation are usually more valuable than a trip or toy you might be tempted to buy on credit. If you consider the views of a partner calmly, without having your mind made up in advance as to your response, and then decide on the basis of logic that his or her position is wrong—fine. The danger lies in disregarding any opinion that seems to go against your own inclinations without giving it a careful examination.

COMPROMISES

Compromise may be hard for you to swallow, Aries, but you are capable of seeing it as the best means to clear the decks for future action. You tend toward an all-or-nothing attitude; you should have it written on your wall in large letters that such a point of view always leads to nothing. Time shows you the legitimacy of the other person's position, particularly in romantic squabbles that take a bit of waiting before the dust settles. When you maintain your detachment, it becomes clear to you that an unbending stance only serves to prolong unpleasantness, which you are anxious to conclude. Often you will come out ahead by demonstrating your willingness to meet the other party halfway.

INHERITANCES

Aries usually does not make excuses for inactivity—indeed, you are seldom inactive for long enough to require them. This is a good thing when it comes to the possibility of inheritances—let it be business as usual regardless of the fact that you may inherit. A steady, conscientious attitude will attract this source of future security to you—showing off or a demanding attitude will not. No one is easier to refuse than an angry Aries. As a rule inheritances or money gifts come to you from unexpected sources or in larger amounts than you had expected. A project or creative work undertaken with your mate or partner can catch on commercially to your delighted surprise, or you may find a satisfying and lucrative position through your in-laws, constituting gifts that you put forth effort to receive, and as such are often the most rewarding. Aries is happiest when occupied. Even if you should come into enough money that it becomes unnecessary to work for a living, chances are that you will not become idle—you will simply take advantage of the opportunity to put your energy into something of your own choosing, which affords you personal satisfaction.

TAURUS

TURNING POINTS

Taurus doesn't like to be taken by surprise; the predictable outcome is always preferable to touch-and-go situations, which might be more exciting but are less safe. You will hang on for an unreasonably long time to outmoded relationships, attitudes, or personal habits simply to prove (to yourself as well as to others) that nothing and no one can force you if you don't want to change. You do not avoid confronting change or those who bring it, but you will contest it all the way if it is not what you have in mind. It is in the Taurean makeup to demand a voice in whatever is going on; often it is hard for you to accept that it may very well go on regardless of your agreement or disagreement. Taurus also can cultivate, with excellent results, a natural matter-of-factness and fatalism that acknowledges what has happened is now history and is probably supposed to happen.

INTIMACY

There is much pride involved in Taurus' romantic and sexual expectations, both for self and for lovers. You expect a great deal in the way of consideration from a partner, and you will not be trifled with. Behind a strong surface reliance on good performance, there is a very soft Taurean who treasures little gestures and gifts—simple and kind words—and has to learn not to demand so much. You tend to convince yourself that you must have things just so; you can make yourself miss out on much that is worthwhile if this position is unbending and unwilling to concede.

RELATIONSHIP ENDINGS

Admitting fault or wrongdoing is torture for a Taurus, who feels that simply to state, "I was mad," "I was jealous," or "I forgot" excuses his or her offense. A natural conservatism makes you stubborn when it comes to ending or resolving a situation, but it also keeps your mind's eye on problems—you won't rush out and leave your partner to bear the burden. Your deep romanticism lends marriage and live-in relationships a great importance to you that grows with time. You don't like to see these relationships destroyed, and realizing that a partner really intends to leave is often what finally causes you to make a long-resisted change in habits or attitude.

NEGOTIATIONS

Your point of view is that it is up to the other party to invite negotiations and to attempt to convince you of the rightness of their stances. When you are called on to defend yourself, particularly if you are accused of not making conciliatory efforts or of being unfair, your anger flares and peaceful Taurus becomes a charging bull. Watch out—often this criticism is justified. You don't look good in a rage and are slow to anger, but once aroused you cannot control your tongue and may say things you will regret for a long time afterward—as well as losing legal ground and alienating others.

JOINT FINANCES

Taurus enjoys money management as an activity in its own right. You like to feel on top of financial affairs, knowing what you have to work with. This also holds true for personal and family finances as well as those connected with your business. You can slip into the dangerous habit of regarding jointly held monies as exclusively your own, feeling that your mate or business is borrowing his or her share from you. Obviously, this creates a touchy situation if not courting disaster outright.

Cautious in all matters relating to investment, you may anger partners by blocking or delaying activities they are ready to engage in and by implying that their assessments of opportunities are inferior to your own.

COMPROMISES

When it comes to the necessity for compromise, Taurus regards everything from the standpoint of pride and saving face. Your thoughts, plans, and ideals are so concrete to you that to modify them is tantamount to requesting that the sun be dislodged and painted a different color. Practice, dear Taurus, having an analytical attitude that scans a proposal first —just because you consider compromise in your own mind doesn't mean that the other party knows you are "weakening." There is no need to feel threatened by the mere possibility that his or her offer is acceptable. The good side is that you won't make a move until you believe things are right for it—so you won't sell out your own interests (except through stubbornness).

INHERITANCES

The strong ties Taurus maintains with family members are almost certain to bring material benefit somewhere along the line. Don't lose this potential gain by taking a proprietary view of the possessions or assets of a possible benefactor. Your obvious respect for family tradition can bring you into the favor of distant relatives who develop an intuitive sense of trust in you as one deserving of the familial wealth. But don't wait around for it and show too much patience! Reveal yourself to be a deserving recipient through continuous diligence and careful stewardship of what you already have—this, not the anticipation of gifts to come, will make you a really legitimate heir.

GEMINI

TURNING POINTS

Gemini needs to develop a scale on which to measure changes and turning points, as these airy folk seem to be daily going through a whole new phase. You need to come up with a way to filter out the superfluous and determine how much of what is going on is mood shifting, how much is the opinion of others making themselves felt, how much is just sheer distraction from living on this planet. Focus on what is truly important in your personal cycles. You are quick to delineate what is going on inside you, be it in your family, education, or social life. However, maintaining willingness to take action to direct the process consciously is difficult.

INTIMACY

You are attracted by what is fresh and novel, but only the most distant Gemini doesn't respond to simple, heartfelt gifts and gestures from a familiar partner who wants to satisfy your desire for surprise. If it is not satisfied, or if you are still in a wild-oats stage of development, you restlessly seek new relationships, leaving behind those that seem too mundane or routine. Your charisma draws attractive lovers into your presence; stop for a minute to decide just what level of intimacy you really want with the next one before plunging ahead.

RELATIONSHIP ENDINGS

Gemini is great at beginnings; endings, not so great. You are not unconcerned with the feelings of your future ex-partner, so you drop hints in advance—subtle ones at first or big ones that cause him or her to panic —at which point you deny that any problem exists, not ready yet to make the final break, setting up even more unpleasantness to deal with later. If your warning signs are observed, the best the other party can do is often just to realize that you won't tolerate any impediment to your freedom, drifting along with you toward an ending. Gemini's problem is allowing this drifting to continue indefinitely, waiting for the other person to realize it's over—and possibly to make the break rather than your doing so. When it is you who is being dropped, especially if there have been efforts at reconciliation, you keep returning, in mind if not in body, to try to snatch moments of the old feeling back—showing the rarely seen Geminian desire for security.

NEGOTIATIONS

If you want to shine, Gemini, go to the field of negotiations, because you are a master. You have an inborn skill at and love of debate and barter. As a labor or management representative you are the best. In your own affairs you have a tendency to prolong family business and romantic matters longer than necessary, wanting to be sure that all facets are adequately covered. Chances are no situation can be talked into complete mutual agreement, so work at quickly reaching an active resolution, which is acceptable if not thrilling to all concerned. Be careful when taking on the role of negotiator for others, particularly couples—it is easy for you to take sides and lose good relations with one party or sit up nights giving the matter more attention than it is receiving from those who are actually involved.

JOINT FINANCES

Joint finances cause you some trouble because you like to see money produce results and are impatient when others would rather scrimp and save. As you see it, solutions are always at hand no matter how tough the spot you're in—so you are a good influence on the morale and optimism of financial partners. Besides, there's not a creditor alive who Gemini can't outrun; this bodes either a truly creative handling of finance or a life of hotel rooms and assumed names. Tread with care and make sure your mate or business associate(s) gets a real 50 percent say in things so that you don't get too carried away.

COMPROMISES

In trying to cover too many bases at once, Gemini can give away too much in terms of self-esteem and integrity. This is not necessary for a good compromise; try to limit yourself in commitments to friends, family, and others. Embarrassing sessions of confession, apology, and making new agreements will occur less frequently. Gemini is more willing than most to consider another's point of view; frankness on the part of the other person always brings out the best in you.

INHERITANCES

Gemini maintains faith that the right attitude will attract what is necessary for material wealth and security. It is rare that you will receive gifts or inheritances beyond your reasonable expectations, but the expected sources generally do come through. You may find yourself presented unexpectedly with business or social opportunities, which come your way in the form of real-estate dealings, recommendations by and to people in high places. These don't supply you directly with money, but with ways of using your talents and ingenuity to feather your nest, pleasing your quick mind by giving it something new to work on, or eliminating intermediate steps by putting what you desire in your hands.

CANCER

TURNING POINTS

For Cancer the approach of major change is marked by increased fretting and anxiety. You have trouble regarding turning points, even those that are going in your favor, with equanimity and rarely welcome them emotionally, even though your mind may tell you that the right thing is happening. The Cancerian temperament, naturally conservative, holds to the past. Although a change may be positive, it is equated for you with a loss of control over whatever the situation has been. The topic can be discussed with you, and you will see all points clearly—including those that show how the change will favor you—but still you must overcome a fear of losing your power over circumstances when the familiar becomes less familiar. You prefer to see such a transition take place one step at a time, but it may actually be better for you if it happens more quickly and is over before you have time to develop an ulcer.

INTIMACY

Cancer has a phobia about the exposure of intimate feelings and habits —things a mate or close associate should never bring into discussion with other family members or friends. A therapeutic situation is the only one in which it is wise for the inner workings of Cancer to have anything like a public hearing. The courtship state of a relationship, for male and female Cancerians alike, is what makes or breaks it. If it doesn't make it, there's usually nothing to break. A courtship manner, likewise, can determine the success of Cancerians as married people or lovers as well—

you never tire of seducing and being seduced, and the thrill of romance returns each time to deepen your relationship with your partner. The loud, pushy type turns you off; this one will never meet the inner you, regardless of how long you are acquainted.

RELATIONSHIP ENDINGS

Your aversion to change extends, of course, to endings—especially endings of relationships. This means on the positive side that: 1) you will talk and analyze for the sake of the relationship, 2) you take all relationships seriously, and 3) a normally shy Cancer will become frank to the point of embarrassment about both good and bad feelings when the stability of a relationship is threatened. On the negative side it means that you can hide behind the form of a relationship and take serious difficulties out on your partner with crabbiness and complaints rather than action, dreaming privately of various good and bad possible developments without working to solve the problem. Often you avoid displaying your discontent until late in the game when little chance remains to rectify the situation.

NEGOTIATIONS

Under your soft, compliant surface is a relentless negotiator; your cheerful attitude, real by all means and serving to put others at their ease, nevertheless masks a stalwart determination not to give in when it comes to essentials. Like your neighbor Gemini, you have a certain fondness for debate for its own sake (unless you are simply not a talkative Cancerian). Don't allow this to override a practical sense of when to stop. The love of sparring can drive away a mate or friend who needs a quieter environment, or put off business cronies who despair of reaching an agreement with you.

JOINT FINANCES

Cancer is prone to huge enthusiasms in financial schemes—too big, often, for partners or associates to lend their support to, alternating with fearful grasping and a pessimism that exceeds the normal bounds of caution. You look for that big break that will set you up for life—or anticipate moment by moment the crash that will end all hope. This makes it difficult for joint ventures and investments to be maintained on an even keel, as your partners become exhausted by your fluctuations. Learn to trust a financial advisor, business manager, or lawyer and the ups and downs will become much more manageable.

COMPROMISES

Letting go of your moorings and putting on the line your views and attachment to routines, past business practices, attitudes toward relationships—this is a frightening area for you. When you and another have finally gone through the process of reaching a halfway point acceptable to both, you are often (if not usually) pleasantly surprised at how pointless it was—much more so than your worry about it. In retrospect, the surrender of some issues for the sake of the healthy survival of something of value seems most sane and seemly. Try to remember this next time!

INHERITANCES

Whenever possible, Cancer maintains close filial ties, referring back frequently to relatives for advice, consultation, requests for and offers of aid. Through this closeness you always come to mind when estates are being divided up or prosperity shared. This often takes the form of real-estate holdings, heirlooms, valuables that reflect a strong sense of the continuity between generations and the strength of family unity. Be ready to work ungrudgingly with siblings, cousins, etc. on final allotments, keeping the air clear for future times when your opinion could well be the one that carries the most weight—something that can evolve from your creating about you a sense of fairness, practicality, and loving respect for the real value of persons and possessions.

LEO

TURNING POINTS

The basic axiom of Leo is to act on what you know and never remain ignorant of anything within your reach. When a life crossroad is reached, Leo is no more exempt from trepidation than anyone else, but this fire native will decide, act, and accept consequences. A less mature Leo still whines and insists that troubles come from without rather than within, if the road taken turns out to be a difficult one. However, experience will season this attitude until it evolves into that of a strong, truly lionlike Leo.

INTIMACY

Leo definitely has a softer self hidden inside his or her brash (or at the very least resolutely self-contained) exterior. Someone should warn your mate or lover, Leo, to watch for a self-congratulatory bravado that extends into the physical relationship; this reveals the part of Leo that is insecure and relies on the effect of showiness and surface confidence. You know what you want in a sexual relationship—this puts the responsibility on you to choose carefully (beware of trying to make a person fit into the mold of your preconceived, ideal partner) and to refrain from running roughshod over quieter, slower-paced types or dominating them simply because it is possible to do so.

RELATIONSHIP ENDINGS

Leo's pride gets in the way when it comes to the ending of a relationship. Although you are considerate of the feelings of the one from whom you are parting company, you are unyielding when you feel you have to go, and your consideration does not make you timorous about stating what your own feelings are. Sudden endings shatter Leo's composure; it is hard for you to moderate your response to the point where you can see what the causes have been and where the responsibility for the breakup really lies. When an ending has been decided upon, you handle the unraveling process well as long as the other person manages to stick firmly to his or her essential position—flip-flopping and vacillating infuriate you.

NEGOTIATIONS

You see the necessity for negotiating to reach mutually acceptable arrangements with others, but often you have trouble participating in them personally. This type of process contradicts your image of yourself in a role of power, the king or queen issuing edicts—to your mind the best way of resolving disputes. Counseling is probably your best recourse in marital difficulties, whether what is in question is the marriage itself or the division of property, custody, etc. In business situations things go more smoothly if you have an arbiter present and active; a partner or your lawyer should present your case and communicate your positions for you.

JOINT FINANCES

Leo is a firm advocate of loyalty to friends, family, and business. You will, in what some would regard as an unlikely fashion, often place too much trust in the handling of funds by friends. As you see it, you have bestowed the royal approval on these friends to dispose of the money as they see fit. On the positive side, your willingness to take risks pays off; when things go negatively, debts are accrued and friendships lost. The absolutely independent Leonian avoids joint financial activity altogether, missing out entirely on the benefits available from it, passing up opportunities, and aggravating his or her mate. Even Leos make mistakes, and a husband or wife whose opinion is ignored or blatantly unsolicited— and then turns out to be right—will usually not hesitate to point it out to you.

COMPROMISES

The perfectionist streak in Leo has trouble accepting a world where shades of gray must be lived with—clear black and white seem so much more desirable. Once a situation has been resolved, Leo can be counted on to play by the new rules. Although compromise puts stress on your sensibilities, you are forthright in spelling out your own needs and stating that certain problems call for resolution. Here you have something to teach more timid folk: nothing can be worked out until all parties concerned are aware of it.

INHERITANCES

The proud Leonian is not one to beg favors from rich relations. You earn the respect of those with holdings, as they are likely to shun those who grasp and scurry to ingratiate themselves, and welcome your presence as that of one who is not waiting for them to kick the proverbial bucket. Though no word is spoken, no promises made, unexpected wealth may well come your way from such contacts. Your aloofness asks people to take you as you are and they look past your faults to the integrity of this stance. Material benefit tends to come to you less often as cash than in stocks, investments, and accounts that are slow to mature, providing for you in later years and at crucial moments when most needed.

VIRGO

TURNING POINTS

Virgo's course of action when a turning point is reached is to hold back the emotional reaction until he or she has a chance to analyze and evaluate the different choices that are now possible. This is a fortunate and beneficial trait, Virgo, as your decisions don't suffer from impetuosity and you manage to take care of ramifications which more impulsive signs would have to look back on with regret at having failed to see them. On the other hand, you will often do what you see as your duty, not allowing personal fulfillment or emotional satisfaction to enter the picture—and thereby miss out on important sustenance for yourself. You are able to make decisions quickly, though you may prefer to hesitate before taking action, letting circumstances decide for you.

INTIMACY

It may seem to many people that Virgo has no real intimate life with others; all discussion of sexuality, anger, even happiness, takes place in the abstract as if it made no difference to you what your share of these things might be. As long as issues can be settled philosophically for the world at large, you seem to say that no problem remains over which to be troubled. The truth of the matter is that you have a soft, caring nature —in romance particularly—but this will disappear each time you have drawn close to someone if you insist on submerging it beneath a surface of unconcerned invulnerability. If you conceal your needs and desires, playing the martyr, resentment will set in at their not being met—without the other person's ever having known what was missing. Indeed, if someone intuits correctly the way to your heart, you will often deny that he or she has found it, bringing disappointment and frustration to you both. Stop that practice!

RELATIONSHIP ENDINGS

It is rather hard to take Virgo by surprise; endings, though they may sadden you, don't often come as a shocking blow. You may not reveal your perception that an end is at hand to your mate or partner, or even consciously to yourself; a certain timidity when it comes to converting knowledge into action may cause you to allow yourself or another to slide into dissatisfaction without taking decisive steps to improve matters or prevent a break. Virgos are very concerned with proper beginnings and endings. You don't want an angry estrangement and will always work toward a fair mutual view; you will take the time to discuss and analyze for that purpose.

NEGOTIATIONS

You are great at negotiating. For being fair and objective, making concessions and compromises, you win the prize—as long as it is on paper. However, when these agreements commit you to changing cherished habits, you fuss and fume at having to keep them—and as likely as not, will imply strongly that you were coerced. Often Virgo does better as a negotiator for other people; you have a good mind for detail, and when it is someone else's business or investment deal you are handling, you have the distance from it which is necessary for real objectivity.

JOINT FINANCES

Virgo is a good partner to have in joint finances. You avoid indebtedness and incautious speculation, functioning best with air signs as they widen your perspective; they take an analytical view of things as you do, but they move faster and are more adventuresome. A too impetuous partner will feel that Virgo is always pulling him or her away from possibilities and is something of a wet blanket, haggling too much over what appears to be trivial considerations.

COMPROMISES

A Virgo has the patience to see the potentially advantageous outcome of compromise. Present limitations and settlements may be all that are seen by a more volatile sign, but you have the future in the picture already and are not dismayed. You keep a close eye on your own interests, but beware—anyone who is fooled by that pleasantly offhand manner will try to take advantage! Virgo's mind works at full speed to compute all the factors in a given situation, positive and negative. You are not bull-headed and will agree to concede even when it means that things will not be 100 percent in your favor, as you are capable of understanding the validity of the other party's desire to have things go well on his or her end. Often you will surprise a former partner or associate by offering things that you could have held on to for yourself, as you realize that you don't need to play for points or to take as much as possible simply because you can.

INHERITANCES

You are likely to benefit more from gifts or inheritances at intervals throughout your lifetime than to receive a bonanza in your old age. Smaller yet frequent gifts come your way and increase your social and business mobility—and chances are this suits you just fine. Certainly, you have no objection to wealth and its trappings, but if you are truly pragmatic, you will not unwittingly outsmart yourself by molding your character or channeling your attention to please possible sources of money or property. The most intricate schemes of this nature will backfire. Keep away from family squabbles and intrigue and your proper share will come to you.

LIBRA

TURNING POINTS

Libra finds it hard to ignore anything that is put in his or her path, seeing the fabric of life as a cohesive whole and therefore viewing each thing as a part worthy of consideration. As a result you face changes directly; the need for them is looked at with care and the available choices scanned. You strive to attain a position of equilibrium as soon as possible, but often you will let an issue sit and stew in your brain rather than accept any watered-down alternative to a business, social, or personal ideal. Take a cue from your zodiacal opposite Aries and make a leap once in a while, trusting your ability to improvise.

INTIMACY

Libra senses that a sensitive and considerate partner will go through good and bad days, allowing a balance to be established. The mood in the air brings you a clear mental perception when you or a partner are dissatisfied; however, an abhorrence of rocking the boat will often as not keep you from bringing it into the open. Needed talks are delayed when this occurs—and the part of you that is not being expressed is what accounts for any sense you may have that your sexual nature is not being lived out to its highest potential. Your dislike of being an alarmist or sounding selfish is enough to keep you from doing so; give yourself time to explore your feelings freely and to develop the needed rapport with your mate.

RELATIONSHIP ENDINGS

Facing up to the finality of an ending, and to the necessity for one, is tough going for Libra. You see all the angles, all the reasons, but this doesn't stop you from feeling just plain lousy about it all. Situations of this nature serve to make you aware of the need to give your emotional self more freedom of expression without feeling guilty or self-indulgent. Allow your emotional state the same time and attention you give to your mental attitude—otherwise you'll end up giving it more attention as your needs become more persistent.

NEGOTIATIONS

Negotiation is Libra's middle name. You have mastered the art of putting opposing parties at ease, convincing them of their right to sincerely hold their positions and to argue for them, and then sitting them down to talk with one another. However, this instinct for the role of negotiator should not run your life. With the best of intentions you may alienate friends and build hornets' nests by being in the middle. Your mate or lover(s) can lean too much on your talents of mediation; don't try to stoically bear the whole burden, as it does not help the other person to have his or her work done by another.

JOINT FINANCES

Libra is willing to incur debt and take reasonable risks for the sake of joint or group financial investment or goals. You provide such a venture with an excellent perspective on pros and cons and are not the grasping type. Good word spreads about your skill and your fairness. Your own best interests may suffer when you make casual promises, not taking the time to consider their possible detriments until you have committed yourself. If this should occur and you are not in a position to reverse any steps without worsening things, use it in the future as a lesson in giving your word or support only when you understand all the possible ramifications.

COMPROMISES

You will let go—of people, possessions, or just a point—without resentment in order to make for smoother sailing. The meaning for you of social position and good reputation is closely bound up with your idealism; your resistance stiffens at compromise when it is a point of true honor, which appears to be demanded as a sacrifice. Society's estimation of your qualities—and the quality of your success—is highly important to you, not wanting yours to be a wild story of success that happens against all opinion and expectation. A larger perspective than that of many of your contemporaries gives an edge to your financial aptitude; temporary setbacks often lead to a boom for you later on.

INHERITANCES

Surprise is usually not a major factor for Libra regarding the inheriting or transfer of family wealth; if there are surprises they will be small ones. What comes your way are traditional family holdings, which you receive as the next in line, particularly homes and business property. Antiques, precious goods, and novelties generally are not what Libra inherits or receives on a large scale as gifts; rather it is more safe items whose value is not of a widely variable nature. Stolid Taurus is the sign associated with inheritance in a chart of your own sign, making you heir to stability and long-standing assets. If you know that you will inherit wealth, don't let the expectation of this good fortune slow down your immediate efforts to make your life what you want it to be. The positive energy you expend in that direction now will make what you receive later an even more considerable gain through consistent movement and good timing.

SCORPIO

TURNING POINTS

Scorpio roots down and hibernates as the time of big change approaches. Others must forgive your uncommunicativeness during such periods; those who do not have a thorough familiarity with your temperament and reactions are left to figure out what is happening as best they can. Of course, it will be fairly obvious if the turning point is an external one, relating to your social or business life, but if what is going on is an internal process, your motives can seem dark and unclear. Advice does not often seem valuable to you, but try not to become angry if it is given —those around you mean well. Let them know that you are working right along on the problem. You relive the past vividly, mulling over dramatic and meaningful episodes for a long time afterward to assure that you have gleaned everything possible from what took place.

INTIMACY

The mythology surrounding the sign of Scorpio most always alternates praise and condemnation for these natives as sexual dynamos, obsessive and hypnotizing. These are labels which all but the most immature Scorpio takes with an enigmatic smile. It is true that Scorpio as a sign embodies emotional intensity and a singularity of purpose. Sexuality for you is a creative experience, helping you to loosen fixed moods and attitudes. Flighty or extremely sensitive types can be overawed by you; but you are very self-sufficient and take pleasure in being alone as well as in being sexually involved. You are generally not the bed-hopper of popular lore.

RELATIONSHIP ENDINGS

The Scorpionic propensity for reflection, mental rehearsal of scenes, and deep attachment to patterns makes endings traumatic for you. Still, you really do want to solve the whys of a breakup or a business failure. It is hard for you to envision your feelings changing—this is a fatalistic slant of mind, but your determination will usually pull you into taking whatever action is necessary to set yourself on the road to healing and new ventures. You are capable of avoiding a paranoid attitude and are always better off when you do so.

NEGOTIATONS

During negotiation Scorpio needs others around to lighten things up; otherwise the positive traits you have in this area—love of justice and an innate sense of rightness over personal preferences—succumb to stubbornness and the desire to see the other party get what they deserve. You are patient and will listen, as well as having specific goals in mind; your long span of concentration is impressive to others. But often it is difficult for you to disassociate yourself from the matter at hand, so that when it is time to move on to new business, you are still stuck in the past and will keep others from continuing until you are satisfied.

JOINT FINANCES

You prefer to handle money matters on your own, although you will undertake a joint venture after tediously careful preparation. It is essential that you have real trust in your partner; otherwise you will wind up devoting so much time to the project, feeling that only you can take care of it properly, that you can easily feel that you deserve all the benefits accruing from it. Make sure that an equal agreement is followed through as an equal effort. These partnership dealings often pay off well, as you are willing to accept temporary debt—even a temporary simplification of lifestyle (which some Scorpios have known to like better and stay with!) —in order to wait for an investment to mature.

COMPROMISES

Scorpio tends to part grudgingly with anything or anyone, even if it is only from habit. Your mental side knows that in time things will have to change anyway, or that it is inevitable for you to have to deal with a particular lesson eventually. Tell this to your emotional side when it wants to cling to outmoded situations or return to them inwardly after a reasonable time has elapsed. When you must divide property or decide on custody matters, a supreme effort should be made to keep the logical aspects of the proceedings in the forefront of your consciousness. Use a list of points or have a third party there to mediate; analyze using the basic premise that no one party can have it all—anything to maintain, within yourself, an objective view.

INHERITANCES

Inheritances or gifts of money come in such a way as to increase your scope of action, to widen your horizons, and rarely to reinforce old patterns or projects. Even when you plan or attempt to use such funds for activities within what has been the daily pattern for you, events seem to move in a fashion that alters your plans and your intentions! Don't shut off opportunities by making presumptions regarding those who are in a position to pass holdings along to you. In some cases there may be conditions that you must satisfy in order to receive or inherit material wealth, such as taking a position in a relative's business (or an in-law's) or pursuing some educational goal.

SAGITTARIUS

TURNING POINTS

Sagittarius chases down changes like a big-game hunter, tackles them and milks them for all they're worth—the bigger the better. You take a courageous view of turning points and transitional periods; in fact, you actually seem at times to bunch together factors that compel new beginnings. Major change does take its toll on you in pressure and tension; your irritability and short temper at such times tax the resources of your mate and friends as well as your own.

INTIMACY

Sagittarius will not hide his or her physical needs in an intimate relationship. You tend to please your partner, which helps to sustain the sexual part of the relationship. You tend to see yourself as less moody and finicky than you actually are, which can be a real chore for a lover or partner. Make up your mind to accept that your body goes through its cycles just like everyone else's. A time of relative disinterest or a desire for private introspection (rare enough for some Sagittarians) is not an automatic indication that it is time to seek elsewhere for intimacy. You adjust quickly to the energy and temperament of new partners; you desire freedom of action and extend this right to those with whom you are involved. A tendency on your part to lecture cools off torrid romances.

RELATIONSHIP ENDINGS

The need for a feeling of security causes Sagittarius to hold on to fading situations and relationships, although the intuition and momentum required to face facts and begin a new phase quickly are always at the disposal of this fire sign. If you are the one who is dissatisfied with an arrangement, be careful not to be wishy-washy and vacillating, prolonging an uncomfortable situation until it becomes unbearable (often this is done in the hope that the other party will make the final break out of sheer desperation). Work out your interior dialogue until it is clear in your own mind what you really think and feel. Then, if it is a matter of ending what cannot be repaired to your satisfaction, be prepared to carry out your decision—yourself.

NEGOTIATIONS

A philosopher by nature, Sagittarius possesses an endless capacity for sticking to an issue, whether it be personal, political, or related to business. This, of course, can be carried too far—with Sagittarius, what can't? —and become mere quibbling or talking just to hear one's own voice. Use your strong intellectual abilities to formulate a cohesive picture of what is going on; then, keeping a definite goal in mind, convince the other party (or the opposing parties if you are negotiating for others) that essential agreement is already at hand and that all is needed is a few minor adjustments.

JOINT FINANCES

The abundant Sagittarian energy is an asset in joint and group financial undertakings, but it can also be a hindrance to them. Your momentum and optimism create opportunities for you and your partner(s), and you willingly combine time and money in cooperative efforts—too willingly, perhaps—as you can get carried away on a golden vision, ignoring details that require serious consideration. You prefer that your partner be the one to handle the minutiae, but then you criticize him or her for being negative and unimaginative. There is a tendency, too, to enter into ventures privately with joint monies, telling yourself that you are borrowing for a cause that can't fail to benefit everyone. All too often such action backfires, incurring not only financial loss but loss of your partners' trust in you as well. Chances are a really good deal doesn't need to be concealed from anyone in the first place!

COMPROMISES

The aforementioned philosopher in you heartily endorses compromise as a wonderful practice, recommending it to everyone. You will formally make all the necessary concessions, but upon reflection—or when it comes time to apply them—you find it hard to stick to them. A streak of perfectionism makes you want each thing in its proper place, and all too often this means that you want to keep it when you have agreed to give it up! When you are really ready to commit yourself to a compromise, you let go quickly and with little effort, relieved to be free of old business, working out agreements without hesitation or reluctance.

INHERITANCES

In matters of inheritance you tend to benefit indirectly; it is your mate who receives money or property. Maybe a relative or in-law loans funds to you, or you join with him or her in business, or he or she asks you to be the manager of his or her new estate. When you do come by money directly, the spending of it is very much subject to your whims. It is likely to disappear quickly, and you will hear no advice regarding its use. Even when, as is usually the case, you are involved with others in the acquiring of wealth and the spending of it, you will have definite ideas of your own and will not wish to feel restricted by the caution or differing approaches expressed by them. There may be provisions requiring all parties to be in agreement before funds are spent or permission granted by a lawyer. Don't use up your share, as well as your time and energy, in continual contests.

CAPRICORN

TURNING POINTS

Turning points and major alterations of pattern and emphasis are taken in stride by Capricorn—much more so, in fact, than changes of habit or relinquishment of personal preferences. In the business world or when it comes to moving to a new location or home, you keep your eyes ahead and push right through. In personal matters, having to accept the loss of parents, having to change your own attitude on some social issue, or make peace with the new viewpoint of a mate or close friend, you are extremely sentimental at best; at worst, you hold on with a vengeance in the name of tradition. The softer, nostalgic side of your attachment to things as they have been, makes you an excellent caretaker of valuables and of values.

INTIMACY

Those who wish to enter an intimate relationship with Capricorn should be duly warned in advance—this native can really live up to the stiff, sourpuss nature of astrological lore. More often than not, serious Capricorn (who may not be a more liberated mate's cup of tea) contains an equal portion of imp, delighting in surprising you with gifts, practical jokes, or a romantic and expensive evening out. The Capricornian shyness and reserve shouldn't be poked fun at too soon after meeting this earth sign—he or she will withdraw all the more. To one who is patient will be shown the sensual, warm side of Capricorn, longing to share real intimacy. He or she is fearful of rebuffs and also of erring in the choice of in whom to place trust.

RELATIONSHIP ENDINGS

Capricorn has a reputation for terse, sudden good-byes. What comes out as an on-the-spot decision has probably been mulled over for quite some time in his or her mind before emerging to confront a stunned partner. You work things out in your own mind until you are sure of your decision and all points that apply, and then you announce what you have decided. You don't take such matters lightly and despite a seemingly impenetrable outer shell, you do feel remorse at hard endings. When it is you who is being left by another, suddenly or otherwise, you draw back into yourself like a turtle, for what is usually a long adjustment period with no dates, often little social contact of any kind, particularly after a divorce. Counseling is good at a stressful time of parting, helping you to know when you are ready to re-enter the social sphere.

NEGOTIATIONS

It is hard for Capricorn to see why discussions and negotiations are needed; you feel it's quite plain what needs to be done by everyone concerned. You are not unconcerned about others and their needs and are realistic enough to know your own limits, but you trust your own mental processes the most. You handle large-scale bargaining better than negotiation of personal affairs and are more at home in politics or labor management than in deciding who will do what chore around the house.

JOINT FINANCES

Capricorn's secretiveness makes dealing with this sign in financial matters rather difficult. You have your own ideas, and often you don't even want to bother explaining what those ideas are! Also it is not easy to participate in a money matter with someone who can't stand to have anyone know how much he or she has available for use. You have excellent long-range planning ability and are a very accurate budgeter—Capricorns abound in accounting firms. Cautious in investments (to the point of making no moves in many cases), you need a partner who combines an analytical approach, reassuring to Capricorn's sensible nature, with the willingness to take risks. Otherwise you may never enter the world of finance except to earn your living. If speculation puts too much of a strain on your nerves, you are probably better off without it, though the world will be deprived of one very capable financial operator.

COMPROMISES

It is possible that Capricorns don't compromise because they are never convinced that his or her position is wrong. When you make concessions, it is out of allegiance to a higher ideal such as family unity or the good of your business. You will sacrifice but not compromise. This holds especially true in personal relationships. You will endure much for the sake of your marriage or another close tie, though seldom withholding criticism, always believing within yourself that your way would have been preferable.

INHERITANCES

Capricorn is capable of being a bit presumptuous about getting what is "rightfully" yours in the way of family wealth. Your point of view is not without validity, but the passing along of holdings is a very personal matter, as you will discover when it is time for you to divide your own estate. You may surprise yourself with the decisions you make. Inheritances coming to Capricorn often take the form of prized family possessions with more of an emotional value than a monetary one. This is fine with you, as you have a deep respect of such treasures and will cherish them for their traditional meaning, selling them only after much serious consideration in the face of necessity or when it means a really great advantage to you and yours. When cash comes your way, try branching out—seek trusted help in a solid investment rather than hiding what you have received under the mattress.

AQUARIUS

TURNING POINTS

Aquarius delights in the heightened pace and sensations which accompany the pivotal moments of a changing situation. Unless the change is depriving the Aquarian of something or someone dearly loved, this native adapts quickly, thriving on what is new and different. You enjoy making a mental review of what you experience at such times, envisioning potential patterns and plotting what your next step should be. Remember that most others move at quite a different pace and view events in quite a different manner—don't get on your high horse at what seems to you to be their lack of appreciation of the rare and exciting atmosphere a turning point has brought to you. You seek always the hidden or essential order in shifting and changing events. The security in life for you consists of what you are able to learn rather than what you possess.

INTIMACY

Aquarius needs freedom of action regardless of how close his or her relationship with another might be. You have a strong instinct for socializing, which a quieter, more conservative mate or lover may find difficult to live with. Still, you can easily perceive when a relationship is foundering and will—if the person with whom you are involved is of high priority to you—put out much effort and make many adjustments of your own in order to heal things. Even in a romance of the earthshaking variety, you tend to hesitate before making any commitment to putting things on a domestic, day-to-day level. Idealistic Aquarius wants to be sure before embarking on a venture of such seriousness (and it is serious to you despite your love of and flair for the unusual).

RELATIONSHIP ENDINGS

Restlessness, combined with the repeated experience of people and situations not reaching your expectations, can bring you more in the way of endings than you like or want to deal with. It may seem to you that this repetition is out of your hands, but it definitely is not! Try giving yourself, at the very outset of an incipient relationship, just a day away from the person in question to take a good look and ask yourself whether you believe this can really work. The key is that regardless of what you perceive the potential of someone to be, if he or she is nowhere near realizing it now you are not likely to be able to bring such a change about. Besides, who wants to spend hour after hour (year after year) trying to change someone?! Aquarius handles sad endings better than most; you are able to detach yourself—after or even during the shouting—and take an honest appraisal. It is rare for an Aquarian to resort to unfair or coercive means to try to prolong a dying relationship.

NEGOTIATIONS

The Aquarian love of debate (or quibbling, as some would have it) shows itself to good advantage when negotiations are in order. With a sharp eye on details and another on general goals, you keep the process going to a conclusive resolution that usually is satisfactory to all concerned. You are able to keep the proceedings interesting so that no one becomes impatient through boredom. Aquarians make good intermediaries for other people's disputes, handling personal and business negotiations with equal facility. You will abide cooperatively by whatever the results may be, though often you may wish to negotiate further or on a continuing basis.

JOINT FINANCES

Your strongly directional energy and sudden enthusiasm may strain relations with financial partners, but as an Aquarian you are able to listen well to criticism and change your course if it seems appropriate. Your partner may be required to draw up a joint budget, as you tend to prefer an improvisational approach, which is a nice way of saying that you are not adverse to flirting with monetary disaster. In a group effort you provide a creative element; someone has to be willing to spend and invest, Aquarius.

COMPROMISES

Aquarius doesn't go down without a fight. You have more endurance than most and will follow up every last detail of a compromise after all others have faded. Aquarius is perfectly willing to let go of habits, concede issues in romantic affairs, and try new business tactics: "Just convince me," you say, "though there are several points you've made that are contradictory, two that are illogical, and three others that display attitudes you should have changed by now."

INHERITANCES

Aquarius burns day-to-day energy on pet projects and scant funds on long vacations. Inheritances coming your way are timed to pay off creditors or fix the car. They arrive with incredible timing just as a need arises for them. This may rankle a bit in your brain, as you've a closetful of grandiose plans the money might have funded. The pain fades quickly, however, as you appreciate a new, stable point from which you can now catapult on to new adventures. You are appreciative of well-meaning efforts to control your use of wealth, but you resist them successfully.

PISCES

TURNING POINTS

Pisces can clearly see the need for a change; you may even have a premonitory sense that one is on its way. To keep your balance emotionally, you step back and regard the event in a detached, though feeling, manner, but you are not as adept at actually severing a connection as you are at forming an interior picture of doing so. Old ties, habits, and attachments beckon to you to stay and retain them. With infinite pathos the beautiful, rich experiences so recently yours pass before your inner gaze, and you feel you cannot bear to let them slip into the past. Even on a mundane level there is reluctance in you to part with what you have put yourself into in the way of work, emotion, or even habit. Decisive action, more than observation, will gain for you a positive control over your responses when situations reach their turning points. Try to develop the ability to take such action; you already have the knack for sitting back and riding through changes when this is the appropriate thing to do.

INTIMACY

Although you may not boldly come out and say so, you love exploration and experimentation in your intimate life. It is most helpful to you to be close to someone who will draw out an articulation of your needs and desires and encourage you to be forthright about them. Otherwise you are prone to drifting into the arms of new, still mysterious loves. As you are sensitive to the moods of your partner, his or her frankness will bring out the same in you. Be careful not to put up with insensitive behavior beyond a reasonable time in which to try to fix things.

RELATIONSHIP ENDINGS

Pisces hesitates to be the one to end a relationship; you are fearful of having to go through loud, angry scenes, as well as finding it difficult to be sure that leaving is not a mistake. Combine these with a general Piscean inertia, and endings can be a long time coming even if they are inevitable. Check carefully to ascertain whether you've kept the other person in touch with your disgruntlement—it helps if the news does not come as a shock. When it is your partner who decides to leave, you may react in a supposedly un-Piscean manner: after the initial response you bloom, no longer having to hold the tension and doubt of the pre-breakup period inside.

NEGOTIATIONS

When you take too much time to consider and review negotiation proceedings, you are likely to let go of more than is necessary or desirable. You lose control of the momentum of the discussion, and with it your initiative to take or retain control of the results. To balance this you are good at spotting the right moment to let go of specific items or points that will balance well with your gains in the end. You will concede if possible rather than prolonging the proceedings. You prefer to keep matters out of court to keep a friend from becoming only an acquaintance, an acquaintance from becoming an enemy.

JOINT FINANCES

The cooperative dynamic in finance often seems too elusive for Pisces to get a good grip on. Particularly in the case of the more reclusive sort of Piscean, you tend either to hoard everything in your possession, arranging the situation at hand to keep the total power of decision for yourself; or you surrender everything to your partner or partners, feeling that the hustle and worry involved are more trouble than they are worth. Others may seem so eager to be involved, they might as well be enabled to enjoy it all the more. Neither course will necessarily result in bad handling of the funds that are available, but the efficiency of joint ventures is interfered with when all parties are not in balanced cooperation. The personal side of your undemanding nature makes for smoother sailing than partners would have with other signs.

COMPROMISES

Pisces prefers compromise to butting heads or shouting matches. You keep your hold on the essentials of your own position by subtly maneuvering around a more aggressive bargainer. In family hassles Pisces can provide a soothing voice that cools things down to the point where antagonists begin to wonder what the problem was. Don't strain your own equilibrium, however, by always playing the go-between—there is more wear and tear on you from the problems of others than may be readily visible.

INHERITANCES

For Pisces inheritances or gifts of money bring chances to solidify his or her position in society, to make connections that were not possible before, to broaden the sphere of social mobility. In many cases such wealth leads to marriage, or to the enhancement of a business that is just the right touch to make it a success. Whatever the gift is to be used for, the timing is perfect. When opportunities of this nature are passed by for the sake of salting the inheritance away for old age or the proverbial rainy day, you will likely end up spending it all, bit by bit, and then wishing you had used it for your original plan.

CHAPTER NINE
Personal Growth

DREAMS, ASPIRATIONS, DISTANT HORIZONS, and goals all come together in this house of the zodiac, forcing you to change, alter your style, and grow to meet the various obligations or circumstances presented to you. This is the portion of your life with the most potential for fluctuation; conversely there is more self-determination here than anywhere else in the chart. You can be your own Pygmalion, creating a work of art that comes to life. Where the eighth house teaches you to make decisions, the ninth one convinces you to expand your hopes and wishes and to be constantly upgrading yourself, reformulating those decisions in the process. The way in which you approach self-improvement is also outlined, for many times the execution is as vital to success as your skills.

Your philosophy about life and your values are found in this chapter. For people who fail to take into account these powerful life elements, they end up doing double the work. Your psychological makeup is defined, along with the ways you use psychology on yourself and others. How you respond to motivation, and how you motivate yourself is also factored into your personal growth.

Long ago this house was strictly the sphere of travel and, interestingly enough, in-laws. In ancient times marriage was one of the key purposes of travel, and that is why in-laws (who necessitated this travel), and legalities were associated with this part of the chart. Today, higher education and professional occupations—which both force people to travel and/or move—are considered to be part and parcel of this natural quest for self-improvement. Confidence, risk-taking, and luck comes from seizing the moment and riding these natural tides to their conclusion.

Continuing education, retraining, and updating your skills are all functions of this area of growth, and are important themes for everyone in the coming years. Use this information to uncover how to open new doors, and push through the barriers standing in your own way of achievement.

ARIES

LUCK

Aries is periodically overcome by fits of fatalism, when you start to feel that things will never go your way again (if, indeed, they ever really have). However, Aries doesn't mind dealing with a little depression once in a while—it makes for good mental housecleaning. As your faith in the possibilities available to you increases once again, your mood balances, and it seems not at all impossible for fortune to smile upon you. You don't really like to think of it as luck headed in your direction; simply having energy and momentum building inside is enough for you, although others attribute your astonishing success to luck. You are confident of your abilities and are satisfied. The break you anticipated happens before you have a chance to label this luck or just excellent preparation.

INTELLECTUAL ACHIEVEMENTS

Curiosity is therapeutic to you; you cure your doldrums by diving into new fields, often at random. You are apt to delve into esoteric subjects off the beaten path of your day-to-day business. You glean what is essential to you and move on, letting what you have learned filter down on its own into your subconscious, where it finds a niche and beings to grow roots. Often Aries will study a topic bit by bit, every few months reading one more book, every few years enrolling in a class or seeking the wisdom of one versed in whatever the field may be.

PERSONAL GOALS

The goals of Aries are as high and ambitious as they are undefined. You have a directional type of drive, which tackles things step by step, one at a time. Pursuing a goal in this manner is satisfying to your own standards. It is not that your aims are always ambiguous, or that you never have a specific pursuit occupying your attention; rather, you honestly accept that things—including your own desires—are very much subject to change. Who knows what tomorrow will bring in the way of replacing one idea with another? (Some signs think they know!)

TAKING RISKS

Whether big or small, dramatic or mundane, the thrill of foraging into uncharted territory is one which Aries never tires of undertaking. It could be a new job, a new mental attitude, a new romance—the stakes only enhance it for you. You do have your fears like everyone else, and so can slip into a rather braggartlike persona as a cover for holding back from taking action. You build character by refraining from building yourself up, letting your actions speak for themselves.

TRAVEL

One way or another, Aries usually manages to do a good amount of traveling. Usually it takes a combined form that includes books, thoroughly exploring a city by bicycle or on foot, and some long-distance trips. You tire easily of the lounging tourist role and will insist on ditching the tour and striking out on your own or with whomever is brave enough to go with you. Let your fellow travelers beware—Aries can't forget what work remains to be done at home and may suddenly be seized by a desire to cancel the trip and go do it.

SELF-CONFIDENCE

An intriguing aspect of Aries folk is their tendency to underestimate the amount and the quality of the self-confidence they possess. Often you will envy your fellow fire signs, Leo and Sagittarius, for their confidence, not realizing that just about all other signs wish they had your share! Remember, confidence rests not on the absence of insecurity but on the ability to improvise. Fear may well be there—and it's a good thing, because we would never know we were sticking our necks out until we got our heads cut off—it's facing up to it that counts. If you envy those who seem supremely self-confident, check out how many foolish disasters they bring down on themselves. Or look to see how often they attempt anything out of the ordinary, anything that requires real self-possession. Perhaps their calm surface owes something to a lack of excitement in their lives.

HIGHER EDUCATION

Aries likes to see results produced by learning and study. This may lead you to start out and then change direction several times in the course of your education. Or you may find that you end up in a different field from the one you originally had in mind, in order to be pursuing what seems to be the most complete use of your time and energy. The Arian brand of enthusiasm can be overwhelming to your instructors. It is not unusual for Aries students to be shuffled around or ignored by unresourceful teachers, as enthusiastic students can be a problem! You aren't particularly interested in getting or having a diploma of any sort of pedigree simply for the sake of being able to say that you have it. You won't think twice about dropping a course of study near its completion if it has begun to seem superfluous or boring to you. Often you will undertake serious study of a favorite topic late in life, bringing to it a depth and duration of concentration you never thought yourself capable of in youth. This can result in recognition for you, appreciated though unexpected, including honorary degrees or invitations to speak before those who have more formal education than yourself.

TAURUS

LUCK

Luck is a tangible thing to Taurus, something which is included in the plans and attitudes of this earth native. Often a Taurean will perform specific rituals to insure luck in business or during traveling—private touches added to the process of preparing for such activities. When luck does not come your way, Taurus, you look around for someone or something on which to place the blame. When it does come you are quite content to assume it was entirely due to your own efforts. Outwardly you are phlegmatic about the possibilities ahead, while inside you turn over all factors in your mind, slowly and carefully, trying to project the outcome. This is good only up to a point; after a while, it's better to try putting the matter out of your mind and resting while the actual happening unfolds.

Intellectual Achievements

It has often been said that necessity is the mother of invention. The first one to say it probably had a Taurus in mind. You are full of questions, but as a matter of course you don't often wander about in the realms of the abstract or the mystical. Your motto is that every question has its answer, and you seek answers on pet topics or in problem areas of your life—practical ones that can help you and make you more knowledgeable. You are not impatient in your search for explanations, but you are apt to decide on a second-best answer rather than maintain the tension of being unsure.

Personal Goals

Taurus formulates specific goals. Often you don't have a grand-scale end result in mind but will plan a series of achievements and then wait and see what each brings. Most Taureans can use a bit more flexibility in their plans, as circumstances almost always press for modification of even the most carefully considered details. You would rather stick to your original plan—just because it was the original one—which causes you needless discomfort as a result of inevitable changes. Those whose advice you will listen to are few and far between, but you do find models whose ideas you test against your own. You don't generally like to make important decisions in isolation.

Taking Risks

Taurus loves security, but if the odds are good you will take a risk. You need time to build up your nerve before such a venture rather than jumping right in, but you will jump (carefully) once you feel ready. You achieve a good sense of self-satisfaction through being able to weather the trials of taking on a new career, a new home, or public involvement. You carry within yourself a secure focus that anchors you—stubbornly! —to your own ideas, ideals, and habits. It is rare that you will take a chance on something that carries with it a real sense of serious risk or danger for you, but when you do, you persevere bravely to the end.

Travel

Not restless by nature or often seized by wanderlust, Taurus still loves to travel but is very happy to get back home. Your first choice of a place to visit is one where friends are waiting to greet you or where some manner of prearranged contact is already made through social, business, or political connections. Just taking off into the unknown is not a Taurean type of activity. When you do travel, you retain the vivid, moving impressions and experiences that you gather. These may be few in number—indeed, you may feel the urge to travel only once or twice—but they are unforgettable treasures in your memory.

SELF-CONFIDENCE

The victories and defeats of the past strongly condition a Taurean's present attitudes regarding his or her worth and ability. All incidents of note in your life have a very real, physical presence in your consciousness. They are building blocks for your character and self-image, and with them you put together the personality with which you face the world and its challenges. Once you have committed yourself to a course of action, there is nothing so threatening as to cause you to back down, although you may refuse to enter an obviously safe venture because of a previous letdown in a similar situation.

HIGHER EDUCATION

Taurus respects education but does not want to be educated into an ivory-tower sort of position for which there is no real need or demand. Although you may be a brilliant student, you tend to set for yourself only moderate goals in academic life and to work at a level not too far above the norm. This is not to say that you deliberately waste your intellect on unimportant matters or that you are unwilling to work; indeed you will often tackle a very difficult field purely to experience the dedication and challenge involved. It is just that steady progress suits your temperament better than academic fireworks. You prefer not to stand out too much from your peer group, and so will hide your light under the proverbial basket—though an astute teacher or counselor may well stop it and encourage you. You will respond to such encouragement as much to please this mentor as to benefit yourself, but you are happy doing so only if allowed to maintain at least a relative anonymity.

GEMINI

LUCK

Gemini, luck is your handmaiden, your ever-present helper and companion. It isn't that you avoid mistakes and setbacks (though Gemini can tend to think that he or she is going to avoid them from now on), but rather that you can feel luck coming and be prepared for it at precisely the right moment. If it isn't coming, you will go out in search of it—and you are sure to find something, though it may not be exactly what you had in mind. You probably come as close as anyone ever gets to understanding the nature of good fortune and putting it to use. Try some mental imaging combined with relaxation to minimize the reckless careening with which you are all too familiar.

INTELLECTUAL ACHIEVEMENTS

Restlessness is all that holds Gemini back from fully exercising an intellect that will take in as much information as might be desired. You often lack the patience to see a project through, to finish a class or a book. This has a good side when a source of learning has only a limited amount that is valuable for you to receive; you are able to skim through and extract that amount from the rest. You work hard at organizing and synthesizing knowledge in order to be able to present it in an articulate and intelligent manner.

PERSONAL GOALS

Gemini experiences periods of confusion and an overflow of conflicting goals, but you always come through them, usually with your objectives at least somewhat clarified. Counseling is a good idea for you in career matters. You find it very helpful to have someone who can help you chart out and organize on paper all that is awash in your brain, pointing out conflicts and contradictions you might miss amid a mass of seemingly unconnected ideas. Whatever your ideals are, your drive is to realize them. Don't allow yourself to dream away your time, using it only to plan and prepare rather than getting down to business.

TAKING RISKS

Risks are exciting to you as you love to be jetting off into new adventures, discovering new social sets, trying your skills in new business or educational fields. In your private life you need to develop an inner review process that keeps relationships fresh by bringing out problems to be worked on in a constructive manner. This can replace a Geminian tendency to hop into multiple romances, a thrilling type of risk, perhaps, but one that rarely leaves you with anything substantial to show for it.

TRAVEL

Gemini can be found pouring over travel posters, pamphlets, newspaper and magazine travel sections, National Geographics—the exotic exerts an irresistible pull on you. You will sometimes use the prospect of travel to goad yourself into taking positive, decisive steps in your work or professional life, telling yourself that you will see the place of your dreams with the money you make. In your private life you use the goals of cruise or vacation to inspire yourself and your mate to secure or maintain freedom of movement.

SELF-CONFIDENCE

How do you translate all that verve, spunkiness, and enthusiasm into true confidence? You have moments of complete assurance, but the next morning you awake to the sound of uncertainties and doubts in your mind. Take your current objective apart, examining it bit by bit, waiting for your self-reliance to catch up with you. Or look at it this way: if you accomplish what you have set out to do, who needs confidence? Of course, if what you want is some of that nice strong calm feeling, you can do it by knowing that your actions line up with your self-respect. You've already got the guts to reach out for what you know you really want. Eventually, you'll stop worrying about making everything absolutely perfect and concentrate on the fact that when you do your best, that's all anyone can expect of you—including yourself.

HIGHER EDUCATION

Higher education for Gemini is a desirable but often elusive dream. Short-term trade school, career-training seminars, an occasional class— more often than not, these are all you take the time to actually complete. Or your own research gives you the information you seek. And this is not bad! Try to make the things you learn relate and reinforce each other rather than being a series of fragments. You are likely to discover an underlying order in your pursuits that you didn't know was there. You desire excellence, but remember that the most prestigious attainments in the eyes of the academic world often lock those who have reached them out of many opportunities—they are overqualified! You can find the excellence you seek by determining your own standards, and then taking the necessary steps in pursuing it. And chances are that if you take this course of action, there will be no problem with becoming bored and taking in only a superficial cross-section of your selected field. Your interest, which motivated you in the first place, will not wane through having to wade through details that have little meaning for you.

CANCER

LUCK

When fair winds blow, Cancer is all aglow with new-found energy, ideas, and enthusiasm. Just as quickly, a downward turn in luck sends our poor Cancerian to the depths of gloom to grumble and wonder, "Why me?" More than anyone else, Cancer knows that moods and attitudes are actually creative and can bring opportunities within reach or cut them off completely. You can harness your powers of concentration, Cancer, to direct the shifts of your various moods into a balanced state of alert readiness, which draws good luck to you.

INTELLECTUAL ACHIEVEMENTS

The little Cancerian crab scuttles into a secure niche to be safe and unthreatened by elements or enemies, but the truth is you can't resist peeking out to see what's going on in the fascinating, though risky, world. Make sure you keep up a steady stream of those peeks into new areas of social and romantic interaction, new creative outlets, even new changes in your self-image. A certain amount of risk-taking eliminates the ways in which you have allowed yourself to get into ruts, the things you are subconciously dissatisfied with; the things you'd really love to do if you only dared will automatically buoy you up emotionally. You actually possess more daring than you give yourself credit for having.

PERSONAL GOALS

Cancer contains a definite curious streak (not to be confused with an odd streak, which you also contain). You are, however, always working toward stability and security, both inner and outer, to feel safe as you consider new points of view. You seek those underlying values and traditions that can serve as a base for intellectual activity. These are philosophical values that you organize and assign mentally; yours is not a restless intellect that searches for the unusual for its own sake. You want to know the inner nature of things, for your nature seeks always to burrow into the heart of a matter (or a person) and nestle there.

TAKING RISKS

You have many goals, some very specific and others that occupy a background position in your thoughts, which are crystal clear. Others may be vague but contribute nonetheless to your general sense of direction in life. Mostly you are moving toward something to call your own—a family or family business, a home, a community service activity—something that reflects the constant interplay of your desires for your own benefit and that of society. Perhaps the hardest thing you may be called upon to do is to digest criticism of your treasured ideals without an angry response, as your goals are closely bound up with what you consider the central themes of living.

TRAVEL

Travel for the Cancer native often takes the form of a search for the perfect home. You love to absorb the atmosphere of new lands, to live among people and share their lives—this is a strengthening and revivifying experience for impressionable, humane Cancer. You plan your itinerary carefully, taking note of all resources, and fret about making sure your home will be secure and looked after if you are leaving for more than a short time. Should you be fortunate enough to take a trip and not have to worry about the home front or a rigid schedule, this footloose and fancy-free traveling opens a wider and more enjoyable sphere of possibilities than you have dreamed you could experience.

SELF-CONFIDENCE

Cancer is confident while on his or her own familiar turf. On the shaky ground of new or uncomfortable territory, the negative Cancerian traits are apt to begin to emerge—a sharp tongue, vindictiveness, and old-maid fussiness. People may not care for this, but what do you care? You are out of sorts and have no intention of pretending that everything is just fine. Actually you do care, and you can benefit by practicing a technique for a more constant inner balance. Repeat to yourself: "I am not under attack. Modifying my values and attitudes will help me to grow."

HIGHER EDUCATION

Cancer attaches much importance to the effort that goes into securing higher education. It may take a while for you to clear away your timidity, the wishes of parents, the advice of counselors, etc. Once your own personal preference has gained the foreground, all systems are go. If getting a degree is of prime importance to you—and to many Cancerians it is—you will invest so much of your emotional energy in it that it may be wise to postpone marriage or having children until you have reached your goal. Keep romance as low key as you can during school—or at least during its critical stages. An upheaval in your love life can derail your concentration and your ability to work, causing frustrating delays and anger at yourself.

LEO

LUCK

You take your luck very seriously, Leo. To insure that you get it, you exert yourself through a positive attitude and hard work, keeping a sharp eye on the world around you. Through superstitious habits and rituals that you employ for a good theatrical performance, you work for a cooperative customer or just an all-around lucky day. When misfortune occurs or your wishes don't come true, try to realize (though this is hard for proud Leo) that there is a principle at work which limits and frustrates you in order to clear away immature attitudes and reveal false trails that lead you nowhere. You haven't failed—it is simply that the venture that didn't work out was not worthy of you.

INTELLECTUAL ACHIEVEMENTS

Like your fiery Aries cousin, you break out of ruts by channeling your energies into new enterprises. You are more systematic than Aries, however, and will follow up on something that has attracted your interest and stimulated your curiosity. This pursuit may suffer numerous interruptions and you may be sidetracked for years from actively engaging in it, but the idea never dies, and sooner or later you will bring it to completion. You reject any limitations on your intellectual life that others might try to impose. You strive always to relate your research to real life and actual needs, and you do so in an idealistic and broad-minded manner.

PERSONAL GOALS

Leo sets high standards on performance; these serve both as goals and as guides for daily behavior. Your friends would be glad to be the first to tell you that you don't always have to live up to them, but they are there, and they are real. You need to put a curb on your tendency to lecture people, trying to persuade them to change their own values. You can also ease up on yourself. As long as you seriously attempt to reach your ideals, you can fall short of them and still shine. It is really the quality of your goals that counts, and your sincerity in wanting to realize them—perfect enactment of them is not necessary in order for you to complete the business at hand.

TAKING RISKS

Leos often judge themselves according to their willingness to take risks. Competing parts of your nature come into play here—your fiery courage against your fixed notions of consistency and maturity. You want to know whether it is appropriate to take a contemplated action or whether it is beneath your dignity. As a result you refuse some chances and then wonder if you have let yourself down. Sometimes you take the risk and then panic before the returns are in, sure that you have lost everything forever. This applies to social situations, as you like to follow your natural inquisitiveness but have an equally strong desire to stay in settings that are safe for you.

Travel

Leo loves travel for the sake of adventure, and if you are traveling alone for enjoyment it can be as exciting as your wildest desires. When travel is necessitated by business or other matters, which are not pleasure-oriented, you have problems making full use of the time. Stress and hassles have a way of following you, refusing to stay home regardless of your plans and resolutions. The same applies for relocation, especially when it results from your work, but if you get things in order in advance the inconvenience can be greatly reduced if not eliminated completely. Finish up the old and then get off to a brand-new start. Without old dead weight clinging to your consciousness your trip or move will succeed.

Self-confidence

Those close to Leo would probably say that he or she has an overdose of confidence. You do tread through the jungle with a sure step, but this is not due so much to sureness as to preparedness. You also meet life with a great sense of humor that absorbs worry and enables you to release it. Don't confuse self-confidence with fixity of purpose—it is entirely possible to have your mind inflexibly made up to do the wrong things. You experience difficulty in rare situations when you find yourself having to convince others of your fortitude. Most of the time, however, people see you as calm and collected even when you don't feel that way yourself.

Higher Education

Leo regards higher education as being closely tied in with two equally important approaches to life—idealism and pragmatism. You are always seeking to synthesize these two modes of thinking and to employ them simultaneously under all conditions. Education seems to be a potentially perfect blend, applicable to both the outer and the inner you. You will listen to counseling, but the style of your counselor is the controlling factor in determining what you do with the advice you receive. If you feel that heavy-handed tactics are being used or that the person advising you is a know-it-all, you rebel and head in the opposite direction from his or her suggestions. This could lead you down a less preferable road, but once started you usually finish. It's better to put your stubbornness at the service of your inspiration.

VIRGO

LUCK

Virgo is of two minds where luck is concerned: one is a naive reliance on luck, admitting that good fortune can't always be present and that you must simply hope for the best (or at least for a break once in a while); and the other is your analytical and rationalist mind, which dismisses the whole idea of luck with a vengeance (especially in bad times) and consigns all circumstances to chance or the need for a practical approach. Trust your mind to always plan ahead, Virgo, and to be able to improvise quickly. Let go of worry and just take the next step. You don't have to wear a smile twenty-four hours a day, but it would help to dump that big sack of negativity.

INTELLECTUAL ACHIEVEMENTS

You apply your own carefully constructed standards concerning the indulgence of curiosity. You have a unique inner world of knowledge, which you have accumulated by yourself. However, you are just as inquisitive as the next guy—it is your interests that differ—so don't be overly critical of the curiosity of others. It is not unusual for you to disdain any reward offered for what you have achieved for your own satisfaction. This is admirable, but don't hide your light too stringently. Take the risk of letting other people see your accomplishments.

PERSONAL GOALS

Virgo's goals are definite and not usually of the grandiose variety. What others see as a modest accomplishment may afford you the greatest satisfaction to achieve. Watch out for the tendency to be snobbish when comparing your aims and values with those of others. You are contemptuous of show-offs and tend to make this a classification that includes more people than may be fair. Although your self-reliance is a good quality when it comes to evaluating your aims, you do need some kind of outside opinion against which to measure your views. The observations of a respected and trusted person can be extremely helpful to you, as your cautious nature often assumes that a desired objective is too far away or too dangerous when it is neither. What fulfills you is the right thing for you; intuitively you know this and most of the time you follow it well.

TAKING RISKS

Changes of perspective and uncritical, wholistic views of life—what you might regard as the property of your zodiacal opposite Pisces—hold a great fascination for you. However, it is so comfortable and safe to remain detached and analytical that more often than not you choose that option. Risks are taken on the inside, in your thoughts and feelings, before they are enacted in new enterprises in your outer life. The real risk is not the actual venture but the process of preparing yourself for it; once this is done, you take the actual step with decisiveness.

TRAVEL

Virgo is a careful traveler—no rainy nights in a tent for this native. You head for the cultural centers of each city or country you visit. Having an ear for language and an eye for style, you always make an effort to blend. Still, many a Virgo prefers the familiar scenery of home to any exotic locale. Those who venture away regularly are working at stretching the Virgonian boundaries. Even a world-traveling Virgo can be quite content with sitting back and observing the curious behavior of the natives rather than spending all his or her time gadding about the tourist spots.

SELF-CONFIDENCE

Although you are capable of handling surprises well, you prefer not to have to deal with them. You would rather contend with what is presented to you from a familiar stance and on known territory; it is when you are pulled away from this comfortable space that your confidence is shaken (and no one may know it but you). Intellectually you can work through a new situation as quickly as any, but emotionally you cling to slow transitions and predictable outcomes. Keep your objectives clearly in mind and use them as the stimuli for taking care of whatever may occur. Consider the details that arise to interfere as secondary. Although you may not always be smoothly complacent at the way you handle them, you will do fine.

HIGHER EDUCATION

Virgo has the patience and the mental discipline to take any degree he or she desires at any college or university. The inhibiting factors, if any, are usually family pressures to go into a particular field (which can make you want to rebel), indecision as to the field you really want to study, and the pressures of financial considerations. It is possible for you to pursue an academic course just far enough to get yourself settled in a comfortable level of employment. Then you can go on to amazing lengths of research and study on your own, even securing coveted honors through sheer achievement, which would ordinarily be out of reach except through conventional channels.

LIBRA

LUCK

Libra has a nicely balanced attitude when it comes to luck and the process by which it is encouraged to be a frequent if not perpetual factor. You don't overwork to make your luck—for this really wouldn't have anything to do with luck—and you also don't overworry that your attitude may not always be keeping you in perfect readiness to receive it. You are not the sort to push yourself through a sixty-hour work week because of money or a notion that the morality of hard labor will bring fortune to your door. You do not strive to keep a safety net around yourself to the exclusion of enjoying life. You aim for an interplay of correct mental attitude, communication, and fair play to ease yourself and others into prosperous and peaceful circumstances. This makes you capable of assessing the limits of yourself and others, so that you can avoid getting lost in self-blame or guilt if a venture falls through.

INTELLECTUAL ACHIEVEMENTS

Libra spends quite a bit of time, starting in youth and continuing through adult life, in researching, testing, and constructing an idealistic philosophy and the intellectual tools with which to take on life's problems. Mostly you are concerned with social interaction, wanting to know how to interpret and deal with people's attitudes and shortcomings. You see yourself as a mediator between higher ethics and knowledge and the pragmatic contingencies of everyday life. Your research is not merely a hobby, nor is it a dry, abstract topic for the intellect alone; it is the basis for your whole approach and response to living.

PERSONAL GOALS

You probably have not one but several complete scenarios of preferred lifestyles and life situations, which you would eventually like to have, each one containing a series of alternatives should one or more aspects not come through. These pertain to marriage, business, family, and social concerns. Librans put a great deal of effort into their imaging. If you want to see your goals realized, verbalize them—don't let them take a back seat to the plans of your mate or family members. Chances are that if these loved ones were aware of your desires they would want to help you bring them into manifestation. Take a cue from those who are more vocal about what they want to do. You would also do well to avoid becoming lost in speculation, refusing to take the first step if all is not the way you pictured it. Go ahead with your plans—the end result may not be identical to your original idea, but it could very well be better!

TAKING RISKS

In a risky situation Libra sees all the advantages as well as all the dangers so clearly that it is hard to make a decision. Often circumstances will force your hand after you have vacillated without coming to any conclusion of your own. This isn't necessarily a bad thing, as often patience will bring just a bit of clarifying information that is needed. Still, you've kept track of missed opportunities and know what should have been done differently—use these lessons now. Rather than taking mental risks try asking yourself revolutionary questions. Ease hazardous elements into your life with preparedness, and the hazards will be greatly minimized.

TRAVEL

Travel occupies Libra's mind in a productive and positive manner. All sorts of resolutions are formalized while you are away from daily pressures. Gaining a new perspective, you determine not to fall back into old ruts, Re-enter your life and work at improving it rather than staying abroad and finding a new home, although this does hold a certain appeal for you. You are a good traveling companion, willing to share the costs, side trips, and problems as well as the fun.

SELF-CONFIDENCE

Libra, you know you can out think them all. You assess new situations quickly, but it is hard for you to say, "I know what to do" and demand credit when it is due you. You manage difficulties well, getting by in better shape than most, but you can tell when recognition that should have been yours has gone to someone else. It takes only one time of refusing to back down—those around you will expect you to stand up for your rights in the future and the pressure will have been lifted permanently.

HIGHER EDUCATION

Libra lives for knowledge. You dislike being in the dark about anything and will head for the library, school, or a quiet place to meditate as a first step before taking action. If you want to complete a course of formal education, don't allow yourself to be deterred by external pressures; following it through to completion will do wonders for your self-image. Even if it seems beside the point now, you have too good a grasp of the possibilities available to you not to put them to good use. You are well-suited to a teaching role, especially in areas of higher learning.

SCORPIO

LUCK

It is perhaps because you watch your interior states of mind so closely, Scorpio, that to other people—and even to yourself—you seem to brush off any suggestion that attitude has a creative influence on good fortune. "If I get the job I get it; if I don't, I don't," says Scorpio, "and whichever way it works outs is the way it was meant to be." This point of view is fine as long as you don't store up resentment at the things that don't work out, and if you consciously regard any situation as a test that will ultimately open new doors. Remember that it is your concentration and dedication which maximizes the element of luck.

INTELLECTUAL ACHIEVEMENTS

Scorpio likes to appear self-contained, and you can do so to the point of smugness. A searching question is what turns your mind toward investigating the validity of your own notions. Rather than searching restlessly for new frontiers, Scorpios prefer a day-to-day confrontational testing to prove the correctness or weaknesses of their philosophies of life. This testing ranges from the most profound beliefs to the details of social etiquette; it can make you difficult to deal with at times, as you will often adapt the very "show me" stance with others that you reject for yourself.

People assume that this comes from disdain toward them and their beliefs; in reality it is your way of connecting and discovering bits of information rather than the cynicism it appears to be.

PERSONAL GOALS

Like your zodiacal opposite Taurus you have fixed objectives, although they don't necessarily constitute a complete overview of your projected life. You focus completely (perhaps too single-mindedly and without enough of a long-range view) on an immediate goal; this allows you to reach many of your chosen plateaus, as your mind remains engaged in the pursuit of what you want until you have obtained it. If your focus is too narrow on the other hand, you can become disillusioned upon realizing that reaching the goal has not satisfied you in the way you thought it would. Speculate more on variations in your approach and in your envisioning of end results, in order to demonstrate to yourself that there are desirable alternatives to every plan.

TAKING RISKS

When it comes to risks Scorpio makes little show and much grim determination—yet you are not unaware of the impressive effect of your impassiveness. Actually this is a bit of a show in its own way, as you would confess to playing for some effect at least once or twice when encountering danger in the presence of some less ferocious folk. You are cautious when checking out the scenery over the next hill; in fact, you may well decide that it's not worth the possible trouble. When you do make a move it is with the full strength of your estimable will. You understand the need for risking existing stability too well to treat the process lightly.

TRAVEL

You carefully research your choices for travel. You may even wind up with some disappointments if you decide too completely just what you will do and what you will gain from a trip. Although your vacations may be few, you head for exotic and memorable places where you can burrow in and participate in the life of the natives. You accept changes in your lifestyle, which widen your experience. Meeting and mingling with foreign people and customs enables you to assimilate these new additions to your repertoire of living. You are resourceful when it comes to traveling on a shoestring—a good travel trait.

SELF-CONFIDENCE

The complaint is made of Scorpio that he or she will knock you on the head with a large, heavy stick to demonstrate Scorpionic self-confidence. You do come on strong, but as often as not it is in a quiet and determined manner, not a bullying one. You know you can do it—what you don't know is whether it's really what you want. Examine your priorities: what needs to be done, not necessarily what you would like to do, is probably what you will benefit from most.

HIGHER EDUCATION

Scorpio usually assigns education a supportive role, while the real work and risks take place in the business world or in studies you undertake on your own rather than in a formalized setting. You use higher learning as a safety net, and to have this you will carry a course of study through to completion. Schooling can also occupy a place of enrichment in your life, enhancing it through artistic accomplishments that relate indirectly to your chosen career. This is fine, but when you can align the two, you have a very powerful combination indeed. This unity of purpose enables you to direct your energies dynamically, widening the significance of each accomplishment because you have brought the fulfillment of differing needs to bear on a single target. It is not unusual for Scorpio to have a successful artistic career, which he or she has not planned for, using the education received in other areas to deepen the content of the creative work and lend expertise to the business end.

SAGITTARIUS

LUCK

Sagittarius, like Gemini across the zodiacal wheel, has an unbounded belief in the ever-ready presence of luck as a tool to use. Sagittarius will initiate action, check the dials, and take off on a wing and a prayer. And to the consternation of your earthbound friends Virgo, Cancer, and Taurus, your mission is usually a success! Be careful that you do not, in the name of a creative and positive mental attitude, shoulder your mate or family with too great a burden in the way of attending to the basic details of life. In other words, don't let them sweep up after you while you are more gloriously occupied.

INTELLECTUAL ACHIEVEMENTS

The Sagittarian mentality challenges itself to maintain a reservoir of curiosity and study in the face of daily pressures to attend to business. What others don't see is that you intend to apply your findings to your professional or family life. Study groups are a good idea for you, as the others involved will help you to spot inconsistencies that you have a tendency to miss. Give yourself a periodic check to see if you are actually enacting your ideals and theorems in life or whether you are letting them remain in an abstract and unapplied form.

PERSONAL GOALS

You have goals aplenty, Sagittarius. As a mutable sign, however, you shift easily with changing circumstances and will alter future plans accordingly. A constant factor is your restless spirit, which can undermine hard-won consistency or progress for the sake of avoiding a rut. Trust yourself to fashion your life creatively; sticking with an enterprise to its completion is a needed practice for you.

Taking Risks

What else is life made of but risk? Such is the declaration of brave Sagittarius. But there are legitimate risks and the unnecessary kind, and you have a fondness for both. Remember that the dullest types of tasks and responsibilities have to be faced. The risk here is the feeling that you will lose the wide perspective and the freedom of movement which you value so highly. This, not your exotic escapades, could be the biggest risk ever to confront you. Take it on with the same adventuresome spirit you bring to more glamourous undertakings.

Travel

Sagittarians incorporate travel into their lives as if life without it didn't exist. If you enjoy traveling, this is reason enough for doing it. If you don't relish it for its own sake, your concentration and patience are too easily disrupted at home and at work if you don't get a change of scene. Like your astrological neighbor Scorpio, you have a yen for faraway, marvelous lands. You should always plan on taking extra time (and money) in case you decide to stay longer or to make extra jaunts along with your planned itinerary. This is frequently the case as Sagittarians have a nose for the unexpected and the exciting and don't want to miss opportunities to experience them.

Self-confidence

You rebel against the idea of past defeats, especially in relationships and in money matters. This limits your self-confidence, but only temporarily —given enough interest and just a bit of encouragement you are off and running again. This short-term sensitivity can be intense, however. You have less of it than most signs, but you are human after all, and any past misfortune does leave a tender spot. You may not be consciously inhibited by such an occurrence, but watch your reaction if someone reminds you of it! "It most certainly does not bother me," you shout, belying your words with your whole demeanor. You can muster up enough confidence to get by under even the most difficult of circumstances, but often your companions must endure a grouchy and unpredictable Sagittarian until you are back on solid ground.

Higher Education

Although your high energy level and enthusiastic good cheer can tackle job, home, and education all at once, your nervous system rebels—as does your husband, wife, roommate, or anyone who spends any length of time in your presence. Financial aid and scholarships take away a burden that lurks in the back of your mind and disturb your concentration on your studies. Investigate what is available, including the good will of relatives, but be sure you pay back any debts incurred in the process, otherwise that burden will return and be magnified. The fields of law, medicine, philosophy, and political science hold the greatest attraction for you, and there is no teacher so great as an inspired Sagittarian. You may take time off from studies to fulfill some other area of life. You are better than most at re-entering school with a rekindling of your original interest, and are often better prepared to apply yourself and finish it.

CAPRICORN

Luck

On one level Capricorn tends to just push through problems, arguments, and unlucky turns of fortune with a brusque, uncommunicative manner, leaving others to soothe hurt feelings and arrange solutions. You consciously hesitate to see a less querulous attitude as necessarily inviting more opportunities, finding it difficult to accept that receiving good thoughts and affirmations from friends lightens the atmosphere as well as clearing the way for improvements. This closed-off manner acts as a mask for what's going on inside—painstaking efforts to define those beliefs and actions that reinforce and encourage good luck.

Intellectual Achievements

"Bah, humbug," Capricorn sneers at new discoveries, fanciful speculations, and theories—perhaps even at astrology! Then disguised as an Aquarius, you head for the library and stay up for days on end reading all you can get your hands on about the preposterous subject. You take intellectual life seriously and can be so rigid and complacent as to consider only that which affirms what you already think. But this attitude, which others might refer to as "too Capricornian," is one cause of your gruffness—you are too devoted to learning for its own sake to be able to kid yourself into thinking you're being objective when you're not! When others are involved in your dilemmas, you are most likely to leave them hanging while you solve them for yourself inwardly and then announce the results.

Personal Goals

Capricornians can set their goals so high as to be out of sight—and at the same time can watch every step with infinite attention to detail. When either aspect predominates, the result is an unhappy Capricorn. On one side there is the brooding dreamer who can deal only in absolutes—this one wants to get there all in one leap and doesn't mind if it's over a thousand-foot chasm. The other pole is the pragmatic type who refuses to look up from the dirt and dust and thinks the sky is a myth invented by silly and inconsequential folk. Both types are caricatures, but both extremes exert a pull on Capricorn, who is truly content while working toward a special goal in a balanced and methodical manner.

Taking Risks

Capricorns never ask others to take risks they would not take themselves. You watch the approach of a risky situation carefully to ascertain the need for a move or a change, judging what your response will be well in advance. Risks that are too sudden for this preparation can trip you up, but most Capricorns get right back on their feet, dust themselves off, and matter-of-factly deal with the surprise as best they can. You tackle risks without any great fanfare. Keeping your cool under fire is one of your finest traits and is most enjoyable to you.

TRAVEL

If bitten by the travel bug, Capricorn starts first with his or her own country and then works outward. You prefer to have a profession that allows you to travel rather than being a touristy type who travels for recreation. Often you are a solitary traveler, preferring to experience the trip without the distraction of companions. You enjoy freedom of movement, as well as the freedom to stay in one place and go nowhere at all except within your thoughts. You will go with a wad of money or just a pack on your back—all you need is to know in advance what type of trip it will be and what you should expect to encounter. You probably have a few close friends who know you to be a good traveler; often if these are moneyed folk, they will take you along gratis.

SELF-CONFIDENCE

You are confident, Capricorn, that you can reach your goals, handle stress, and face enemies. In tackling them, however, you let yourself become submerged in working out each detail and planning every response down to the last punctuation mark. It is this which overwhelms you, undermining your self-confidence. "I know I can handle this," you sigh, "but there's so much to do." You don't have the panicky response of fire or air signs, which displays a loss of confidence, but your spirits drop and you stop communicating and become irritable. The key to solving problems of confidence is to engage the situation at hand more directly rather than talking it out to yourself.

HIGHER EDUCATION

Capricorn has a deep respect for academic subjects. In-depth knowledge and critical and analytical techniques offered by the highest degree in your field are usually a top Capricornian priority. You seldom branch out into unknown subjects, wanting rather to enrich existing knowledge and tie it in with your career interests. Management, investment counseling, architecture, and music all attract Capricorn, and you have the organizational skills to utilize them. You do your best studying when there are no interruptions, and are willing to scrimp and save to take your schooling in one long stretch with no breaks.

AQUARIUS

LUCK

The topic of luck is fascinating to Aquarius. Enacting the positive, renewing attitudes in your own life is a high priority for you. Doing so may be more elusive than it seems in the idea stage, as Aquarius is a chaser and has trouble accepting that the object of a chase tends to run away at the same speed as your pursuit. A more relaxed approach allows you to make full use of your intuitive mental abilities, and to put together what seem to be random occurrences into a coherent pattern, which points to the most profitable and beneficial path to take.

INTELLECTUAL ACHIEVEMENTS

Aquarius loves to snoop out exotic and little-known topics. You have a craving to be in the middle of what most people would consider the outer fringe of accepted knowledge. You will take on a teaching role in order to communicate your findings to the less adventurous. You travel your own path, studying a topic to your own satisfaction, not relying on diplomas, rewards, or recognition for stimuli. You become impatient at the way others hold on to old attitudes and can easily slip into the habit of lecturing them. You want to shake up those who are stubbornly self-satisfied and are an automatic challenge to the Aquarian mentality. It helps to realize that you can't change anyone's mind, but you can question someone intelligently and provide a nudge toward a broader prospective.

PERSONAL GOALS

You have a notebook's worth of goals, being always in the process of replacing old ones, revising still relevant ones, and excitedly adding more. Your imagination, a real strength that you should consciously make good use of, bounds ahead, ever on the lookout for new possibilities—often it is Aquarius who sees what others miss. Try not to leave too many projects unfinished, as you will then have to face difficulty with new ones as past commitments reassert themselves, diverting your attention. This can cause you to form the habit of impatience as well as to have continual trouble completing work.

TAKING RISKS

Aquarians are willing to take risks, but it often happens that they don't perceive the nature of what they are getting themselves into. To correctly assess the degree of risk in a venture is the key for maximizing the benefit of all your ideas and projects. Watch a tendency to let the idea of risk, its glamour, draw you into situations where, once you have gotten your feet wet, you realize you don't want to be. Get out of habits that slow down your decision-making process, even if it means running out of the room with your hand over your mouth instead of blurting, "yes!" You can trust your natural curiosity to bring you all the excitement you can handle. You don't need to work at it.

TRAVEL

You are not a solitary traveler, and once at your destination you want to make friends and seek out a circle to join. This natural sociability makes you welcome wherever you go. Remember that you will want some time by yourself eventually to move at your own pace and savor your own thoughts, so don't overextend yourself in the flush of a new scene and new friends. Generally, you prefer to avoid tours and prefer to get together with one or two acquaintances with similar interests for seeing the sights and exploring new places. A fixed schedule makes you restless, as do rigid time limits, but these restrictions can ease money pressures, which you may underestimate.

SELF-CONFIDENCE

Aquarius, though no more secure or insecure than other signs, is acutely aware of the size and shape of his or her self-confidence—where it is lacking, where it is in control. This native has two drives (the strife between them generates the Aquarian brand of self-doubt or lack of confidence): the need to feel united with a group, to share its outlook and participate in its activities (this can be a club, society, spiritual organization, profession, or social movement), and the need to feel unique and independent. The ideal situation, of course, is to find a group that allows for and appreciates your individuality. If this is not available you resolve the dilemma by incorporating into yourself that knowledge you receive through temporary associations with groups or by being a friend and visitor but not a member.

HIGHER EDUCATION

You have a great deal of admiration for those who complete the higher education process, as well as for the concept of higher learning in itself. Your utopian and somewhat rebellious self prefers, though, to carve out your own realm of knowledge rather than accepting someone else's. There are many alternative schools that will give you this freedom while providing you with skills and information that might be slow or difficult to obtain otherwise. Education provides Aquarius with an important means of exploration; you benefit from it by gaining patience, self-confidence and a chance to focus your talents in an authoritative manner to constructive ends.

PISCES

LUCK

If you are a Pisces you have seen repeated proof of the way in which mental outlook contributes to the number of hurdles you face and how difficult they are to encounter. You know that good luck always appears as a good opportunity. Pisces, whose intuition sniffs out which direction to take, knows that his or her chosen road, with all its twists and turns that hide the destination, will nonetheless lead to the right place. There is difficulty when you hesitate to act for two reasons: first, if you are fearful of tests and problems that may have to be overcome; second, if you don't seem to override the inertia that makes the place where you are now seem like the only place to be.

INTELLECTUAL ACHIEVEMENTS

When it comes to curiosity, there are two types of Pisceans: the fish who floats motionless in order to absorb every pattern of light and sound around it; and the restless one who is always on the go, trusting to the interplay of all six senses for guidance (particularly the sixth). In both cases Pisces is aiming at extracting the essential lesson from all experience; you know that encyclopedic lists and preconceived ideas only keep people from learning fully what each moment of life has to offer. You don't need to accumulate such details for yourself—don't burden yourself with them for the sake of making impressions on others.

PERSONAL GOALS

Pisces loves to envision possibilities, to daydream endlessly, projecting all the nuances that a career or personal goal might present. You will imagine all the benefits and all the difficulties—although hardship has little bite when one can conjure up a solution at one's leisure. A Piscean who fixes on only the positive or only the negative possibilities becomes either an unrealistically utopian visionary or a worry-laden fretter who avoids choosing any direction because of the unpleasant things that might happen. Write on your wall in big letters, Pisces, "My imagination is creative, and it is fulfilled when I act on it."

TAKING RISKS

As stated above, Pisces can be the consummate worrier, not lacking in physical courage but filled with imagined terrors that cloud the picture of what a potential risk might entail. Once you have decided—and the moment of decision for Pisces always has a sudden and unmistakable clarity—you share the determination of your fellow water native, Scorpio, setting one foot after the other with single-minded concentration. You are capable of achieving an overview that accepts both the dangers and the benefits of your course of action equally, not demanding a happy ending—or a tragic one—and knowing there will always be a tomorrow with surprises in store.

TRAVEL

The timid Piscean stays at home, letting a vivid imagination do the traveling. This can be satisfying, but actually being there has a charm all its own. The active Piscean is quite a rover, often settling in a favorite foreign country for good or living in a succession of them over the years. Once bitten by the travel bug, you have trouble getting back into the familiar home environment. Pisces saves scrupulously for travel; you like your schedule to be open-ended so that you can wander about as your whims suggest.

SELF-CONFIDENCE

Probably your most forceful mood will never bowl anyone over with its intensity, but your sign is often inaccurately portrayed as being unable to stand up to the slightest challenge. True, you are sensitive and impressionable by nature, and you dislike hassles as much as anyone; you need to choose your steps carefully for self-protection. But your nature equips you also with stamina and patience, as well as the ability to find a dry cave and weather out the fiercest storms—this at times when others would change course too soon. Cultivate this quiet strength, and others will see and respect it.

HIGHER EDUCATION

The prime objective for Pisces in higher education is the fulfillment of the inner self. This is followed by your career interests, and you are happiest when they overlap. Social sciences, psychology, medicine, and the fine arts are naturals for you, and pursuing a course of learning enriches your imaginative scope as well as giving you the confidence that you can meet respected people on an equal basis. You may be surprised at your hidden abilities in the physical sciences, particularly the theoretical branches of biology, math, and astronomy. Although it may not be a financial necessity, part-time work during school gives you a needed change of pace.

CHAPTER TEN
Achievement

IN ANCIENT TIMES, this tenth house was that of the father, the family patriarch, and from him it extended to leadership in the home, then in the community, and also to state affairs. The role of leader and a person's standing in his or her career were closely linked, especially in more simple times. Now achievement—exemplified by leadership, accomplishment, and clout in whatever field you choose—more clearly reflects what personal attributes are defined in this house.

Surely ambition, power, politics, and leadership are still in vogue today, but these don't have to be interpreted in either positive or negative terms. These are energies which must be expressed in some way, for if you don't have some outlet to display all of your traits, a part of the personality's beauty is lost.

Homemakers have homes and children to show their contribution to society; business people have their work; artists have their crafts; entrepreneurs have the products they sell; and those in the service professions have the help and comfort they give others. Many times people become dissatisfied with their careers, when the recognition for their duties goes unspoken, wrongly interpreting this as unhappiness with their professions or daily life. Using your natural talents for getting recognized, gaining (and delegating) responsibilities, and altering your environment to make it more favorable may turn boring jobs around.

This is the portion of your life associated with a career, a life direction and a conscious choice about how you want to contribute to the world. It does not represent work for work's sake—that can be found in Chapter six.

Prestige and honors can come in any shape or form, but the way they arrive will come through efforts expended *as if* you were pursuing a career goal. Don't pass over this chapter no matter what your aspirations.

ARIES

CAREER POWER

To get in touch with a career most in harmony with your own basic nature, bear in mind that the sign Aries is noted for love of pioneering and exploration, a drive to live exuberantly in the present, and an appe-

235

tite for immense physical activity. You could be happy in the field of architecture, assuming the work is with an innovative firm. Investigative reporting could spark your interest, especially as a war correspondent, or a career in the military may provide an outlet for your dynamic energy and interest in weaponry. The field of sports and athletics could prove quite appealing, particularly if it draws upon your independent effort rather than integration with a team. Desk jobs will probably leave you cold as your activity level is high and could be a superb asset in the right job. Other possibilities are psychiatry, psychology, engineering, mechanics, and dentistry. Surgery, especially dealing with the head, could also be a fulfilling profession.

GETTING RECOGNITION

The need for recognition exists in all of us, but the ways in which we try to receive this can vary widely. Aries loves to be the leader, and recognition to these natives often comes through having loyal followers. Associates will be attracted to follow you by your sincere enthusiasm, certainty of purpose, and dynamic energy. Although you sometimes make the wrong choices due to impulsive decisions, your followers see a rare and highly prized quality of honor in you and are forgiving of the occasional error, recognizing your innate integrity and desiring to be part of your powerful creative processes. They will learn to stand clear when you are in motion so as not to be overwhelmed by your cyclone of activity, but will get into motion themselves as they are affected by the blast of raw Mars energy. Medals don't mean a great deal to you, but the freedom to act does, and will be a most satisfying recognition of your worth.

AMBITIONS

Aries is a sign generally associated with ambition, but not the plodding type associated with Capricorn natives. Ambition in the sign of Aries is closely related to the enthusiasm and vigor which give you the drive to surmount obstacles. Your ambition is connected with the present, not some future day in which you will reach your final goal and resting place at the top of the heap. You are, above all else, a starter and an initiator of action. You most certainly want to succeed, and it is that ambition that propels you forward, but then you would like to succeed at many things during your lifetime, and chances are that you will do exceptionally well at anything you see through to completion. The danger here lies in your impulsiveness, which can often motivate you to dive into something new before a previous effort has reached fruition.

WORKING ENVIRONMENT

As an Aries you will require a working environment that is full of stimulation. It is often said that desk jobs are not for Aries—and rightly so—for this will place him or her in a bondage, causing dissatisfaction, then unrest, and finally an explosive break. Aries needs a place with immense activity and noise. You seem to thrive on what others might consider noise pollution. A good deal of freedom is also necessary for your best performance. This applies to both physical and mental conditions which, when flexible, can bring forth your great creativity and dynamic strength. Physically, your work environment should have a feeling of substance. A delicate, pastel office with cute knick-knacks would be totally alien to your nature, and you may well destroy them by intention or accident. You want a solid, large desk, quality tools, and a lot of light and fresh air.

Employers

As an Aries you are quite independent by nature and can often be found as the head of your own business or free-lancing in the field of your choice. You can be a shining star in the employ of another as well, but the work should allow you plenty of independence, including the freedom to be flexible in your working hours. Although you can make it working alone, you can add an extra dimension to your career by employing or working with others who can fill in the spaces often left vacant as you rush into the job at hand. The loyalty of others actually means a great deal to you, though often this fact goes unnoticed beneath your dynamic presence. Being rather impulsive yourself, you can understand the need for change in others and are likely to be understanding if they would occasionally like a weekday off, but will be glad to work on Saturday instead. In fact, that would suit you just fine, as you need an employee who will give an extra hand when the rush is on.

Responsibilities

You feel a strong sense of responsibility toward your business, especially if it is one you have created through your own efforts. It is an extension of yourself and deserves your full support. Aries is approachable by others, thus facilitating the development of a wide network through which you may develop future contacts and help others within your sphere. Outgoing and positive, people enjoy having you around and feel good about helping you out, as you have been understanding of their circumstances in the past. You could be in a position to become a mentor for another if that person earns your admiration through his or her personal integrity. You will be quick to advance an employee who shows spunk and ability, particularly if he or she has been loyal to you, as loyalty is a quality for which you have great appreciation.

Community Service

The Aries individual is generally motivated to lend a hand to others less fortunate than himself. The radiant, outgoing warmth of the Aries woman is suited to working with the public in a service capacity. Having the vitality and the open heart to contact a wide range of individuals, your high degree of motivation becomes contagious to others who are often inspired to offer generous contributions to the cause. This is a result of your belief in yourself, as well as the validity of your group affiliation. You would be excellent at breaking new ground for a community service organization, as possessing the energy to get things started is typical of your sign. You may find satisfaction in supporting a community group involved with sports activities such as the YMCA or YWCA. Another possibility for those of you with school-age children could be the PTA.

TAURUS

CAREER POWER

Characteristics to consider when evaluating career placement are those most fundamental to your sign. In the case of Taurean types, you will function best in areas dealing directly with the material world, especially where accumulation of objects or symbols of value are concerned. Kindness, patience, and tenacity are all innate qualities that can serve you well in your livelihood. The building trades are particularly well-suited to your personal expression, as they allow creative manifestation through use of the earth's resources. The natural and environmental sciences, including agriculture, horticulture, farming and animal husbandry, will draw upon that same inner understanding of the earth. Your administrative skills could be utilized both in managing the finances of others through banking or investment, and in positions of responsibility at the federal, state, or local levels. Your ruling planet Venus gives you a fine sense of beauty and appreciation of music, which could be applied to many areas where aesthetics are desirable or marketable.

GETTING RECOGNITION

The need for recognition is universal, but each individual perceives the acknowledgement of merit differently. Recognition of your worth by others gives you a deep satisfaction, but it is not something you strive for outwardly. It is the expression of certainty in everything you do that is so appealing to people as well as the warmth and patience you show to others. You do, of course, want to make all the right choices, but not so much to gain the approval of others as to satisfy your own inner need for stability and security. By satisfying these needs in yourself, they are automatically extended into your environment and provide a much appreciated sense of solidity to all around you. When recognition comes in the form of promotion or gratitude from others, you are usually taken by surprise, and people admire you even more for not being smug about it. A job well done gives the satisfaction you most appreciate.

AMBITIONS

Taurus is usually not considered to be the ambitious type, yet even without that trait natives can build their career right to the top of any field. What causes you to accomplish so much is a seemingly bottomless desire to accumulate objects and symbols of material value and establish a solid, immovable foundation. Your persistence is legendary, and combined with your stubborn unwillingness to change often produces a phenomenal amount of power and influence. With the increased availability of upper-level positions for women, many of you could gravitate with typical Venusian grace right to the top. You have the capacity to methodically plan your course for the future and the tenacity to stick with it unwaveringly.

WORKING ENVIRONMENT

Ruled by Venus, planet of harmony, you will find it important to work in an environment that is both functional, to satisfy your earthy practicality, and tastefully appointed to suit your aesthetic sense. A harsh, dirty, or discordant atmosphere will go against your basic grain, and though you have the strength to endure such conditions, they do not favor your peace of mind. Comfort is important to you as well, so if moving to a new office be sure to work closely with the decorator to assure that the surroundings will be in harmony with your fundamental nature. You will be considered a fine asset by others in your work environment, as you display both strength and an inherent warmth to which others easily respond, but be aware that you possess an awesome capacity for destruction if pushed too far. Try to avoid lengthy buildups of minor irritations that can lead to explosive behavior.

EMPLOYERS

Those in the sign of Taurus have the rare gift of common sense and a persistence that usually allows them to do quite well in their own businesses. If this is your sign, you probably innately understand how to establish a company, how to finance it, and how to manage it. Overall, your warmth and ability will be appreciated by your employees. Although your tendency toward stubborn resistance can be exasperating when new ideas are being considered, your adherence to solid business sense turns out to be the wisest decision in the long run. In the employ of others, you will be considered dependable and personable, and could be a delight to your boss if he or she happens to be an impulsive idea generator who can't seem to take care of the mundane details. You could be a helpful stabilizing influence.

RESPONSIBILITIES

If any sign is characterized by a fine sense of responsibility, it is Taurus. Coworkers will be delighted to discover that not only do you have a good insight into the workings of the company, but you can be trusted to fulfill any commitment to which you've given your word. This is all involved with your patient desire to make the environment a secure one. Amazingly, despite what other less single-minded individuals may do, you will continue in your path of building and accomplishing, and could well be the major reason anything gets done. Your example to others is a good one, especially in the case of other employees who intend to be reliable and thorough, but have never developed the necessary qualities. In this case you could serve as a marvelous role model. Capitalize on your stability, as it is a rare gift in these changing times.

COMMUNITY SERVICE

Taureans are often the pillars of strength upholding the activities of public service organizations. You are the epitome of the responsible citizen and will feel happy to support the integration of your community. The home is important to the Taurus, as is the locale surrounding the immediate home. Any place where you or your family may tread in the local environs becomes an extension of the home and thus deserves your interest and contribution to its general welfare. If you own your own business, donations to nonprofit organizations can offer tax breaks that are quite attractive. Your excellent business sense knows this is an area that can be both financially and emotionally satisfying. Your own personal warmth and sincerity will draw good responses from others, which is helpful when approaching possible benefactors.

GEMINI

CAREER POWER

Career placement is always most satisfactory if the basic modus operandi of your own sign is carefully considered and integrated into the work through which you earn your income. Geminis do well in fields allowing free reign to their inquiring minds as well as their physical requirements, which demand swiftness, flexibility, and activity. You are superb in any area concerned with communication and contact with the public mind. Language arts, news, and the media are all indicated. Occupations requiring persuasion such as public relations, sales, advertising, and politics will all capitalize on your skills. With your ceaseless movement, the travel and transportation industries could be beneficial, as could work in education, especially teaching languages. In business, retailing would be natural as would work in the computer field, particularly with software. Entertaining would capitalize on both your communication skills and your quick wit.

GETTING RECOGNITION

The ways in which Gemini experiences recognition is usually directly related to the mental realm. Most of your satisfaction in life comes through verbal and intellectual exchange, and your rewards and signs of recognition will be the reflection of your mental abilities. A quick and data-packed conversation will leave you feeling alive, vitalized, and fulfilled, whereas a dull response from another can give you an empty, dissatisfied feeling. An employer who allows you the freedom to zip about, attending to many tasks, is acknowledging your competence and value. Not one to stick around long for anything, including praise, you will accept your recognition in terms of the freedom it can buy for you. You have a strong capacity for detachment and a cool logic in recognizing your own value and are not likely to be overwhelmed by the compliments of others.

AMBITIONS

The sign of Gemini is not considered to be ambitious in the usual sense of the word by striving for personal recognition and attainment. Yet there almost seems to be a type of ambition in your zeal to make connections between ideas and people. Your ruling planet, Mercury, known by the ancients as messenger of the gods, propels you outward into the environment of your locality to receive ideas and communications and carry them to other places. In this, you will find the keynote for the type of work to which you are best suited. The accomplishments you seek—and they are usually not the type planned with an eye to the distant future—are connected strongly with the present, with dissemination of ideas now, with reasoning and responding. Your dexterity in these areas is usually the only security you need, as it can bring you activity, interest, and income throughout life.

WORKING ENVIRONMENT

A feature to give strong consideration in your working environment is that of change. If anything works against your own innate abilities, it is repetition and stagnation. Repetition of situations that strain your highly sensitive nervous system can be quite detrimental to your health. In your place of employment, you will do well working with a wide variety of individuals and circumstances which allow your innate dexterity as full a rein as possible. The decor of your office should always be tasteful, contemporary, and have an atmosphere of airiness, giving you a feeling of openness rather than confinement. There should be plenty of opportunity for movement, as this is a basic feature in your mode of operation. Glass-walled, high-rise structures will suit you just fine, especially if you work on one of the higher floors. Try to maintain good air quality in your office, perhaps through use of a negative ion generator, which will add life and vitality to the air and help protect your lungs from damage.

EMPLOYERS

The basic characteristics of Gemini keep things active within a company. You are likely to present new ideas and innovations at an alarming rate, and can quickly penetrate the suggestions of others to ascertain their true merit. These are skills that could bring much reward and satisfaction in the field of management, but conversely, might prove to bring you considerable frustration if your job is behind an executive desk. Other factors in the chart could modify this, of course, but generally, based on sun sign alone, Gemini is better suited to types of work that allow enormous amounts of freedom of movement, both physical and mental. You could make it in your own business if teamed up with someone who complements your own active temperament with a stable, common-sense approach. Working for others just may be what will give you the most freedom to be yourself.

Responsibilities

The type of responsibility you handle best is that which is connected with your own inner drive and strong reasoning power. You may find it difficult, if not impossible, to plod through tasks requiring tedious and repetitious work and could very well find yourself leaving the task again and again in order to get stimulation elsewhere. On the other hand, if given work that demands much action with quick, incisive reasoning powers, the job is easily accomplished through interest, if not responsibility. There could hardly be a more important consideration in any kind of business than aligning the worker to the type of work to which he or she is naturally suited. This in itself inspires individuals to take responsibility, as they will be achieving satisfaction by doing something pleasurable to themselves. If you employ others, keep this in mind.

Community Service

Gemini's well-known communication skills can find a creative outlet in the field of community service. Work with nonprofit organizations often requires a tremendous amount of footwork, both in soliciting financial support from other agencies and in inspiring individuals to contribute their time and talents to the group effort. Gemini excells in this area and can receive great personal satisfaction from the actual work itself, knowing that your efforts are going to help others. With your keen reasoning powers, you will be able to help plot the future course of the organization. Clarity of thought is extremely valuable here, as public funds are usually involved and it is important that they are used wisely for the good of the community. The public will evaluate your decisions and actions and will appreciate the sound logic that you have applied to the situation.

CANCER

Career Power

Considering your most fundamental strengths is essential when planning for a career, particularly in relation to the peace and security the right career can mean for the Cancer native. The moon's rulership gives a fluctuating quality to your life, primarily influencing your emotions and feelings about life. You are a manager of situations by nature and have a nurturing quality, which manifests through your personal and professional endeavors. You appreciate tradition and cultures and would thrive in most areas connected with these. Museum work is a specific example. Occupations connected with domestic concerns are excellent and could cover many professions related to food, clothing, shelter, and survival. Natural resources from the earth and the sea will attract you as will many phases of the diagnostic and healing arts. Motel work, real estate, and housing all focus on the need for care and nurturing, which is a natural expression of your sign. Supporting and furthering women's affairs could work well for you.

GETTING RECOGNITION

In the case of the Cancerian, recognition is strongly entwined with material and emotional security. You are an extremely capable and responsible worker and appreciate hearing about it from others. You also want to see it reflected in your paycheck. Material accumulations are supremely important to you because they provide a feeling of security that is notably absent in your sign. You probably are the best worker in your group and therefore wish to be rewarded financially or you will have to do something highly unlike Cancers and find a new job. If the rewards for your work are not equal to your effort, you see it as an insult. Rather than being recognized for speed or courage, you will be noted for your marvelous tenacity and ability to create a solid career. You have a deep need for the respect and admiration of others and will enjoy their recognition of your worth.

AMBITIONS

One does not generally think of the Cancer as an ambitious person, yet this sign often does extremely well in the business world due to other motivations. The well-known ability of the crab to hold on firmly illustrates your ambition, even at the risk of losing a claw. Your main driving force is toward security, and this can be a powerful ally in the business world. You have a phenomenal ability to envelop and contain that which you can use to advantage in securing solid work situations. To gain an understanding of your ability to succeed, consider the crab again. Inwardly soft and vulnerable, it is protected externally by the armour of the shell, which renders it invulnerable to attack from outside sources. Your emotional interior is likewise vulnerable, but the face presented to the world can be formidable, allowing you to accomplish things that would make a less protected individual shudder.

WORKING ENVIRONMENT

A primary ingredient to consider wherever you work is the element of calm. With a predisposition to see the worrisome side of things, you should make every effort to elminate any influences that could bring out your tendency to be overconcerned. In decor you will no doubt appreciate the traditional or the antique, but always in the best of quality. Objects with cultural significance will enrich your feelings about your home away from home—the office. You may feel most at ease with a fair amount of solitary time, but on the other hand can be quite the administrator when the situation requires. Your adaptability can be utilized in work where change is necessary, but within a fixed structure. Here your imagination could have expression within a context of security so important to you. You probably will prefer an environment that does not require a lot of interaction with extreme personalities.

EMPLOYERS

The Cancerian possesses a rather improbable combination of personal qualities, which can suit you well to a career in the home or to the intense demands of executive-level positions. In the business game you are in it for the money and are not inclined to disguise the fact. Your sense of what people need and what they're willing to exchange for it is phenomenal, and can be the very key needed to open the door to the financial security you so ardently desire. No one dupes you, nor are you inclined to fritter valuable time away in frivolous activities or conversations. Every moment can be used in making money. You could be a fine asset in the employ of another as well, for those very qualities which single you out as an executive will make you most valuable in any working environment. Your paycheck usually reflects this value.

RESPONSIBILITIES

Part of your real value in the marketplace is your ability to take responsibility, a quality your employer wishes was contagious. Obviously, not much will be accomplished unless there are those willing to put their names on the job and see it through to the finish. You realize that in being reliable you will be, in essence, opening the door for promotion and a raise in pay, which is what business is all about. Your humor regarding others who do not demonstrate this ability is not great. In your mind, there is no excuse for inefficiency, and anyone who works for you had better line up with your expectations if the job is to continue. You are extremely fair with coworkers and compassionate, too, but this will not cause you to accept inferior work from others.

COMMUNITY SERVICE

Cancer types should feel quite at home working in a community service position. It is natural for you to be associated with the public, and your innate desire to nourish and support family environments could flourish here. You have managerial abilities, which could find excellent expression in a wide range of organizations from the largest global service groups to the local PTA. You will intuitively understand the need for high-quality extracurricular activities for school-age children, and by contributing your skills to such groups as the YMCA, YWCA, scouting, and the PTA you can do much to enhance the lives of future generations. Your abilities will allow you to integrate the activities of different community service groups, thus making the best use of available funds while creating a rich experience for all. Providing a little security in your community can be a marvelous contribution in these unsettled times.

LEO

CAREER POWER

For true fulfillment through career, you should ascertain the inherent traits of your personality and strive to align your life's work with that harmonic. Power and self-expression are at the root of Leo's fundamental nature; when combined with your territorial imperative, it can produce a dynamic business situation. You could be successful in all areas of money and finance, or in corporate management in any type of business or industry. Public administration is another possibility. Your flair for drama indicates a facility for entertainment, the visual or performing arts, and the fashion industry. The luxury trades could be quite appealing, especially with furs or gold jewelry. Gold mines are another possibility for Leo. If inclined toward the healing arts, you would probably do best in the areas which bring in substantial income, such as surgery or counseling. Work with young children is strongly indicated.

GETTING RECOGNITION

Each of us requires a different amount of recognition to keep his or her gears oiled, but the amount required by Leo runs a bit above the average. Leo is grand and he or she knows it; and Leo thrives on hearing about it. A natural dramatist, your most satisfying recognition often comes from having an appreciative audience, whose applause seems to spur you on to even greater heights. However, the adulation of others is not the only reward on which you thrive. Your expansive lifestyle requires an adequate income and, as your ability to be dramatic is often connected with the spending of money, you want to see your efforts amply rewarded in a monetary sense. Nor are you stingy with what you have. Your deep warmth of heart and sincere concern for others makes you quite generous, and here is another area in which the wise will be appropriately grateful for your benevolence. Even if your finances are less bountiful than you would like, you can still fare well if given sufficient strokes on your Leonine mane.

AMBITIONS

One would certainly consider Leo to have a great drive toward success and accomplishment. In a word, you are ambitious. Emanating from your solar nature (Leo is ruled by the sun) is the awesome energy that breathes life into every endeavor and continues to sustain it throughout its existence. Not one for moderation, you will (often without intending to do so) be a prime mover wherever you are and will easily attract a broad sphere of influence. You could view yourself as a nucleus by nature and, taking this key, align yourself with an area of work that draws upon this power to vitalize within a wide range. With such a placement, your ambitions will most easily be realized by magnifying yourself and manifesting your ideas through others. You may have to be careful with the more easily overwhelmed individuals with whom you associate, as solar power can be quite awesome, but your warmth and good nature are usually adequate compensation to those around you.

WORKING ENVIRONMENT

You will want your environment to supply plenty of room for you to expand and a goodly number of opportunities to relate to other people.

Your influence is beneficial and can do much toward expanding your business if directed along positive lines. Leo does have an ego that others must deal with. But if you do not flaunt this to an extreme, people will accept it as part of your work environment. Most Leos respond well to colors related to the sun—orange, yellow, and gold. You will appreciate a boldness and richness of decor, and superb quality should surround you both at work and at home. You thrive on action and accomplishment; as a mover and an organizer, you should try to work where those qualities may flower. Avoid dark and stagnant environments as they antagonize your natural solar energy.

EMPLOYERS

Leo is among those usually considered to be good executive material. Originally associated with kingly powers, Leo continues to earn this designation by conferring upon its natives a strong affinity for leadership and authority. Certainly, you are well equipped to lead and would thoroughly enjoy the prestige connected with such a position. Your warmth of heart is enjoyed by everyone, and provided your ego doesn't become cumbersome, others will be attracted into your presence by a glowing solar vitality. Even as the sun nourishes the earth, you have a rejuvenating effect on everyone within your sphere and are a welcome element in any environment. You can be equally as successful working for others as in being captain of your own ship, and will add your leadership qualities wherever you are placed.

RESPONSIBILITIES

As a Leo you will shoulder responsibility with a natural dignity and grace and are capable of accomplishing much. Others consider you an inspiration, and with the good will you generate in groups, a great deal can be accomplished. When placed in positions of authority, take care that your position does not cause your leadership to degenerate into bossiness. Few things can be more unseemly than a bossy Leo. Remember that those whom you lead will follow willingly, but only as long as there is justice to all. At the first sign of pushiness on your part, the whole endeavor can fall apart, and you will be left with the responsibility but no coworkers to help carry out the program. You could make quite a contribution to the world by sharing your understanding of leadership with children, most of whom have not learned that skill in these permissive times. It is a quality that is needed, and many could benefit through your efforts in working with a small group.

COMMUNITY SERVICE

As a Leo you could make a fine contribution to society in the area of community service. Inclined by nature to create and organize, you could be a prime mover in getting projects off the ground. Your enthusiasm and imagination will be contagious to others, creating a wave of energy that can manifest marvels even if funding is limited. You may enjoy working with a little theater group, or perhaps with a children's drama group, helping them to build confidence in their own creativity. You rather like a gamble and probably won't let adverse odds stop you if you have a terrific inspiration to bring to life. Your solar energy will bring it to fruition. You will recognize the need of all age groups to have some kind of healthy physical activity, and can be quite energetic supporting and participating in sports programs. Let your energy expand in helping others to enrich their own lives.

VIRGO

CAREER POWER

In selecting a career it is wise to carefully review your zodiacal strengths and inclinations in order to best capitalize on your innate assets. You are usually intellectual, your sign being ruled by the planet Mercury, and have fine powers of discrimination. You are attracted to the essential purity in things and are concerned with cleanliness and health. These qualities suit you well to the diagnostic and healing arts, which provide a wide span of occupations from research to actual medical practice, therapy, and nursing. Lab work will probably be appealing, especially if it deals with chemicals. You could do well at jobs connected with inspecting, health and safety, and educational institutions. Fields involving work with numbers, such as bookkeeping and accounting, would draw upon your skills, as would the area of engineering. Virgo types are often suited to work with animals in care and breeding. Service is the keynote of your sign and should be a factor in whatever you do.

GETTING RECOGNITION

Virgo is a natural server and does not require a great deal of public acclaim for the purpose of ego-satisfaction. Since you generally ask nothing for yourself, your visible recognition usually comes through increases in pay and position, although you are not ambitious and are usually quite happy to work where you are. You are aware of your current market value, however, and are not likely to stay around where your skills are undervalued or your efforts unappreciated. Your work often provides the satisfaction you need, and your value becomes obvious as your work environment increases in organization, approaching perfection as nearly as possible. A well-run ship is immensely rewarding to you, and to see your superiors advance due to your efforts provides a real satisfaction. Monetary rewards are important to you, but mainly because of your desire to be secure against ill health or loss of funds later in life.

AMBITIONS

As a sun sign it can be safely said that you are virtually without ambition in the sense of climbing to the top or desiring personal aggrandizement. Yet you have a compelling motivation to do things thoroughly and with an efficiency that is truly awesome. Rather than high placement you wish to be of service to others through your work, a far more noble ambition than receiving public acclaim for your position of authority and influence.

You work behind the scenes, and in the last analysis could be much more important to the success of a group than the person who has great flash but can't get the organizational aspect together. Recognizing that all things work together for the ultimate good allows you to do marvelously well in your particular position, and thus build a firm foundation on which a solid organization may be built.

WORKING ENVIRONMENT

Above all, you will appreciate cleanliness and order in your work environment. There is no place in your life for objects with no useful function, and you will be happiest if the frills are left to someone who appreciates them. You can do extremely well in a superbly organized office or can be the one who can make order out of chaos if given the opportunity to do so. Virgo can be a perfect complement to an individual who has a multitude of terrific ideas, which are scratched out on napkins and scraps of paper, but somehow never quite get collected into a form that allows them to develop. Your ability to focus allows you to take the scattered energies of others and integrate them into a useful form. There should be a certain amount of harmony and quiet in your work place, as too much discordance can be extremely draining on your nervous system.

EMPLOYERS

Virgos—like every other sign—can be found in every imaginable type of work, but they are not all using their inate skills in the most creative and productive ways. You have abilities that could be quite valuable in high company positions, but you seem to be much more content using your fine skills to further the careers of others. If you find the thought of an executive position appealing, then by all means go for it. You have a genuine concern for others, which would be welcome at any level of employment, and your ability to persist can assure you a good foothold once established in the desired position. You have a unique ability to process vast amounts of data and could be an asset to any company as a secretary or possibly working in the research field where there is much information to consider. By all means, allow yourself to go as far as your heart desires.

RESPONSIBILITIES

When given an assignment by your employer, you will work methodically and consistently until the work is completed with absolute perfection. Virgo can handle the responsibility; and this sign can fulfill it with a precision and clarity that can awe others. If you want quick, clean work handed to you with a smile, give the task to a Virgo. The fact that others do not necessarily come up to your standards can be somewhat distressing because your makeup does not easily accept sloppy, slow, or second-rate work. When dealing with your own employees, remember that you have been gifted with a precise eye for detail, but others may not have that same ability. It is easy for you to become nit-picky about things and drive other personality types crazy, so allow for the differences between people and try to restrain unrealistic expectations.

COMMUNITY SERVICE

If any sign has everything needed to be the heart and soul of community service, it is surely the sign of Virgo. Naturally inclined to help others, you could find this type of work extremely rewarding and satisfying. Nonprofit community groups often fail to fulfill their potential due to lack of planning and organization, and it is especially in this area that you could lend valuable service. Many willing hands and hearts are needed if the members of a community are to care responsibly for themselves and others. Virgo understands this and will work harder than most to contribute to this type of group effort. You are a specialist and would do well focusing on a particular area of activity, rather than branching out to encompass a wide scope of endeavors. Health is a focus in your life and could be a direction to investigate where the public is concerned.

LIBRA

CAREER POWER

In order to integrate your natural abilities and tendencies into the practical aspects of earning a living, it is wise to carefully consider the natural traits of your sun sign. Libras are well-suited to partnerships and will strive for equilibrium in all facets of life. These characteristics are needed for work with the public, and your greatest success will come in this area. Arts and services connected with the use of leisure time would be a good field for you, as would work in the liberal arts, especially in a teaching capacity. An aptitude for persuasion would incline you toward a variety of public relations jobs, including dealing with the law, sales, and politics. With Venus as your ruler, you will have a fine sense of aesthetics, which could be cultivated in the fashion and beauty fields, decorating, the graphic arts, or any place where personal appearance and refinement are significant factors. Acting and diplomatic skills fall naturally into your realm and could be career directions.

GETTING RECOGNITION

For many signs, outward recognition is not particularly important, but the sensitive Libra wants to be well-received at all times. You have a deep need for personal approval, as being accepted by others is part of your ceaseless drive to achieve harmony in all things. You desire to be acknowledged as refined and elegant, which indeed you are, although in the business world you can be absolutely ruthless in driving toward your goals. You recognize your value to others in their efforts to make your life pleasant and your environment harmonious. An invitation to an exquisite dinner can mean much to you and can be a reward in itself. But with all your seeming passivity, you are practical and know the value of financial rewards. These you expect and will strive for, and can actually become rather unpleasant if your expectations are denied. You are fair-minded in all things and will advance financially in one way or another. You know your worth and want others to recognize it as well.

AMBITIONS

Libra is not considered to be one of the ambitious signs, yet through a highly developed power of persuasion, you are able to get just about anything you want. Your main strivings in life are for refinement and justice, and most of your endeavors are in some way connected with these. Your ambition, if it could be called that, to establish elegance and beauty wherever you are is viewed favorably by society and is often an asset, which moves you far in the business and professional world. Especially combined with the deep desire for equity and an acceptance of others, it becomes a powerful combination that can lend your career a strong upward impetus. A fine sense of discrimination is yours as well, but you must be somewhat cautious about your impressionability lest it lead you into unfavorable situations. Draw on your innate sociability to support you in career advancement.

WORKING ENVIRONMENT

Your working environment is an important issue to you. As with Venus-ruled desires for harmony and beauty, you will be highly responsive to these influences, and likewise devastated by the opposite qualities. An unpleasant work environment will set up such antagonistic waves that you will find it extremely difficult, if not impossible, to cope. Everything in you gravitates toward peace, so give this trait strong consideration when evaluating various careers. The harmonious or discordant vibrations given off in your work area will have a direct effect on your productivity. Working with people will be a natural for you, especially if it is connected with beauty or with negotiation in some way. Partnership is natural for you, and close work with others draws upon the innate abilities of your sign. You can go far in a twosome.

EMPLOYERS

Libra is a fairly versatile sign and can do well in many positions, but traditionally this sign is considered to be one of partnership. Your sign seems to thrive on interrelating with others, and with your innate sense of balance or justice you are able to build a superb working relationship. You have a notable taste for elegance and luxury, and often your business successes are the results of the desire to surround yourself with expensive objects. Regardless of the motivating factors, however, you can quickly move from an entry-level position right up to that coveted spot you have set your sights on. With your smooth manner and attractive appearance, you will be welcome anywhere, and even those whom you may use a little to get what you want probably won't mind too much.

RESPONSIBILITIES

Despite the apparent easygoing quality of Libra types, there are not many jobs they can't handle—and quite effectively at that. Once focused in a direction, they can take great responsibility upon themselves, but make sure that plenty of time for enjoying the finer things of life is included in the schedule. In any kind of decision-making process, Libra will go to great lengths to evaluate the merits of all sides, but may carry this process on to such length that the decision is never made. Perhaps you would be better at bringing all the facts to light and leaving the final decision to another, as in the case of an attorney who produces and evaluates the facts, leaving the verdict to the judge. You aim to shoulder your responsibilities in such a manner that the work may be accomplished in an atmosphere of intelligence, harmony, and mutual effort among all involved.

COMMUNITY SERVICE

The influence of Libra adds a touch of class wherever he or she appears, and individuals of this sign could contribute a bit of beauty often needed in community service work. Due to limited funding, public facilities often lack the finer touches that make an environment special, but with Libra's natural flair for the aesthetic this shortcoming could be easily surmounted. Given the most basic of materials, you can often come up with marvelously imaginative ideas, which can beautify the premises at little cost, while at the same time giving others the chance to express their own creativity in making a nicer place for all. At community banquets or social events you will be the perfect host or hostess, making everyone welcome and at ease, while seeing to it that the decor is exquisite and the food tasty and attractively served. This ability can be particularly valuable when entertaining those of philanthropic inclination.

SCORPIO

CAREER POWER

As a Scorpio you have a particular intensity about everything you do, and thus should give extremely careful consideration to an appropriate career. If your work is not compatible with your natural abilities, great frustration could occur with a tendency to express itself in a destructive manner, either inwardly or in your visible life. With an innate insight into the subconscious and subatomic, you could do quite well in such diverse fields as psychotherapy and research into the organic or inorganic areas of science—any place where there is a mystery to be penetrated or something of the unknown to be brought to light. This could apply to investigative work as well, especially in the crime areas. Any work related to the military/industrial complex would be natural, and also some areas of healing, particularly surgery. You could enjoy working with finance, taxes, and insurance, especially where heirs are involved, or in trades that deal with removal, sanitation, purification, or death. You will probably feel most comfortable working behind the scenes in some way.

GETTING RECOGNITION

Recognition by others seems to be an important feature in most of our lives, and can certainly be a strong motivating factor for future successes. With Scorpio recognition from outward sources is meaningless, as you answer only to your own values, and the standards of most people fall far below your self-imposed set. You have a penetrating insight into the motives of others and know immediately if the praise given is insincere. If the recognition is indeed shallow, you will not only be unaccepting of it, but will be insulted that anyone has considered you so superficial as to take the adulation seriously. The mildest consequence of such an event is that you lose all respect for anyone who offers you recognition for an action which does not meet your own exacting standards. The one area in which you are likely to accept the recognition of others is that of power. You know you carry a mysterious power and you don't mind if others recognize that fact, but you would appreciate the acknowledgment much more coming from someone who knows what power is.

AMBITIONS

In viewing the Scorpio native it is important to distinguish between ambition and intensity. One could not actually call your sign ambitious, yet you love to succeed and approach everything with such a single-minded intensity, appearing to bulldoze your way to the top. However, this is unlikely; although you understand power well and know how to wield it, you prefer to keep a low profile. You are much better suited to being the power behind the throne than the figurehead who looks impressive but is, by virtue of his position, consistently open to public scrutiny. Your designs are best carried off under the cloak of anonymity. Although not always understood by others, you are well aware of the great freedom inherent in invisibility, as without being known you are not exposed to the psychic energy drain of other people's interpretations of your methods and goals, their opinions, or of your own personality, which you prefer to keep to yourself.

WORKING ENVIRONMENT

Scorpio is associated with birth, death, and regeneration, and your work should draw upon your innate understanding of these processes. You will probably be happiest in a job that allows you some amount of time that does not demand social interaction. You are inclined to look deeply below the surface in all things, and as social exchanges are by nature superficial their value to you is limited. You appreciate a certain amount of calm in your work environment, but are surprisingly able to put your intense powers of concentration to work despite the chaos of external surroundings. In relating to others you tend to be rather severe, yet have great patience with what you see as merely human weakness. You will probably feel most useful in work that deals in some way with the unseen, the unknown, the mysterious, the underground, the subconscious.

EMPLOYERS

Individuals born in the sign of Scorpio are highly independent by nature. Natives of this sign live life on their own terms, and no amount of outside influence is going to change that to any significant degree. This independent spirit often causes you to create your own employment, do freelance work, or go into business for yourself. Your sign gives all the dynamic and aggressive energy of your ruling planet, Mars, and will lend strong support to any venture you undertake. Those in this sign often have a certain harsh edge to their personalities, which can make working in groups difficult. You prefer the background scenes and usually would rather keep a low profile than to be out front gathering all the recognition, but also losing your freedom to the demands of the public. Your desire to delve beneath the surface is better suited to lone work.

RESPONSIBILITIES

Dealing with responsibility comes quite easily for most Scorpios. Along with your intense personality comes an equal intensity in everything you do, including your commitments to others and an unshakable loyalty to those whom you admire, respect, or who have helped you in the past. Scorpio will never forget a kindness—or an offense—and you will always carry a sense of responsibility to one who has gained your favor, alert to any way in which you may repay the kindness. Raising children can be a career to Scorpio, and parents of this sign feel highly responsible for the welfare of their children. They can take great pains to see that their children are raised in a manner which will give them strength for their own futures. This sign can be trusted with many responsibilities and will perform extraordinarily well as long as his or her honor is not betrayed.

COMMUNITY SERVICE

The unique focus of Scorpio will often allow this native to serve the community through work with prisoners or other institutional groups. This sign has an innate understanding of the unseen, the underground, the subconscious. In fact, you could be attracted to work in an area directly connected with crime, such as investigation or prison work. You may have a special insight into the minds of the maladjusted, and thus may be able to provide helpful counseling to those in such circumstances. Not uncommonly, you have a certain unusual rapport with children and juveniles who are in trouble with society, and by gaining their confidence could help them form new and more positive directions in their lives. You have an enormous amount of energy under your usually calm exterior, and when focused for the good of the community could provide the needed dynamism to get things done.

SAGITTARIUS

CAREER POWER

As a Sagittarian you would work in many fields, but you should be aware of your basic temperament and abilities in order to best focus your energy. Movement is extremely important to you in the physical sense and as a future-oriented tendency in everything you do. Since you love to travel, your work could easily be in the international scene, studying and teaching languages or actual service in a foreign country. The scientific and esoteric areas of futuristic studies will be appealing and could incorporate work with space or astrology. Having a strong philosophical and theological inclination, you could become deeply involved with religion, particularly in a scholarly sense. Teaching and research are both natural for you, as are the arts of communication and language. Working with animals, especially the larger varieties, appeals to you, making veterinary medicine a good choice. The law, international finance, and education are all fields in which your fundamental skills could be utilized.

GETTING RECOGNITION

Everyone desires to find his or her place in the sun, and Sagittarius is no exception. You seem to find yourself on stage quite often; in fact, you seem more at home on stage than off. The favorable response of an audience, whether in the theater or in real life, warms your heart and inspires you to give even more of yourself for the enjoyment of others. This could well be the form of recognition that pleases you most. The freedom to carry on work at your own pace and with your own style of perpetual motion will be a type of recognition you deeply appreciate. It demonstrates the faith and trust of others that you will honorably fulfill your tasks even if it is in an unfamiliar manner to them. The Sagittarian will appreciate recognition through monetary rewards, but this is not his or her main driving force. You are too fond of change to spend year after year on a job merely because security is at the end of the road. Your security is in the ability to deal with change and challenge in a creative way.

AMBITIONS

Unlike the other fire signs of Aries and Leo, you are not necessarily thought of as ambitious, but you do have that fiery drive that keeps propelling you forward and expanding your circle of influence. You have the ability to see an opportunity immediately, and you are bold enough to leap into it with no more than a moment's consideration. This can produce quite a variety of changes in your life, but this, too, is something you welcome with open arms. Your tendency is toward expansion, and you can go quite far without the solid type of ambition connected with some of the other signs. Anything that you become involved with must have a forward motion or you will not be with it for long, as your basic nature inclines a strong need for locomotion. Growth is most likely to come through your own aspirations and tendency to aim far beyond your present placement.

Working Environment

An ideal work environment for the Sagittarian is the world at large. Not one to be confined or limited, you will want the freedom to touch many polarities and to express yourself through a variety of modes. Not only is it essential to your temperament to have this liberty for its own sake, but your own inspiration and productivity is increased through multiple contacts. Those of your sign even seem to think better on their feet; if in a confining environment you can get some relief by walking around a lot during the day. You are a good-natured sort and usually add an element of humor to your workplace, thus endearing you to coworkers. You are not terribly exacting when it comes to decor, but it should at least have a feeling of energy and expansiveness, not the look of a dusty vault. Look for a career with plenty of movement and interaction with other people, which you need to stimulate your mind.

Employers

As a Sagittarian you will often find yourself in the employ of others rather than owning your own business. The reason behind this is your seemingly limitless appetite for travel and change, which keeps you moving at a frequency that prohibits the establishment of a solid foundation. You get on quite well with others and are welcome in many places, which even further provides incentive for change. One job can become quite tedious for you action-oriented individuals, unless it happens to be in a field where your natural desire for movement can be expressed. Your fine intellect needs to experience a variety of stimulating situations as well, thus becoming a suitable companion for your body. You have a marvelous, persuasive ability and can easily promote yourself into higher and higher positions in your company or from job to job, each in a different location.

Responsibilities

Sagittarians feel a strong responsibility toward the intellectual development of humanity. You understand the importance of developing the intellect and of being aware of the earth as a community both physical and spiritual. Your aim is high as depicted in the symbol of your sign, the archer with bow aimed at the heavens, and you desire that all persons should become in touch with the highest aspect of their natures. To this end, you accept a certain responsibility to humanity as a whole. Responsibility connected with the material world is not as great, as it is not uncommon for you to view physical possessions as a source of limitation and an impediment in the path of your freedom to get up and go whenever you choose. Your real responsibility is to the soul of man rather than to his transient accumulations.

COMMUNITY SERVICE

With your love of travel, Sagittarius, you could easily be found spreading your love of humanity to the far corners of the earth. To you, the world is one big community in which you feel quite at home. Always a teacher by inclination, you could do wonderfully well working with groups to help them upgrade their living standards. Creative change sparks your enthusiasm, inspiring you to expand your efforts to help those who have received less than the rest of society. You are naturally merciful to others without becoming a bleeding heart. With refreshing optimism, you approach the knottiest of situations eagerly, working to develop and expand available resources, that others may benefit. Your eye is ever to the future, and this focus can be valuable in helping to keep projects from bogging down under the weight of momentary difficulties. Your aspirations can be an inspiration to many.

CAPRICORN

CAREER POWER

The sign of Capricorn, ruled by Saturn, manifests a solid, earthy quality and a strong sense of definition. In order to be successful in a career, you will want to put these qualities to work for you. Occupations connected with the earth in some way will be quite satisfying. Your ambition will drive you to the top in whatever you do, but your work should be in an area providing a great deal of stability. Your natural ability as a manager could direct you into many areas, but you are especially well-suited to business and finance, big business or industrial management, and administrative positions connected with labor. Property, real estate, and construction all draw upon your attraction to the earth and could work well with your understanding of economics and mathematics. Regulatory and correctional services would utilize your ability to discipline and create structure, while the physical sciences could give you a satisfying contact with the earth.

GETTING RECOGNITION

While recognition is unimportant to some signs and satisfying to others, to Capricorn it is the prime motivator, the compensation for self-denial and hard work and the very reason for existence. Capricorn is the ambitious one, the climber using every person and situation to work his or her way to the top of the mountain. Do you care about recognition? You need a full dose and at frequent intervals. Rather quiet and apparently unassuming on the surface, others can almost see the inner processes moving when praise is given you. Visibly digesting and absorbing it into your being as nourishment, you radiate a satiated glow. Of course, this is all done in a low key, and at a casual glance one could scarcely believe that such a seemingly quiet and refined individual could thrive in such a way on public adulation. It's your life blood. In the early stages of development, you are quite content to humbly accomplish rather mundane work, but that is only because you have already plotted your entire life's course and are merely biding time until the predetermined moment of success and power.

AMBITIONS

If there is a sign that has ambition written all over it, Capricorn is surely the one. The drive toward ambition operates at every level of your existence, and even if success is thwarted you will still retain the tendency to climb. It is not uncommon for those of your sign to be found in executive positions, and it is usually a combination of knowing how to use people as stepping stones and dogged hard work that gets you there. The smell of success is sweet to you, but often your focus in that direction is so intense that your personal life suffers, being repeatedly put on the back burner while career interests are pursued. You usually show a natural dignity, which causes others to trust and believe in you and helps further your goals. Capricorn is known as the "executive sign,"and it's easy to see why.

WORKING ENVIRONMENT

The kind of work environment that will be most satisfying to you is one with predictability and a solid foundation. You will expect everything to run according to regulation and can become quite distressed if things are otherwise. Your ruling planet, Saturn, is associated with structure and form, and you will be extremely aware of these characteristics in all aspects of life as a result. Since career is a main focus, that is the area in which these things become most important. You will be a strong steadying influence in your work environment and can, by your example, help others to become better disciplined and organized. You will need to curb your tendency to criticize others, as this is not usually well received even though you may view it as constructive. Your surprising wit can save you from being too heavy an influence on coworkers.

EMPLOYERS

In the realm of astrology, Capricorn is known as one of the "executive signs." This is due in large part to your being associated with the earth element, which provides a stable foundation for all growth and production. The "executive" designation indicates work with others, and in this company you are usually to be found. Capricorn loners are rare, not because they are tremendously social creatures, but because the external climb to the top requires something or someone to climb on. This is why you need to be involved with other people. You are a true disciplinarian, and as such have little trouble keeping your organization in line, though you do tend to appear quite stodgy to those free-spirited individuals in your company. You have fine executive qualities, including the ability to plan wisely and to see plans through to completion. Try not to smother your employees with your own traditional views, as their innovative ideas could well be money in your pocket.

RESPONSIBILITIES

Taking responsibility is in the natural realm of the Capricorn. You are a broad-shouldered person with the capacity to carry much responsibility and to work persistently and hard to achieve the desired goals. Once you make a commitment there's no turning back, and though it may take an enormously long time for you to finally make that decision, it will have been given scrupulous consideration, and be both sensible and financially sound. Herein lies the secret of your success: you accept the work, the responsibility, and the rewards that come as you watch yourself bypass the competition. If affiliated with others through family or career, they are part of your overall plan for success, deserving to some extent, your care and support. They will have this as long as they act in a manner you feel to be correct.

COMMUNITY SERVICE

As a Capricorn you are heir to administrative skills par excellence. In addition you have a deep concern for your performance as viewed by the public, and you would be fulfilled by a community service occupation, which places you in a favorable position in the public eye. Your ambitious drive to succeed could work well here, if you have a humanitarian leaning. If you are not so inclined, you would still climb to the top and satisfy other basic urges. The chamber of commerce would be a likely place to find Capricorn working to enhance relations between business and the community. You could also work well with the elderly, especially in helping them to arrange the practical concerns of their later years. For the aged, it is of primary importance to have their estates dealt with in a businesslike manner and in keeping with the seemingly endless rules and regulations imposed by government regulations. Your administrative skills and business savvy could be a real blessing here.

AQUARIUS

CAREER POWER

As an Aquarius you have a unique type of future orientation, which is connected with humanity as a whole in the context of opening the door to the new and unexpected. In considering a career you will want to give this unusual ability an opportunity to blossom for the benefit of humankind. You could do extremely well as an entrepreneur, especially in a contemporary field such as computer science. You are imaginative and innovative and could express these qualities in the physical sciences and technologies including nuclear physics, meteorology, and electronics. Communication is another area in which your skills could be used, including broadcasting, the media, and teaching, particularly in technical and higher studies such as metaphysics. Social sciences will capitalize on your attachment to humanity and could allow you to be of real service to the world. Humanitarian causes will inspire you, especially in connection with associations, civil rights, feminism, and philanthropy. In the healing arts, radiology and work with nervous disorders and mental health would be indicated.

GETTING RECOGNITION

Recognition is like a form of food to many persons, and it is surprising to what lengths many of us will go to acquire it. The Aquarian receives recognition through the different, the unusual, the futuristic, and the bizarre. Regardless of income level or social position, the Aquarian would hate to be viewed as the same as most folks. This is not to say that you view the masses in a condescending manner. Quite the contrary, you are more likely to be their benefactor. The type of recognition you desire is connected with the surprising and unusual. You are an individual who needs much freedom, and if given it will often make a notable contribution to the betterment of humankind, or the further development of the arts or sciences. Your recognition often comes from afar, as those in close proximity are often so affected by your unpredictable ways that they fail to see the ultimate benefit of your work. But this, in itself, is a form of reward. After all, it is in being different that you express your unique individuality.

AMBITIONS

Aquarius is not considered to be an ambitious sign, but you do have a great deal of energy to invest in your fields of interest. Your overall concern is for humanity as a whole rather than the self, and with Uranus as your ruling planet, your energies could easily be directed into some revolutionary form of expression. This could even include political or social revolution on a large scale. If there is an ambition in your life, it could well be to thrust inspired, progressive ideas of an unconventional nature into the eye of the public consciousness. Your penchant for experimentation can spark an ambition for a new discovery and the accompanying intellectual thrill that makes your life worth living. You are an unbiased soul who will direct your desire for reform toward the betterment of the masses rather than for your own self-aggrandizement.

WORKING ENVIRONMENT

You require a great deal of freedom and understanding in your work environment, though perhaps acceptance would be a better term than understanding. There are few who can really understand your ways, but there are more who could accept them under the right circumstances. Coworkers are attracted to a certain mystique that radiates from you and is enhanced by an apparent aloofness, which is actually no more than detachment. Your friendliness and helpfulness are welcome in any environment and can further your own interests, but be careful not to get so caught up in the quest for the unusual that you lose sight of what you set out to do. Your work situation should include access to the tools you need to pursue your goals and should allow plenty of physical and—

even more importantly—intellectual freedom. Try to locate yourself in work that will allow you to fulfill your visions.

EMPLOYERS

As an Aquarian you will likely find yourself in a number of interesting and unusual job placements during your life. Yours is one of the signs that enjoys variety and change, though more for what it can do for humanity than for the sake of change itself. You can often be found working on your own in some self-conceived business or creating a new and unusual art form, but just as often you could be deeply involved with some humanitarian cause, which keeps you busily working with many other persons. The living breath of humanity draws you like a magnet, and can be an area where your world-changing ideas can begin to manifest themselves. Most of your ideas are so far advanced for the time that it may take years, decades, or even centuries before the rest of the world catches up to you. In your deepest being, you want a utopia for all humankind and will give your life's energy to see it develop.

RESPONSIBILITIES

You have a sense of responsibility of a sort, but not the same spine-compressing kind associated with the solid and steady earth signs— Capricorn and Taurus in particular. Your responsibility, as you see it, is toward the earth and its peoples, the solar system, the universe. Your ruling planet, Uranus, ties you firmly into the fate of humanity, and regardless of your personal career expression it will probably in some manner be connected with the advancement of the human race as a whole. Radical imbalances in living conditions among the earth's peoples are sources of discontent for you. The misuse of planetary resources, pitting one nation or culture against another, distresses you deeply and inspires you to put your unique type of creativity into solving these imbalances.

COMMUNITY SERVICE

As a sincere humanitarian, Aquarius could easily find the majority of his or her lifetime devoted to some type of direct or indirect service to society as a whole. It is always your inclination to help others, and with your characteristic liberalism you could find yourself on the forefront of the newest, world-saving movement. Your work is geared more to the masses than to the individual and more to reform than to continuing the same well-known methods of dealing with social problems. There is a complete absence of bias in the Aquarian nature, which makes you an ideal candidate for working with a variety of cultures and races. There is a magnetic mystique about you that can be an asset in public relations. People may often accept your unconventional approaches to the public merely because they are attracted to you personally. This can be a key to planting new seeds of world service in a manner painless to your colleagues.

PISCES

CAREER POWER

In order to best utilize your Piscean attributes, you will want to take a close look at your zodiacal tendencies and make a firm decision as to how these may best be used as creative energy in the world. Your high degree of sensitivity can work for or against you, so it is important that it be used in a positive way. Naturally artistic, a career in one of the arts could be most satisfying and fulfilling. These possibilities could include writing fiction or poetry, music, dance, painting or sculpture, and photography. Filmmaking and set design would be crafts that draw upon your understanding of illusion. Counseling and guiding are innate capacities, which could help many and could be connected with your spiritual inclination. Institutions of confinement such as hospitals and prisons can be places where Pisces' talents can be used. You can be quite persuasive in an inoffensive way and may do well in selling, advertising, or managing. Entertaining and the theater are other areas where your creativity and insight could shine.

GETTING RECOGNITION

Some form of recognition seems to be necessary for those of us who have not yet retired to a high Himalayan cave to commune with the essence of all life. Even the mystical Piscean finds he needs a good deal of reinforcement from his or her fellow travelers here on planet Earth. Pisces isn't native in his or her Neptunian driftings, and would be quick to identify false recognition when given it. But in the fields where you excell, particularly the various arts, you will be greatly appreciative of recognition for the quality of your insight or the technical skill with which you handle your medium. Although nebulous in many ways, you know good art when you see it, and even realize its current and future value in the world. A certain amount of recognition will help to alleviate the nagging insecurity which can drive the Piscean into unhealthy habits or abuses of the body. Monetary rewards are nice, of course, and will offer minor notivation, but the type of recognition most appreciated relates to the beauty and harmony of your sign.

AMBITIONS

The Piscean nature is the very antithesis of the hard-driving ambition associated with Capricorn. Your nature is much more ascetic and universal, and you would not be particularly effective commanding a bevy of employees or dealing with the intense decisions required by corporate executives. Your gift to the earth is much more poetic and sensitive in the artistic sense. The Piscean whose major concern is accumulating vast material resources is rare. In fact, it is an area of life that is often difficult for you to deal with. You are, however, quite resourceful and have well-developed powers of persuasion, which you can use so artfully that a person may not realize your influence. There is a certain mystical glamour about you that can attract a benefactor who could help further your career in the field of art. However, you need to discipline yourself to take care of life's mundane practicalities, if for no other reason than your own peace of mind.

WORKING ENVIRONMENT

Pisceans require a great deal of peace and quiet in their work environment. You have a strong sensitivity to the discordant and can become extremely overstressed if subjected to such environments for very long. Harshness is something with which you do not deal well. The decor of your workplace should reflect your temperament and have a soothing quality that blends well with your own spirit. The brash, noisy, or unbeautiful can be most irritating and will certainly not inspire your best efforts. Coworkers usually enjoy you very much and are quite often uplifted themselves by your natural compassion and understanding of their feelings. You are unselfish and remarkably flexible—characteristics that permit you to blend beautifully in a variety of situations. Focus on a career that allows you to develop your own innate qualities to their fullest.

EMPLOYERS

As a Pisces you have an unusual combination of characteristics, some of which suit you well to working in the employ of another, and others which almost demand that you proceed on an independent course. You probably benefit the most by associating yourself with an individual or company that can provide a structure within which your work may be done. Quite often those of your sign show great promise in the arts, particularly visual art, music, poetry, and dance. In these fields it is almost essential to retain the services of an agent or promoter who can make the contacts necessary to assure that your art or craft will produce an adequate income for you. This is an invaluable service, as often the Pisces is temperamentally unsuited to business dealings. The heart of a poet is at its best in other realms. There are some marvelous Piscean business persons, so be open to that possibility as well.

RESPONSIBILITIES

Responsibility is something Pisceans would just as soon not have to think about. It is all too mundane and too difficult. Your real sense of responsibility is likely to be related to one of the artistic fields in which you make yourself available to the mystical vibrations of your ruling planet, Neptune, bringing these exquisite perceptions into the public eye. It is probably difficult even for you to determine just exactly where you feel your responsibility lies—if indeed it lies anywhere at all. Your highly intuitive capacity inclines you to be a receiving unit for the world, and your artistic sense inspires you to create beautiful works of art based on these most unusual revelations. You are truly the poet's poet, the artist's artist, the creator of divine illusions and mystical myths, which bring humanity into contact with its own subconscious.

COMMUNITY SERVICE

As a Piscean you have an inner understanding of individuals and of mankind as a whole. This gives you a certain universal approach to life that can be beneficial in working for the benefit of the immediate community or assisting humanity in a larger scope. Your insight into mass psychology will show you how to approach the public on matters concerning the welfare of the local or world community. Your own flexibility will allow you to work contructively with others without too much weight placed on your personal desires. You have managerial skills that could be valuable in working with social institutions, especially when fortified with your considerable persuasive ability. You may be attracted to work involving prisons, asylums, or other institutions characterized by confinement. Resourcefulness as part of your basic makeup is always a prime asset where public monies must be wisely used.

CHAPTER ELEVEN
Friendships

ASSOCIATIONS, COMPANIONS, and the social interaction with people at work can aid or hinder your success. But there are other benefits of friendship that are sometimes overlooked in our active lives. Friends are a reflection of what you'd like to be yourself; whom you choose to associate with reveals much about yourself. Additionally, how you relate to the different signs tells you what zodiacal prejudices you have. In fact, finding out a nemesis may guide you in developing what you need to learn to move into your new phase of life.

For that reason, this is the house of the visionary, of the dreamer of future delights, of the idealist and emotional voyeur. Astrology explains the difference between a success and a failure as the difference between complete participation in life and a desire to sit on the sidelines. Hobbies or activities you enjoy with your companions all force you to do something, rather than to watch life. If you are someone with few friends, you might make up this lack by finding interests that prod you to pursue new activities.

Another facet of this side of your astrological nature, and long overlooked, is how this area of life delineates where your own special genius lies. As much as friendship is a linking with another, so genius is the linking of ideas together in another (or novel) fashion. For artists, writers, designers, and inventors, the way you approach friendship is often the way you approach creative matters. Those with writer's block or stalled on projects may notice that surrounding yourself with harmonious people and complementary signs may jar you out of your inertia. Secondly, activities or projects that are connected with your lucky signs are miraculously positive, regenerative, and inspiring.

Hosts and hostesses who populate their parties with their most compatible signs will find that their social occasions improve dramatically, bringing greater acceptance and community visibility.

ARIES

FRIENDSHIPS

Aries has a loner streak that surfaces occasionally, making this air native restless for travel and seclusion. Most of the time, and when you are not feeling desperate for some time or space alone, you have a correspond-ingly strong need for the company of one or two intimates. You are usually not one to build up a big crowd around you on a regular or even frequent basis, but you like to inspire and be inspired by a few close friends.

Friendships with the Different Signs

You have a most enjoyable affinity for your fellow fire signs, especially other Arians. Some would think arguments and clashes of will might characterize these friendships, but this need not be the case because the fiery natures are capable of sustaining a fast-paced and innovative rela-tionship, sharing agreement and disagreement alike, taking changes, whims, and opinions in stride. Cancer has the same combination of shy-ness and spontaneity that you do, alternating and unpredictable. You may become annoyed at this, but you understand it and are in basic sympathy with this water sign. Capricorn and Scorpio share a great deal in common with you, which may turn out to be a mutual learning process with potent lessons for both. If this friendship is persevered, rewards in the way of loyalty and positive growth will result.

Social Goals

Your reputation goes before you, Aries, wherever you go. This can often be unfortunate, as your combativeness in the past closes doors to you in the present. You may feel driven to say, "I'll just climb right over every-one," striving to reach the top just to show them. Remember that your idealism and the drive to achieve your aspirations impress those above you. If you simply persist in working toward your goals, you will gain the necessary recognition despite obstacles—so don't place needless ones in your own path!

Groups and Associations

Aries livens up a group but may find it difficult to be truly comfortable in one. Compromise and patience are not tools that you use habitually in a social setting, though you give of your time and energy selflessly. You are happier with a few close friends among whom you feel free to express what you truly think and feel—even when this is criticism. You appreci-ate people who want to hear what you really think, and who will treat you with the same straightforwardness.

Inner Circles

Those to whom you feel truly close, who have your confidence and confide in you, form a tight, close group around you. Here you share openly; and you defend each other as fiercely as you may fight over your differences as to political, ideological, or simply common-sense ways of approaching life. Your Arian need for time by yourself serves to ease any pressures of too much contact; your intimate associations, if few in num-ber, are long-lasting and rewarding ones.

SOCIAL CLOUT AND PRESTIGE

The demands of social prestige pull Aries in several directions. You love recognition, although you are not necessarily fueled by a big drive for money or power—real importance for you lies in whether or not your inner ideal of excellence has been realized. You are ambivalent toward the mantle of influence and affluence and may not wear it gracefully. Often the Aries drive will pursue and gain public adulation and then squirm under the responsibilities that accompany it. It is easiest for you to live with recognition that comes from the expression of talents and brainwork, or actions based on your original ideas. This can come from a small yet select circle of those who value your work, as opposed to a more widespread but less worthwhile acceptance or renown.

SURPRISES IN LIFE

An Arian tendency to ignore the infinite complexity and subtlety of social interaction is almost sure to bring surprises your way—both the pleasant and unpleasant varieties. The actions of others, which seem logical to them, can throw you off guard—this can be anything from a thank-you note for some kindness you hardly noticed you had rendered, to a red-faced, loud lecture on some way in which you have given offense. Un-expected events and changes in your life toss you off on tangents, some-times long ones, and often cause you to trace a zig-zag course through life. You are resilient and resourceful, however, and possess the ability to make this course the best possible one for you. It might even be said that the element of surprise molds and shapes the Aries life, throwing before you the beginnings on which you thrive and leaving it to you to complete each cycle with the full use of your potential. Avoid indulging in an attitude that you are being somehow picked on by life when things don't go according to what you expect—it's a lot more fun to consider them to be new challenges, which are well within your ability to meet. After all, you have survived everything that has come your way so far!

TAURUS

FRIENDSHIPS

Taurus enters friendships cautiously, wanting very much to have close friends yet needing all relationships to fit into an already envisioned mold. You define personal contacts according to your own private hier-archy, usually having a favorite friend at the top of a mental list, followed by others in order of preference. A shy surface conceals a very gregarious person; Taurus loves to share and to interact but wants to be sure that everything is quite correct first. This does not necessarily refer to propri-ety of an externally defined nature, but rather your own judgment as to how each acquaintance will affect your life. You tend to be more loyal to the ideal of friendship than to any particular person. When you feel that this ideal has been violated, you will spurn a friend or play a drawn-out game of ignoring him or her until sufficient time has passed for you to

recover from hurt feelings and assess the situation—and to extract payment for the offense! See that you do not become devious in this, causing
yourself to lose worthwhile friendships by keeping a confusing distance
rather than bringing grievances into the open.

FRIENDSHIPS WITH THE DIFFERENT SIGNS

You have an almost automatic liking for other earth signs but may have
trouble relating with them on a long-term basis, as they embody your
own brand of unyielding stubbornness. Water signs, particularly Cancer
and Pisces, provide you with a warm, emotional climate as well as helping you to loosen up and relax. The third water sign, Scorpio, can challenge you in a direct manner, which raises your hackles. This sign is your
zodiacal opposite and, like Taurus, is a fixed sign—you have much in
common and this friendship can be lasting if not always smooth. You are
more comfortable at a distance from air and fire signs; these may stimulate you, and mutual admiration may be present, but the atmosphere is
usually too disruptive for your liking.

SOCIAL GOALS

Taureans believe implicity in social hierarchy—and therefore function
well under its strictures. You know how to obey the rules, pay your
dues, and climb up rung by rung. When less earthy types object to
aspects of this it surprises you, as you see such social structuring as
logical and fair—the survival of the fittest, the most tenacious, the
knower of the ropes. If upward movement is easy for you, lateral motion
can be tough; getting into new social settings in which you must revise
your habits and attitudes is nervewracking to Taurus. You would prefer
to keep everything on an even keel, with no sudden shifts—unless they
are engineered by you! Remembering the importance of keeping a wide
perspective is essential to your sign in terms of keeping open to opportunities and being flexible enough to continue being useful in a constantly changing environment.

GROUPS AND ASSOCIATIONS

You weigh the pros and cons carefully before entering into any group
association or activity. It is important to feel that you can maintain your
personal integrity as part of a group—not only as far as your ethical
standards go but also in that you do not wish to be forced (or even asked)
to alter your habits or opinions. You may have many constructive ideas
and methods which make you an asset to a group; you accept the leader
role willingly and expect to be followed once you have been chosen. The
most enjoyable way for you to receive such a position is to be coaxed into
it, knowing that you are really wanted for your own unique qualifications
and be praised for your many fine qualities. Overdoing this attitude can
cause you to become a drag on the group impetus, forcing everyone to
pause and dole out the attention you feel is your due—or to experience
your manner of long-suffering, unappreciated martyrdom.

Inner Circles

When it comes to a close circle of friends, you like to choose from those in your work environment. This serves the dual purpose of showing you in advance what a person is like under day-to-day conditions, including those of stress and of making your position at work more secure by cementing relationships there. Often Taurus requires much time in establishing a close tie. You must work out all kinks in communication—including some that have not come up but might according to your perceptions—and get used to the idea of allowing someone new to have an equal share of preferences and opinions honored. It is sometimes difficult for you to allow for this quality between persons, not because of any feelings of superiority (these would probably prevent you from forming the friendship in the first place), but through reluctance on your part to share attention with another. You derive more strength and support from close friends than you often admit, either to them or to yourself.

Social Clout and Prestige

Taurus believes in using social standing to whatever advantage it may bring. You dislike being contradicted and so can become rather stuffy, even snobbish, with those who disagree with you. You take your accomplishments seriously and will not shun recognition through false modesty, success, substantial contributions, or involvements with charities.

Surprises in Life

You tend to resist looking for an overall pattern in events that take you by surprise. Wanting things to be pleasant, you can miss the point of needed lessons and end up having to experience them repeatedly. Try to steer a steady course through the changes that occur, and don't be too hard on friends whose lives undergo sudden change. They may have something to show you in the way of taking the unexpected in stride.

GEMINI

Friendships

Gemini has a wide circle of friends; your curiosity about others, their motivations, propels you outward. Even those with whom ordinary powers of observation would consider that you have nothing in common are numbered among your friends. You are willing to share all manner of troubles as well as joys for the sake of friendship; and you are accepting of foibles and eccentricities and would more often than not cause more reticent signs to hold back. You do, however, keep a secret scoreboard and will occasionally or periodically drop one or more friends because of old hurts or even a sudden irrational need not to feel in a rut.

Friendships with the Different Signs

You always seem to be surrounded by fire signs, as they are attracted to your speed and brightness. You share such high energy and spontaneity with Aries and Gemini in particular; a sense of mutual timing of even ESP can characterize such a friendship. With earth signs there is an exchange of widely differing viewpoints. There is less excitement here so your earth cronies may be fewer than those of more shifty types, yet these are reassuring relationships despite quarrelsome moments and maddening impasses. Relate carefully with Scorpio and Capricorn—they resist your investigations and could strike back later on, catching you off guard.

SOCIAL GOALS

Gemini wrote the book on using social connections. You move with fluidity in a variety of environments, able to feel at home at any level of society and to make others feel at home with you. You quickly and intuitively draw lessons from what you see and experience, assimilating the language and customs of every group or foreign country with ease and rapidity. The obstructions you meet to your social ambitions stem from a lack of clearly defined, long-term goals. You often don't follow through on your own efforts and commitments, and can even spur opportunities arising from your own successes with a certain perverse glee.

GROUPS AND ASSOCIATIONS

A cooperative attitude keeps you in the good graces of others, helps to energize them, and brings them together. You advance yourself well in this kind of activity; your problem is that you frequently lose sight of the limits of your nerves and energy. Riding a wave of heady optimism you plunge headlong into too many commitments, and you already have quality kinks to work out in that department without adding more in the way of quantity.

INNER CIRCLES

You are able to number quite a few people as your intimates. People must get past your joking attitude, your refusal to take anything seriously, before they get to the inner you, but you are adept at communication and genuinely share yourself with others, opening their ability to share with you as well. Your quickly changing focus may cause a regular turnover among your inner circle. Former friends may abound who have been estranged from you by a seeming duplicity on your part—while to you it seems only that they have misunderstood your intentions.

SOCIAL CLOUT AND PRESTIGE

Gemini's ability to spread out in many directions simultaneously brings prestige through being known, at least among a select circle, for a variety of accomplishments and achievements that are notable for the way in which they are reached. Personal grace opens doors for you rather than any heavy-handed drive to the top or any utilization of an existing position as a motivating power. You need to pare your goals down to essentials and to be clear on them in your own mind. Don't be flippant about the responsibilities inherent in any attainment. Examine also your real reason for wanting a particular advancement or opportunity. If you cannot respect yourself for going after something, the chances are you won't really enjoy it once it is within your grasp.

Surprises in Life

If anyone can get used to surprises, it is Gemini; so many of them occur in your own life that they become simply the normal course of events. You, in fact, are the one who usually generates surprises for others. This can continue for years, but eventually something will come your way that will surprise you on a large scale, leaving you elated or sobered, as the case may be. These come in the form of changes with family, mate, or lover. Often it is that someone rejects a role you have put him or her in, taking it for granted that the situation was agreeable to everybody concerned. Karmic situations mirror themselves in the life of Gemini, receiving in alternate cycles the same treatment that you have given to others. This repetition can be stopped or at least greatly reduced for you if you will seriously consider what others expect from you, whether or not you encourage this expectation (and if it is one that you accept), and how others will react if you do not do it. It will also benefit you to look for the lesson within any hurt you receive rather than dismissing the other person involved as having been of no consequence or taking advantage of you.

CANCER

Friendships

Cancer asks much from friends in the way of tolerating piques, grouchy periods, and oblique behavior. In return, however, your friends receive warmth, sincerity, and an insightful and perceptive feedback for their ideas and feelings. There may be frequent flare-ups between you and your friends, but making up comes quickly and naturally to you. You do need to avoid trouble with certain sensitive ones who cannot handle such ups and downs—important relationships can be lost as a result.

Friendships with the Different Signs

The more outgoing Cancer native is attracted to fire signs, though loud ones. You enjoy more of a variety of activity than may show on your placid surface, and you like being carried along by the enthusiasm of fiery folk. A quieter rapport and a long-term intimacy can be had with Scorpio, Capricorn, and Libra—these signs, though diverse, all have the patience to last through Cancerian mood shifts. Gemini and Aquarius prod your sedateness; you may find this troublesome, but good lessons are often to be learned here. With Aquarius in particular you have a strong, intuitive friendship, especially with an Aquarian of the same sex as your self.

SOCIAL GOALS

Cancer is prone to funks, often long ones, and at the same time is very much concerned with having a successful image in the world. This leads, when uncontrolled, to worry and too much self-criticism and to socially ungraceful moves that don't leave a good impression on influential people. Balance the serene part of you with the part that stamps, is sarcastic, and impatient. People enjoy you for yourself—faults and all—and you gain good ground if not driven by anxiety.

GROUPS AND ASSOCIATIONS

Group interaction is beneficial to you despite the fact that you may find it difficult. You have precise ideas about the way things should go and what your function should be—often too precise! When barriers are lowered and true relating occurs, you can partake of a unique type of sharing in which the ideas of all concerned blend and complement one another for a creation that is greater than the sum of its parts. A compassionate nature leads you to social work, providing relief for the needy. Cancerians are often found in volunteer situations, deriving much joy from bringing a bit of companionship or aid into the lives of those who have little. Don't let a need to further your own interests or keep personal projects in the foreground dominate you. Correspondingly, don't let them be overshadowed by playing the martyr to everyone else's needs.

INNER CIRCLES

Your truly close friends are few but very close indeed. You may have a wide circle of acquaintances but not many share your inner life with you. From those who do, you demand loyalty and confidences that are strictly kept. It is helpful to the Cancerian nature to take a mental step back occasionally to remind yourself of the positive addition a friend is to your life, as it is easy to take a close contact for granted. Check to see that you are not growing too finicky, driving friends away because you do need them! If you have a doubt or a grievance, air it—a momentary unpleasantness can clear the atmosphere and restore harmony between you and someone you love.

SOCIAL CLOUT AND PRESTIGE

The rights and responsibilities that go along with wealth and status may at times seem overwhelming to you, but you will not refuse them. Indeed, the closer you come to them, the more naturally you seem to take them in stride. If strongly motivated by career or other social factors, Cancer directs energy skillfully toward reaching an influential position. Keep your friends and family close while engaged in such a move, and listen to their counsel. This will help you to avoid becoming too wrapped up in your own view, aiming for something that is smaller than what you deserve, or losing the respect of people who count through intolerance or sarcasm. Remember that if there is something you would like to see changed in an organization or social structure, you will have a better chance at it from the inside. You will be trusted and respected more there than from outside and below where sound criticism can be dismissed as the mere sour-grapes ranting of someone who can't make it. Direct your desire to make corrections with care, and you will find yourself in the position to accomplish real improvements.

SURPRISES IN LIFE

Cancer rolls right along with surprises—perhaps too much at times. You tend to take the unpleasant ones as evidence of utter and eternal failure and loss; the pleasant ones indicate that from now on everything will go your way forever. It will help to be more phlegmatic, to set your mind on a higher plane and a longer perspective. Sudden shifts can then be fit into a larger framework and can be seen as significant parts of a continually developing whole.

LEO

FRIENDSHIPS

Leo believes in being loyal to friends and supporting them against all comers. You want to demonstrate openly to your friends the appreciation you feel for them and will do so in many forms including direct praise, gifts, and putting in a good word for them with others. The Leonian consciousness builds a friendship along certain fixed lines; those who don't fit the bill are dismissed, but you will never lead anyone falsely in the pretense of real liking. You may not have a large pool of friends, but you choose a variety of types of people from different lifestyles.

FRIENDSHIPS WITH THE DIFFERENT SIGNS

Your most harmonious relationships for companionship and the sharing of the inner self are with direct, self-motivated signs such as Aries, Aquarius, and Libra. You dislike the company of those who seem snobbish to you, and you also avoid spaced-out or fretful types. This is a good thing, as these bring out the worst in the Leo temperament in terms of intolerance and impatience, not to mention feelings of smug superiority. Pisces, Virgo, and Cancer tend to affect you adversely in this manner, irritating you with complaints and what to you is a lack of centered attention to the matter at hand. For serious, long-term friendships you have a lot to share with Capricorn and Taurus, although there will almost definitely need to be a relaxation of wills to maintain harmony.

SOCIAL GOALS

Leonians have a clear perception of the steps in the advancement of business and social interests. You quickly understand what kind of relationship is necessary and with which person, as well as how open or how formal you will need to be. Don't become obsessed with proving your excellence in the social area—sudden changes of pace come hard, and you may find that you have just stepped off a cliff.

GROUPS AND ASSOCIATIONS

Leo yearns to be a leader, a figurehead, among the members of any group or association to which he or she belongs. The mass of detail you must take on in assuming such a role can be mind-boggling, requiring the acquisition of competent assistants or secretaries, but to Leo these are the only visible trappings of success, desirable in their own right for this reason. You are charismatic, good at attracting attention, funds, and publicity. Beware of taking yourself too seriously when recognition has come your way; it can lead you into silly strutting that undermines your credibility and tempts people to laugh behind your back.

INNER CIRCLES

Watch the tendency to want to be the ruler of your circle of close friends. You offer your time, home, and affection generously. Don't lose the love and appreciation of intimates by making them feel you are extracting payment in the form of their subservience to you. You enjoy generating excitement among your friends, introducing them to new sights, music, theater, and each other. Remember to balance the rush of events with the flow of communication that comes with quiet times. The shared ideas and feelings of others give depth and strength to your confidence which can be shaky, and help bring to you the maturity of serious reflection and a sense of commitment.

SOCIAL CLOUT AND PRESTIGE

You will play the role of Mr. (or Ms.) Big to the hilt. You have worked for what is now yours, but it is wrong to ignore or minimize all the aid you have received in getting it. Resolve to strengthen the side of your character that moves you to seek noble and charitable causes and throw your support behind them. When you have truly committed yourself to a cause, you will risk all—even your good name for it. Don't let yourself be duped into thinking that you are gaining real prestige in situations where others are actually pulling the strings. They may be playing on your fondness for public acclaim in order to use your energy and abilities. There is no need for putting on airs of false modesty—indeed, this is often the greatest show of egotism—but it will benefit you most to receive honors and compliments diffidently, showing that you are grateful to be appreciated. In this way you can openly show your enjoyment of recognition without gloating.

SURPRISES IN LIFE

The surprises that come to Leo often take the form of the removal of what you have taken for granted. A supposedly solid job, friendships, or social positions will melt away, revealing that it has been illusory all along. The lesson in such a shock is that the wrong aspect of the situation has been given importance; you fix your attention too much on surface detail, glimmer, and glamour. Free yourself from the necessity for such hard knocks and realize that you have been fooled by no one but yourself. You have the clarity of perception with which to accurately evaluate a situation before involving yourself. It is a matter of taking serious stock of what is or is not a valid priority, and often this will mean relinquishing something that appeals to you in the way of feeding your ego. On the positive side, you can be surprised to discover that you are liked and needed simply for yourself, with no frills or social motivation involved.

VIRGO

FRIENDSHIPS

Virgo longs for the close ties of intimate friendship but must overcome both shyness and habit-bound opinions to have them. You are cautious about revealing yourself to others, often making friendships take long in forming for you. Although you and another may be on very cordial terms for some time, it takes a while for you to feel and act truly at ease. Your usually calm and affable exterior brings many acquaintances to you, particularly in your work environment and sometimes from your home neighborhood, but there are few whom you would really covet as your friends. You tend to accentuate the fragility of friendships by putting emphasis on trivial or imagined slights.

FRIENDSHIPS WITH THE DIFFERENT SIGNS

Pisces and Libra make pleasant company for Virgo; you enjoy low-key, harmonious times without pressure or conflict with them. You get a kick out of the liveliness of Gemini and Sagittarius and derive pleasure from traveling in their extravagant wakes. They do loosen your tongue, making for squabbles as well as agreeable chatter. It is a rare Virgo who can match the emotional fervor of Aries, Leo, or Cancer. You are more likely to find quick, inflammatory romance with these and to become annoyed or burnt out by their intensity.

SOCIAL GOALS

Virgo prefers a background type of social position, though one that carries with it a good amount of respect. You impress others with your innate sense of etiquette and decorum (a Virgo not displaying these is often deliberately refusing to do so). You advance slowly but surely, often on the coattails of a boss whom you are helping to be more efficient. If you overcome your reluctance to put yourself forward, you will be surprised at the positive response you receive from tactful self-advertisement and assertiveness.

GROUPS AND ASSOCIATIONS

Participation in a large or small group affords you the opportunity to join in while at the same time maintaining partial anonymity. Service organizations were designed for Virgos, as you can feel useful and contribute ideas and effort without being in the position of star or innovator. You possess a tireless and conscientious dedication to whatever your chosen cause may be. Literal-mindedness causes you to be a strict follower and enforcer of rules and guidelines, making you a great worker and sharer but not at your best as a public-relations person or fund-raiser.

INNER CIRCLES

The Virgonian imagination, often underestimated, shines in the presence of close friends. You achieve much in the way of creative projects when working with those with whom you share a strong liking and mutual interests. Those friends who are still with you after the tests of time have seen and accepted the emergence of all the little Virgonian quirks (for which your sign is famous) and have gotten past the petty habits and inflexibility lurking behind your placid, social face. You are truly at home with them, often more so than with blood kin, in-laws, or acquaintances of long standing who have never penetrated past the social courtesies with you.

SOCIAL CLOUT AND PRESTIGE

Virgos often have more sway over the opinions of others than they realize. As long as you don't undercut your own credibility and stature with small-minded stances, you will enjoy the spontaneous respect of those around you, often being the one to whom they come for advice and support. People are impressed by your careful preparations and obviously sound perceptions. Virgo rarely takes the showy route. You don't come across as being socially hard-driving or aggressive, but often you do risk adopting a snobbish attitude, which clearly proclaims that you know best. Chances are that if you wait to be asked for an opinion, it will be better received than when you thrust it upon unwilling ears. A silently disapproving air will serve to alienate others with almost no exceptions.

SURPRISES IN LIFE

The unexpected usually comes to Virgo in positive forms in the social and business spheres. Others take notice of your abilities and fine performance and present you with raises and advancements, or at the very least, praise and opportunities. The biggest surprise for you is when you state your goals plainly and those in positions of authority respond with enthusiasm, implementing your ideas and looking on you with favor henceforward. In your personal life surprise is apt to take a less benevolent form. Especially with a mate or partner, you need to be aware of your fabled Virgonian finickiness. A close personal tie can pop suddenly and completely out of your life as a result of feeling overly criticized by you, unable to live up to your fastidious standards—or simply unwilling to do so! You may take it for granted that an often repeated request, ignored or belittled by you, has as little importance to the one making it as you do. You will discover to your chagrin that your refusal to acknowledge it has been the last straw as far as the other person is concerned. Keep in mind that you must give as much cooperation as you expect— and that the results of not doing so are the responsibility of no one but yourself.

LIBRA

Friendships

Acquaintances become friends easily for Libra. Your obvious concern for them draws them in, as does your willingness to listen. You like to bring people together, forming a group of friends with whom to share a constant exchange of new places to go and things to do. Watch out that you don't try to accomplish too much in the way of accommodating your friends, keeping them busy, managing the cooperation of disparate personalities. You can overtax your own nerves as well as fail to let people think and operate for themselves, causing fatigue for yourself and incurring the annoyance of those who feel they are being moved around like chess pieces.

Friendships with the Different Signs

Earth signs, though aggravating to your logical mind, are a good complement for you. They provide you with endless opportunities to unravel their obtuse and mysterious motives and processes. Pisces and Cancer are warm and supportive, although there are frequent spats with them as well as mood encounters to resolve. Fire signs provoke Libra to stop fooling around or persist in a perfectionist attitude. These can become enduring, respectful friendships.

Social Goals

Libra has a clear mental grasp of the needs and inner workings of social structure, whether in business, club, or society in general. You make intelligent and helpful criticisms, although often they do not further any personal goal of your own, as you either have not formulated a goal in a cogent manner or feel guilty at your need to be recognized. It is perfectly all right to be interested in success—and perfectly fine to admit it! As long as you are consistent and honest, you can rest assured that you are not taking advantage of a friendship simply because something you do to help others might eventually benefit you as well.

Groups and Associations

Your service-oriented motivation makes you an asset to any association, group, or organization to which you belong. You make an excellent advisor or coordinator, as your articulate thinking and speaking enable you to present a good case at benefits, rallies, and other events where bringing together the strength of diverse people is needed. You also help to attract political and social support for whatever your group is working to accomplish. Librans are often found in political lobbies, social service organizations, and other associations directed toward the public welfare. You may waste time deliberating over which group to join and what your role should be once an affiliation has been made, having a perfectionist attitude that gets in the way of decisive action.

INNER CIRCLES

Libra revels in the company of truly close friends and confidantes. You bare your soul in conversation with intimates and expect the same degree of revelation about their lives. You remain a constant friend, but you may find that those close to you will periodically evaluate whether you are putting out too much energy and emotional involvement, and tell you when you are straining yourself by trying to give too much. Conversely, your friends may sometimes feel that you expect too much from them. Don't let your own practical affairs fall to ruin by concentrating only on others. You will find yourself concealing resentment toward them, which you do not want to feel, and they will resent your giving more than they are able to give in return. On the other hand, if you have a strong, centered outer self to reflect the person you are inside, your friends will be able to relate to you on a more equal footing.

SOCIAL CLOUT AND PRESTIGE

Libra does not shy away from the weight of responsibility—in fact, you enjoy it. Don't let yourself become a martyr, though, as this will cloud your judgment. Like your zodiacal neighbor Virgo, you have little or no craving for the maverick-hero role, and you aren't interested in getting a lot of notoriety. If you desire prestige, it is in order to get results. There are not many Libras who are interested in social position for the adulation or envy it can bring. You delight in working behind the scenes, coaching those who are in the spotlight and watching them enact your plans. The greatest satisfaction comes to you when a client, friend, or protégé follows your advice and gains success and happiness from the result.

SURPRISES IN LIFE

It nearly always shocks you when someone becomes angry at a white lie that you have used for the sake of maintaining peace or restoring a calm surface. The surprise comes first, and then you clearly recall having had this same problem before, tracing the details of your thoughts perfectly. The problem is in taking action at the appropriate time, which in some cases may mean undergoing a brief but painful confrontation for the sake of a deeper, long-term harmony. The other side of the coin is the fact that stored anger inevitably brings an outburst that is out of proportion to the situation. You will feel better about expressing your real views for a few strained moments rather than glossing over them. You have an ideal for yourself that consists of harboring no resentment, and will approach this much more closely by airing your feelings without delay.

SCORPIO

FRIENDSHIPS

Scorpio, though solitary and anxious to maintain personal routines, desires the company of close friends. Those who would draw near to you must accept a great deal of natural reserve. You may limit yourself to one or two close friends at a time, not wishing to overspend time or energy and cautious to retain a private inner space. As long as you have some good outlet for your feelings of sharing and companionship, you are satisfied, not needing to have a crowd around. Often one friend of yours will never meet another, and it is rare that you will discuss matters between them. You prefer not to be talked about when you are absent and have a distaste for doing the same to other people. Only when you are angry at the conduct of a friend or have ended a friendship unpleasantly will you stoop to vilifying a person in his or her absence—and then you are capable of doing so with a vengeance.

FRIENDSHIPS WITH THE DIFFERENT SIGNS

Although difficult in romantic situations, Aquarius and Leo match Scorpio in strong temperament and so are satisfying as friends. Earth signs create stormy relationships with Scorpio, but these may abide for years despite differences. With Gemini and Libra you tend to have friendships that are one-sided, with one party putting forth all the effort that goes into maintaining contact. Pisces makes a less tempestuous friend for you than does moody Cancer. Your water sign friends are ideal for your privacy policy—even if they are acquainted, they tend to spend much time actively ignoring each other.

SOCIAL GOALS

Scorpio intuitively heads for weak spots in the social fabric and pushes right through, moving into a desired position. Beware that your head doesn't swell over minor successes and cause you to tackle situations which are out of your depth. Your best advertisement is a well-done job; as refinement in the social graces may not be your strong point, you can be overly blunt with people. Your reserve, if it is projected well and does not appear to be a contemptuous aloofness, inspires others to have confidence in your quietly knowledgeable manner and few but well-chosen words.

GROUPS AND ASSOCIATIONS

You are extremely choosy when it comes to joining or participating in group or club activities. You don't want to waste either time or effort, as there is always some private endeavor or pastime that you feel might be more worthwhile. Once you have decided to be part of a group, however, you will work harder than anyone. The mutual support of the group becomes part of you, and you part of it. Your natural reticence doesn't impede your willingness to try group counseling or therapy, which can become valuable tools and training for you in understanding other points of view and cooperating with them.

INNER CIRCLES

Your inner circle is very small—possibly only one friend with whom you are truly intimate. Scorpio doesn't want his or her secrets to get around.

A more evolved Scorpio type will refrain from burdening a friend with personal matters, choosing instead to keep it inside. This puts distance between you and others, which you may view as being preferable to any unpleasantness your confessions might cause. Asking a Scorpio to talk doesn't work nearly as well as proving loyalty by taking the time to let it happen. Loyalty is the highest virtue to Scorpio, who never forgets a slight or kindness.

SOCIAL CLOUT AND PRESTIGE

Social clout is a tricky area for Scorpio, who often misjudges his or her own impact on others. You want to play the part of a social sledgehammer for egotistical reasons, and will reach for a leadership role, confident in your ability to sustain it. If you are mature, you will follow the law zealously, as you have had graphic experience of what unlimited power can do. If you wield your influence for its own sake, you are drawing such experience to you. It probably won't take too many lessons of this kind to revise your approach in the future.

SURPRISES IN LIFE

A major surprise in the life of a Scorpio may be to discover that you have wasted much valuable time searching for enemies or obstacles that didn't exist or were minimal. Too often Scorpio makes a rash judgment. You assume that if others are interested they will approach you, but this is not necessarily the case. You may seem so self-assured and remote as to cause others to think you prefer your own company. The realization of such things can change your life for the better. Don't lose the benefit of it by indulging in too much self-reproach. Put it to good and permanent use on your behalf by examining each subsequent situation with new eyes. Let it help you to accept a place of your own choosing where you are both comfortable and well-received.

SAGITTARIUS

FRIENDSHIPS

Sagittarius invites the world over to visit. Variety is the spice of life for you, and your times with friends are lively and argumentative. Although you converse and confess freely—often too freely—you save your real self for a mate or one special friend. With all others you disguise yourself with a smokescreen of intrigues and catastrophes.

FRIENDSHIPS WITH THE DIFFERENT SIGNS

The air signs provide Sagittarius with a fun pace of bickering and excitement. Aquarius in particular will share adventures with you, but even this nonconformist doesn't go quite as far as you do into the realm of the outrageous. You yearn for someone who can be both a confidante and a sort of anchor for you. Cancer fulfills this need when the priority is emotional security; Leo provides a professional, calm outlook for you. The obtusiveness of Capricorn and Scorpio befuddles you, making it hard for you to relax—and talk between friends should be more than mutually fending off judgments.

Social Goals

You move freely in most social circles. Your ebullience is contagious, and you manage to charm even those from drastically different lifestyles, economic levels, and points of view. Your restlessness, however, can undo successes as quickly as your unbelievable mixture of personability, audacity, and wild luck has attained them for you. Make sure your reputation doesn't have a chance to catch up with you—even Sagittarians can talk themselves out of just so many predicaments. An inbred respect for tradition comes to your rescue when in your chosen social setting; you abide by the rules though you may flaunt them elsewhere.

Groups and Associations

Sagittarius wrote the book on etiquette and the function and importance of cooperative group projects. You have the ability to formulate and then structure new groups—art associations, ecological projects, and therapeutic support groups are only a few that Sagittarius can put together. You are capable of doing whatever you set your sights on, and you like to see the whole family or block involved. And you have a fine eye for unifying many talents to a single purpose. The handling of money and personnel problems are better left to others rather than to Sagittarius, who cannot see the trees for the forest. Yours is a world of ideas, although you do have the energy and enthusiasm to put those ideas to use on an everyday level. The strictly mundane details can be left to a trusted friend or associate who won't risk all on a cosmic chance.

Inner Circles

Your energy level tends to set the pace for your group of personal friends. You look to these friends for criticism, advice, and reprimands, which you won't accept at home or in your business environment. You don't reject friends for lecturing you; indeed, you seem to go out of your way to behave in a bizarre enough fashion as to force them to do so. However, you are not likely to follow their advice until you're good and ready. When your friends are scolding you, Sagittarius, you are the center of attention. If they don't mind that, neither do you!

Social Clout and Prestige

Sagittarius has no quarrel with the natural order of those who succeed in making the rules. This philosophy allows for action, and Sagittarius always seeks a fair viewpoint and generous scope in which to act out. Regardless of relative social position, your place in life is usually highly visible—you somehow seem to remain, beaming, in situations that make people gape and exclaim. You dream of accolades for just and wise policies proven by time and results. If you are willing to make the necessary concessions to the world of everyday affairs, you are fully capable of creating these policies, at least among those with whom you do connect.

SURPRISES IN LIFE

Poor Sagittarius is surprised when what was dismissed as a petty and inconsequential issue reasserts itself with a bang—and it is usually the sound of a door slamming as someone makes an exit. The complaint will probably be the same: "What was important to me emotionally, you scoffed at—while you claimed to be getting no support." Perhaps even more annoying to Sagittarius than the loss of a relationship is when your freedom-loving nature is repeatedly drawn back to the same lesson. It's not as if you aren't aware of what the universe is trying to tell you, but you wish to test things out to see exactly how far you can really go. Standing out there on the corner in the cold rain with no money in your pocket, no job, and no one whom you could possibly call at this hour of the night—you are sure to think of something, and it just might work.

CAPRICORN

FRIENDSHIPS

If Capricorn gathers a large group of friends, most likely they will be from your work environment. This is where your strongest interests lie, and your knowledgeability about your job makes it rewarding for others to exchange views with you. You are prone to sudden and often rather long silences; these are not meant as an affront to those around you, but you tend not to explain them and friendships can be strained. You protect your own, Capricorn, defending your friends and guarding your privacy jealously. You love the warmth and comfort of friendship but always keep a large reserve for solitude. It is with reluctance that you share space and possessions with another, only becoming accustomed to it after a long period of time. You may never lose this hesitation completely.

FRIENDSHIPS WITH THE DIFFERENT SIGNS

A friend to you is someone to bang heads with, and someone who also has his or her own need for long stretches of time spent in solitude. Aries, Scorpio, and mature Leo types fit the bill for you. More easeful and casual relationships are to be found with Virgo and Pisces; the atmosphere with these signs is quieter, calmer, though perhaps the closeness you feel with them is not as deep as with more solitary folk. Air signs provide you with a humorous, argumentative, lively, and satisfying time; grouchy, opinionated Capricorn may simply ignore them at times but there's lots of good energy exchanged. Aquarius can be your noisiest but most satisfying friendship.

SOCIAL GOALS

Capricorn doesn't believe in wasting time trying to please social acquaintances. Improving and socializing for the sake of current properieties is not a Capricornian trait. You want to put your efforts into more useful activity. You see yourself as deserving of a position of authority when your background has given you sufficient training. Respect is satisfying to you, not adulation or personality-based fame. You can miss much deserved recognition through being unwilling to observe social graces. Capricorn is quite capable of forfeiting advancement or acknowledgement that only requires a word or a smile to obtain.

GROUPS AND ASSOCIATIONS

You watch your time so carefully that you may never become a joiner, feeling that your private pursuits demand all your free time and attention. Others may see you as being uncaring; this is not the case. It is simply that you want every shot to count and see no value in spreading yourself too thin. When you see a chance for truly useful action, you will accept a leading role in which you efficiently guide a group of your peers. You are not fond of too much public contact and prefer having someone do your handshaking and baby-kissing for you, making many positions unsuitable or just not to your liking. You do best as a big fish in a small pond.

INNER CIRCLES

Your real friends may be fewer than others think. Capricorn keeps his or her own counsel and conceals any favoritism that is felt. The people who are close to you do more for you than you sometimes realize. You need to pass along to others your carefully worked-out thoughts and to have partners-in-action. Take care to give your friends signs of your appreciation from time to time so that they don't begin to feel neglected or to think that they have overestimated the depth of your friendship.

SOCIAL CLOUT AND PRESTIGE

When Capricorn holds court, the axe falls; you are not one to hesitate in the use of power or influence. You do take your position seriously, and you resist falling prey to whims and moods, which earns for you a reputation as a potent personage who has earned his rewards. It is possible that out of shyness or a misanthropic attitude, you may avoid applying the influence of your position to social questions or to attracting the public eye. Often when a Capricorn does accept a very public placement, it is with resignation and personal sacrifice, relinquishing the preferred climate of solitude and anonymity for the sake of something that needs to be done.

SURPRISES IN LIFE

After much planning, care, and forethought, you may be faced with the surprise that one of your goals has very different results from those you had in mind. What you have built turns out, in its manifestation, not to be the thing you built in vision. This can pertain to something you have done for the sake of others—and their response is not what you thought it would be. Or an inner need of your own, subjugated to what you decided was a more worthy cause, reasserts itself with new strength and intensity. In either case the battle goes on with yourself, largely unnoticed by those near you. Those who would view you with an unsympathetic eye must admit, when faced with the facts, that you do not bluster your way through. Faith and resignation, combined with a true conviction in the rightness of your actions, enable you to withstand shocks and disappointments. Diffidently contain your elation at the pleasant surprises that come your way, and prefer to enjoy quiet satisfaction rather than a visible celebration of goals attained or dreams realized.

AQUARIUS

FRIENDSHIPS

Aquarius is truly democratic—perhaps to a fault. You associate with all types of people, even at a cost to yourself, in order to avoid seeming intolerant or being accused of making value judgments on the attitudes of others. At best, you are able to be choosy, and to do so without becoming snobbish. The Aquarian penchant for detached analysis frequently leads to your taking on the role of analyst for friends who parade their troubles by for your inspection. You will patiently explain a point again and again, but the pressure can lead to sudden ruptures between chums. This is especially true if you come to feel that someone who continually asks your advice is enjoying his or her predicaments (and having you for an audience) and has no real desire to make the changes required for improved conditions.

FRIENDSHIPS WITH THE DIFFERENT SIGNS

You often have more of an affinity for your fellow mixed signs—Taurus, Leo, and Scorpio—than for the other air signs. This doesn't mean that you and the fixed folk have quiet, restful times, but you enjoy the altercations, perhaps more than they. The peaceful, harmonious hours are spent in the company of Cancer or Virgo, quieter types who in their own ways put a premium on effective communication as you do. Cancer provides feedback for your emotional life and values your perceptions highly; Virgo shares with you his or her intuitive, pragmatic viewpoint. Both hold the promise of being long-term friendships for you, continuing in mutual growth.

SOCIAL GOALS

There is more shyness and unsureness in Aquarius than is readily apparent or is usually attributed to this sign. When new and familiar situations follow one another too closely, Aquarius tends to think in terms of which facet of the self to put forward and can stumble and look awkward. Still, your open social attitude enables you to fit into various situations well. Frankness and curiosity about people spread a positive image of you.

GROUPS AND ASSOCIATIONS

Your energy is more extroverted than that of your zodiacal neighbor Capricorn, but you share with this sign an idealism regarding close relationships, which makes you very selective. The problem is that you can forget what is all right. It is even a good thing for you to pick and choose, but you may find yourself promising your time and attention where you don't really want to be and then cancelling out when you come to your senses. Then others begin to pass the word that you are insincere, that you don't come through in a pinch. Similarly, you are willing to perform a variety of tasks, which someone else might shun without a second thought, getting your hands dirty or hiding away in a back room licking envelopes, but your spirit of enthusiasm doesn't last too long. Aquarius needs to employ his or her brain in order to remain interested. Your social conscience leads you into ground-breaking areas of community service; here you happily join with those of like vision to work toward common goals.

INNER CIRCLES

You are serious about the efforts needed to deepen the lines of communication between yourself and your friends. More casual friends can't handle the intensity, but those who share your drive toward mutual revelation become lifelong partners and companions with you; the closeness and sustained energy of these relationships is hard for other signs to imagine. Incorporating the events and situations of your respective lives, your friendships are ongoing conversations that span years, continuing without hesitation even if there are long intervals between the times you and your friends can see one another.

SOCIAL CLOUT AND PRESTIGE

Aquarius will strive for a position of authority or seek influence in a public sphere if doing so is allied with a cause or an ideal. You put yourself at the service of a particular conception of social duty with single-minded devotion. Even Aquarians however, are not exempt from the danger of self-deception, and selfish motives can intrude. You fall prey to the latest mood of the country or community too easily at times. Be on the lookout for this tendency and don't let it push your point of view around. Often your greatest influence comes from an example you may not know you are setting. Regarded as a trendsetter, Aquarius seems to first do what will later be done on a large scale. You are a forerunner, not of the bizarre but of the acceptable norm of the future, always resisted at first by those who fear change.

SURPRISES IN LIFE

Finding out that you are human after all can come as a shock to Aquarius. You can surround your shortcomings for a long time with a large edifice of rationalizations, social causes, and parental responsibility for your behavior—but sooner or later your analytical eye will fall on yourself. A brave Aquarian puts this discovery to good use. A more immature type will run wildly from career to career, place to place, relationship to relationship, trying to discover his or her trustworthy self.

PISCES

FRIENDSHIPS

Pisces delights in unearthing new layers of friends' personalities, hearing their secrets, being in their confidence. You have an aura about you that inspires others to place their trust in you and reveal what no one else, perhaps, has heard or will hear. However, you are not above worming hidden facts and feelings out of intimates and then repeating what you have sworn silence about—not out of malice but rather through a lack of discretion and an impulse to share what you know. People find a sympathetic nature in you that is genuine and hard to come by, but please stick to good ethics concerning their rights.

FRIENDSHIPS WITH THE DIFFERENT SIGNS

Gemini and Sagittarius try the patience of Pisces, taking you on wild goose chases and barging in at all hours of the night with new disasters —and you love it! Earth signs make for mutually beneficial friendships with you; Virgo and Taurus especially bring you durable and steady relationships. Unless you are a very vibrant type of Piscean, Aries, and Leo, and Aquarius may simply move too hard and fast for you to maintain a long-term friendship with them, although they challenge you positively with their ideas by presenting you with such persistent energy to deal with.

SOCIAL GOALS

By riding the social currents Pisces can go far, as long as he or she retains a clear sense of direction and staunchly refuses to sell out in the ethics department to please others or to get ahead. Don't ignore your conscience; maintain your integrity; stand up for your needs and beliefs. Others see you as a nonthreatening personality so you don't need to hold back to keep from intimidating them.

GROUPS AND ASSOCIATIONS

You function well in a group setting, as you cooperate readily and understand the need to sublimate your own desires for a common goal. Keep a strong hold, however, on your own perspective; only by retaining your individuality can you remain effective as a constructive member. The Piscean curiosity and spiritual leanings lead you often to study and research groups in occult and psychic matters, organizing educational readings, presentations, films, and art shows for the public. You will also meet others at these functions who share common interests.

INNER CIRCLES

The inner circle of your truly close friends is smaller than you may think. For the good of all concerned, define for yourself the nature of your relationship with each friend; clarify it so that neither party asks or expects more of the other than is reasonable. Misconceptions in this area can lead to major problems and disillusionment. Your moods may lead you to withdraw at times when friends have requested your time and energy, which you have agreed to give them. It is hard not to be offended by such behavior, although you rarely do it as a personal affront—there is simply much pressing inner business going on. Try to verbalize this to your friends, gently stressing that you would not intentionally hurt or inconvenience them.

SOCIAL CLOUT AND PRESTIGE

Pisces can fool others—and themselves—by hiding from the desire to attain an eminent social or business role. Be frank and don't stand in the shadow of your mate or business partner and claim that you were made to advance yourself against your inclinations. Whether they are ingenious or ill-considered, your actions, words, and plans are your own. You have the knack for having a steady keel in the midst of chaos; thus you are well-equipped to be in a decisive and prestigious role. Often this will afford you more in the way of privacy and the freedom to live your own life than if you remained in a lesser position.

SURPRISES IN LIFE

When it comes to surprises, there are two types of Pisceans: one is surprised by nothing, the other by everything. Both have a sense of wonder about life and invite startling and novel people and incidents into their proximity, sometimes passing up romance or financial opportunities to do so. The fatalistic, unsurprised type is chagrined to see the vital interests he or she might have pursued in retrospect, thinking the outcome predictable and adopting a "why bother" attitude. The surprised Piscean sees that he or she had an inner filter all along that could have shut out the flow of distracting episodes, allowing time and concentration for digging in and getting down to business. The great thing about retrospective realization is that you always get another chance. Put what you have learned to work the next time around, and you'll be pleasantly surprised to find that you can utilize your mature new perspective to direct your life with skill. And there will be no shortage of delightful and interesting things and people to continue to highlight the passage of time and the development of your mind.

Chapter Twelve
Inner Self

THE INNER SELF—the hidden side of our natures—and the unconscious are the aspects of personality of the twelfth house. In astrological literature, this has been called the house of "self-undoing." This is an oversimplification, as well as an example of downright negative interpretation. For this inner self is the self of the mind. It is the guardian angel, the secret mentor, the super ego, and the part that religion plays in our lives.

Unconscious motives are revealed here. By finding out how you tend to fall into unintentional habit patterns, you can avoid these pitfalls and use the psychic energies released by this knowledge to get what you want with far less trouble.

In this treasure chest of activity exist the miracles, the surprising benefits, and the last-minute rescues that we all have up our sleeves. It is the Aladdin's lamp, the magic carpet, and the fairy godmother all wrapped up into one. However, it is also the king in beggar's clothes, meaning you must learn to see beneath appearances to really get the benefits of what this house represents.

This leads to the other key points of this chapter: intuition and psychic abilities, which exists in this area of your personality. They can only be released when you come to grips with your inner world. Remember it is your endowment to have psychic talent. Although each sign has more luck using a different psychic channel (ESP, intuition, precognition, visions, meditation, yoga, and the I-Ching are just a few), you can gain confidence from better understanding this particular portion of your mind.

Secret enemies can be figments of your imagination in real life. Learn not only who but what actions (which you might even perform unbeknownst to yourself) are particularly antagonistic to you. How to deal with rejection will illuminate how to deal with all types of setbacks, especially assaults to personal esteem.

ARIES

COMPULSIVE ASPECTS

When a matter that has been stewing inside Aries explodes, you go from a complete stop to a hundred decisions per second—some good and some bad, most of them necessary. There can be trouble when the stewing period is too short. You neglect to complete trains of thought and to observe what conclusions are based on, making for hasty moves and often ill-considered words. You tend to label people as either friends or enemies based on snap judgments. Your choices are drastically narrowed, often unnecessarily, by overly impulsive action. You tend to channel all your energy into one effort and then give up if you fail.

INSPIRATION

If you belong to an orthodox type of religious or instructive group, you will develop your own version of the teaching, an inner life that tends toward mystical interpretations. You follow your chosen path passionately, contentiously fueled by the Arian need to tame conflicting desires, satisfy a confrontational spirit, and protect the frailty of your human ego.

BEHIND-THE-SCENES ACTIVITY

Aries always retains an inner spark of calmness and joy that is not driven to impress or impose upon others. This can exist in relation to artistic activity, family happiness, or simply an ability to extract vital spiritual strength from the environment during moments of quiet or even of sadness. You accept that this part of your nature may be uncommunicable to others, or nearly so, and therefore are not pushed by it into self-destructively futile efforts or projects.

MYSTERY

It is not unusual for Aries to have secret career goals or private projects to work on in the home or in relationships. You probably don't formulate these clearly even to yourself for fear that they will seem silly or impossible, though they are of high importance to you. You approach them, not bit by bit as might be expected, by waiting for a prime moment and then leaping into furious activity. Vivid childhood dreams and aspirations are carried forth in this manner to adulthood to be exploded into reality with your Arian fervor.

SECRET ENEMIES

A loose tongue and hasty judgments may have angered others who retain injured feelings while you move restlessly on, sometimes conscious of their resentment but often oblivious to it. You can train yourself to contain your own anger and your surprise when confronted with a problem out of your past. Impediments facing you are frequently of the leftover variety. You possess the ability, through sharp senses and a quick faculty for concentration, to recognize and resolve such a situation.

HANDLING REJECTION

Aries flares up at provocation, then recovers quickly. You lose the trust of others by undermining their image of you through temper and impulsive actions. Such a rejection is a serious matter to you, although you usually refuse to admit it. The thought of it rankles and casts a cloud of self-doubt over you. Your reaction is similar when another is selected over you in business or love matters, or when someone simply finds you unsuitable for his or her needs, though no rival is involved. You will feel better if you acknowledge your hurt and resentment, thus being able to work through them with the clarity of knowing consciously that you are doing so.

EXTRASENSORY EXPERIENCES

The latent intuitive or psychic abilities of Aries need a balanced attitude, open-minded yet not gullible, for development. It is helpful to you in these matters to make use of some calming practice, which enables you to sift and channel your energies so that they don't erupt out of nowhere. Don't let skepticism cause you to reject others' evaluations of your dreams and perceptions.

TAURUS

COMPULSIVE ASPECTS

The literal mind of Taurus leads this earth native to try to stuff the world into a predetermined mold. You see this as logical ordering, but behind the order are desires, security needs, and self-interest. Repetition establishes a pattern that constitutes fact for you. Once within such a pattern you feel it should not be changed, and you will cling to it tenaciously, clashing with mate, family, friends, or business cohorts over the issue of maintaining it. When change occurs despite your efforts, you consider it unfair. You may realize later that it is unfair to others to expect them to abide by strictures you impose.

INSPIRATION

You accept what has been given to you in terms of religious or spiritual instruction, following it devotedly. At some time you will need to investigate the limits of your belief, to test yourself, as otherwise you are apt to simply adhere to accepted concepts of good and bad as dictated by creed. If you give no thought to the actual merits of your religion, you are in danger of becoming lazy, disregarding aspects which may be bothersome or even harmful to you. You deny the group to which you belong the benefit of sincere, carefully considered critique.

BEHIND-THE-SCENES ACTIVITY

Any hidden processes you engage in are likely to be related to family tangles. You automatically draw so much from your background and environment that working such problems over internally can result in curious attitudes and directions taken in other areas, while home patterns remain the same. Social and family relations are kept somewhat hidden as to ups and downs. You present a face to the world that shows only what you wish them to know about what is taking place in your life. You devise effective ways of facilitating the movement of events without

making it obvious to others exactly what is happening with you personally.

Mystery

Taurus possesses a grim determination to push forward objectives
which, though you are not a loner, can crowd friends out of close emotional proximity to you. Because of your very private way of doing
things, your social face is amiable, but the least frustration grows inside
if given no outlet. A good side of this is that outsiders underestimate
your resolve and then are pleasantly surprised to see you persevere and
get results. All your methods stem in truth from a romantic, beautiful
vision of the way things should be, and it is your effort to make things
that way.

Secret Enemies

Absolutism and reluctance to compromise create walls around you.
Claiming that others have erected them, you believe that your way is
right and should be maintained. Consider whether you put yourself at
the service of others—which you indeed do—in an understanding and
flexible way, or whether you expect to have what takes place be on your
own terms. Enemies pass from the scene as time goes by, but a taste of
unpleasantness lingers with you. Their presence, not seen objectively by
you, is translated into your sense of unfairness at the difference between
your view and what is actually the situation.

Handling Rejection

Behind the stolid exterior of Taurus is a sensitive, proud heart. When
rejected you pout, mentally going over and over the slight you have
received. It is fine to consider the validity of others' criticism, but it
should not be allowed out of proportion. Listen to what is said and apply
what seems appropriate, and let go of wanting everyone to see things
according to your sense of rightness.

Extrasensory Experiences

Taureans have a graphic dream activity with a literal, often precognitive
nature. You fit your dream experiences into your already existing spiritual framework or, if agnostic or atheistic, take a psychological view of
the symbolism. Your extrasensory ability takes the form of momentary
ESP or visionary flashes rather than asking for constant communication
with others.

GEMINI

Compulsive Aspects

When an aspect of life becomes stifling to you, Gemini, or when the
attitude of a family member or coworker seems patronizing or even
overly complacent, you rebel. Anything you sense as being inhibitory or
of a stagnant nature switches you into a frantic mode in which you

attempt to throw off the restriction you feel. This comes out as a sudden change of direction or plans, needless argument, or a struggle for no apparent reason. This aspect of your personality has probably been active within you since earliest childhood.

INSPIRATION

Your restless desire for exploration usually will lead you away from any orthodox or conventional framework of spiritual instruction, although you are likely to return to it periodically to recharge and reevaluate. The excursions you make on your own serve to show your true spiritual needs and what must change in your inner and outer worlds. Trust your perceptions, taking care that they do not become submerged beneath the pressure of social assumptions.

BEHIND-THE-SCENES ACTIVITY

Gemini can be quite often involved in a secret romance, whether this is extramarital or socially frowned upon for such reasons as differences in race, background, or age. You are able to handle multiplicity without feeling a need to integrate the various aspects of your life, although you dislike the idea of being accused of deceit should one ever become aware of the other. You may have the courage not to rationalize the situation so that it appears the fault lies not with you but with the objection of others.

MYSTERY

In a hidden part of yourself, you are seeking Cancer-like roots, Taurus-like stability. This is fuel for the ways in which you surprise those whom know you, as you are generally considered to have little care for security. There is a valiant side to this, which you may miss, observing only your pain or confusion or oversimplifying things by considering only whether or not you are enjoying yourself.

SECRET ENEMIES

Your greatest secret enemy is most often yourself. You propel yourself into risky situations, needlessly repeating lessons and cycles, allowing the charm and flattery of others to mislead you. This is nebulous and difficult to seize hold of or control. Try drawing up charts showing your goals, listing the crises and repetitions you have experienced. This can graphically show you what the pattern is and how to avoid it.

HANDLING REJECTION

You assimilate a rejection quickly and bounce back. You may be more hurt than you let on, but you're not going to let it stop you. Childhood rejections affect you the most deeply, undercutting the fragile sense of security to which you privately cling.

EXTRASENSORY EXPERIENCES

Many Geminis manifest a psychic or intuitive gift, not so much in the form of revelatory experience as in an automatic, externalizing process that shows in your artistic work and your interpretation of the work of others. It also shows in an ability to identify symbols within the workings of society, which are crucial and revealing of the spirit of the times.

CANCER

COMPULSIVE ASPECTS

Cancer is strongly reactive to ideas, people, and challenges, which stems from a fear of the unknown. You are prone to acting as if attacked under relatively light pressure, and you are always on guard against falling into depression. Yet it is by overreacting and becoming hysterical that you prime yourself for a depressive collapse or long moody period. You expect others to consider protecting you first, furthering their own interests second. You become suspicious of close ones, as people predictably are not likely to cooperate with this system of expectations.

INSPIRATION

Your spiritual roots are taken with great seriousness, whether you accept them unquestioningly or ruthlessly investigate their validity. Your attitude depends on childhood experiences—whether religion was warm and nurturing or dogmatic and cruel. If there was little or no influence in this area, you possess great clarity in selecting a path or may remain without formal connections.

BEHIND-THE-SCENES ACTIVITY

To satisfy home and security needs and also to find fulfillment in a career or some means of expressing your inner self to others, you often pursue a dual course. A natural dreamer, you may work out much in the way of experience on a mental or fantasy level, which is high in creative potential. Within Cancer is a volatile, articulate person who may or may not meet the outside world.

MYSTERY

Cancer interacts with the world through his or her feelings, responding with empathy and understanding, going through much pain and frustration at all the unhappiness of others. Your mate and close friends will discover in you an obsession with finding ways to aid in alleviating world suffering. Those who do not know you well will see only your outwardly self-concerned, alternately quiet and crabby, surface.

SECRET ENEMIES

You find it difficult to conceal your reactions, which brings most antagonisms—and antagonists—into the open. You suffer not so much from your enemies' efforts to hurt you directly as from injuries to your reputation and the loss of positive contacts, who might have been allies or at least neutrally helpful coworkers or acquaintances.

HANDLING REJECTION

Cancer's feelings are hurt too easily to forget offenses. You are apt to take things seriously that were never meant that way, developing phobias and resolutions to cut people off somewhat arbitrarily. On the other hand, you draw close to others in times of crisis when matters of opinion are subordinate to a central issue or need. Make the effort to establish more solid, independent criteria for making evaluations of people and their actions.

EXTRASENSORY EXPERIENCES

Cancer's intuition is downright scary. As a child the Cancerian may have had telepathic experiences, which startled his or her family, and especially one parent so much that he or she backed away from this very natural talent. To develop aid in reusing this natural skill, be a bit more trustful of those twinges of insight. Of all the signs, Cancers are most likely to be able to guess a person's sun sign.

LEO

COMPULSIVE ASPECTS

Leo acts out feelings and convictions, taking as necessity an expression and making reactions and responses known. You don't necessarily rush into this externalization process but will not change course once you begin. A somewhat weak sense of what is or is not a real priority often results in your forcing clashes and confrontations without positive results.

INSPIRATION

You are rarely content to be merely one more invisible member of a church or spiritual group. If there is no room for individual expression, you will look elsewhere. A traditionalist by instinct, you regard those of radical persuasion with mistrust. Your outspokenness and the usual atmosphere of churches will likely make you seek a group that conforms pretty much to your standards. You believe in the importance of ritual and of recognition and will not hide your light under a basket.

BEHIND-THE-SCENES ACTIVITY

Leo searches out a sphere of activity that brings some special acknowledgement, influence, or position of authority. You will forego financial gain and don't mind being a big fish in a little pond. You find much satisfaction in volunteer work; an ideal situation for you is to be able to participate in theater or music that provides community aid. You may perceive hypocritical qualities in yourself but will conceal them to maintain a tough, no-nonsense image to the rest of the world.

MYSTERY

You desire to channel your drive and sublimate your ego in helping others. By instinct you are divided in mind about this, wavering in your reluctance to lose out on the spotlight. You cover your tracks, wanting to show a seamless exterior without contradictions. By nature you want to draw others to yourself and bring your own importance to light, but you also feel much inward pressure to act selflessly without thought of reward—to be loving and generous toward all.

SECRET ENEMIES

The proud airs and presumption of Leo stir up envy and make people feel that some wind should be taken out of your sails. This can result in needed lessons in humility. Watch carefully for signs of this need and you will save yourself much in the way of embarrassment and humiliation. Although someone may harbor an unspoken resentment toward you for a while, your energy eventually generates an open contest. You recover as soon as possible from the realization of another's hostility, which is of great help to you. Forget the dramatic denunciation of your adversary, as it is only likely to add fuel to the fire.

HANDLING REJECTION

Leo's pride is hurt by rejection, the blow being felt mainly in your self-image. You have an instinctive reaction to ignore a slight you have received, which is good, but not to the point of blanking out all criticism—some of which may be beneficial. Refusal to face a rejection squarely will undermine your sense of stability.

EXTRASENSORY EXPERIENCES

You are a communicator of your intuitions and insights more than a receiver of the extrasensory messages of others. The testimony of others, even in interaction with you, is filtered and sorted to fit with and validate your own searching and conclusions. The famous Leo, Carl Jung explored the subconscious analytically, acting as a medium, not of the predictive or fortune-telling type but for the revelation of universal structures.

VIRGO

COMPULSIVE ASPECTS

Virgo mentally carries on a running commentary of everything seen, thought of and heard. While in the company of people you feel comfortable with, you verbalize the inner critique freely; otherwise Virgo retreats to a safe distance and then spouts criticism. From a secure work or family position, aloofness, often with a vindictive streak, keeps others in line as far as you are concerned. Your compulsion is to avoid having a generous attitude toward others, and this is in conflict with a more outgoing, altruistic side of your nature.

INSPIRATION

You are inspired by the enactment of values and virtues in everyday life; mundane activity is the ideal milieu for spiritual expression for you. Virgo does not believe in faith without works, and you have this expectation for others as well as yourself—not hiding your disapproval at their failure to live up to this ideal. You take a scholarly, philosophical approach to faith and church, which stirs up unsettling questions that you are always muddling over privately.

BEHIND-THE-SCENES ACTIVITY

Outwardly conservative and disliking to make waves, Virgo investigates alternatives to inherited and socially accepted beliefs through reading, correspondence, and esoteric groups. You desire to keep secret such intimate and revealing behavior, to keep it separate from day-to-day social activities. Your secret interest can run to the occult or to extracultural religions, which you continue to mock when with friends and associates.

MYSTERY

Virgo is deeply sensitive, wishing to accommodate everyone and help others along and cleanse them of faults. You stay on the lookout for ways to break with the past without offense or disrespect, although you do toy with notions of more explosive behavior. What stays hidden from others is a passionate commitment and urge toward freedom; this pushes your timid and retiring outer self along into settings you would normally pronounce too adventurous or unconventional.

SECRET ENEMIES

You are not above gossip and verbal sniping, and you attract the same to yourself. Watch out that your attitude does not fuel the wrath of antagonists, as many others are more confrontational than you. An open battle may begin for which you don't have the strength. Give yourself a break from your routine in order to get fresh air and lend perspective to troublesome situations.

HANDLING REJECTION

Outwardly Virgo may simply shrug when rejected; inwardly you review your own behavior and attitude to see what fault may be there. Often you will avoid contact with the person involved, although you are hurt and wish you could air your feelings.

EXTRASENSORY EXPERIENCES

If you have set up a framework for yourself in which to understand the psychic and extrasensory, you may begin to experience some of what you study and investigate. You take a cautious approach, sensing that there are lessons to be gained from such phenomena. Meditation is an aid in opening the mind to the worlds beyond the senses. Your earth sign literalness may, if unaided, delay the development of potential abilities or submerge them in skepticism.

LIBRA

Compulsive Aspects

Libra strives constantly to make everything all right for everyone—and often you will ignore yourself in these efforts. Your generous intentions can result in an unintentional duplicity—you see alternatives very clearly and frequently have shifting opinions, from which friends may withdraw. Give yourself a timetable for decisions; this will ease the weight on others of resolving your inner dialectic.

Inspiration

Libra has a perception of the truth behind symbols and rituals. You work to unite this inner knowledge with group participation and the compromises that go hand in hand with community activity. You may be in the position of an instructor or healer, living with a deeper religious life than others think prudent or correct, although they are drawn to you for those very qualities.

Behind-the-Scenes Activity

You are likely to accumulate a body of knowledge that runs counter to the accepted norm, which can emerge as your own written work over a lifetime. Your thesis is always the unification of idealism with a far-reaching reorganization of social and economic life, as you long for a harmonious and plentiful existence for all, based on spiritual principles of goodness and understanding.

Mystery

Libra possesses a relentless intellect that rarely shows. You inwardly desire decisive conflicts in which clarity is achieved and order established. Outwardly patient, you would like to see self and society propelled forward by leaps and bounds, with cautious planning rendered unnecessary by everyone suddenly grasping the truth of the need for change.

Secret Enemies

It is unusual for you to attract outright anger or violent behavior from others; what you receive in the way of negativity is mistrust. A tendency to meddle, thinking only that you are helping, can be an alienating factor, causing those involved to be constantly wary that you may interfere. Inconsistency, hesitation, and backpedaling, due to indecisiveness, can also make others suspicious of you, thinking that you alter your position for reasons of self-interest.

HANDLING REJECTION

You keep a bagful of reasons on hand in case you should strike out—so you are very understanding when someone puts you down. This is fine up to a point, but you need to develop the inner confidence to shake off unreasonable criticism and unpleasant partings. Scourging yourself only builds resentment which, unacknowledged, continues to grow.

EXTRASENSORY EXPERIENCES

Libra brings a natural sophistication to the divining of dream material and the understanding of psychic experiences. Your sense of wonder and curiosity are fully alive, keeping your mind open. What you experience usually contains symbolism that is relevent to you personally, helping you to act decisively in your own life, and also helpful to others in conveying similar lessons through your interpretations.

SCORPIO

COMPULSIVE ASPECTS

Scorpio contrives tests to determine the motives of others, closely observing their actions from an undetected position of watchfulness. This is done to ascertain whether or not a commitment is genuine, or what the person's real attitude toward Scorpio is, determining any concealed hostility. Scorpio carefully measures the injuries and offenses received from another. This sign can be unkindly blunt or completely uncommunicative, forcing others to keep their distance.

INSPIRATION

If you are a Scorpio, you have deeply explored your religious heritage, perhaps not in a particularly objective manner, but rather evaluating it on the basis of your experience. If interested, you will add ideas and beliefs from other cultures to your spiritual framework. Scorpio is traditionally said to have a strong interest in magic and the occult. You make the most use of whatever you are given, extracting the most potent experience possible from your spiritual practice.

BEHIND-THE-SCENES ACTIVITY

Although you desire and enjoy involving others in activities (or at least having them view the results of your own) you feel compelled to organize and carry them out in secret by yourself before letting others in on them bit by bit. As with your zodiacal neighbor Libra, this can pertain to research designed for teaching others or a political effort for social improvement.

MYSTERY

Frustration and cynicism are in a conflict within you against an almost unlimited capacity for fidelity and devotion to a person, an ideal, or a philosophy. You would probably describe yourself as singular in purpose; the duality is hidden inside yourself.

SECRET ENEMIES

It is possible that Scorpio creates more enemies than any other sign, both knowingly and unknowingly, through relentlessness and suspicion born of Scorpionic secrecy. You cannot believe that others are as tough as you are and may attempt to squash an adversary with the force of a penetrating look or an acid comment. You sense and exaggerate the presence of covert enemies to a point that can border on paranoia.

HANDLING REJECTION

Rejection can be traumatic to Scorpio, as this fixed sign often sees his or her own traits and values as absolute. You prefer criticism to come from within yourself, not from someone else. You do not let go of relationships or patterns easily and will brood over and review at length something that has not ended well or against your wishes.

EXTRASENSORY EXPERIENCES

Scorpio's intense, inner activity generates powerful and compelling dream symbols and an ear for astral activity. You can grow suspicious without a discipline that clarifies the nature of these occurrences; usually you do not mention them to anyone until you have sorted them out alone.

SAGITTARIUS

COMPULSIVE ASPECTS

To put it mildly, Sagittarius is prone to the exaggeration of reactions, attitudes, expressions, and facts. You tell stories even you have trouble believing. Still, it's better than having to move point by point over details or to simply say, "I was wrong." You don't have the patience for all that slow plodding, and you feel a need to avoid pressure and constriction on your freedom of movement. A matter-of-fact manner is anathema to Sagittarius; your exaggerations put pressure on others to solve problems for you—starting with telling you that you are exaggerating.

INSPIRATION

Sagittarius searches for absolute eternal values with which to order society. You have a far-ranging scope of intellectual interest in religion, philosophy, and anything pertaining to the mystical and sociological, which to you is a natural and necessary blend. Belonging to some community of shared beliefs is a priority for you. You stir things up socially with observations that are blunt and frequently arrogant in tone.

BEHIND-THE-SCENES ACTIVITY

It is not unusual for your sign to carry on more than one "exclusive" relationship, keeping each secret from the party (or parties) involved with the other. You explain this as being essential to your freedom of movement. You are quite capable of keeping most or all extramarital or even live-in affairs platonic, although you don't always do so. It is important to you that your mate or partner see that you have a code of honor.

MYSTERY

Sagittarians rely on traditional values. Your interests seem so broad and radical to others that it is hard to believe you possess a rigid formula by which you proceed, outwardly belittling the narrowness of the ethics and practices of contemporaries. Others who embody this combination of restlessness and security-seeking are made your intimates and confidantes.

SECRET ENEMIES

Unintentional rudeness and judgmental remarks, not delivered in anger but leaving others muttering over their ruffled feathers, are the elements that make up Sagittarius' enemies. It dawns very slowly on you that something is amiss in this department. You may have difficulty healing things over with injured parties—as by now the offending attitude and comments are ancient history to everyone but yourself.

HANDLING REJECTION

You appear to be unconcerned that it is hard to tell when a rebuff has registered. Those who know you well see that it takes the form of irritability, quarrelsomeness, a critical stream of commentary—rarely a frank discussion of your wounded feelings. Once things are finally talked over, you recover quickly, carrying no grudges.

EXTRASENSORY EXPERIENCES

A natural curiosity combined with a philosophical bent incline you more toward evaluating the experiences of others in extrasensory areas than to generating your own experiences. It is most likely that you will need others to trigger realizations of this nature in your consciousness. Your antennae are always out for people's input in all areas of interest, as you are a social—not a solitary—being, and thrive on sharing with others.

CAPRICORN

COMPULSIVE ASPECTS

Capricorn confuses intimates with an unspoken assumption that others must intuit and adapt to his or her needs without their ever being verbalized. This earth native reacts indignantly when the expected mind-reading is not done, thinking that something so obvious is being inconsiderately neglected. Capricorn emanates a stubborn aloofness, which stems from the need to balance the desire to be loved and accepted with an obsessive concern with inner strength and order.

INSPIRATION

Capricorn searches inwardly for spiritual freshness within the limits of a conventional or orthodox religious framework. The approach is often scholarly, as you respect the words and work of those who have established a reputation for knowledgeable commentary and interpretation. For any ethic or philosophy to be sound, it must carry with it a practical benefit. God must do His part if you are doing yours.

BEHIND-THE-SCENES ACTIVITY

Like your fellow earth sign Virgo, you will disguise any unconventional activity behind a mask of conformity. You want to wait until you have done something right or have become as secure in a position as possible before showing your connection with it to anyone.

MYSTERY

Capricorns, for all their respect for the status quo, love improvisation and the expression of a humorous, perceptive view of humanity. Behind your solid facade you are always ready for new adventures, and want them to take place according to your own timetable and on your terms.

SECRET ENEMIES

Your air of benign unconcern can be taken for snobbery or dislike, making others feel that you are scorning them. Hesitancy about sharing your emotional self adds to this—people think that you don't trust them, that you have a low regard for their views and feelings. In your work environment, your efficiency may cause envy among associates; this is intensified if you tend toward bossiness or are visibly ambitious in seeking upward mobility.

HANDLING REJECTION

In an instinctive, earthy way, your first reaction to rejection is, at worst, to think of a way to get even; at best, you try to find the optimum way to direct your energy into making up for what has been lost. Your hermit-like style inclines you to withdraw; your real feelings are worked out inside yourself rather than in discussion.

EXTRASENSORY EXPERIENCES

Capricorn combines a wise type of insight into the psychic realm with a sometimes undeveloped emotional perspective to balance and humanize it. You assume the role of teacher easily and well in this area, rarely letting egotism cloud your relationship with your students. Your dream images tend to be convoluted, multi-leveled, stark, and often sensual, giving you much to contemplate in your waking hours.

AQUARIUS

COMPULSIVE ASPECTS

Aquarious turns relatively unimportant details of day-to-day living into cosmic issues, seeing a significance in them that goes beyond a simple sequence of events. You are often inconsistent in this, causing others to be caught off guard. There is a connection between what you bring forward and the matter at hand, but often there is no real need for it to occupy center stage.

INSPIRATION

You draw in an eclectic manner from all spiritual sources available, with an eye for the unfamiliar. Once inspired, you are eager to spread the news. If you are within an orthodox religion, you become restless, striving to see the community live out the principles embodied therein.

BEHIND-THE-SCENES ACTIVITY

Like your friend Sagittarius, you can be attracted to the concept—and the reality—of multiple relationships, the difference being that you are more organized and usually more out in the open, although no less (and sometimes more) bizarre. You commit yourself in a real way to each person and wait to see things worked out regardless of the stress involved for all concerned.

MYSTERY

Aquarius secretly longs to put out the fire of having to be absolutely unique and to break out of all stereotypical roles. You have a positive acceptance within you, which can lead to effective action. It is afraid to come out because of the big club wielded by the wilder Aquarian self.

SECRET ENEMIES

Aquarius covers so much ground among so many people that if some carry grudges against you, they are scattered far and wide. You carry no malice within you so that you are unlikely to create any lethal enemies. When someone with a large bone to pick does show up, you are startled by the element of surprise this contains for you.

HANDLING REJECTION

You approach rebuffs and rejections ideologically, looking for flaws in your own theories, performance, and presentation. You move through such an experience quickly but may miss the point of a needed lesson by refusing yourself any emotional response or distance in which to contemplate the issue for clarity, and therefore a true inner reconciliation with what has occurred.

Extrasensory Experiences

Your ruling planet Uranus puts you on a natural wavelength for the extrasensory. Aquarius is the sign of the magician, the explorer, the scientist blended with the mystic. You seek to codify and articulate what are often graphic and overwhelmingly real psychic experiences and dreams. You view your own and others' understanding of these as being equal and interdependent.

PISCES

Compulsive Aspects

Pisces would rather not engage a problem too closely or have to act in a very decisive manner. You prefer to remove your consciousness a step, hoping the issue will resolve itself. You dislike putting yourself on the line and will even deceive those close to you to avoid having to do so. You tend to confuse the expenditure of energy with a selling-out of ideals or the giving up of peace of mind, as if anything requiring much effort were ethically wrong.

Inspiration

Piscean intuition seizes hold of the mystical element in any religious environment. You can get caught up in the handling of psychic clutter rather than applying yourself to the discipline you have chosen to follow. You have a direct response to symbology, particularly when it is visual, needing no dry explanations to reveal inner meanings to you.

Behind-the-Scenes Activity

Being mysterious is attractive to you. Those who know you may be surprised when you reveal a major relationship that has existed in secret for some time, or you may engage in a business or artistic project that you share with no one. You desire to make an effect on the physical world, to use it well and to have some control over it. Others only see your philosophical self; meanwhile, you labor away in a surprisingly disciplined manner to leave your mark on the world.

Mystery

You are shrouded in mystery—what remains inside is a person who wants to proceed calmly through life, to take things pragmatically, step by step. A part of you would like to see yourself with no more daydreams, mental confusion, or the moods that can paralyze as well as enthrall you.

Secret Enemies

When you attract hostility to yourself, it is through misjudging your effect on people, through ignoring their needs. Although you avoid clashes for the sake of inner peace, your lack of willingness to confront leaves you unprepared to deal with an antagonist when one surfaces.

Your consciousness swings between two poles: the innocent, incredulous Pisces who cannot imagine having an enemy, and the suspicious, para- noiac Pisces who sees enemies everywhere.

HANDLING REJECTION

You are so receptive to people's impressions of you that criticism and rejection can have a strong hold on your imagination. Try to work toward an ability—you do have it—to see things from a detached overview that lets critics and adversaries swell and crash as they will, knowing that the disturbance will soon subside.

EXTRASENSORY EXPERIENCES

You are prone to letting the experiences, views, or teachings of others control your own psychic life. You are very much aware of your inner life and that of others, but allow your evaluation of your position to be shaped by outside information rather than by what is already inside. A specific practice is helpful to you, both in keeping you from going beyond the depth you are ready for and in strengthening and clarifying your perceptions.